ESSAYS ON NORTHEASTERN NORTH AMERICA, SEVENTEENTH AND EIGHTEENTH CENTURIES

Any examination of the history of northeastern North America in the seventeenth and eighteenth centuries must take into account three central, interacting sources of influence on the region's development: the colonial, the imperial, and the aboriginal. Thus, while the relationship between native inhabitants and colonial settlers helped to define Acadia / Nova Scotia and New England in this era, it was also shaped by wider continental and oceanic connections.

The essays in this volume deal with the widely varied forms of colonial habitation throughout the region, the manifold expressions of imperial exchange with this colonial world, and the persistent process of aboriginal engagement with the growing non-aboriginal presence. John G. Reid argues that these complicated processes interacted freely with one another, making northeastern North America an arena of distinctive complexities in the early modern period. Reid also explores the significance of anniversary observances and commemorations that have served as vehicles of reflection on the lasting implications of development in this era.

These essays offer a fresh perspective on the region and a deeper understanding of North American history.

JOHN G. REID is a professor in the Department of History at Saint Mary's University.

JOHN G. REID

Essays on Northeastern North America, Seventeenth and Eighteenth Centuries

With contributions by Emerson W. Baker

UNIVERSITY OF TORONTO PRESS
Toronto Buffalo London

Toronto Buffalo London
utorontopress.com

ISBN 978-0-8020-9137-6 (cloth)
ISBN 978-0-8020-9416-2 (paper)

Library and Archives Canada Cataloguing in Publication

Reid, John G. (John Graham), 1948–
Essays on northeastern North America, seventeenth and eighteenth centuries / John G. Reid ; with contributions by Emerson W. Baker.

Includes bibliographical references and index.
ISBN 978-0-8020-9137-6 (bound) ISBN 978-0-8020-9416-2 (pbk.)

1. Maritime Provinces – History – To 1867. 2. Acadia – History. 3. New England – History – Colonial period, ca. 1600–1775. 4. Indians of North America – History – 17th century. 5. Indians of North America – History – 18th century. 6. Canada – History – To 1763 (New France) I. Baker, Emerson W. II. Title.

E46.R44 2008 971.01 C2008-903468-6

The University of Toronto Press acknowledges the financial assistance to its publishing program of the Canada Council for the Arts and the Ontario Arts Council.

University of Toronto Press acknowledges the financial support for its publishing activities of the Government of Canada through the Book Publishing Industry Development Program (BPIDP).

Contents

PART THREE: ABORIGINAL ENGAGEMENT

PART FOUR: COMMEMORATION

Acknowledgments

It is always a pleasure to thank those who have provided support along the road towards publication. Because this book is a collection of essays written at various times since the 1970s, I have included specific acknowledgments in the introductory notes to each chapter. My sincere thanks to everyone named there. I especially thank my friend and colleague Emerson W. (Tad) Baker for agreeing to the inclusion of two essays of which he is co-author.

I am grateful to all the editors and publishers of journals or collections in which certain of the essays were previously published for kindly granting permission to re-publish here.

As I revised the essays, the Patrick Power Library of Saint Mary's University proved to be, as always, a congenial space with an efficient and gracious staff. In the office of the Department of History, Marlene Singer was characteristically generous with her skills and advice as the manuscript came together. The Research Committee of the Faculty of Graduate Studies and Research at Saint Mary's provided an important and timely grant in aid of publication, which I gratefully acknowledge.

At the University of Toronto Press, Len Husband provided invaluable encouragement and good counsel, Frances Mundy steered the book efficiently through the final publication process, and John St James contributed many improvements as copy-editor. Two anonymous Press readers also made nuanced and much-valued recommendations.

My debt to my wife Jackie Hicks is always too great to portray adequately, as also to my children Jane and Robert.

Maps

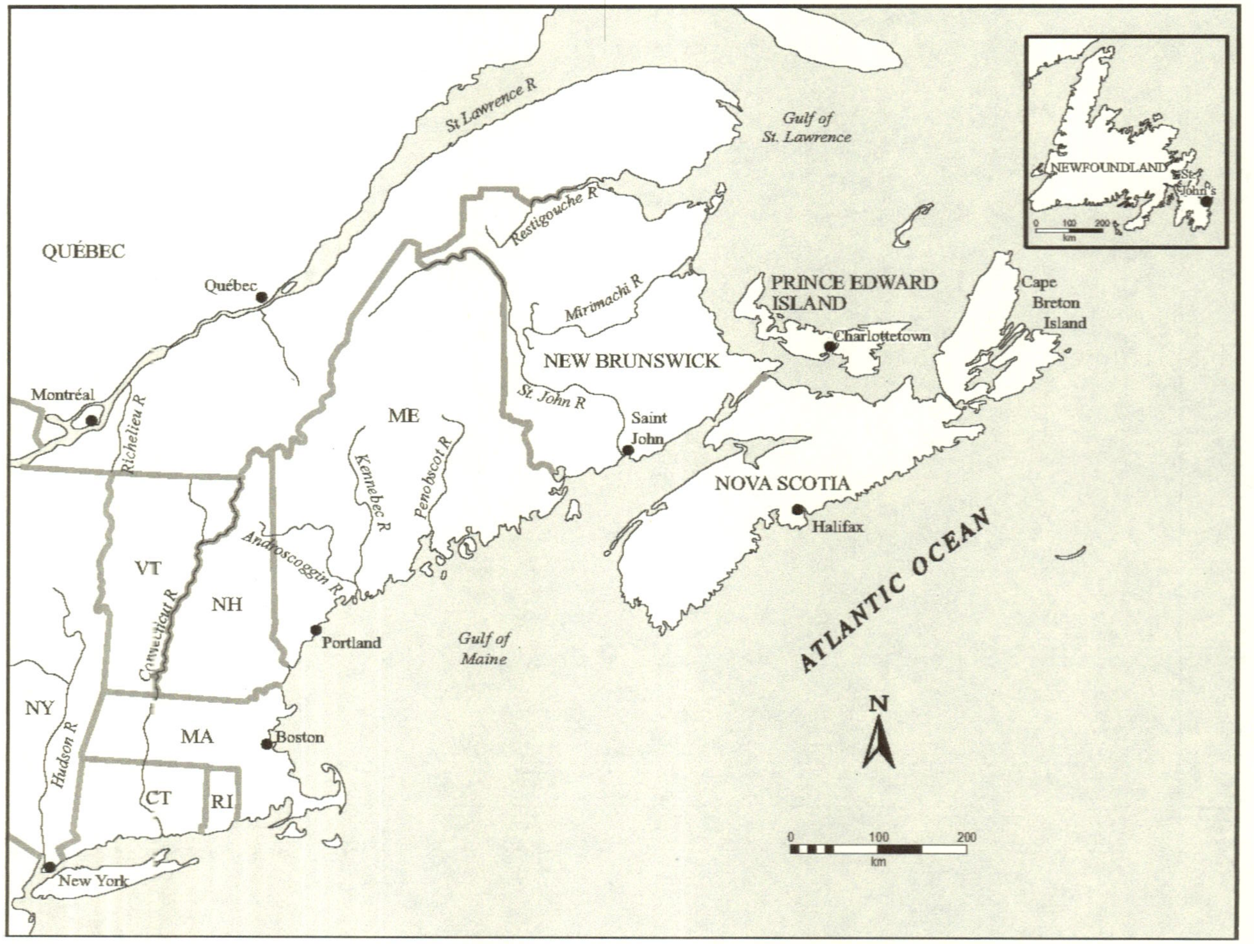

Map 1 Northeastern North America, modern boundaries

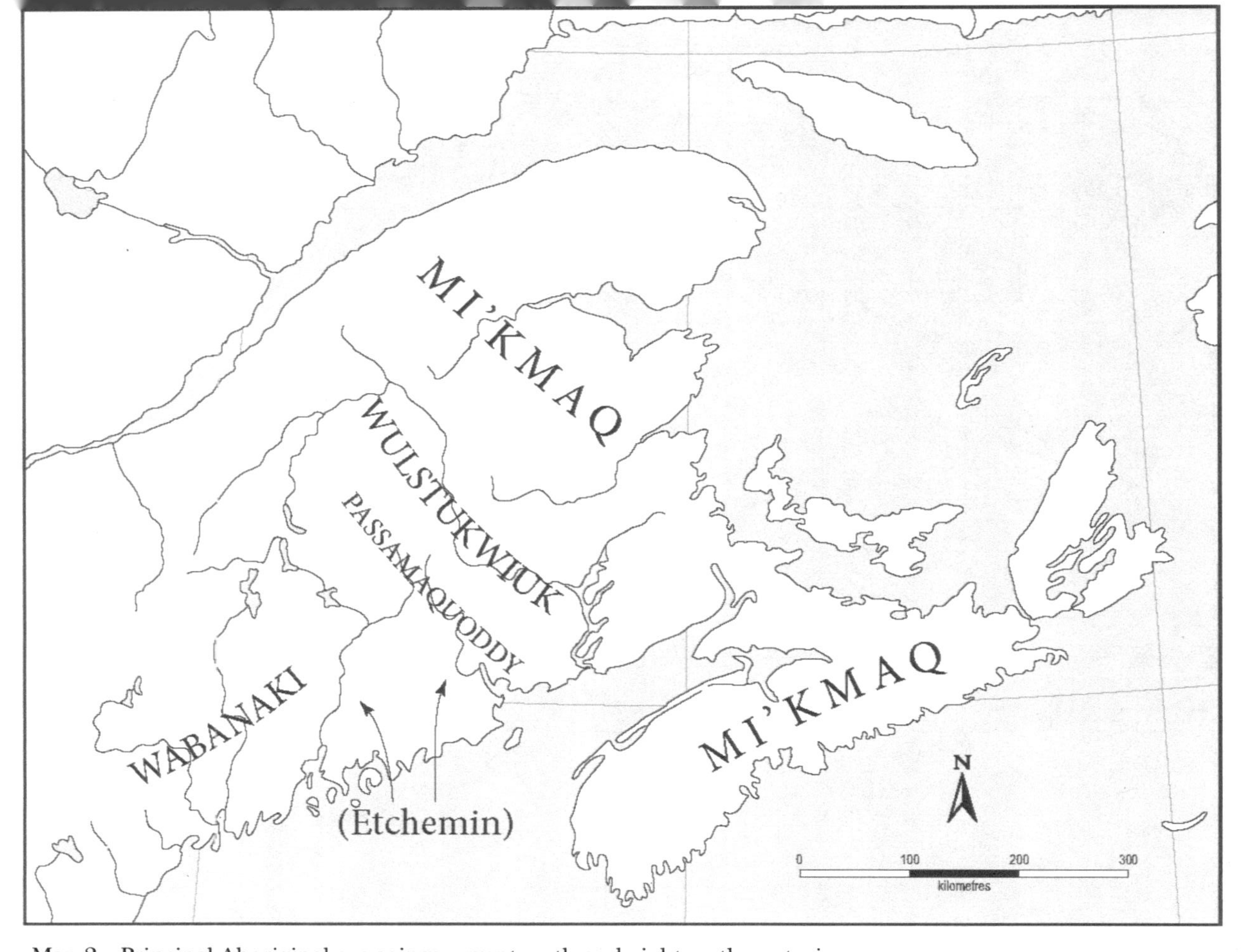

Map 2 Principal Aboriginal groupings, seventeenth and eighteenth centuries

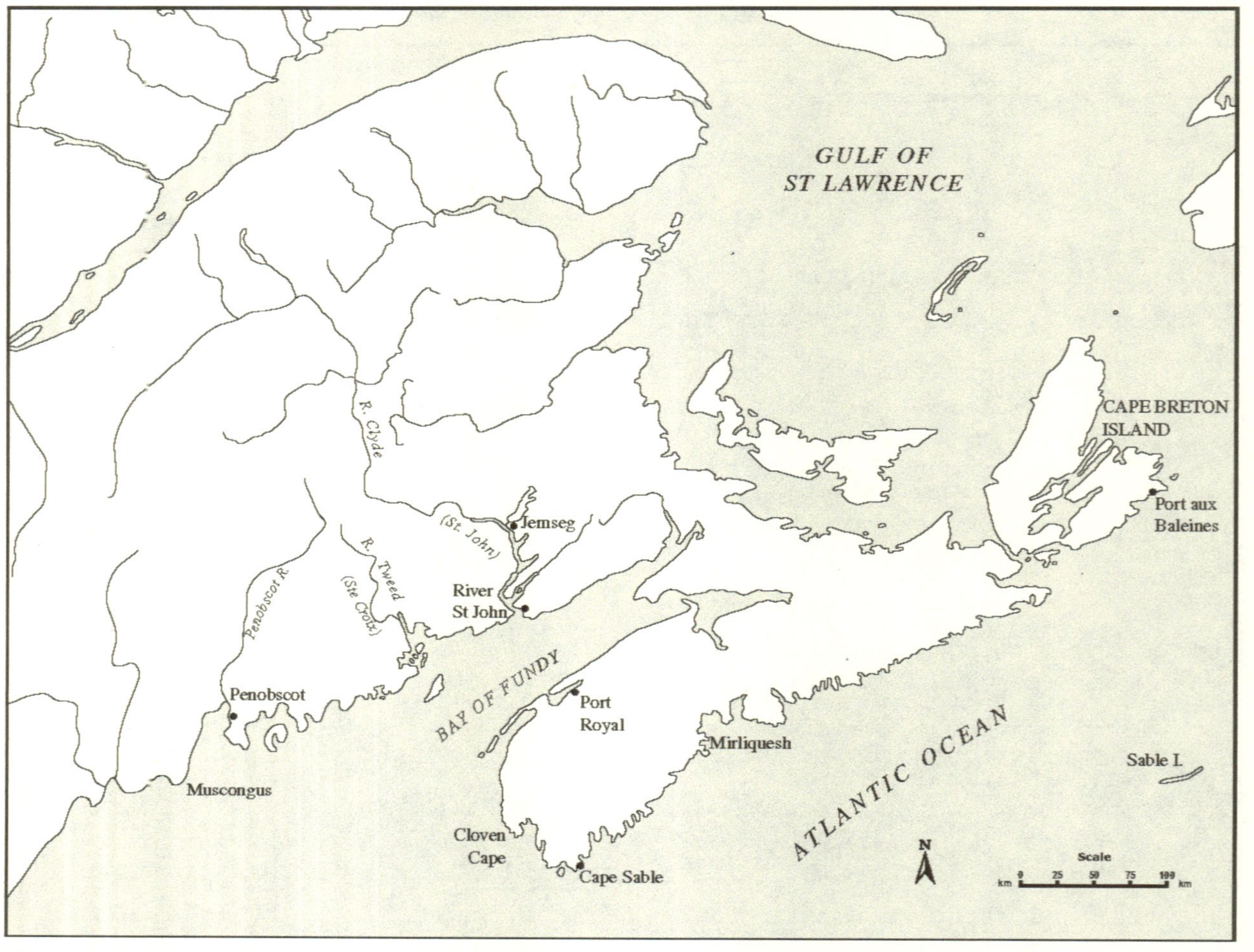

Map 3 New Scotland (Nova Scotia), seventeenth century

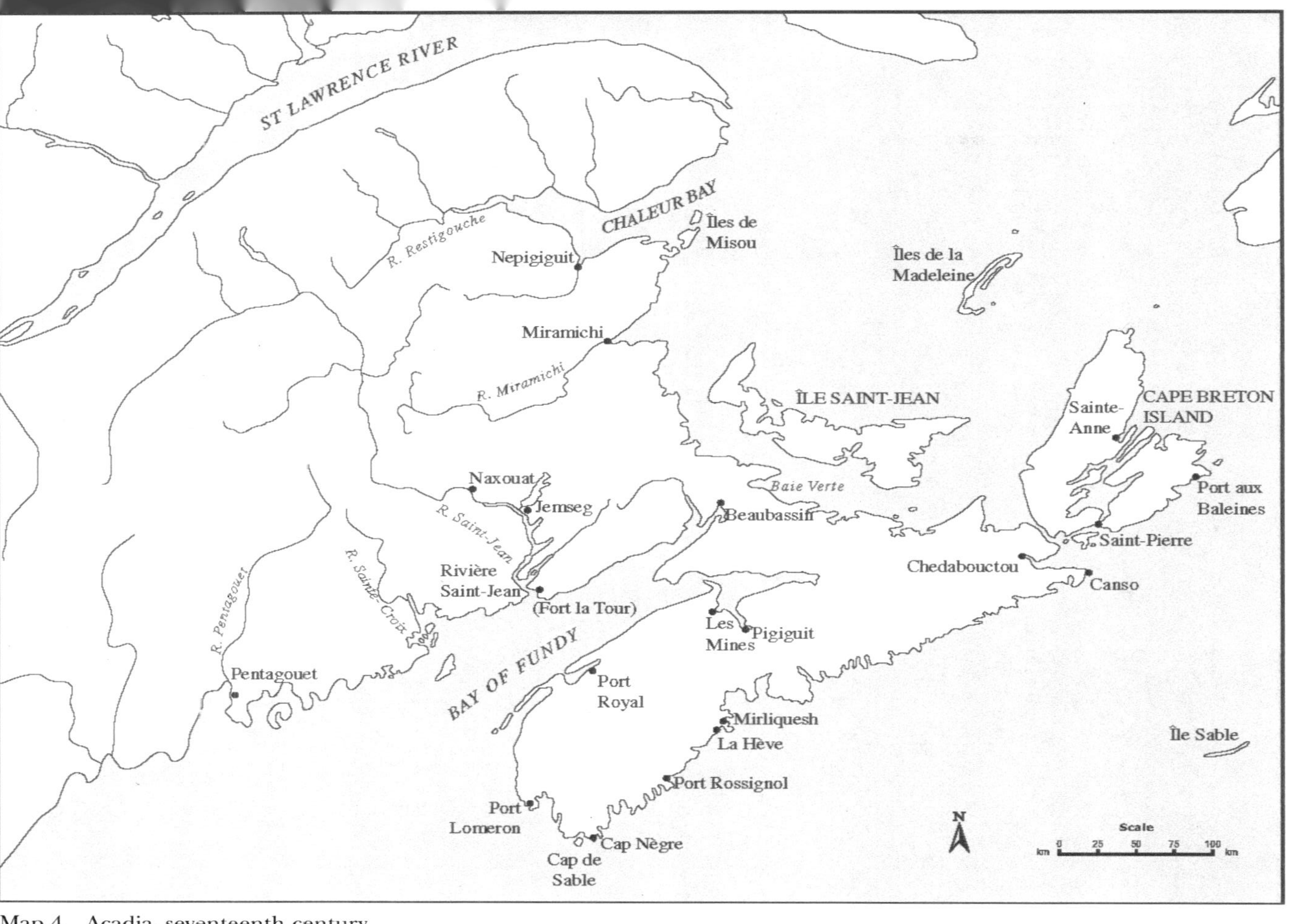

Map 4 Acadia, seventeenth century

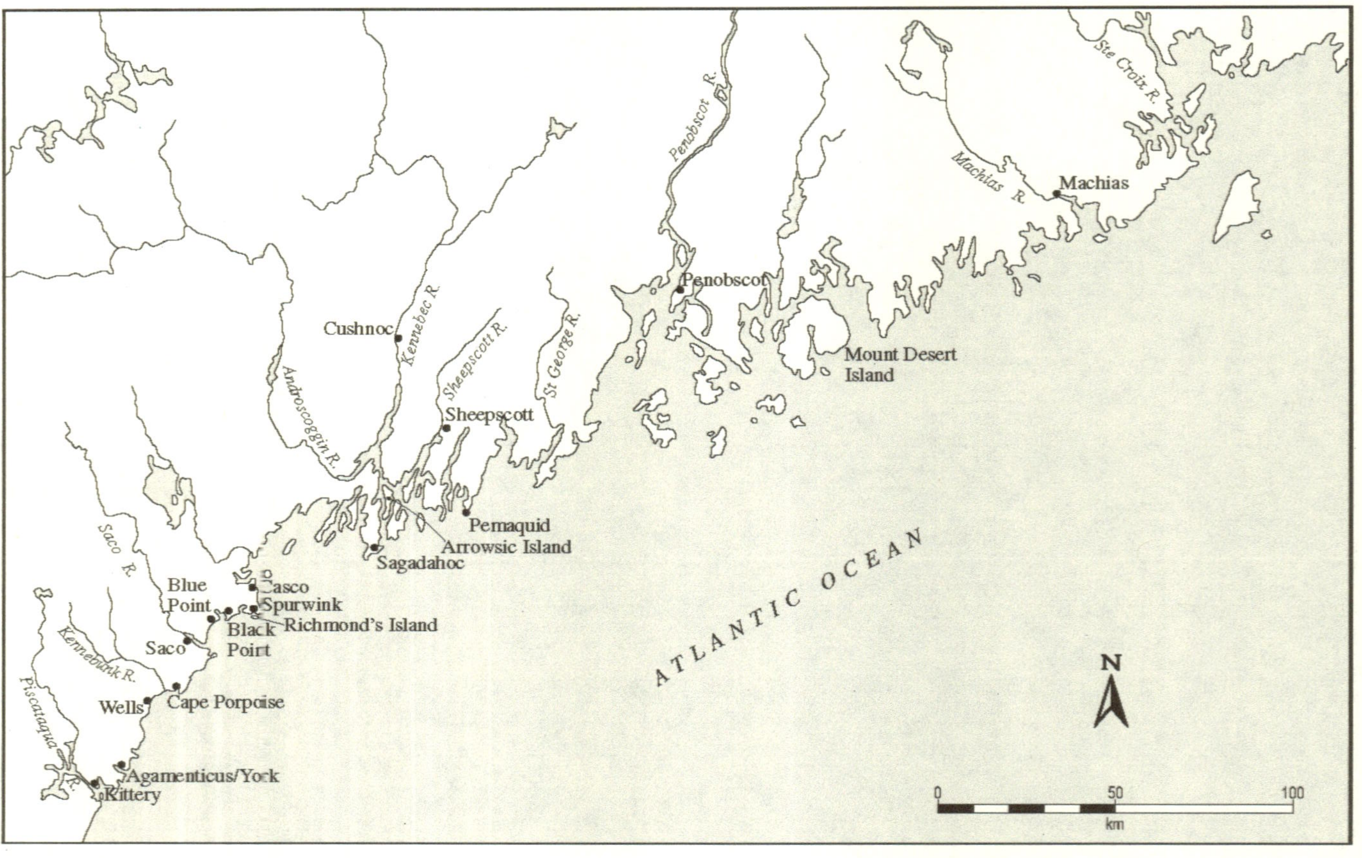

Map 5 Maine Coast, seventeenth century

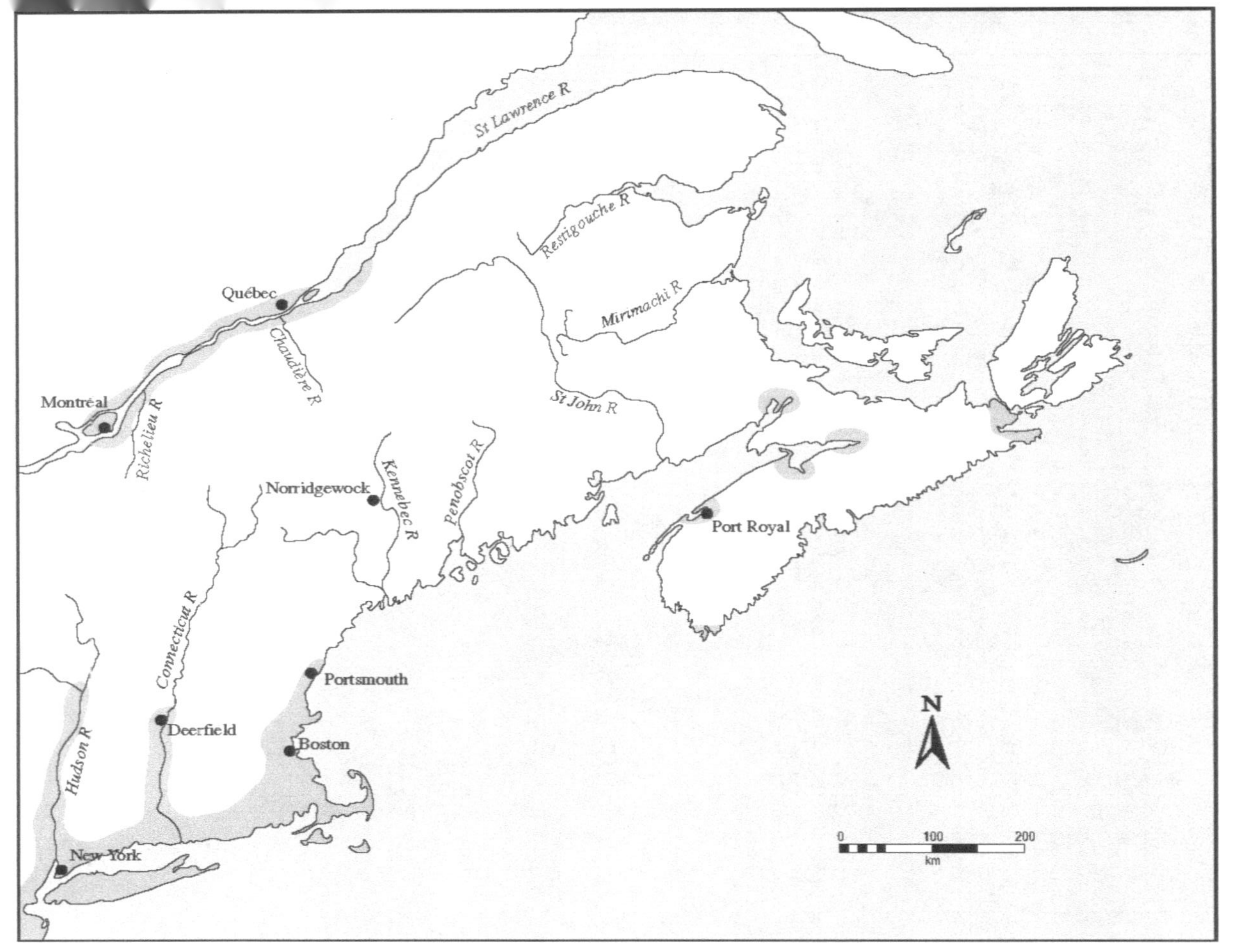

Map 6 Northeastern North America, showing approximate bounds of European control, 1700

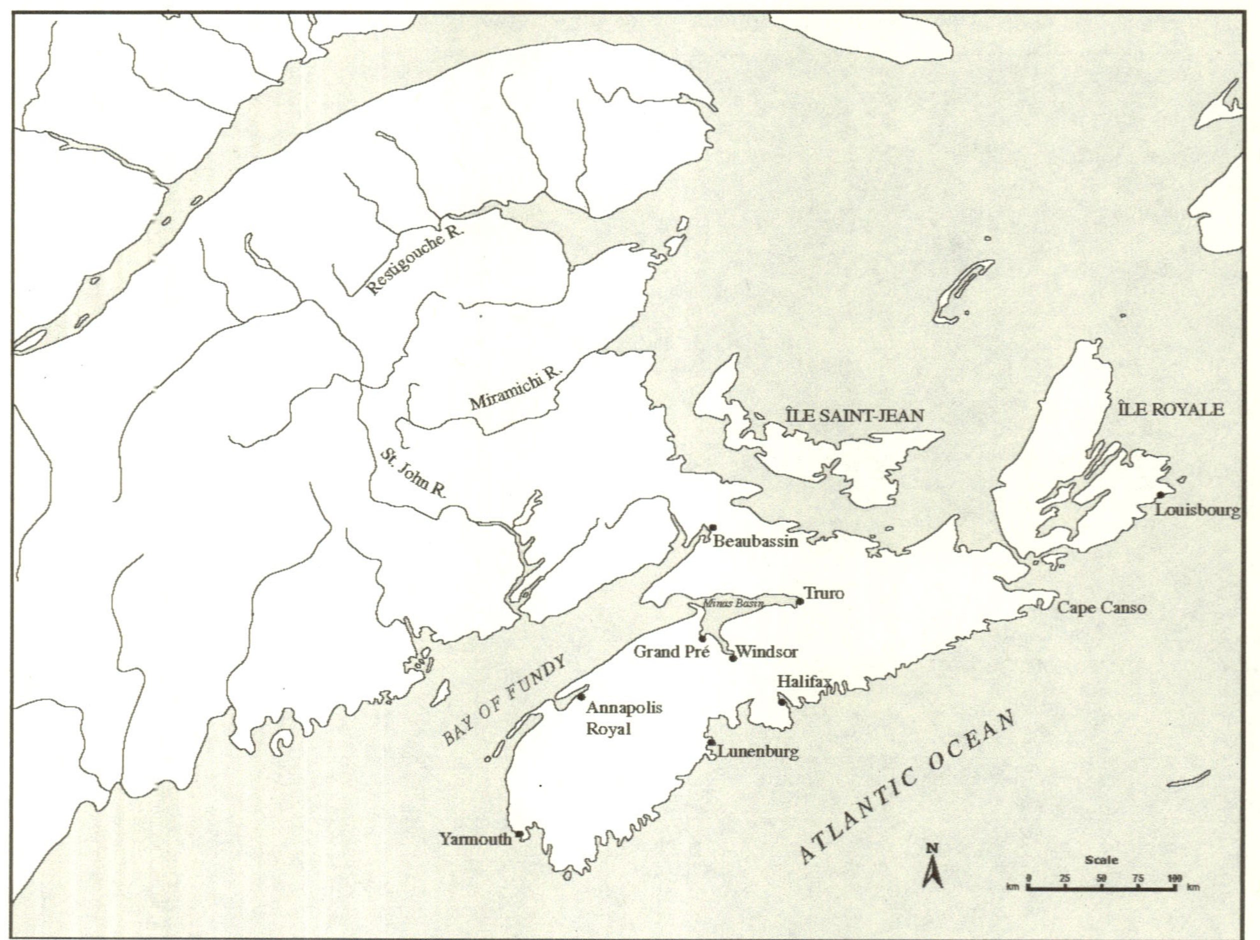

Map 7 Acacia/Nova Scotia, eighteenth century

ESSAYS ON NORTHEASTERN NORTH AMERICA,
SEVENTEENTH AND EIGHTEENTH CENTURIES

1 Introduction

This book has two distinct origins. In part, it is a record of work compiled since I began serious study of northeastern North America in 1970. However, it also responds to the 400th anniversaries that fell in 2004 and 2005. The summer of 1604 saw a group of colonists established on St Croix Island in the name of the French colony of Acadia, some distance upriver on the river of the same name that today divides New Brunswick from Maine. It was a disastrous venture, with all but ten of the participants suffering from scurvy and only just over half of the original eighty living to see the spring. During the summer of 1605, the survivors joined with a few newcomers to inaugurate a more lasting site at Port Royal, on what later became known as the Annapolis Basin in today's Nova Scotia. Port Royal too had troubled beginnings, although for different reasons. Scurvy remained a threat, but the abandonment of the settlement in

---

Earlier versions of this Introduction were delivered to the Graduate/Faculty Colloquium of the Department of History at Dalhousie University, to the 2005 Annual Conference of the French Colonial Historical Society / Société d'histoire coloniale française, at Acadia University, and to the Imperial Seminar of the Institute of Historical Research in London. I am grateful to all these audiences for their engaged and constructive comments, and especially to Jerry Bannister and Norman Pereira for their apt proposals in matters of terminology.

In the Introduction and throughout the book, northeastern North America is defined as indicated by map 1, encompassing in modern terms New England, the Maritime Provinces of Canada, the island of Newfoundland, and the portions of Québec and New York surrounding respectively the St Lawrence and Hudson valleys. Within that wider area, however, the geographical focus of the studies collected in the book reflects my especial interest in new England (particularly northern new England) and the Maritimes.

1607 was the direct result of the revocation by the French crown of the fur-trade monopoly held by Acadia's proprietor, Pierre Du Gua de Monts. Port Royal would be tenuously re-established three years later by a different though related French group, although by that time de Monts – acting through his lieutenant, Samuel de Champlain – had begun a small and equally precarious post in 1608 at Quebec.[1]

The Port Royal anniversary of 2005 had added poignancy, since that summer and fall also marked the 250th anniversary of the first phase of the deportation of the Acadians. It was no accident that 2005 saw the publication of a number of major studies in Acadian history by authors such as Naomi Griffiths, Ronnie-Gilles LeBlanc, and John Mack Faragher.[2] The *Grand dérangement* was marked by a formal act of commemoration at Grand Pré on 28 July 2005, sponsored by the Société Nationale de l'Acadie.[3] The historical importance of the Acadian expulsion, with which this volume deals only tangentially, is self-evident, even though there remains considerable scope for debate over its causation and over the subsequent processes that led both to a substantial Acadian return and to the creation of a far-flung Acadian diaspora. The commemoration, like its predecessor fifty years before, had elements of both solemnity and celebration. The 1955 ceremonies, while necessarily recognizing the suffering that had taken place two centuries earlier, were designed largely to celebrate not only the Acadians' survival but also – in the context of the efforts of the Société Nationale to launch for Acadians a new era of national consciousness and prosperity – the essential modernity of Acadians as a people of the 1950s.[4] By 2005, although celebration of Acadian achievement remained a prominent theme, the sombre implications had been firmly underlined by the long-awaited issuance of a royal proclamation that acknowledged in December 2003 the Crown's role in precipitating the *Grand dérangement*, with its immense human cost.[5]

Yet the 400th anniversaries of 2004 and 2005 had their own distinctive characteristics, and raised a complex series of questions. Not only did the anniversaries highlight the French origins of the earliest colonial ventures in northeastern North America, with their implications for the eventual development of the flourishing Acadian society that was disrupted by the *Grand dérangement*, but also they marked a critical phase of the encounter between empires and aboriginal societies – which had its own extended consequences. Just as the Acadian dimensions of the anniversaries were inevitably modulated by their falling between the royal proclamation of 2003 and the 2005 anniversary of the deportation, so the relationship between aboriginal nations and the state stood at a delicate pass. In 1999 the Supreme Court of Canada, in the case of *R. v. Donald Marshall Junior*, had recognized the treaty-based right of Mi'kmaq and Wulstukwiuk individuals to earn a 'moderate livelihood' from fisheries.[6] A further important judgment on logging rights under the same treaties of 1760 and 1761, in the interrelated cases of *R. vs. Stephen Marshall et al.* and *R. v. Joshua Bernard*, was expected during the summer of 2005 and was delivered on 20 July, just four days after the main commemoration of the landing of de Monts and Champlain at Port Royal. Although the logging cases went against the aboriginal defendants, the public prominence accorded them served to underscore the importance of reaching a stable, negotiated resolution of outstanding native-rights issues that were bound up with the entire process by which European imperial claims had been initiated in the early seventeenth century and then intermittently asserted over the centuries to come.[7] The increasing importance of negotiated solutions was exemplified in Nova Scotia by the signing of a tripartite – Mi'kmaq–Canada–Nova Scotia – Umbrella Agreement in June 2002, marking a milestone in the ongoing Mi'kmaq Rights Initiative and leading some five years later to the conclusion of a more detailed Framework Agreement as a blueprint for negotiations.[8]

That the 2004 and 2005 anniversaries would have complex and sensitive implications was not apt to come as a surprise. The 1990s had provided examples of just how intense debates over anniversaries could become, notably when competing notions of celebration and commemoration were at issue. Most international in its implications was the 500th anniversary of the first transatlantic voyage of Christopher Columbus, marked in 1992. Early indications that a celebration might be in prospect, reminiscent perhaps of the Eurocentric public expositions of a century earlier (including the famous Chicago World's Fair of 1893), brought about a decisive response from Native American organizations and others who advocated solemn commemoration as a more fitting approach to a sequence of historical events that had brought disaster to so many native inhabitants of the Americas. As James Axtell noted soon afterwards, the debates not only altered the tenor of the anniversary's observance but also stimulated an 'outpouring of Encounter scholarship,' which formed a lasting result of the quincentenary.[9] More recently still, and closer to home, the 250th anniversary of the founding of Halifax had been marked in 1999 amid unresolved tensions. The celebratory tone pervading the advance planning for the event prompted the Assembly of Mi'kmaq Chiefs to refuse participation in the ceremonies, pointing out not only that the establishment of Halifax represented in itself an encroachment on Mi'kmaq land but also that it had led directly to the offering of bounties on Mi'kmaq scalps by Governor Edward Cornwallis.[10] Again, the anniversary left a significant scholarly and creative legacy exemplified by a multidisciplinary exhibition at the Art Gallery of Nova Scotia, mounted with Mi'kmaq participation, and a new history of Halifax, but these were ventures independent of the official observance.[11]

There was also another way in which the complexities of the 2004 and 2005 anniversaries had been anticipated: through historical analysis of the ceremonies marking the anniversaries of a century before. Extended treatment had been given in earlier years to the related observances in Quebec in 1908, commemorating the establishment of Samuel de Champlain's habitation there, by H.V. Nelles and Ronald Rudin. For Nelles, writing in 1999 on the Quebec tercentenary as a facet of Canadian nation-building, an 'essential pluralism and multivocality' prevailed.[12] While the governor general, Earl Grey, led the imperial apologists who sought to concentrate the pageantry narrowly on benefits purportedly flowing to all Canadians from the outcome of the battle of the Plains of Abraham, a variety of *Canadien* organizations contested this focus by emphasizing both the tercentenary as such and the survival of French Canada following the conquest of 1759. Native performers recruited to play the roles of their ancestors, meanwhile, succeeded in expanding their participation to assert the dignity and value of the native contribution to any kind of founding mythology.[13] Rudin, writing four years later, explored *Canadien* celebrations over a more extended period beginning with the ceremonial reinterment of the remains of Bishop Laval in 1878 and ending with the tercentenary. The tercentenary itself, for Rudin, was characterized by a disconnection between the imperialist-influenced historical pageants and the more accessible processions and demonstrations that honoured the Catholic and francophone character of the *Canadiens.* Those who looked on the official pageantry with suspicion, or who objected to the substantial admission charge, were sufficiently numerous to be conspicuous by their absence.[14]

The observances of 1904 – which extended to Annapolis Royal and thus largely pre-empted any further major events in 1905 – were then examined both by Rudin and by Greg Marquis, in complementary articles published in 2004. Rudin's portrayal of a series of events that set out to celebrate a sense of shared progress in the context of early-nineteenth-century Maritime industrial capacity, and yet could not avoid tensions over the relative significance of the Protestant de Monts and the Catholic Champlain in setting the foundations for later prosperity, also took note of significant exclusions. Even at the ceremonies in Annapolis Royal there was no Acadian speaker, while in Saint John any necessity for including aboriginal participants in the reconstruction of Champlain's landing was neatly avoided by recruiting members of a local rowing club to dress up as what one participant described as 'sham Indians in canoes.'[15] For Marquis, who studied the tercentenary observances in Saint John from the time of the anniversary itself until the raising of a statue of Champlain in 1910, the affair reflected 'a blend of provincial patriotism based on Loyalist roots, contemporary imperialism and an emerging Canadian nationalism that embraced the "romance" of New France.'[16]

While, as Marquis showed, this ideological cocktail again elided the Mi'kmaq, Wulstukwiuk, and Acadian significance of 1604, it did owe a considerable debt to historians who assembled in the Saint John area for the occasion. The Royal Society of Canada met in nearby Carleton, and the New Brunswick Historical Society sponsored meetings that included addresses by representatives from the equivalent societies in Maine, Nova Scotia, and Quebec. Members of the Acadian elite such as Senator Pascal Poirier were among the speakers, while a special issue of the Saint John–based historical journal *Acadiensis* included a substantial article by Montague Chamberlain on the aboriginal peoples of New Brunswick. Yet there remained, in the historical meetings as in the official celebrations, a strong preoccupation with the Loyalists as the real founders of Canada, admittedly with Champlain as a worthy predecessor.[17] Historians would also be prominent in the ideological contests associated with the Quebec tercentenary, as francophone writers sought to adapt the works of Francis Parkman to give a heroic and a clerical gloss to the evolution of New France, while anglophones such as George M. Wrong portrayed the experience of New France as a romantic and integral phase of the history of Canada.[18]

Historians in the early twentieth century were not, for the most part, university-based. Although Wrong, already long-serving as department head at the University of Toronto, was the exception who represented an incipient shift towards the proliferation of academic historians, history was still more likely to be written by 'clergymen, lawyers, and journalists who regarded themselves as men of letters rather than narrow professionals.'[19] Albeit in the context of a small literary elite, such authors were fully accustomed to writing for, and speaking to, audiences that were public rather than academic. A century later, increased rates of literacy, when combined with the availability of affordably priced books and the development of the electronic media, meant that history could be directed to a much wider public. At the same time, history as a professionalized discipline had grown to be substantially represented in every university. The two phenomena, however, were disconnected. Academic historians had little obligation to communicate with a general audience, and many of them rarely did so. Thus, while it had become a frequent complaint of the historians that popular perceptions of the past – as represented, for example, in approaches to anniversaries – were dominated by outdated ideas and inadequate research, the reciprocal complaint was that professional historians wrote obscurely and often only for each other's consumption. There was no widespread agreement as to how to bridge the gap. It was true that a major public debate such as that over the Columbian quincentenary could transcend the schism at least temporarily, but whether the 2004 and 2005 anniversaries would generate a capacity to do so remained a question as the time approached.

In the event, academic historians had no cause to maintain that their interpretive viewpoints were excluded. Neither did their expositions predominate, but it would have been foolish to expect that they would. Anniversary observances, by their nature, are negotiated events. Participants intend them in part to showcase selected portions of a usable past, to focus attention on the issues and conflicts of the present by constructing the past accordingly. Historians, as citizens, may or may not sympathize with the goals that come into play, but their role and responsibility as historians is to act as guardians of the dispassionate and ethical use of historical evidence and as advocates for hard-won and currently defensible interpretive insights. Events preceding and surrounding the anniversaries provided substantial opportunities for doing so. The Federation of Nova Scotian Heritage, for example, joined with the Nova Scotia Museum to sponsor a largely attended conference in May 2003 on the theme *Anniversaries That Work: Content and Connections.* Bringing together representatives from museums, local historical and heritage societies, tourism organizations, and anniversary planning committees, the conference heard (among other speakers) from historians working in a range of relevant fields. The discussions were generally agreed to have been productive on all sides.

The most prominent observances in 2004 took place along the St Croix River in Charlotte County, New Brunswick, from 26 June to 4 July. The central events belonged to the first day, when aboriginal and Acadian cultural and political leaders joined at the Saint Croix Island International Historic Site with local residents and high-level representatives of the governments of Canada, France, and New Brunswick for a rain-soaked but impressive commemoration.[20] The equivalent ceremony in 2005 was held at the reconstructed Port Royal habitation on 16 July, in the context of a summer of Mi'kmaq- and Acadian-related displays and activities in the Annapolis Royal area.[21] Between the two were held a number of related events, including at least two that offered further opportunities to academic historians: a lecture series in August 2004 at Petite Riviere, on Nova Scotia's south shore, which had been an early landing site of the de Monts expedition, and a conference held at the New Brunswick Museum in September 2004 entitled *Encounter 1604*. At the same time, an innovative research project mounted by Ronald Rudin involved filming major commemorative events and interviewing participants. As well as potentially providing documentation for those who might be involved in marking the quincentenary in 2104 and 2105, the product of Rudin's work was an hour-long documentary film examining the 2004 anniversary and the debates it generated.[22] The film quickly gave rise to a debate of its own, as its concentration on the anniversary as a framework for the assertion by Passamaquoddy natives of an identity and a presence on the land on the Canadian side of the St Croix river prompted a response from Ronnie-Gilles LeBlanc, who argued that a legitimate Acadian perspective had been obscured.[23]

In short, the anniversaries of 2004 and 2005 had much in common with the marking of all such historical milestones, in that they were complex and at times contested events. Yet they were characterized in general by a widely shared determination to avoid the more exclusive elements of the ceremonies of a century earlier and even of some of the more recent anniversary celebrations. There was general recognition that, as well as marking developments that had profound significance in Canadian history as such, these events had a particular and legitimate importance for Acadian and aboriginal communities. For Acadians, especially in the long-standing historical context of productive coexistence between Acadian communities and their Mi'kmaq neighbours, there was proper reason for a celebration, even though tempered by reflection on the sombre implications of the 250th anniversary of the *Grand dérangement*. For aboriginal inhabitants – whether Mi'kmaq, Wulstukwiuk, or Passamaquoddy – who were in the process of reasserting treaty and aboriginal rights that had long been ignored, commemoration of a fateful series of developments could be combined with a cautious sense of assurance that 'despite the influence of the newcomers, we as a people have survived, changed but intact.'[24]

In addition, the anniversaries had afforded to historians and scholars in related disciplines some clear opportunities to participate in surrounding discussions, and perhaps even to influence their tenor. My own contributions, for which I will claim the former but not necessarily the latter significance, form the final section of this book. In brief, they argue that the assertion of imperial claims and the onset of colonization did not immediately alter the fundamental reality of aboriginal territorial control. They contend that one of the principal keys to a realistic understanding of the events of 1604–5 and of the developments that flowed from them is to recognize the essential fragility of both imperial pretensions and attempts at colonization. They also portray these developments as demanding a northeastern North American context for effective historical analysis, and appraisal over an extended period, rather than a more restricted geographical and temporal framework. And they maintain that what took place in 1604–5 did not unleash an inexorable series of consequences that was somehow preordained. Rather, there were many possible sequences, and uncertainties of cause and effect persisted over time. For all these reasons, there was no basis for triumphalism as the anniversaries were marked, but every justification for reflection on a significant historical turning point.

That these essays come at the end of the book rather than at the beginning reflects an effort to substantiate these arguments not only in the context of the discussions of 2004 and 2005 but also through my own studies reaching back another thirty-five years. I have been fortunate in living through a number of important historiographical evolutions. When I began studying early modern northeastern North America in 1970 I considered myself – in the now curiously outdated phrase of the day – an American colonialist, or at least an aspiring one. As such, it was not easy at the time to see any acceptable option but to respond primarily to a historiography that focused on the New England colonies, to a lesser degree on post-1664 New York, but disproportionately on those areas of concentrated English residency that stood within a day's march (which was not very far in the seventeenth century) of the shores of Massachusetts Bay.

My own interests were not exactly in this area, either geographically or historiographically. I was interested in northern New England, and especially in the nascent English settlements of Maine; as time went on, this interest extended further northeast to encompass Acadia / Nova Scotia. I was attracted by imperial history, and even by the legacy of the Yale-based 'imperial school' associated with Charles McLean Andrews.[25] There was a sense in 1970 that for, a young colonialist, both of these interests were guilty pleasures that should not be overly indulged. It was true that Charles E. Clark had just published *The Eastern Frontier*, although the extent to which the book would soon prove to be a turning point in the development of a distinctive historiography for northern New England was not yet clear.[26] It was also true that a knowledge of the work of the imperial school might be considered useful for the filling in of prosaic but necessary institutional background, and as an outmoded body of scholarship against which the glories of colonial community studies could be savoured. Beyond that, however, imperial history was decidedly out of fashion as a dimension of the colonial past. Aboriginal history was even more disconnected. Although historians such as Douglas Edward Leach and Alden Vaughan had quite recently published on the troubled relationship of New Englanders with native inhabitants, there was nothing in the work of either author to suggest that aboriginal societies had anything but peripheral significance vis-à-vis the English colonies.[27] Indeed, there was a lingering sense, soon to be dispelled by the work of such scholars as Axtell, Francis Jennings, and Wilcomb E. Washburn, that the aboriginal past was properly the preserve of ethnologists rather than of historians as such.[28]

As the United States– and British-based historiographies of the late twentieth century evolved, it was not only aboriginal history that underwent a transformation. Aboriginal history saw the most immediately dramatic changes, as Jennings's vigorous 1975 denunciation of the victimization of the Pequot, the Wampanoag, and others at the hands of ruthless Puritans opened the door for more nuanced treatments of the dispossession of aboriginal groups to make way for New England settlement. Especially influential was William Cronon's *Changes in the Land*, which offered in 1983 a sophisticated environmental analysis of the erosion of the ecological basis for existing aboriginal society, while authors such as Neal Salisbury and John Demos demonstrated the insights arising from cultural study: notably of, respectively, the religious dimensions of aboriginal culture and the cultural attractions of aboriginal society even for captured colonists.[29]

The study of empire, meanwhile, enjoyed a revival that stemmed from the emergence in British historiography of a 'new imperial history' based on elements ranging from John Brewer's examination of the 'fiscal-military state' to the launching of wide-ranging reconsiderations of the nature of empire such as that of P.J. Cain and A.G. Hopkins and the drawing of insights from the eighteenth-century Asian experience of empire through the works of authors including C.A. Bayly and P.J. Marshall.[30] The publication of the first five volumes of the *Oxford History of the British Empire* in 1998 and 1999 consolidated and refocused a still-expanding historiography, while also giving rise to renewed debates centring on the use of economic, social, and – increasingly – cultural analysis to offset traditional institutional approaches to the nature of empire.[31] Colonial history in northeastern North America has also gained since the 1980s from the wider perspective of the 'Atlantic world' approach, which by the early years of the twenty-first century had gained sufficiently in sophistication and diversity as to generate both geographical and theoretical subdivisions.[32] Integrating themes from all four continents bounding the Atlantic Ocean from east to west, studies of the Atlantic world have provided a wide variety of contexts for colonial development, as well as connecting imperial and colonial activity.[33] The Atlantic approach has also facilitated new studies of the significance of oceanic spaces themselves, and of the exploitation of their resources through fisheries.[34]

Yet even the Atlantic-world approach, with its praiseworthy linkages of imperial with colonial – and, indeed, imperial with aboriginal – analyses, has limitations that are inherent in its focus on the ocean and its rims. In his tellingly entitled *Facing East from Indian Country: A Native History of Early America*, Daniel K. Richter advocates a 'visual reorientation' by which the Atlantic ocean can be seen as peripheral to the aboriginal history of the continent not yet known as North America to the vast majority of its residents.[35] Much as the notion of the Atlantic world has opened up the colonial history of North America – including northeastern North America – to the realities of a wider system of social, economic, and cultural exchanges, there remains a profound historiographical separation between two respective principles, even though each may be valid enough in its own terms: the principle that the elucidation of the Atlantic exchanges has a unique explanatory power and the principle that the 'Old World' of aboriginal North America has a continuing and legitimate centrality throughout the early modern period.[36]

Over the same three to four decades, however, the largely Canadian-centred historiography of French-influenced areas of northeastern North America has followed a different path, prompted or at least affected by the simple impossibility of understanding French colonization efforts in isolation from their imperial and aboriginal contexts. The attainment by colonial settlements of any substantial degree of autonomy from imperial and aboriginal influences was inseparable from the kind of defensive stability, environmental change, and economic complexity that came with dense and rapidly growing population. While it is highly debatable to what extent at any given time the British colonies had crossed thresholds in these respects, and notably in regard to military defence, the colonies that made up New France were conspicuously less heavily populated.[37]

Thus the many studies, recent and not-so-recent, that have set French colonization in its wider contexts. One measure of this phenomenon can be found in the work of authors who have worked seriously and contributed innovatively to either imperial or colonial history – or both – and to aboriginal history. An early example can be found in the too-often overlooked but pioneering work of Robert Le Blant. The author of a long series of important articles on seventeenth-century transatlantic commercial linkages, Le Blant during the 1930s was the biographer not only of the colonial governor Philippe de Pastour de Costebelle but also of the third baron de Saint-Castin. While Le Blant obviously did not have the benefit of later ethnohistorical techniques, he nevertheless interpreted Saint-Castin's career in the full context of his adopted Wabanaki identity.[38] Another biographer of a prominent French colonial governor, this time an iconoclastic treatment of the comte de Frontenac, was W.J. Eccles. As well as writing other major studies of New France and of French imperialism, Eccles – with the spur of being called as an expert witness in a major native-rights legal case – later became a leading exponent of aboriginal history and the author of the ground-breaking article 'Sovereignty-Association, 1500-1783,' in which he affirmed the persistence of aboriginal sovereignty and land title despite the existence of New France.[39] A third example is the work of Bruce Trigger, who was looking east from Indian country long before the phrase was coined. Author of the definitive ethnohistory of the Huron, Trigger subsequently offered a far-reaching re-evaluation of French imperial outreach, emphasizing the role of traders as opposed to state officials and missionaries.[40]

Yet, if over the longer term there has been a significant historiographical distinction in that the study of the French-influenced areas of northeastern North America has prompted a diversity even within the bodies of work of individual scholars that would be unusual in the study of the British-influenced areas, there have nevertheless been convergences in recent years. The Atlantic-world approach has extended its influence far beyond the British Atlantic, as Kenneth J. Banks's recent culturally oriented study of the eighteenth-century French Atlantic has clearly demonstrated.[41] Another important departure has been the launching of borderlands studies, which by their very nature imply comparative and cross-cultural analyses. For the early modern period, Richard White's celebrated *The Middle Ground* deservedly continues to exert a strong influence, with its depiction of commercial, political, and cultural interactions in areas of only incipient non-aboriginal settlement.[42] Moreover, authors such as Karen Ordahl Kupperman and, most recently, Evan Haefali and Kevin Sweeney in their study of the Deerfield raid of 1704, have introduced sophisticated multifaceted perspectives to the examination of, respectively, cultural identifications (self- and otherwise) and military/diplomatic collisions in areas of British influence.[43] And Alan Taylor's volume in the Penguin History of the United States, *American Colonies*, offers a broad North American synthesis embedded not in the national project that Taylor explicitly disclaims but in 'an Atlantic perspective, environmental history, and the ethnohistory of colonial and native peoples.' Taylor's even more recent *The Divided Ground*, moving forward from White's earlier insights and from existing borderlands historiography, has fashioned a bold and convincing reinterpretation of the nature – in an aboriginal context – of the emerging post-revolutionary border between the United States and British North America.[44] Meanwhile, important syntheses of the French experience of the Americas and of related non-French peoples, by Gilles Havard and Cécile Vidal and by James Pritchard, have even more recently reached publication.[45] Havard's *Empire et métissages* has also brought a new clarity to analysis of the significance of aboriginal–French relations – formal and informal – in the Great Lakes region. 'Le Pays d'en Haut,' argues Havard, 'n'était ... pas un poids mort ou une zone de déperdition pour l'empire [français]: il était sa chance. La faiblesse du peuplement français, loin d'y être un handicap, constituait en effet l'une des conditions de l'alliance, laquelle soutenait la Nouvelle-France.'[46]

Yet significant questions remain. Is there any prospect of solidifying these convergences so as to measure the degree to which the overall human experience – in all its cross-cultural complexity – was comparable between French- and British-influenced areas of northeastern North America in the early modern period? Is there scope for discussing ways of thinking about the processes at work in this time and place while doing equal justice to the Atlantic world and to the eastward-facing aboriginal reality, and to areas of both heavy and light or non-existent colonial settlement? The essays that follow suggest, from varying perspectives and in diverse contexts, that a useful starting point is to separate for analytical purposes – but consistently juxtapose – the closely related processes associated with the colonial, imperial, and aboriginal facts in northeastern North America. Specifically, I propose that attention be focused on colonial habitation, imperial exchange, and aboriginal engagement.

Colonial habitation was a phenomenon that, from the early seventeenth century onwards, had a pervasive influence. The term can be used to capture a wide variety of situations in which western Europeans resided for short or long periods of time in northeastern North America, and also Africans in limited though locally significant numbers.[47] The range would extend from the relatively dense and partly urbanized populations that were emerging by the early eighteenth century in Canada, Île Royale, southern New England, and New York, to the rural and resource-harvesting clusters that existed elsewhere. It would encompass everything from overwintering to multigenerational settlement. There are, of course, certain difficulties involved in adopting such a generalized term, notably arising from its coarse texture. To what degree can the experience of an eighteen-year-old fisher from Barnstaple or La Rochelle, who expects to measure his stay on Conception Bay or Chedabucto Bay in terms of one or at the most two or three winters, really deserve to be put in the same interpretive basket as the patriarchs (or the matriarchs for that matter) of families such as de Ramezay, Winthrop, or van Rensselaer?

Yet the usefulness of the term 'colonial habitation,' I would argue, lies in its offering a counterweight to two common but flawed notions of colonization: the idea of the colony as an essentially institutional phenomenon, the creature of the imperial state; and the Whiggish belief that small-scale colonial communities must necessarily, unless they should fail, be the prelude to the growth of larger ones and thus form part of the ineluctable process by which North America became a colonized space. The institutional view of colonies is belied by a number of strands of recent scholarship, but by none more clearly than in analyses of Acadian society. Studies by authors such as Naomi Griffiths, Maurice Basque, and others have revealed the complexities – the cohesiveness and also the fault lines – of a substantial and diverse residential community that organized itself largely independently of formal institutional structures, or at least in an ongoing process of negotiation with them.[48] As for small size, the recent study of seventeenth-century Newfoundland by Peter Pope has surely established once and for all that residential communities do not have to be large or even rapidly growing to have a critical historical significance in the North Atlantic world. Not only has Pope demonstrated that both planters and servants were central to a trade economy that linked the Atlantic coast of Europe to both New England and New France, but also that – the small size of the community notwithstanding – a planter on the scale of Sir David Kirke of Ferryland (who in a previous phase of his life had been one of the 1629 conquerors of Quebec) was 'a big fish in what was then a very big pond.'[49] Colonial habitation rightly commands considerable attention from historians. Residential communities were central to many important processes of change in early modern northeastern North America, not least because by definition they involved population movement and some form of environmental alteration. But any realistic appreciation of their significance cannot avoid taking into account the enormous variation in shape, size, and texture of life that they encompassed.

Imperial exchange, a term that owes much to the central insight of 'Atlantic world' scholarship that transatlantic influences could travel in either direction with multiple trajectories, can be associated in part with the operation of the state in its manifold forms. At times the state might seek to promote colonial settlement and the economic development of colonial communities, though not necessarily – as James Pritchard has recently argued with respect to the French state – to any great effect.[50] At other times and places, the state might actively discourage settlement, as the Port Royal colonists in Acadia found out in 1607. The state might seek to intervene actively in a political or military sense – whether to govern subjects, to make alliances with aboriginal neighbours, or to attempt coercive measures against either – or it might have recourse to less active strategies such as co-opting members of colonial elites to act as its agents.[51] All of these initiatives could have unpredictable results on either side of the ocean. Yet imperial exchange involved much more than the activity of the state. Commercial enterprise was the origin of much, though not all, of the outreach of western Europe into the wider world during the early modern era. Some areas of northeastern North America, with Newfoundland the clearest example, were so closely tied to commercial outreach that the state long maintained a profound ambivalence towards colonization. Even those areas that experienced colonization on the level of, say, Canada retained important linkages with transatlantic trade. Louise Dechêne, in her study of seventeenth-century Montreal, maintained that 'Canada was created by merchant capital as an offshoot of metropolitan interests to which it remained subservient,' while Dale Miquelon's study of the Dugard merchant house of Rouen pushed well into the eighteenth century and identified a different kind of middle ground, 'where the economic sphere overlaps with the social.'[52]

Clearly too, imperial exchange could take cultural forms, ranging from religious missions and movements to the melding of legal cultures.[53] Also partly cultural, though also involving the independent enterprise and sometimes the genetic legacy of – typically – male sojourners is what can be described as informal empire or, in the suggestive phrase often used by historians of Portuguese imperialism, 'shadow empire.' The temporary or permanent assimilation of such individuals as, in the northeastern North American context, the baron de Saint-Castin into indigenous societies could result in new patterns of interaction and kinship.[54] The phenomenon is of course also comparable with the formation of fur trade society in more northerly and westerly reaches of North America.

Critical to our understanding of colonial habitation and imperial exchange is the equally persistent process of aboriginal engagement. Without, of course, suggesting that aboriginal history in the early modern period can be evaluated only by measuring responses to what was at first a highly peripheral non-aboriginal presence, nevertheless in northeastern North America in this era the non-aboriginal intrusions were persistent enough to emerge as a substantial factor placing demands on aboriginal leaderships. The demands could take many forms, ranging from requests for trade and alliance to the dilemmas presented by assertions of superiority, land appropriations, environmental degradation through agriculture, and even military aggression. The responses were just as varied, and often delicately nuanced. Commercial interactions would frequently underlie cultural or military alliance. Warfare and diplomacy could be opposite sides of the same coin when dealing with imperial officials. In varying circumstances, aboriginal inhabitants might welcome colonial residents to the extent of seeking kinship ties with them, might withdraw as far as possible from any form of direct contact – in effect, in a case such as that of the Beothuk, disengagement became a form of engagement – or might simply decide unceremoniously to expel the intruders. All of these approaches presuppose that aboriginal decision-making was able to take place in a context where realistic choices were available. This was not true at all places and times, notably where epidemic disease undercut populations at critical times or where large bodies of colonial settlement brought about sudden environmental degradation. The area known to the English as southern New England was the scene of a lethal combination of these factors, compounded in its results by highly effective military action, notably against the Pequot.[55] Yet this, like the establishment of a substantial colonial population itself, was a local phenomenon. Despite the historiographical importance of Francis Jennings's impugnment of the ruthless use of Puritan military force, the norm in northeastern North America was that the non-aboriginal presence retained a marginal quality well into the eighteenth century.[56] The adaptive ability of aboriginal polities long continued, with local exceptions, to be expressed in wilful decision-making.

Colonial habitation, imperial exchange, aboriginal engagement: each of these was or became, I suggest, a pervasive phenomenon throughout early modern northeastern North America. All of them, however, were processes rather than structures, the variations within each were considerable, and they were interactive. Thus, there were many distinct combinations that shaped the human experience at different times and places.[57] Yet, northeastern North America remains an arena of distinctive complexities of human interaction in this period. Not only were there environmental differences separating northeastern North America from neighbouring areas but also human ones. Further north, the sparsity of colonial habitation persisted until a much later era. Further south, the presence of Africans in large numbers made for an equally important but distinct series of interrelationships. Further west, the transition to a more intrusive form of colonial habitation was played out in a later and entirely different diplomatic and military context. Early modern northeastern North America, diverse as were the combinations among the processes unfolding there, provides in my view a manageable and logical basis for historical study, and an opportunity to bring together strands of interpretation – colonial, imperial, aboriginal – to a degree that would have been unimaginable to an American colonialist of decades gone by. Similarly, anniversaries such as those of 2004 and 2005 provide an opportunity to reflect on the lasting implications of historical developments that were just as complex and contested as the processes of negotiation that surround anniversary observances themselves.

In adapting essays of varying age for inclusion in this book, some previously published and some not, I have avoided making fundamental revisions. My working principle has been that any piece that was clearly unable to stand on its original merits did not deserve a place in the collection. Nevertheless, as well as correcting any errors that may have come to light, I have not hesitated to refine the essays in matters of detail and in any areas where more recent scholarship has provided relevant insights. These emendations range from simply providing endnote references to updating certain interpretive passages, but none of them alters the central import of any essay. The first group of essays deal with colonial issues, focusing primarily on the early and middle decades of the seventeenth century and on the colonies I initially studied: Acadia, Maine, and New Scotland. Emphasized throughout is the fragility of colonial habitation. The second group, which includes one essay co-authored by Emerson W. Baker, addresses imperial questions reaching into the early eighteenth century. Beginning with the ability of one prominent individual to use empire as a tool of social mobility, the section also explores the malleability of imperial claims and the negotiation of British imperial authority with non-British peoples as an element of imperial exchange. The third group, dealing with aboriginal matters, again includes an essay co-authored with Baker. Taking up again the issue of negotiated relationships, this section emphasizes the military power and diplomatic sophistication that was mobilized in the interests of aboriginal engagement well into the second half of the eighteenth century. The final group of essays builds on the contentions of the first three, and represents my response to the anniversaries of 2004 and 2005. Not primarily research-driven, these essays were designed rather to contribute to the negotiated character of the anniversary commemorations in which historians engaged with participants who brought other perspectives to the table.

Beginning with an essay questioning the interpretive value of a purely linear approach to the process that began in 1604–5 and advocating a cautious exploration of counterfactuality as an interpretive device, this section concludes with discussions of the significance of anniversaries as opportunities to consider the career of Champlain and the development of Acadia. A short Epilogue advances some final reflections.

PART ONE

Colonial Habitation

2 Sir William Alexander and North American Colonization

On 12 February 1640, Sir William Alexander, first Earl of Stirling, died in London, at the approximate age of sixty-three years.[1] His death was probably the only way in which Alexander could have obtained release from the host of difficulties that plagued the last years of his personal and public life. As Charles I's principal secretary of state for Scotland, he had been deeply involved in that monarch's efforts to impose an unfettered episcopacy on the Church of Scotland. In 1639 he had travelled north with the king during the first campaign of the so-called Bishops' War, when Charles had failed to overawe the Covenanting army with what turned out to be a display of military weakness rather than strength. Had he lived, Alexander undoubtedly would have been caught up in the crisis that led to the English Civil War. At the same time, his personal affairs were chaotic. So complete was the bankruptcy that had stemmed from his expensive efforts at North American colonization in earlier years that creditors may well have outnumbered other visitors at his deathbed. It seems that the presence of creditors disrupted his funeral in Stirling, and so great were his debts that by 1641

This essay was originally delivered in 1990 as a public lecture at the University of Edinburgh, sponsored by the Centre of Canadian Studies, to mark the 350th anniversary of Sir William Alexander's death. It was the only time when my parents, along with three of my Scottish aunts, heard me deliver a lecture. Ged Martin, then Director of the Centre, was my host, while Allan Macinnes, now of the University of Strathclyde, made valuable comments on an earlier draft of the text. The essay was first published as a booklet by the Centre of Canadian Studies, with the encouragement of George Shepperson and the support of the Agent-General for Nova Scotia in the United Kingdom.

the Scottish parliament had had to strike a committee to deal with the claims being made on the Stirling estate.[2] Thus, despite the bright promise that had seemed to attend Alexander's early career as a poet and a royal official, it would have been hard at the time of his death to find any observer willing to pronounce his life a story of success. Nevertheless, Alexander had been a leading participant in Scotland's short-lived attempt in the 1620s and 1630s to attain an overseas empire. While unsuccessful, this effort had at least inaugurated the title of 'Nova Scotia,' which came to be applied more lastingly after the British conquest of Acadia in 1710. As a founder of sorts, Alexander has been given more generous praise posthumously by filiopietistic Nova Scotians than he ever enjoyed during his life. This essay will not join in the praise – historians are not usually by nature that way inclined – but it will seek to do more than just bury him over again. At a remove of 350 years from his death, and in the light of recent historical research and analysis, Alexander can be seen as a significant figure, albeit in ways that would not necessarily have been of his own choosing.

The biographical details of Alexander's life can readily be outlined, as he has not lacked for biographers. From the mordant satire of Sir Thomas Urquhart – who in 1652 wrote of Alexander that 'it did not satisfy his ambition to ... be esteemed a king amongst poets, but he must be king of some new-found-land; and like another Alexander indeed, searching after new worlds, have the sovereignty of Nova Scotia' – to the more recent and scholarly works of Thomas H. McGrail and D.C. Harvey, Alexander's career and personal characteristics have been described and debated.[3] A member of a not insubstantial landed family, Alexander was born in the Clackmannanshire village of Menstrie. Educated in Stirling and perhaps at the Universities of Glasgow and Leyden, he quickly found a powerful friend in his feudal superior Archibald Campbell, Earl of Argyll. Argyll, who was shortly to become notorious for his role in the brutal suppression of the Macgregors, introduced Alexander to the Scottish court and to King James VI at about the turn of the seventeenth century.[4] Alexander consistently sought social and political advancement, and he accomplished it. Part of the credit was due to Argyll, and to Alexander's marriage to Janet Erskine, a kinswoman of John Erskine, Earl of Mar, who was close enough to James VI that he was one of the chief architects of James's accession to the throne of England in 1603.[5] However, Alexander also took an active part in advancing his own aspirations through his skill as a poet.

The progression from poet to government official might not seem at first sight to be a natural one. Nevertheless, under a king who himself had solid literary credentials and who presided over a continuing bureaucratization of the government structures of Scotland that opened many new opportunities for office, the linkage was not so surprising.[6] Alexander's reputation as a poet has not worn well over the centuries. The inclusion of two of his sonnets in the Oxford *Book of Scottish Verse* assembled in 1966 is about the most that could reasonably be expected in any modern collection.[7] In 1603, however, the publication in Edinburgh of his *The Tragedy of Darius* earned him a respectable reputation, and a portion of this work may have provided Shakespeare with the inspiration for one of the crucial passages of *The Tempest*.[8] Over the ensuing eleven years Alexander published a series of other volumes of poetry that assured him of his place among the most prominent Scottish writers of the day and earned him selection by James VI as co-translator with the king himself of an edition of the Psalms.[9] Throughout this period, Alexander advanced steadily through positions in the royal household, received a knighthood in 1609, and in 1614 was appointed to his first position of real power as master of requests for Scotland. Formally charged with screening petitions directed to the king, the master functioned in practice as royal secretary. The role of the office had become more important after James VI's removal to London as James I of England, when the master of requests became a powerful intermediary in communications between the king and his northern kingdom. For Alexander, membership of the Scots privy council followed in 1615.[10] Thereafter, until the end his life, he retained office and favour. Named secretary of state for Scotland by Charles I in 1626 as part of that monarch's effort to govern increasingly through court officeholders rather than the existing administrative structure in Scotland, he was ennobled as Viscount Stirling four years later and became Earl of Stirling in 1633. Finally, in 1639, he gained the additional title of Earl of Dovan.[11]

Of the many indications of royal patronage that Alexander received, however, a number of the most conspicuous were related to his advocacy of North American colonization. First interested in Newfoundland, Alexander secured title from the Newfoundland Company to a large area of land on the south coast, extending westwards from Placentia Bay.[12] There, he wrote in 1624, 'I had made a Plantation ere now, if I had not beene diverted by my designes for *New Scotland*.'[13] The New Scotland scheme, much grander than anything that Alexander could have hoped to pursue in Newfoundland, had its beginning in an instruction issued by James VI to the Scots privy council on 5 August 1621. Noting that 'sundry other kingdomes, as like wyse this our kingdome [England] of late, ... have renued their names imposeing them thus upoun new lands,' the king ordered the preparation of 'a signatour under our great seale of the ... lands betweene New England and Newfoundland ... to be holden of us [by Alexander] from our kingdome of Scotland.'[14] When the charter was sealed on 29 September, it defined the territory of New Scotland as extending north and east from the length of the St Croix River as far as the St Lawrence River. Thus, in modem terms, it included the Maritime provinces and the Gaspé Peninsula. 'I thinke,' declared Alexander proudly in 1624, 'that mine be the first National Patent that ever was cleerly bounded within *America* by particular limits upon the Earth.'[15] By his own account, he was 'exceedingly enflamed' by the notion of colonization and by the benefits that might accrue to Scotland. As he declared to English colonial promoters he had met in London, 'my Countrimen would never adventure in such an Enterprize, unlesse it were as there was a *New France*, a *New Spaine*, and a *New England*, that they might likewise have a *New Scotland* ...'[16]

In attempting to bring about actual settlement of New Scotland, Alexander was about to encounter problems of a scope and scale that he was ill equipped to deal with. In the long term, the most serious had to do with counter-claims. Not only were the lands in question already occupied by aboriginal inhabitants, but also the same territory, or parts of it, had been included in grants issued to others by no fewer than three European governments: England, France, and the Netherlands. With the English promoters of New England, Alexander had a cordial relationship and expected no conflict. With New Netherland, the overlapping of claims was marginal. With France, the likelihood of serious dispute was much greater. French colonists had been in Acadia continuously since 1610, and although their numbers were small there was no reason to expect that France would gladly see its title challenged by the Scots.[17] A more immediate difficulty faced by Alexander, however, was simply the question of how to begin the settlement of the new colony. Basic but demanding tasks had to be undertaken: arrangement of shipping, provision of supplies, and recruitment of settlers. The first of these was quickly accomplished, as Alexander found a suitable ship in London in March 1622 and sent it to Kirkcudbright, in the south of Scotland. Despite a sharp increase in food prices in the early part of that year – associated with the dearth that would lead in 1623 to famine – he saw the vessel provisioned. The matter of recruitment proved more difficult. 'The very people specially Artizens,' Alexander wrote, 'of whom I stood in need, were at first loth to imbarke for so remote a part, as they imagined this to bee, some scarce beleeving that there could bee any such bounds at all, and no wonder, since never any in that part had ever travelled thither, and all novelties being distrusted, or disvalued, few of good sort would goe, and ordinarie persons were not capeable of such a purpose.'[18]

Not until August did the expedition leave for the transatlantic crossing. Evidence is lacking as to the identities of the colonists who had been eventually persuaded to embark, but whatever they may have lacked in skills and knowledge they did not make up for in enthusiasm. Prevented by a storm from reaching the coast of Cape Breton, the vessel turned back towards Newfoundland. To Alexander's later annoyance, it bypassed the lands he himself had been granted and finally made port in St John's. There, many of the intended colonists decided instead to sign on with fishing vessels for the next season. A few of the 'principall persons' of the expedition left St John's in late June 1623 and spent some four weeks exploring the coasts of New Scotland before returning to Newfoundland and thence to the British Isles.[19] For Alexander, the entire episode was a disastrous failure and – given his futile dispatch of a supply ship from London in March 1623 – an expensive lesson in the unpleasant realities of attempts to settle North America at this time. Undaunted, however, Alexander again made use of his access to royal patronage. On 18 October 1624 a letter went from James VI to the privy council to reaffirm royal support for New Scotland, and to announce the creation of an order of knights-baronets of Scotland, as a parallel to the English order that had primarily been instituted as a means of advancing the colonization of Ireland. The Scottish knights-baronets, the letter declared, would 'agree for ane proportioun of ground within New Scotland, furnisheing forth suche a number of persones as salbe condiscended upoun to inhabite there.'[20] A formal proclamation followed on 30 November, outlining details of the scheme. Each knight-baronet would be entitled to a barony of 30,000 acres in New Scotland, of which 16,000 would be personally held by the knight-baronet and 14,000 reserved for public uses, 'as for the crowne, bishops, universities, colledge of justice, hospitalls, clargie, phisitiouns, schools, souldiours, and utheris.' In return, the grantee would make a payment of 1000 merks Scots (£55/11/1 sterling) to Alexander, and would have the choice of sending 'sex sufficient men, artificeris or labourers' to New Scotland or paying a further 2000 merks.[21]

The knights-baronetcies had more than one purpose. As in other North American colonial ventures of the day, a structure of landholding was to be established that rested on conventional European practices. More immediately, however, this was a money-making scheme. It was designed to yield enough capital to enable Alexander to mount a further expedition to New Scotland. Its success was not great, as there was little demand for the titles – the technical unorthodoxy of which also produced disputes over matters of rank and precedence – or for the properties they supposedly conferred. Royal support for Alexander continued as strong after the accession of Charles I in 1625 as it had been under James VI. It was expressed not only in the issuing of a new charter for New Scotland in July 1625, but also in a series of royal letters encouraging likely candidates to become knights-baronets. One individual was bluntly informed in March 1626 that his personal advancement would depend on accepting the doubtful honour as 'a nixt steppe to a further title.'[22] For all this, membership of the order fell far short of the planned total of 150, and Alexander derived little financial benefit.[23] It was by digging deeply into his personal resources that he succeeded in assembling a small fleet at Dumbarton in the summer of 1627. After long delays, it sailed the following spring, commanded by Alexander's son – also known as Sir William Alexander – and probably in company with an English expedition under the Kirke brothers, which sought to capture Quebec. By November 1628, the younger Alexander had returned, leaving a group of colonists in North America. His father proclaimed in a letter of 18th November that 'my sone, praised be God, is returned safe, haveing left a colonie neare Canada behind him, and I am dealeing for a new setteing forth from Londoun.'[24] Another observer, William Maxwell, wrote five days later that 'it is for certaintie that Sir William Alexander is come home againe from Nova Scotia, and heathe left behind him 70 men and tua weemen, with provision to serve them be the space of one yeir, being placet in a pairt of the countrie quhilk is a natural strenhe.'[25]

On the face of it, it would seem that Alexander's difficulties with the knights-baronetcies had been triumphantly surmounted by this expedition of 1628. As with so many other aspects of his career, however, the reality was more complex and much less triumphant than the appearance. First, Maxwell had been mistaken in the location of the colony, as later evidence makes it clear that it was not located in New Scotland.[26] Alexander's reference to a site 'neare Canada' is too vague to provide any firm indication, although it is part of the evidence that has led some historians to speculate that the Scots may have wintered at Tadoussac, in the St Lawrence valley.[27] The contemporary account of Richard Guthry, however, raises another strong possibility. Members of a 1629 expedition that undoubtedly did reach New Scotland learned, during a brief stop in Newfoundland, of 'the pitifull death of many of our young men, that died [of scurvy] ... The scurvy is a sicknes insident to that country [Newfoundland].'[28] Obscure and fragmentary as the reference is, it suggests that the colonists wintered in Newfoundland – either on Alexander's lands on the south coast, or in St John's. Be that as it may, Alexander had certainly failed once again to settle New Scotland. In the spring of 1629, having settled certain jurisdictional disputes with the Kirkes during the winter by joining with them in the formation of a company to trade on the St Lawrence in a distinct but complementary role to the colonization of New Scotland, Alexander was ready to try yet again.[29]

The expedition of 1629 brought genuine success to Alexander at last, though it was incomplete and turned out to be short-lived. On 24 May the fleet left the port of London, from which Alexander had been hoping to organize his 'new setteing forth.'[30] After stopping in Newfoundland, they reached Cape Breton Island in early July, and one group of colonists was left to settle at Port-aux-Baleines, near the later site of Louisbourg. Commanded by James Stewart, Lord Ochiltree, the colonists of this short-lived settlement were apparently the product of recruiting efforts in England rather than Scotland. Later described by Alexander himself as '60 or 80 English,' they included some eight families of Brownists – congregrationalists who wished to separate from the Church of England.[31] The presence of the Brownists was an unwelcome surprise for the leaders of the expedition, and they were harshly denounced by one as 'factionists and schismaticks ... good Lord deliver all plantations from such people.'[32] Within weeks, however, the matter had become unimportant, as the Port-aux-Baleines settlement was seized later in the summer by a French force under Captain Charles Daniel. Some of the colonists were repatriated to England, and others taken as prisoners to France.[33] The younger Sir William Alexander, meanwhile, had proceeded to Port Royal, on peninsular New Scotland, with the other body of colonists. They arrived at the end of July and quickly fortified the site. For more than three years, it would accommodate the Scottish colony.

Of New Scotland and its colonists during these years, evidence is sparse. The first winter, as so often in North American colonial ventures at this time, brought disease and death. In 1630 Claude de la Tour – a French colonizer who had lived in Acadia for many years and who for a time identified himself with the Scottish colony, to the point of accepting a knight-baronetcy in 1629 – reported that 'il estoit mort trente Escossois de septante qu'ils estoient en cet hyvernement, qui avoient este mal accommodez.'[34] Certainly the elder Alexander betrayed his anxiety in February 1630 when he confided to the Earl of Menteith, president of the Scots privy council, that his son's 'saftie or ruine' depended upon whether supplies could be immediately sent to New Scotland.[35] Yet there were other, more positive, indications. The colonists had quickly established a cooperative relationship with native inhabitants, a prerequisite for the survival of the small settlement. The summer of 1629 saw a series of visits to Port Royal by Mi'kmaq and possibly Etchemin parties for trade and gift-giving, and late in the year the Mi'kmaq chief Segipt departed with his family for a visit to the court of Charles I.[36] With the few French who still lived in Acadia, led by Charles de la Tour (the son of Claude), there was no such accommodation. La Tour, who had long since moved away from Port Royal, maintained a settlement at Cap de Sable, in the southern part of the peninsula, and in 1631 built a fortified trading post at the mouth of the St John River. Even so, he was in no position to threaten the Scots militarily. Rather, the opposite was true, as a Scottish expedition from Port Royal was successful in seizing the St John fort in September 1632.[37] This action confirmed the growing strength of the Scottish colony, and justified the verdict of a lieutenant of the La Tours who had reported in 1631 that 'les Escossois ne se resoudoient point à quitter le Port Royal, mais qu'ils s'y accommodoient de jour à autre, et y avoient fait venir quelques mesnages et bestiaux pour peupler ce lieu qui ne leur appartient que par l'usurpation qu'ils en ont faite.'[38]

In the final phrase, however, was contained a reference to the issue that would eventually bring an effective end to the New Scotland colony. In April 1629 the interim peace treaty of Suza had brought an end to two years of war between France and the kingdoms of Charles I. When negotiations began for a final treaty, the French claimed the restitution of both Canada – which had been occupied by the Kirkes since a successful attack on Quebec which they had carried out in July 1629 – and of Acadia. On the question of Canada there was no argument, as it had obviously been seized after the peace had been concluded. On New Scotland, or Acadia, there were lengthy negotiations, during which Alexander argued that the Scottish colonization of Port Royal was not a violent seizure but a peaceful occupation of an area long abandoned by the French and now belonging to him by virtue of his charters of 1621 and 1625. Eventually threatening the peace itself, the issue was finally settled by what the British negotiators regarded as an honourable compromise: 'If Sir William Alexander wolde exchange that Seate [Port Royal] for some other upon the same coast, and not far distant from the porte Royall, and some meanes were found to indemnize him of parte of the charges hee hath been att to make his plantation, it may bee that wolde give them [the French] satisfaction here in pointe of honour.'[39] It was on this general basis that agreement was reached, and eventually embodied in the treaty of St-Germain-en-Laye in 1632. Alexander would order the evacuation of Port Royal, though without any formal abandonment of the Scottish claim to New Scotland. In the event, the Scottish colonists were brought to England in a French vessel early in 1633. Alexander himself received a series of honours from the Scots crown that were intended to preserve his prestige intact, including his patent as Viscount Stirling, and in early 1632 a royal warrant for £10,000 sterling was issued in his favour, 'for satisfaction of the losses that the said Viscount hath, by giveing ordour for removeing of his Colony at our express command.'[40]

The warrant was never paid, and a subsequent licence granted to Alexander to mint copper coins proved to be as unhelpful to his personal finances as it was damaging to Scotland through the currency debasement it produced. Nor, despite frequent royal assertions to the contrary and the confirmation of all of Alexander's rights in New Scotland by the Scottish parliament in 1633, was there any question of re-establishing the Scottish colony at Port Royal or anywhere else.[41] France had quickly proved to have every intention of securing its hold on Acadia. Its commitment to re-establishing its North American colonies had been consistently underestimated not only by Alexander but also by the British treaty negotiators. The compromise that was intended to satisfy the French on a point of honour was, in reality, a concession that was fully exploited in the dispatch of some three hundred French colonists to Acadia under the leadership of Isaac de Razilly in the summer of 1632.[42] Nor, given the state of Alexander's finances, would he have been in a position to re-establish New Scotland even if the French had held back. Repeated attempts during the 1620s had depleted his resources, and the knight-baronetcy scheme had done little to help. From 1632 to 1638, a further thirty-three knights-baronetcies were conferred, but following the demise of the Port Royal settlement the order could only be seen as a grasping effort to recoup Alexander's losses by selling meaningless titles. By late 1638, in the context of the worsening religious crisis in Scotland and the possibility of civil war, a committee of the royal council of war had recommended that a prerequisite for the raising of a royal army was the 'taking off all such projects as yield his Majesty noe considerable proffit and are grievous to his Majesties Subjects.' Among the taxes and monopolies listed were the 'Baronets of Nova Scotia,' and although the order was never suppressed, there were no further additions to it after December of that year.[43] Thus, New Scotland declined into obscurity. While it was true that the name of the colony survived in its Latin form to be applied in later years to parts of the territory that Alexander had sought to colonize, the term Nova Scotia had no further connection with Scotland except insofar as the province of that name received Scottish immigrants in the vastly different historical circumstances of the eighteenth and nineteenth centuries.

For Alexander himself, the collapse of his chief colonial venture did not end his interest in North America. Both he and his son William continued to be involved in trading and colonization schemes, ranging from a trading monopoly on the St Lawrence River and the gulf – awarded in 1633, when France was once again in full control of that region – to a large land grant obtained from the Council for New England in 1635. The main part of the grant extended from the St Croix to the Kennebec River, to be named 'the county of Canada,' but it also included Long Island, now to be known as 'The Isle of Sterling.'[44] Alexander was in no position to take advantage of this award, although he may have gained some modest revenue from it, as in 1639 he confirmed the sale of land on Long Island to a number of settlers.[45] In that year he was still hoping for fur-trading profits, but confessed to a correspondent that as yet he had seen no benefit from this quarter.[46] In reality, he was now only a fringe participant in North American affairs. It was true that Alexander and his son were admitted as members of the Council for New England in 1635, and that the council met at times at Alexander's London house.[47] But even this was a distinction that had little substance. Although the council had played a significant role in English colonization during the 1620s, it had been overshadowed since 1630 by the independently launched colony of Massachusetts Bay. In 1635 it surrendered its patent to the English crown and divided up remaining New England territories among its members. Thus, Alexander derived no significant advantage from his membership, other than the grant for the 'County of Canada' which he was unable to exploit.[48] At the same time, his influence in Scottish affairs was also waning. Although never losing office, and continuing to accumulate titles, Alexander became more and more clearly a spent force as the 1630s went on. Increasingly villified for his part in Charles I's efforts on behalf of episcopacy in Scotland – and especially over royal attempts to enforce the use in Scotland of the translation of the Psalms made in earlier years by Alexander and James VI – he became steadily less able to play effectively his role of intermediary between the monarch and the northern realm. On larger questions of state, he was a lightweight by comparison with more powerful figures such as James Hamilton, third Marquis of Hamilton, and the king's English advisers William Laud and Thomas Wentworth. The foundations of the limited influence that he had been able to wield, therefore, were significantly eroded. By the time of his death, honours such as his two earldoms and his judgeship in the Court of Session were just as thin a disguise for his loss of political authority as his North American involvements were for his failures as a colonial promoter, and neither could obscure the accompanying reality of his crippling debts and personal insolvency.[49]

If this seems to be a harsh verdict, it is mild compared to that delivered by Alexander's contemporary Sir Thomas Urquhart. 'The purity of this gentleman's [poetic] vein,' wrote Urquhart some twelve years after Alexander's death, 'was quite spoiled by the corruptness of his courtiership; and so much the greater pity; for by all appearance, [if] he had been contented with the mediocrity of fortune he was born unto, and not aspired to those grandeurs of the court, which could not without pride be prosecuted, nor maintained without covetousness, he might have made a far better account of himself.'[50] Nevertheless, later historians have, on the whole, been kind to Alexander, at least in his capacity as a promoter of colonies. None in recent years has been as fulsome as the nineteenth-century author Edmund F. Slafter, who maintained that Alexander's 'toils of twenty years and his whole private fortune, which he freely bestowed, constituted ... a noble contribution to the experience which was destined to be unfruitful for a period, but which was demanded, in the order of human progress, before American colonization could be crowned with success.'[51] George Pratt Insh, writing in 1922, was more cautious in describing Alexander as 'essentially a man of contemplation who became by misadventure, as it were, a man of action.' Thomas H. McGrail, in a full-length biography published in 1940, admitted that Alexander was 'an opportunist ..., that he was ambitious for material glory, that he was sometimes unscrupulous and occasionally sycophantic,' but regarded these failings as being of secondary importance compared with the bravery with which he pursued his grand though unsuccessful enterprises. S.G.E. Lythe, in 1960, described Alexander as 'the one Scotsman of the time who fairly bears comparison with the Sidneys and the Raleighs of Elizabethan England,' while D.C. Harvey in 1966 identified his 'courage and tenacity' and commented on the New Scotland venture that 'it cannot be regarded as a complete failure so long as the name Nova Scotia survives, and its citizens treasure their armorial achievement and their flag.'[52]

In the light of more recent analysis of European colonial attempts in North America during the early decades of the seventeenth century, however, it can be argued that Alexander's significance does not ultimately depend on the armorial bearings of the modern province of Nova Scotia or even on the personal qualities that he may or may not have possessed. The key to understanding Alexander's historical role is not to attribute to him extraordinary virtues or vices, but rather to explore the extent to which he was a representative example, even an archetype, of the colonial promoter of the 1620s. European ventures in North America at this time – with the exception of the long-established settlements in Spanish Florida – were still tentative. Although, before 1620, colonies had been essayed by the French, English, and Dutch, whatever modest successes had been achieved had been greatly outnumbered by the failures. Difficulties with climate and environment, failure to understand the necessity of cooperative relationships with native people, and failure to establish adequate economic and financial frameworks, had created obstacles time and again. Yet the survival – tenuous as it often was – of settlements such as those at Cupids Cove (Newfoundland), Quebec, and Jamestown gave rise to hopes that the right combination of capital accumulation, effective recruitment of personnel, abundant natural resources, and shrewd management might bring about success on an unprecedented scale. Early colonial efforts in North America had been founded on small-scale private enterprise. Scarcely better capitalized than the merchant concerns that exploited North American fish and furs through the much less expensive means of seasonal voyages, such ventures had consistently failed to support any but the smallest and most fragile outposts. Certainly, none had come close to justifying the massive territorial claims – Acadia, for example, was defined in 1603 as extending from the 40th to the 46th degree of latitude – with which they typically began.[53]

By 1620, new conclusions were being drawn by colonial promoters and would-be promoters. Efforts were made to divide North American lands into manageable units. Although the more fundamental emptiness of European pretensions to ownership of lands that were already occupied by native inhabitants had not yet been grasped – and still has not gained widespread recognition among non-native North Americans even in the early twenty-first century – it had become clear enough that it was ridiculous to attribute vast expanses of land to enterprises that could hardly sustain a tiny year-round trading post. In this context, Alexander's boast that his New Scotland patent was precisely defined by 'particular limits upon the Earth,' as opposed to 'sundry other preceding Patents [which] are imaginarily limited by the degrees of the Heaven,' indicated that he was consciously one of the newer generation of colonizers of the 1620s.[54] Not that this prevented him from repeating mistakes already made by his predecessors. The expedition of 1622–3 was clearly undercapitalized and ill prepared, and Alexander paid a heavy financial price for this miscalculation. Also characteristic of the 1620s, however, was the realization by colonial promoters that adequate financing and organization required state involvement. Earlier colonial schemes had frequently enjoyed what might be described as a neglectful benignity on the part of the state. Still in the 1620s, it was unrealistic to look for direct state investment in such a marginal matter as North American colonization. But there were other ways in which the state could assist: through support in international diplomacy, through delegation of governmental powers to colonial promoters, and above all through provision of inducements and incentives for investment of capital in colonial schemes. There again, Alexander responded in a way characteristic of the decade. The knight-baronetcy scheme, unsuccessful as it was, was a serious attempt to enlist the power of the state in the process of capital formation. In its own way, it corresponded to efforts elsewhere, such as the establishment in England in 1620 of the Council for New England, the chartering of the Dutch West India Company in 1621, and the foundation of the Compagnie des Cent-Associés in France in 1627.[55]

The importance of state involvement meant that, to have any chance of success in the climate of the 1620s, any prospective colonial promoter would be required to have certain personal abilities. One was the capacity to relate colonization to wider matters of state. In this respect, Alexander's government position gave him important advantages. Although his characteristic role was that of an administrator, rather than the more creative function of advising on the greater issues of the day, Alexander was well placed to be sensitive to what the most attractive arguments in favour of colonization would be. Aware of frequent suggestions on both sides of the border that Scotland, by comparison with England, had a surplus of labour that was channelled into unproductive occupations such as serving in foreign armies, he deplored in his 1624 tract, *An Encouragement to Colonies,* the compulsion felt by so many Scots 'to betake themselves to the warres against the *Russians, Turks,* or *Swedens,* as the *Polonians* were pleased to employ them.' Similarly, he continued, 'the *Lowe Countries* have spent many of our men, but have enriched few.' Furthermore, 'the necessities of Ireland are neere supplied, and that great current which did transport so many of our people is worne drie.' The conclusion was obvious: that North American colonization, with the trade and resources it would make available, was a productive use of surplus population that would tend 'to enrich that ancient Kingdome [of Scotland].'[56]

Alexander's reference to Irish colonization was an indication of a further major issue of state to which he addressed himself: the relationship between the crowns of England and Scotland and the Celtic parts of the British Isles. The colonization of Ulster by Scots – mainly Lowland, but also including some Highland settlement, as on the estates of the MacDonnell family, Earls of Antrim – began on a significant scale in the earliest years of the seventeenth century and continued intermittently, Alexander's statement notwithstanding, for a hundred years. For the New Scotland scheme, its significance was partly in providing a precedent for westward colonization and partly in that a significant number of those who undertook roles of leadership under Alexander were veterans of Irish colonization: Lord Ochiltree, commander of the short-lived settlement at Port aux Baleines, was a case in point.[57] Colonization had also been adopted during the reign of James VI as a possible means of subduing the north and west of Scotland, and the search for expedient courses of action in this area was ongoing.[58] By 1629, Alexander had a new departure to propose. 'Whereas ... Sir Williame Alexander, our Secretarie,' read the draft of a letter of Charles I in October of that year, 'hath agreet withe some of the headis of the cheeff clannes of the heighlandis of that our kingdome, and with some other persones, for transporting themselves and thare followers to setle themselves into New Scotland, ... wee doe verye much approve of that course for advancing the said plantaceone, and for debordening that our kingdome of that race of people which in former times hade bred soe many trubles ther.'[59] There is no evidence that any part of this supposed agreement was carried into practice, and yet the existence of the proposal indicated again the ability of Alexander to link North American colonization with the current concerns of the Crown. Arguments such as these, although always accompanied by the more conventional justifications such as that of religious conversion of native people, were at the heart of the campaigns for state support mounted by colonial promoters.[60]

Yet, in a political culture where personal relationships were crucially important, argument was never enough to secure state protection, no matter how plausible the case might be. Successful colonial promoters also required personal entrée to the court and to the small circle of those who exercised power and influence. This was true in Scotland, as it was in England and France. Access could be gained through kinship ties or those of féodalité, as exemplified by two influential French promoters of the 1630s. Isaac de Razilly, lieutenant-general in Acadia from 1632 to 1636, was related to Cardinal Richelieu, chief minister of France at the time, and Richelieu's family of du Plessis was the feudal superior of the Razilly family; Isaac de Razilly's successor in Acadia, Charles de Menou d'Aulnay Charnisay, was, in turn, his kinsman.[61] An alternative was for the promoter to be an individual who had attained position in government through extended service leading to high office, as in the case of Sir George Calvert, Lord Baltimore, who was English secretary of state when he acquired territory in Newfoundland that would later be known as the Province of Avalon.[62] Alexander qualified under both of these rubrics: connected with two powerful families, the Campbells of Argyll and the Erskines of Mar, he also had a long record of personal service to the Crown. Thus, in this further respect, he was a model candidate for the role of colonial promoter. There was, however, another implication of these personal qualifications, which related to the place of colonial promoters in the class structure. Persons who had the necessary state connections would be likely to come from a landed family – though not necessarily a major one – and certainly either from that background or a professional one. This played its part in creating the motivations that impelled these individuals towards colonization. While other motives cannot be excluded – political or religious – one advantage that colonization was perceived as offering was the possibility of combining the acquisition of extensive landed property in North America with the profits that might accrue from transatlantic trade. Colonization, if successful, might gain for the promoter a different kind of entrée: access to the expanding prosperity of merchant capitalism.

To Alexander, who from an early age had been assiduous in devising money-making schemes, the New Scotland charter of 1621 conveyed extensive economic privileges, including trade and fishing monopolies.[63] At a time when Scottish trade, and with it the burghs through which trade was directed, was enjoying significant growth, such entitlements apparently had great value. They opened the possibility of full participation by Alexander in pursuits that were urban, mercantile, and lucrative.[64] Yet, for Alexander as for others elsewhere who sought the same opportunities as he did, there was also a corresponding problem. Nothing in Alexander's personal background or in any of his roles – landowner, poet, officeholder, judge – prepared him to deal effectively with the essentially commercial decisions and dilemmas that colonization frequently entailed. Forced to rely on others, such as merchants and sea captains, for the expertise that he lacked, he soon found out that he could easily become their hostage, as debts and desperation mounted. On occasions when Alexander had to deal directly with commercial matters, as when he sought to finance a supply shipment to his son at Port Royal in early 1630, he encountered difficulties, compounded in this case by the need for him as a Scot to raise money in London. 'I can lift no monie here in hast,' he complained to a correspondent, 'the English marchants never taking Scottish securitie, and the Scotish factours not haveing monie.'[65] Superficially attractive, the colonial promoter's access to mercantile activity involved an effort to straddle the roles of two social classes, and it was an effort that could be uncomfortable at best, disastrous at worst. For a promoter of this era to make money on North American ventures was the exception rather than the rule: Alexander and d'Aulnay were just two who died financially ruined as a result of their endeavours.[66]

The career of Sir William Alexander, therefore, was a significant one in respect of his involvement in North American colonization, but the significance stemmed not so much from anything he did that was exceptional as from the remarkable extent to which he typified the North American colonial promoter of his time. Well qualified, by social background and by service to the Crown, to enter the field of colonial development, he also had the characteristic deficiencies of skill and experience that so often plagued the individuals who did so. Not that Alexander's own shortcomings fully explain the failure of the New Scotland scheme. Understandable miscalculations of the expense of colonization, the outmanoeuvring of the British negotiators by the French before the treaty of Saint-Germain, and sheer bad luck: all of these had an influence. While it lasted, the Scottish settlement at Port Royal was just as successful as any other new colony in North America up until 1629, and more so than most. Yet Alexander ended his days as only a minor participant in colonial affairs, and with only debts to show for his labours over the years. By the time of his death, at least in the context of English colonization, a figure such as Alexander was coming to be seen as old-fashioned. The totally different, and highly successful, model of colonization demonstrated by the Massachusetts Bay colony was one alternative to development along the lines envisaged by a colonial promoter on the older pattern, while the increasing stability of Virginia as a royal colony provided another. In this sense, Alexander was a transitional figure: more knowledgeable and sophisticated than an earlier generation of colonizers in North America, but soon overtaken by newer approaches. Even a transitional figure can merit historical analysis, however, and the career of Sir William Alexander, first Earl of Stirling, ending with his death some 350 years ago, is a revealing one not only for the historian of Nova Scotia but also for the historian of the wider question of European approaches to North America in the early seventeenth century.

3 Environment and Colonization Styles in Early Acadia and Maine

The early colonial histories of Acadia and Maine present striking similarities. Both colonies came under the domination of external forces early in the second half of the seventeenth century. In the case of Acadia, conquest by English forces in 1654 was followed by the domination of Massachusetts mercantile interests during the next sixteen years. In the case of Maine, the colony was directly annexed by Massachusetts between 1652 and 1658, an arrangement that soon became politically controversial, but was subsequently perpetuated in the Massachusetts charter of 1691. In both cases, the domination of external forces was accepted, even welcomed, by significant segments of the respective populations as a solution to the previous disorders. Thus, Acadia and Maine had reached the point by 1650 where both were unable to resolve their own internal contradictions. The purpose of this

---

An extract from an as-yet uncompleted doctoral thesis, this was my first published article. With the encouragement of then-editor Jean Daigle, it appeared in *La Société historique acadienne: Les cahiers*, 7 (1976), 105–17. The approach owed a great deal to my thesis adviser at the University of New Brunswick, Thomas J. Condon, and to his seminar on comparative approaches to North American colonization. Because this is the earliest-written essay included in this book, it is also the one that has been most extensively revised. Not only was my writing style thirty years ago wordier than it should have been, but also the absence of detailed consideration of related aboriginal issues (while justifiable within the limited frame of reference of the piece) needed more explanation than it originally received. Nevertheless, I still like this essay, especially with its environmental reflections. Portions of the essay were later integrated into my *Acadia, Maine, and New Scotland: Marginal Colonies in the Seventeenth Century* (Toronto: University of Toronto Press, 1981), and it was reprinted in J.M. Bumsted, ed., *Interpreting Canada's Past*, 2 vols. (Toronto: Oxford University Press, 1986), 1: 40–51.

essay is to explore the origins of this state of affairs. It will be suggested that the essential cause was a deep inconsistency between, on the one hand, the plans and concepts of the colonies' European promoters and, on the other hand, the realities of American colonization. In particular, the promoters failed to transplant conventional European landholding customs to their colonies. They had hoped to cover their land with tenant farmers and thus to induce a measure of social homogeneity. Their failure in this contributed directly to the extreme fragmentation of both projected colonies, in turn rendering Acadia and Maine unable to retain their distinct status from other colonies.

At the middle point in the seventeenth century, the eastern coastline of North America between the Piscataqua and the St Lawrence Rivers – while occupied primarily by aboriginal inhabitants – was notionally possessed by two discrete European colonies. From the Piscataqua to the Kennebec River lay the English province of Maine; further north supervened an area disputed between English and French, while the French colony of Acadia putatively occupied all lands north and east of the Penobscot river. Both Acadia and Maine, however, suffered from deep internal disputes that had by 1650 reduced them to virtual ungovernability. The several components of Acadia had for a time been brought together by the overarching power of Charles de Menou d'Aulnay Charnisay, who had held official position in Acadia from at least 1638 and in 1647 had acquired wide powers and privileges as 'Gouverneur et nostre [the king's] Lieutenant Général representant nostre personne, en tous les ... pais, costes, et confins de la Cadie.'[1] D'Aulnay had successfully asserted his authority in seizing the bases of rival fishing and trading establishments in Cape Breton and Miscou; but his accidental death in 1650 was enough to revive previous disputes within Acadia, especially in connection with the rival claims of Charles de la Tour, and thus to throw the colony back into chaos.[2]

In Maine, the nearest equivalent to the position of d'Aulnay was that of Sir Ferdinando Gorges as Lord Proprietor. Gorges, a longtime servant of the English crown in colonial matters, was accorded his proprietary charter in April 1639.[3] For a time he was able to govern his province through his kinsman Thomas Gorges, who was in Maine as governor between 1640 and 1643. Sir Ferdinando, however, never himself went to America, and by 1643 both he and Thomas Gorges were embroiled in the English Civil War.[4] Within a few years, the province of Maine had fallen victim to centrifugal forces. A dispute between two rival landowners, George Cleeve and Robert Trelawny (the latter acting through his agent, John Winter) led in early 1646 to predictions of a 'sivill warre' in Maine.[5] Although such a violent conflict never materialized, Cleeve managed to obtain parliamentary confirmation in March 1647 for the setting up of an independent province under his leadership, the province of Lygonia, within the theoretical boundaries of Maine.[6] The area continuing to uphold the authority of Gorges was thus restricted to the three small settlements of Wells, Agamenticus (later known as York), and Kittery in the southern corner of the province. It seems that Wells soon withdrew its allegiance in all practical terms and stood temporarily as a town in its own right – a Maine court record of December 1651 referred to 'the inhabitants of Wells, who formerly deserted this government' – so that the province of Maine was now splintered into three tiny jurisdictions.[7]

Thus, both Acadia and Maine had fallen into disorder and disunity by 1650. As such, neither was in any position to offer effective resistance to external pressures that had by 1658 forced both colonies out of existence for at least the time being. The various parts of Maine were taken over by the neighbouring Massachusetts colony between 1652 and 1658; while this was achieved over the opposition of the remaining officials of the colony, it was certainly favoured by a majority of the colonial residents, who saw a chance of more stable governance and a redistribution of land.[8] In 1654 an English naval expedition under Robert Sedgwick made an easy conquest of the principal settlements in Acadia. After some debate in London, the British government decided upon retention of Acadia, renamed Nova Scotia, and for the next sixteen years the area remained under the effective tutelage of commercial interests based in Massachusetts.[9] Here too, however, there is evidence that the residents of the colony were not averse to the change of government. Many colonists, for example, took the opportunity to migrate further up the Port Royal valley than their original sites, now being released from former seigneurial obligations. This is suggested not only by the evidence of the migration itself, but also by the efforts shortly afterwards of the seigneurial claimant Emmanuel Le Borgne to lure the Acadians away from the English allegiance by giving out lands. A later Le Borgne document complained of difficulties in collecting 'de petits droits seigneuriaux quy leurs appartenoient pour les terres qu'ils ont cedees en proprieté a divers particuliers a fin que leurs abitans fissent un solide establissement et qu'ils n'abandonissent son party pour se jetter en celluy des anglois.'[10]

In the cases of both Acadia and Maine, therefore, the colonies had fragmented by 1650 to such an extent that annexations by external forces were able not only to take place easily, but also to command support within Acadia and Maine themselves. That the colonies were not merely weak, but chronically divided, indicates clearly that the planning of the two had gone radically awry in practice: European conception had failed to harmonize with American reality. This was certainly a problem that was not unique to Acadia and Maine, since early-seventeenth-century colonizing attempts in North America had almost invariably suffered from faulty conceptualization. The earliest attempts had sought to emulate the alluring example of New Spain by finding deposits of treasure and a passage to the Far East. Such concepts as these were soon disappointed. During the 1620s, however, certain influential individuals in both England and France advocated North American colonization for its own sake, as a matter of national prestige and possible national profit. A prime example in France was Isaac de Razilly, a naval captain and Knight of Malta who in 1626 presented an important memoir to Cardinal Richelieu in which he advocated North American colonization on grounds of both diplomatic and commercial strategy; his chief counterpart in England was Sir Ferdinando Gorges.[11] Both Razilly and Gorges thought in terms of recreating European societies in North America, and so the titles of 'New France' and 'New England' took on a profound significance in the mind of each.

When it came to the process of settlement, it was natural that promoters such as Razilly and Gorges should be guided, again in conventional European terms, by the principle of 'nulle terre sans seigneur.'[12] Hence arose the seigneurial system envisaged in the foundation of the Company of New France in 1627.[13] A closely corresponding arrangement was embodied in the chartering of the Council for New England in 1620, and this became the ancestor of the similarly conventional land system that operated under Gorges's proprietorship of Maine from 1639.[14] The immediate question, however, was whether sufficient population could be attracted to the two colonies to make these plans feasible in practice. Where large resources of population did reach America, strong colonies could certainly be created; the most dramatic example in North America is clearly that of Massachusetts Bay, which quickly attracted colonists in numbers that astonished even the colony's leaders, owing to political and religious conditions in England. In Massachusetts, a totally new style of colonization unexpectedly arose from the resulting ability to push aside aboriginal populations already critically weakened by epidemic disease, based on powerful town organizations that granted land to their inhabitants without encumbrance.[15] In

Maine and Acadia, however, more conventional concepts remained, until undermined by the decline of both colonies into weakness and disunity by 1650.

The period between 1630 and 1650 was one of only modest growth in the settler population of Acadia and Maine, and it was also one of great uncertainties. From the scattering of isolated settlements that had existed in 1630, the two colonies had grown some twenty years later to have approximate populations of 350 and 1000 respectively. These populations were by no means homogeneous, and the motivations that had impelled settlement were very varied; the existence also of seasonal populations of fishermen and fur traders added to the diversity. What remained to be seen was whether the diversity would produce a healthy complexity or simply fragmentation. In this regard, there arose the problem – as old as colonization itself – of whether the exploitation of natural resources was compatible with colonization. Colonization as such, in the absence of large resources of population on a similar scale to Massachusetts Bay, required the venturing of large capital sums for little or no immediate return, while resource exploitation could readily and profitably be carried on without recourse to any but the smallest and most rudimentary settlements. Thus, even such an enthusiastic advocate of colonies as Nicolas Denys never progressed significantly beyond the fur trade and intermittent efforts to establish a sedentary fishery: 'Bien qu'on ait crû,' wrote this notable entrepreneur of Acadia, 'que mon principal bût dans toutes mes entreprises en ces pays-là a toujours esté le negoce des pelleteries avec les Sauvages; je n'ay jamais compté là-dessus que comme sur un accessoire qui pouvoit servir en quelque façon au capital de ce qui peut faire dans le pais qui est la pesche sedentaire et la culture de la terre.'[16]

In the face of this difficulty, settlements devoted exclusively to exploitation of natural resources seldom developed beyond the point of being small communal habitations. Even where they did develop further, they were insufficient to satisfy the ambitions of promoters such as Razilly, with his assistant d'Aulnay, or Gorges. The building of new societies in America, the promoters believed, required extensive areas of colonization, covered by tenants holding their land according to conventional European practice. Thus arose the efforts to establish such ambitious projects in both Acadia and Maine. To a degree both were successful, but only in small areas of each colony.

In Acadia, the principal centre of agricultural settlement was Port Royal. Although the headquarters of Razilly, who served as Lieutenant

General of New France from 1632 until his death in 1636, had been on the opposite side of the Acadian peninsula at La Hève, the colony was moved to Port Royal when command was taken over by d'Aulnay, acting at first as agent for the Razilly family and then in his own right. At Port Royal, d'Aulnay took over the former Scottish fort, and agricultural settlement thenceforward grew up on the marshes of the Port Royal basin. 'Il y a quantité de prairies des deux costez,' wrote Denys, 'que la marée couvroit et que le sieur d'Aunay fit desecher.'[17] The reason for the move to Port Royal, while not directly apparent from surviving sources, was probably not based purely on agricultural considerations, since La Hève also offered good land in the form of drumlins,[18] but perhaps reflects a change from the combination of agriculture and fishing to that of agriculture and the fur trade.

On the operation of the seigneurial system at Port Royal in this period, little source material survives. According to the nineteenth-century account of Rameau de Saint-Père, each censitaire at Port Royal received a substantial concession subject to a rent of one sou in perpetuity; remissions by d'Aulnay in order to facilitate the initial process of settlement were later repayable in the form of labour.[19] This description has been followed by other historians, but seems to be derived not directly from primary sources but by inference from sources relating to the seigneurial structure in Canada.[20] What is well established is that d'Aulnay took much personal responsibility for the establishment of French families at Port Royal and for the equipping of the settlement. Much later, in 1687, a number of the oldest inhabitants of Acadia certified that d'Aulnay had settled several families at Port Royal and had caused the building of several ships and installations.[21] D'Aulnay himself affirmed in 1644 that he had at Port Royal '200 hommes, tant soldats laboureurs que autres Artisants sans compter les femmes et les enfants, les Peres Capuchins ny les petits enfans sauvages qu'Il faut nourrir dans le Seminaire estably pour cela. Il y en outre 20 mesnages françois qui sont passez avec leurs familles pour commencer a peupler les Païs dans lesquels ledit sieur d'Aulnay en feroit bien passer d'advantage, s'il avoit plus de bien.'[22]

In another later document, no earlier than 1675, the Le Borgne heirs, who laid claim to d'Aulnay's legacy on grounds of his debt to their merchant ancestor, stated that 'depuis que le sieur de Menou [d'Aulnay] s'est veu seul proprietaire de l'accadie il a faict bastir au port Royal le fort qui supciste, une Eglize, et un Convent, Des moulins, beaucoup de logements, et fait desfricher un nombre considerable D'arpens de terre quy font trois metairies quy luy coustent plus de cent cinquante mil livres.'[23] In this description, the term 'métairie' may well have been used literally, implying a form of tenure by which equipment and land were both provided by the seigneur, in return for rents either in money or in kind, and a sharing between lessor and lessee of the products of each year's farming. This form of lease is best known in New France as an arrangement prevalent in Canada by which an elderly or widowed landowner might continue partially to enjoy the fruits of his land by renting to an habitant who lacked the means to hold land in any other fashion, but was also common in the granting out of salt marshes in the vicinity of La Rochelle and thus could have been readily imported to Acadia.[24] It would clearly have been convenient also for the interests of an ambitious colonizer such as d'Aulnay, allowing him to reap continuing profits from the lands of Port Royal without being distracted from his active efforts to monopolize the fur trade. How far it was satisfactory to the tenants is a different question, especially in view of the availability of large quantities of unused land further up the Port Royal valley. Nicolas Denys, for example, though a biased observer, remarked that d'Aulnay held his tenants 'toûjours esclaves, sans leur y laisser faire aucun profit.'[25] Furthermore, it has been noted above that Le Borgne had great difficulty in holding together any workable seigneurial structure after the tenants' bonds had been loosened by d'Aulnay's death and the English conquest of 1654. For the moment, though, and working with settlers who were at least in part drawn from his own family lands in France, d'Aulnay had a well-established, though small, seigneurial settlement as his home base.[26]

The colony of Maine also developed a small area of settlement on a pattern of conventional landholding by an agricultural tenantry, in this case the cluster of villages in the southern part of the province. This development was rather larger and more complicated than that of Port Royal, involving not the direct effort of a single seigneur to produce agricultural settlement, but the action of several landowners holding ultimately from the grants of Gorges as Lord Proprietor, or in some cases from the earlier Council for New England. In the early years, particularly in the case of those settlements that derived from the Laconia Company – a fishing and fur-trading operation on the Piscataqua River financed by Gorges and others from 1629 to 1634 – this southern area of Maine resembled the settlement of Razilly at La Hève in being based upon a combination of agriculture and fishing.[27] Several of the early grantees had been involved in the Laconia Company, a prime example being Edward Godfrey, who had had charge of the company's fishing operations on the Piscataqua River and became an early settler of Agamenticus.[28] From at least 1638, Godfrey was a major landowner in Maine, and in future years his practice was to sublet land to tenants who would pay either rents or services in return: on 16 February 1651, for example, a grant by Godfrey to one Thomas Waye involved the annual payment of two days of labour.[29] As an English observer, John Josselyn, remarked during his second visit to Maine in the 1660s, 'the people in the province of Main may be divided into Magistrates, Husbandmen, or Planters, and fishermen.'[30] Magistrates in the earlier period between 1630 and 1650 were, with few exceptions, also large landowners by grants from the Council for New England or from Gorges;[31] farmers and fishers in the vicinities of Kittery and Agamenticus – often, according to Josselyn, the same men pursuing both occupations – were their tenantry.

Sir Ferdinando Gorges, too, retained considerable direct interest in his province. Even before the proprietary grant of 1639, in his association with the Council for New England, Gorges had taken similar roles to those of d'Aulnay in Acadia, in providing equipment, settlers, and supplies. In July 1634, for example, John Winthrop of Massachusetts recorded that 'Sir Ferdinando Gorges and Captain Mason [John Mason, a close associate of Gorges, who had similar interests in New Hampshire] sent ... to Pascataquack and Aquamenticus, with two sawmills, to be erected, in each place one.'[32] Again, in late 1636, Winthrop wrote that a ship had arrived in Boston from Bristol; 'but she had delivered most of her cattle and passengers at Pascataquack for Sir Ferdinando Gorges his plantation.'[33] Gorges's continuing interests as Lord Proprietor of Maine from 1639 embraced both dues arising from equipment and direct rents, as Thomas Gorges made clear shortly after his arrival as governor in 1640:

> Rogers [an employee of Gorges] I intend to put into the grist mill as soone as I have it a litle repaired, which mill and the saw mill with a litle cost if they be well mended, as I hope they shall, will bringe in 200 li per an. to Sir Fard: at the least. As yet he hath but halfe the profit. Likewise the smiths mill will bringe in a good round sum, and in the interim he works it and will be every day comminge. Likewise the Rents of the Province will amount to a good round sum in time. Some now pay 10s per an., some 5s, some more, some lesse. At the next Court we intend to confirm all theyr leases and have exact account of arrears.[34]

Thus, in 1640 Gorges was optimistic of the continued working of the structure of landholding he had established in Maine. As in Acadia, however, this form of land tenure had more obvious advantages for landlord than for tenant. In Maine, moreover, the proximity of Massachusetts, with its freer system of land allotment by towns, gave added point to discontent among tenants. Certainly the tenants of John Mason and, after his death in 1635, his heirs, soon welcomed the annexation of New Hampshire by Massachusetts between 1641 and 1643, in that it enabled them to press aggressively for distribution of land by town-meeting grants on the Massachusetts model.[35] Indeed, it seems that from 1643 a form of land distribution similar to that of Massachusetts could be found in Maine itself, in the town of Wells. At the time of the Antinomian controversy in Massachusetts in 1636–7, Rev. John Wheelwright had become a close supporter of Anne Hutchinson, his sister-in-law, and had consequently been expelled to New Hampshire where, with a number of supporters, he founded the settlement of Exeter. When New Hampshire was itself annexed by Massachusetts, Wheelwright and some of his followers fled northwards in 1643. On 14 July of that year, Wheelwright, along with two associates, received a grant from Thomas Gorges as 'trustees' of the town of Wells. This grant, unique in Maine, suggests that the intention was to form a town on the Massachusetts pattern: although the land was held on tenure requiring the payment of rent to Gorges, the internal distribution of land could remain unencumbered.[36] In a real sense, this drove a wedge into the structure of Maine, differentiating Wells from the other settlements where tenants could hold land only on relatively restricted terms and by the direct payment of rents and services.

Even before the establishment of Wells, moreover, discontent had become evident. Writing to Robert Trelawny in September 1640, in the context of the latter's land dispute with George Cleeve, Edward Godfrey advised that 'Yf Sir Fardinando Gorges Cannot rectify you, then make you remonstrance to the Lords Comitioners, get a Comition to those that have pattentes [large grants of land], other wyse noe help; for here planters would have all Common.'[37] That Godfrey had not misjudged Cleeve's intentions is confirmed by a deposition of November of that year in which Cleeve was reported to have declared that 'he would be tenant to never a man in New England.'[38] Robert Jordan, moreover, the son-in-law of John Winter, wrote to Trelawny some two years later that 'in these parts ... actions are passed according to the conceipts of unknowing Planters, without the least referenc to the law, right or conscienc.'[39] This defensive feeling among patentees is further evident in a letter written by Godfrey to John Winthrop in July 1647 in which he complained of 'the rude multitud in waie of common priviledg ...,' and confessed that the more turbulent elements 'ar hard to bee suppressed by our weake power.'[40] Part of the patentees' weakness no doubt arose from what a contemporary observer, Thomas Jenner, described as 'their manifold debts in the [Massachusetts] Bay and else wher.'[41] The patentee Francis Champernoun, for example, although engaged in the mercantile aspects of the Piscataqua fishery, in December 1648 mortgaged half of his lands in Kittery to a Massachusetts merchant, Paul White, for a debt of £200 and subsequently defaulted on the agreed payments.[42] Like d'Aulnay in the fur trade, the Maine patentees were discovering that the fishery afforded insufficient profit to offset the expenses of colonization.

Here, then, was one crucial flaw that threatened the feasibility of the original plans for both Acadia and Maine: in both colonies, the promoters envisaged the holding of land by tenants on forms of tenure that carried restrictions both on the freedom of action and on the potential wealth of the tenant. Moreover, the financial problems of the promoters, and their consequent need for all possible revenues, would effectively prevent them from easing the terms. Among the tenants, on the other hand, such a restrictive system inevitably produced resentment in a seeming context of abundant land uncompromised as yet by serious aboriginal constraints. In Acadia initial colonization of the extensive Fundy marshlands had not aroused the antagonism of Mi'kmaq for whom access to coastal resources proved compatible with an Acadian presence, while in Maine the existing encroachments had strained relations with Wabanaki neighbours without as yet leading to widespread hostility.[43] Maine's colonists, close to Massachusetts Bay – where the displacement of aboriginal population had created the illusion of a greater New England with available land – were especially apt to see the advantages of a freer land system. The behaviour of the Acadian tenants after the death of d'Aulnay and the English conquest, however, demonstrates that they too entertained such feelings.

Moreover, if the landholding structures of Acadia and Maine had internal defects, they also had a further serious disadvantage in their intended role of providing social stability and homogeneity: they were not sufficiently extensive to offset the dangers of fragmentation through geographical dispersion. Although Port Royal and the southern corner of Maine contained the largest settler populations in the respective colonies, they were not dominant social influences. In the case of Acadia, the very shape and configuration of the colony made for fragmentation. The ports of the Atlantic coast of the peninsula and Cape Breton, relatively near to Europe and offering easy access to the best fishing grounds, tended to be centres not of colonial settlement but of the migratory fishery. The rivers of St John, St Croix, and Pentagouet, on the other hand, offered rich resources not so much for agricultural settlement as for the fur trade. The coasts of the Gulf of St Lawrence, moreover, offered opportunities for both fishery and fur trade. Thus, the small settlement of Port Royal was surrounded by vast areas of aboriginal territory that from a non-aboriginal perspective were exploited only by essentially commercial enterprises that depended for their subsistence not upon the land of Acadia, but upon exportable natural resources and upon predominantly European capital and marketing. Hence, the colony was inevitably lacking in economic coherence and offered few prospects of supporting the kind of large-scale agricultural settlement that alone could rectify this situation but was utterly unattainable in the existing context of aboriginal control.

The force of environmental pressures in dividing the colony of Acadia becomes further apparent when it is considered that the situation was not necessarily the result of deliberation on the part of those individuals involved. It has been noted that Nicolas Denys's enthusiasm was for settlement that, like southern Maine, would combine agriculture with a sedentary, American-based fishery; but his fishing, fur trading, and lumbering enterprises on the Atlantic and Gulf coasts, much to his chagrin, never developed in this way. La Tour also, the principal exponent until 1645 of the St John River fur trade, protested in August 1644 that, although he had been accused 'que je n'ay rien fait dans le pays,' d'Aulnay was to blame for this falsehood: 'Car j'ay batty deux Forts et luy m'en a bruslé un et si rien a basty aucun ny defrichée que sept ou huit Arpents de Terre il a aussi bruslé l'Eglise le Monastère contre la teneur de l'arrest qui luy ordonnoit de mettre dans les places hommes qui en puissant repondre et par consequent de les conserver.'[44] The differences between d'Aulnay, La Tour, and Denys as colonizers arose not so much from differing ambitions – La Tour and Denys were no more indifferent to the prestige to be derived from founding extensive settlements than was d'Aulnay to the profits of the fur trade – but from the differing practicalities and potentialities with which each was faced in his principal sphere of activity. D'Aulnay's solution to the problem of fragmentation was to extend his control over all.

As Denys remarked of the St John River, 'le sieur d'Aunay y a traitté de son temps jusques à trois mille orignaux par an, sans les castors et loutres, ce qui fut la cause qu'il en déposseda le sieur de la Tour.'[45] Similarly, d'Aulnay shortly afterwards, in 1647, dispossessed Denys of his current fishing and trading establishment on Miscou Island.[46] The extension of d'Aulnay's rule by military means, however, was not a solution to the basic incoherence of the colony of Acadia: although seigneurial colonization had taken hold at Port Royal, it by no means characterized the colony as a whole; and even the fragile unity that d'Aulnay did achieve was lost with his death in 1650.

In Maine the problem of geographical fragmentation was less acute, owing to the greater compactness of the province as compared with the far-flung coastlines of Acadia. Nevertheless, the problem existed and in important respects it was closely similar to its equivalent in Acadia. The Isles of Shoals, some fifteen miles southeast of the mouth of the Piscataqua River, formed in the early years a counterpart of the Atlantic coast of Acadia in being a centre of the migratory fishery.[47] The most lucrative areas for the fur trade, on the other hand, were known to be in the northeasternmost parts of the province, and beyond the province's boundaries, in the area disputed between English and French. Thus, the area occupied by the proprietorial settlements was, as in the case of Port Royal, sandwiched between centres of the fishery and the fur trade and was likewise hemmed around by much larger areas under continuing Wabanaki control. Furthermore, the economic influence of Massachusetts was very immediate in Maine – much more so at this time than in Acadia – and was essentially divisive. In some ways, the Massachusetts colony provided elements of economic security for Maine, especially in terms of providing a market for produce and a source of essential supplies. However, even these functions were divisive: they ensured that economic interactions would be conducted between Maine inhabitants and Boston, rather than being concentrated in any increasingly complex pattern within Maine itself. The fact was that Maine, just as much as Acadia, lacked coherence and interdependence; that portion in which the projected landholding system operated more or less successfully was fundamentally isolated within Maine, just as Port Royal was within Acadia.

The attempts in Acadia and Maine to introduce conventional European land systems did not fail completely. In each case, communities were established that became the bases of the subsequent settler populations of both regions. Moreover, d'Aulnay at Port Royal, like Gorges and his patentees in southern Maine, had established settlements where the seigneurial structure was a recognizable and important part of colonial organization. Nevertheless, the scale was still very small, and all the problems of settlement had by no means been solved. In truth, the promoters' plans had only partially been fulfilled in the letter, and not at all in the spirit. First, conventional European land structures, when established among the abundant lands claimed for colonies in America, had in themselves created new tensions between landlord and tenant. Second, the small and isolated areas of seigneurial and proprietorial settlement were simply not enough to offset the centrifugal effects of geographical fragmentation. What the two colonies of Acadia and Maine essentially lacked was any solid reason for their existence as colonies in themselves: European conception had never, in either case, been satisfactorily reconciled with American reality. In this situation, internal relationships were freed from the constraints that an evident interdependence would have imposed, and deep conflicts inevitably resulted.

Thus, in this condition of fragmentation, social heterogeneity, and political chaos, the two colonies of Maine and Acadia were ripe for the intervention of any external power. In the years following 1650, the Massachusetts colony became anxious to annex Maine, both for strategic and for economic reasons, and also proved willing to take advantage of the Sedgwick conquest of Acadia to extend its influence, though not its direct rule, even further north. This did not permanently end the separate existence of either Acadia or Maine, as the crowns of France and England made efforts in the later seventeenth century to re-establish the respective colonies. What was clear, however, was that any effort at re-establishment would have to originate from outside the colonies themselves: both were too weak and divided to accomplish any spontaneous act of regeneration. Styles of colonization involving adapted versions of conventional European land systems were not in themselves discredited – the seigneurial system in Canada, and the prevalence of quit-rents in the English royal colonies, are sufficient examples – but in future a much more careful attempt would have to be made to ensure that European plans took full account of the realities of American colonization.

4 The 'Lost Colony' of New Scotland and Its Successors, to 1670

In 1629, two settlements were established in the northeastern North American colony of New Scotland. The first, on Cape Breton Island, survived only briefly before it was attacked and razed by a French warship. The second, at Port Royal, continued until late 1632, when the colonists were evacuated under the terms of the Treaty of St-Germain-en-Laye. No Scottish colonists are known to have remained under the French regime that was now known as Acadia. Only the name of New Scotland (or, in Latin, *Nova Scotia*) persisted, to be revived in mid-century and again following the British conquest of Acadia in 1710. Treating primarily the period to 1670, this essay will argue that the demise of New Scotland was no random event. In the imperial outreach to northeastern North America in this period, resource exploitation predominated and – with some local exceptions – colonization remained a by-product. Colonial endeavours were therefore inherently fragile. Even state support, when it was attained, was chronically vulner-

This original version of this essay was presented at a conference on 'Lost Colonies' held by the McNeil Center for Early American Studies at the University of Pennsylvania in March 2004. The conference gave me an opportunity to revisit some important issues in the history of Acadia and New Scotland, and to argue that the phenomenon of the 'lost colony' – defined by the organizers, Alison Games and Robert Olwell, to include 'failed colonial enterprises anywhere around the globe that took place in the four centuries from 1450 to 1850' – was part of the mainstream experience of seventeenth-century northeastern North America rather than an aberration from any supposed pattern of colonial success. Participants in the conference had a wide range of complementary interests, and I continue to be grateful for insights derived from the papers and discussions. This essay is previously unpublished, and has been edited only to avoid undue overlap with other chapters of this book.

able to the pressures of competing economic and strategic interests. Such pressures were crucial to the undermining of New Scotland, but they also exerted a longer-term influence that was evidenced not only by the failure of an earlier French colony of Acadia in the same territory, but also by the problems encountered by New Scotland's French and English successor colonies. New Scotland was a lost colony built on the remnants of an earlier lost colony, and it was succeeded by the two further lost colonies of French Acadia and English Nova Scotia.

If colonization is taken to be the measure of the significance of a given territory in the Atlantic realm, it becomes easy to attribute limited significance to Acadia / Nova Scotia for either contemporaries or historians. Yet repeatedly during seventeenth-century treaty negotiations, as in the negotiations leading to the later Treaty of Utrecht, its disposition was among the last of the potentially treaty-breaking issues to be resolved. In reality, New Scotland and its successors provide examples of the 'lost colony' as a mainstream phenomenon during what is often misleadingly referred to as the colonial era. Even where densely concentrated colonial populations were eventually established – as in Canada, New England, and New York – they long remained exceptions to a more widespread pattern in northeastern North America by which colonization was initially an atypical product of imperial expansion and never during the seventeenth century became an invariable or even a predominant expression of it. Thus, the problem of lost colonies and of European failure in colonial activity is only a problem if it is assumed that imperial outreach inherently included migration and colonization. With the recognition that this was only one of a series of possible forms of outreach, that extraction of resources was also critically important, and that it was inevitable that there should be false starts and blurring of the various forms, then the lost colonies can be recognized as an entirely normal phenomenon.

New Scotland originated as the project of a single colonial promoter, Sir William Alexander. Although Alexander had previously entertained the possibility of involvement in the colonization of Newfoundland, the charter he received from the Scottish crown in September 1621 defined boundaries extending northwards from the St Croix River as far as the St Lawrence, and thence eastwards. In later geographical terms, it embraced Canada's Maritime provinces and the Gaspé Peninsula.[1] Although Alexander defined his project in explicitly Scottish terms, it was also coordinated with concurrent promotional efforts for New England, and in later years the use of the terminology of 'Great Britain' would signal its harmony with the goal of James VI and I (later of Charles I) to build further integration of the two states on the basis of the 1603 union of the crowns. As master of requests for Scotland at the court of James VI, Alexander was ideally placed to frame his North American venture within the context of this and other current state objectives that would make it an attractive candidate for royal encouragement and support, and he also had personal ties to powerful aristocratic families. Among the basic qualifications for colonial promoters of the 1620s was an array of readily usable connections either at the heart of the state or in major Atlantic ports, but preferably in both. Alexander, although he made strenuous efforts towards the end of the decade to mobilize merchant capital in favour of New Scotland, had his main strength weighted – to a dangerous extent, as later became clear – towards the state end of the spectrum.[2]

Thus, Alexander never personally lacked for state encouragement, and throughout the 1620s this translated into consistent efforts on the part of the Scottish crown to facilitate the colonization of New Scotland in ways that were requested by Alexander and did not imply expenditures from state revenues. Nevertheless, difficulties remained. The institution of the order of knights-baronets of Scotland, a scheme designed to raise funds for New Scotland by conferring titles of honour and lands in the colony to individuals who would make financial contributions in return, had limited success.[3] More productive was the chartering of the English and Scottish Company. Forming an alliance between Alexander and the English/Huguenot Kirke family, the new company allowed the Kirkes to continue efforts they had begun in 1628 to dislodge the French from Canada. This they accomplished in 1629, holding the post at Quebec for some three years. The Kirkes' earlier activities had led to tensions with Alexander, who himself held an extensive Scottish land grant in the St Lawrence valley and was also apprehensive that the Kirkes would extend their reach into the New Scotland region. With the formation of the English and Scottish Company, Alexander was freed from the possibility of English competition in New Scotland and proceeded to send a colonizing expedition.[4]

The expedition of 1629 followed two earlier failures.[5] To underline its importance to Alexander's plans, the venture was commanded by his son, the younger Sir William Alexander. Its goal was to establish two settlements, one on Cape Breton Island and the other at or near the former French post at Port Royal. The numbers of potential colonists were small, though not unusually so for settlement attempts in northeastern North America in this era. Destined for Port-aux-Baleines, the Cape Breton site, were '60 or 80 English,' according to Alexander's own account. A French observer later put the number at Port Royal – who were likely Scots, although there is no firm evidence of their identities – at seventy, of whom thirty had died during the first winter.[6] Fragmentary references suggest that the 1629 groups, to an extent greater than in the earlier voyages, included a significant number of women.[7]

The Cape Breton settlement was troubled from the start. Shortly after its landing, it became sharply divided along religious lines when a number of 'Brownists' identified themselves and separated from the main community.[8] A greater disaster occurred later in the summer, when the small fort constructed at Port-aux-Baleines was stormed by a force commanded by the French sea captain Charles Daniel. Daniel, a member of the Company of New France, asserted the French right to this territory as part of the colony of Acadia. The New Scotland settlement's leader – James Stewart, Lord Ochiltree – later described the attackers as consisting of 'threescore sojours and ane certaine number off savages.'[9] His comment suggests that, as well as suffering the misfortune of being discovered by a powerful French vessel, the colonizers had committed the cardinal error of failing to establish a respectful relationship with Mi'kmaq aboriginal inhabitants. The result was the destruction of the fledgling settlement and the removal of the colonists, some to be released in England and others (including Ochiltree) to be imprisoned in France.[10]

The Scots fared better at Port Royal, despite the ravages of scurvy during the first winter. Here, the construction of Charles Fort was completed by late August on a site across the later-named Annapolis Basin from the site of an abandoned French habitation that had been constructed in 1605 and destroyed by a Virginia expedition in 1613. While the evidence of Scottish–Mi'kmaq and Scottish–Etchemin relations is not extensive, what references do survive invariably indicate a diplomatic and trading relationship. Within the first five weeks of the Scots' arrival, they had at least three visits from aboriginal parties. All were cordial, and characterized by trade and gift-giving.[11] More complex were Scottish contacts with the few French who remained in the region. The habitation destroyed during the Virginia raid of 1613 had been empty or near-empty at the time, as the colonists had been absent on one of their regular resource-exploiting journeys – fishing, fur-trading, or both. Initially staying in the vicinity of Port Royal, probably in a new building close to the original site, they had moved by early 1618 to more southerly coastal areas of the Acadian peninsula. Since the death of Charles de Biencourt de Saint-Just, commander on behalf of his father (the original seigneur of Port Royal, Jean de Biencourt de Poutrincourt), the leading figures among the French had been Claude de Saint-Étienne de La Tour and, increasingly, his son Charles de Saint-Étienne de La Tour. The La Tours held a small fort at Cap de Sable. Alexander had apparently completed an important *coup* after the elder La Tour was captured at sea by the Kirkes in 1628 and brought to London. Alexander persuaded La Tour, in effect, to join him in the colonization of New Scotland, promising knights-baronetcies to him and to his son, and allocating to the La Tours an area of the peninsula that included not only Cap de Sable but also a number of other major harbours and a productive fur-trading area of which the La Tours and the Alexanders would share the profits.[12]

For the Scots at Port Royal, initial indications were that the agreement would hold. One of them, Richard Guthry, wrote in late August 1629 that '[La Tour] with his sonne we expect every houre.'[13] Whether or not either La Tour ever arrived at the Scottish fort, Claude was ultimately unable to persuade his son to accept the knight-baronetcy or the agreement, and in the following year he himself repudiated his alliance with Alexander.[14] Although the failure of the relationship with the La Tours must have complicated matters for the Scots, both in terms of defence and in the establishment and maintenance of fur-trading networks among aboriginal inhabitants, it proved to be a surmountable hurdle. By 1632, they were in a position to take the offensive. In a reversal of the events that had taken place at Port-aux-Baleines some three years earlier, a Scottish expedition from Port Royal captured and plundered the La Tours' other fort – and key fur-trading centre – at the mouth of the St John River.[15]

As yet unknown to the Scots at Port Royal, however, the end of the colonization of New Scotland had already been determined by the recently signed Treaty of St-Germain-en-Laye. Formally ending the war between France and the kingdoms of Charles I that had begun in 1627 and had then been suspended in April 1629 under the interim Treaty of Suza, the 1632 treaty provided that the British crown would restore to France 'tous les lieux occupés en la nouvelle France, l'Acadie et Canada.'[16] Although the Scots crown continued to maintain – as put in a royal letter to the knights-baronets in August 1632 – that the New Scotland colony had been 'forced of late to remove *for a tyme* by meanes of a treatie we have had with the French,' in reality it was never revived as such.[17] Its colonists removed by French shipping in late 1632, it had become a lost colony. Why so? The demise of New Scotland can be explained in part by factors particular to this venture. Diplomatic miscommunication and miscalculation in the negotiations leading to the Treaty of St-Germain, associated especially with the period during and immediately following the fatal illness of Secretary of State Viscount Dorchester in early 1632, played a significant role. The chief British negotiator, Sir Isaac Wake, complained to London in April 1632 that he had had no acknowledgment of his dispatches for five consecutive months.[18] The results were seen both in the wording of the article by which Acadia was to be restored to France and in the ignoring of indications that France had every intention of sending a strong colonizing expedition as soon as the treaty was signed – which it did under the command of Isaac de Razilly.[19]

Outside of these specific circumstances, two further characteristics of the New Scotland venture contributed to its downfall. First, no clear economic rationale had been established for New Scotland's existence. From the beginning, Alexander's strengths as a colonial promoter had inclined much further towards the state rather than the mercantile end of the spectrum. An officeholder who had originated from a landowning family in central Scotland, he had few personal connections with the major ports and apparently failed to hire factors who could make up for his own deficiencies. Furthermore, now as royal secretary for Scotland, Alexander spent little time in Scotland itself. Efforts to mobilize cash in London for his colonial interests were difficult at best, even to the extent he had Scottish bonds to offer.[20] More generally, in the Scottish economy of the early seventeenth century, New Scotland was an exotic plant. Scottish trade was still heavily concentrated in east-coast ports which had networks that were either coastal or spanned the North Sea. Glasgow had not yet emerged as a serious rival. Of Alexander's own colonizing expeditions, that of 1629 had left from England while the previous two had departed from the relatively small west-coast ports of Kirkudbright and Dumbarton. Fisheries, meanwhile, formed an important part of the Scottish economy but were heavily weighted towards harvesting Scottish waters for export to western Europe. An effort in 1617 to form a Scottish company that would have interests in eastern Europe and Asia, but would also seek whale oil in Greenland waters, collapsed in the face of opposition from established English trading companies.[21] When the royal letter of 1632 to the knights-baronets noted that New Scotland 'hath not takin the root which was expected ... partlie, as we ar informed, by want of the tymelie concurrence of a sufficient number to insist in it,' this was an accurate indication that the project had never set down an economic foundation that could mobilize a critical level of support or even convincingly justify Alexander's large expenditures on recruiting, transporting, and supporting settlers.[22]

Alexander's close connections with the state formed in themselves a second characteristic of New Scotland that also affected the venture's longevity. His personal access to state support and patronage – assisted by his feudal and family connections – had been essential to the early stages of the chartering, planning, and attempted implementation of the scheme. The influence of the extent to which this support was personal to him, however, began in the early 1630s to operate quite differently. Alexander, up until the time of his death in 1640, never lost either office or royal patronage. Named Viscount Stirling in 1630, he became first Earl of Stirling three years later.[23] In 1632, soon after the signing of the Treaty of St-Germain, he was granted a monopoly of the minting of copper coins in Scotland, and further patronage awards followed.[24] They were insufficient to save him from overwhelming debts to which the New Scotland scheme had contributed largely, but did indicate a persistent effort being made by the Crown to ensure that Alexander's prestige survived the evacuation of Port Royal without undue damage, and that financial opportunities were put in his way to the limited degree that a troubled treasury could afford.

From the beginning, state endorsement had been indispensable to the New Scotland scheme. The personal nature of Crown support in this case, however, facilitated its shift from New Scotland itself to other forms of patronage rewards for Alexander as soon as the other priorities of the state dictated that it was prudent to remove the Scottish colony. While it had existed, New Scotland's presence in northeastern North America had been as successfully established as in any other conventional colonial attempt, more so than the ones that had failed before it. It was true that the flow of English settlers to New England was creating a new model of colonization based on sustained migration, rapid environmental degradation, and increasingly dense settlement. As yet, however, it was unclear whether this model was either tolerable by the imperial state or sustainable in North America itself. Among colonizing efforts that adhered to the more common techniques of settler recruitment by a colonial promoter, harvesting natural resource items for export, and depending on aboriginal support or toleration for security,

New Scotland had shown significant strength. Its persistence for more than three years gave one indication, as did its relationship with Mi'kmaq and Etchemin neighbours and ability to inflict military defeat on French competitors. However, lack of metropolitan mercantile support and, above all, the subtle but decisive redirection of state support from New Scotland as a colony to Alexander as an individual had proved to be formidable obstacles.

Yet the longer-term seventeenth-century history of the territory named New Scotland by Alexander gives evidence of a still wider interpretive framework within which to define the reasons for its becoming a lost colony. In effect, this was a graveyard for colonial ventures, a seemingly inexhaustible source of lost colonies. The initial French attempt to colonize Acadia, beginning in 1604, had failed for reasons that had some affinities with the experience of New Scotland, although also some differences. The principal promoter in this case had been Pierre du Gua, Sieur de Monts. Here there was no question that the project fitted with an existing area of mercantile interest. De Monts assembled a group of merchants from four major ports and signed them on to the ten-year fur-trade monopoly he had received from the French crown. Experience would show that the solicitation of private subscriptions had serious deficiencies as a means of raising capital in the amounts necessary to launch a vigorous colonial expedition, by comparison with later alternatives such as the Crown-sponsored trading company or joint-stock company. De Monts's total subscriptions of some 90,000 *livres* were sufficient, however, to allow him to lead a small expedition to St Croix Island.[25] Following a disastrous winter of cold and scurvy, the remains of the group set up the habitation at Port Royal in 1605. As in the case of New Scotland a generation later, a close relationship with Mi'kmaq neighbours was quickly formed and fur-trading activities began. Also as in the case of New Scotland but in a different context, changes in the role of the state proved destructive. De Monts's principal claim to royal patronage came through his long-standing relationship with Henri IV, for whom he had fought during the Wars of Religion. However, the chief minister, the Duc de Sully, was personally sceptical of the value of colonization in northeastern North America and was open to the representations of merchants excluded from de Monts's monopoly. When demand for furs, and prices, increased sharply French markets during the first three years of the monopoly, Sully intervened to have it cancelled. The removal of the French from Port Royal followed during the summer of 1607.[26]

The Port Royal habitation was reoccupied by a small group under the seigneurial grant of Jean de Biencourt de Poutrincourt in 1610, but disputes between Charles de Biencourt and Jesuit missionaries damaged the colony's ability to gather either state or private patronage. The raid by Samuel Argall's Virginians in 1613 ensured that Biencourt, the La Tours, and a few other fur traders and fishers would live a tenuous existence, respectively dependent on Mi'kmaq neighbours – Charles de Saint-Étienne de La Tour solidifying this relationship through marriage to a Mi'kmaq with whom he had three daughters – and a small group of individual La Rochelle merchants.[27]

Although by the time of the Scots' arrival in 1629 the La Tours had elaborated their fur-trading operations and consolidated their base at Cap de Sable, Acadia remained a lost colony, from which metropolitan support had been withdrawn. As in the case of New Scotland, the withdrawal of state support had been crucial. In other respects, the two cases differed. In targeting the fur trade, de Monts and the other leading advocates of colonization in Acadia had rightly identified a growing and increasingly lucrative trade that since the 1580s had been of direct interest to merchants of all the French Atlantic ports. There was no difficulty comparable with the eastward orientation of Scottish trade. At the same time, de Monts's personal associations with the state were not as strong as those of Alexander. They rested on earlier services to Henri IV and did not extend either to ongoing metropolitan officeholding or to family and feudal ties to powerful families. For Alexander, the result had been that his personal position in patronage networks was secure, but that in the absence of any economic justification for Scottish involvement in New Scotland the same security did not apply to his colonial interests. For de Monts, the fur trade proved too valuable for his monopoly to escape the protests of competitors, and his influence with the state was insufficient to support the mounting of an effective counter-argument. The consequences were the same for both: abandonment of colonial activity. De Monts did persist for some years in trading interests at Quebec, but only briefly with a trade monopoly there and even then with limited success.[28]

New Scotland, therefore, was a lost colony that had succeeded an earlier lost colony. Its own successors encountered difficulties that offer further comparisons and contrasts. Again, the roles of the state and of merchant investors proved central. Acadia began a new era as a French colonial project with the arrival of the Razilly expedition in 1632. Signs of renewed state interest in the territory had already been seen not only in what were – to the British negotiators at least – unexpectedly determined French diplomatic efforts prior to the Treaty of St-Germain, but also in the first state recognition granted to Charles de Saint-Étienne de La Tour. In 1631 La Tour was commissioned as royal lieutenant-general in Acadia, while Razilly arrived in the following year as lieutenant-general for all of New France.[29] These governance arrangements, intended to be complementary, would lead over time to destructive factional disputes within the tiny elite of Acadia. Initially, however, they indicated the return of the French state (though without significant state investment) to encouraging Acadian colonization. As a colonial promoter, La Tour's qualifications rested primarily on his long-standing merchant connections in La Rochelle and on his proven ability to maintain diplomatic and trading relationships with both Mi'kmaq and Etchemin. His ties to the state were much weaker. Razilly, by contrast, was a figure more closely comparable to Alexander. He was related by kinship to Cardinal Richelieu, chief minister at the time, and Richelieu's family of du Plessis were feudal superiors of the Razilly family. Razilly brought as one of his senior lieutenants another kinsman, Charles de Menou d'Aulnay. Making up for his own and d'Aulnay's lack of direct mercantile connections, Razilly also brought with him the La Rochelle merchant Nicolas Denys, who had taken prime responsibility for fitting out the expedition.[30]

As long as Razilly lived, and continued to exert from the small Atlantic coastal settlement of La Hève the authority of his commission to govern all of New France, the four leading elite figures coexisted. When Razilly died in 1636, it was the signal for fragmentation. While La Tour continued to trade on the St John River, d'Aulnay gathered colonists in family groups at Port Royal. By 1650 – the year of d'Aulnay's own death by accidental drowning – following fifteen years of intermittent recruitment, the Port Royal population had reached some three hundred.[31] Denys, meanwhile, pursued commercial fishing and lumbering ventures in a number of the harbours of the region. Not surprisingly in view of his state connections, d'Aulnay was successful in having his own claim to exclusive governance over Acadia formally endorsed. In 1647 he received sweeping powers as governor and lieutenant-general.[32] D'Aulnay had already inflicted military defeat on La Tour by storming his fort at the mouth of the St John River in 1645, and he set about a successful campaign to expel Denys from his most recent fishing and trading centre at Miscou. However, d'Aulnay's ascendancy was never complete. First, both La Tour and Denys personally survived his attacks.

Second, all of d'Aulnay's efforts, while facilitated by state encouragement, were financially underwritten by a particular merchant house of La Rochelle, that of Emmanuel Le Borgne. Like Alexander before him, d'Aulnay accumulated crushing debts, largely held by Le Borgne. When d'Aulnay died in 1650, Acadia fell apart again, as Le Borgne struggled to recoup his losses by intervening in the colony's fisheries and fur trade, while Denys and La Tour reasserted their interests. Matters were brought back into an uneasy balance only when a small English naval squadron captured Port Royal and certain other Acadian ports in 1654.[33]

Acadia was again a lost colony and, for the time being, Nova Scotia prevailed. This time, there were certain continuities, both with the Acadia that had been launched in 1632 and with the earlier New Scotland. With Acadia, the continuities included the persistence of the small colonial population at Port Royal, though without the French officials, garrison, and clergy. Also, Le Borgne refused to accept that a legitimate conquest had taken place, and continued with commercial activities and occasional military thrusts at Port Royal from the Atlantic coast of the Acadian peninsula. With New Scotland, the primary continuity lay in the co-option of the old Scottish claim – in its Latin form of 'Nova Scotia' – as a justification for the refusal of the English interregnum regime to restore Port Royal to the French.[34] Charles de Saint-Étienne de La Tour, ironically, provided the direct connection through his knight-baronetcy and land grant from Alexander, while Sir Thomas Temple and William Crowne provided, respectively, the necessary state and mercantile connections. In 1656 the three received a patent for 'the Country and Territories called Lacadie and that parte of the Country called Nova Scotia,' with a fur-trade monopoly.[35]

La Tour was soon marginalized, retiring to Cap de Sable where he died in 1663. Sir Thomas Temple, whose patronage value to the venture came not only from a military career on the Parliamentary side during the Civil War but also from a family connection with William Fienes, Viscount Say and Sele, moved to North America, although Boston was the closest he came to any long-term residence in Nova Scotia. Crowne was a Parliamentary supporter, and briefly a Member of Parliament, who had mercantile connections in London. He also took up residence in New England, but confined his trading activities to the western part of the territory designated as Nova Scotia and notably to the Penobscot River region.[36]

In practice, the new Nova Scotia was dominated by Massachusetts commercial interests. 'T. Temple dwells idly at Boston,' scathingly wrote a contemporary, 'and is fooled by them [the Bostonian merchants].'[37] Temple himself persisted in sending optimistic reports to London, although to his kinsman Lord Nathaniel Fiennes he was sometimes more frank. Not only, he informed Fiennes in September 1659, was he having to wage a costly battle with Le Borgne for control of La Hève and by extension of the entire Acadian / Nova Scotian peninsula, but also a recent shipwreck had left him with 'the greatest loss I ever received in my life.' Still, Temple continued to busy himself setting up fur-trading centres around the Bay of Fundy and on the rivers draining into it, which were then operated to the benefit of Massachusetts merchants such as Thomas Lake, Hezekiah Usher, and Thomas Breedon.[38] Lake for one was critical of Temple's retinue of friends and lax control over expenses, urging on him 'a frugall management.'[39] Although the Boston merchant was no doubt justified in his strictures, the deeper reality was that his own growing involvement in the Nova Scotia fur trade and that of other Boston merchants, was also a factor in the inability of Temple to supply satisfactory returns to his London investors. Temple's Nova Scotia was clearly a commercial venture, no matter how the terminology of its founding patent might imply a wider colonial purpose, but it was no simple one. London merchants had provided the initial capital, and should the state's commitment waver, their support could reasonably be expected to be essential. Yet the trade was now largely in the hands of Massachusetts merchants whose local commercial influence was considerable but lacked an imperial dimension.

In 1660 the Restoration abruptly put state support for Temple's Nova Scotia in jeopardy. Temple's earlier state connections – and those of Crowne – were now liabilities rather than assets. A hurried journey to London saw Temple claiming that in the later stages of the Civil War he had secretly worked for the mitigation of Charles I's treatment by the Parliamentary victors – on the very scaffold, he recalled, the king had commended 'honest Tom Temple' to the care of his son and successor – and defending his stewardship of Nova Scotia.[40] His efforts had apparent success, as he ultimately returned to Boston with a new patent as Nova Scotia governor and a knight-baronetcy to boot.[41] However, in reality the price had been high. Temple had had to buy off a rival claimant by agreeing to make an annual payment of £600, and his standing with the state remained uncertain in the event of a serious test. Eventually, in peace negotiations following the second Anglo-Dutch War, the English crown conceded the restoration of Acadia to France in the Treaty of Breda in return for the reciprocal restoration of the

English half of the Caribbean island of St Christopher. Temple prevaricated for three years, but the final surrender took place in 1670 and involved the dismantling of the trade networks that had been established since 1657.[42] Nova Scotia, commercial as its character had primarily been, had become again a lost colony.

Although the sequence of weak colonizing ventures in Acadia / Nova Scotia would persist for more than a century, with only the Loyalist migration finally establishing a non-aboriginal ascendancy, 1670 did mark a turning point of sorts.[43] When Acadia was re-established, it was with a royal governor and with a clear plan to integrate the colony into the commercial and strategic imperatives of the French Atlantic – even though the plan quickly failed and the royal governors were subsumed one by one into New England–oriented trade patterns. The conquest of Port Royal by the British in 1710 was followed by the creation of yet another Nova Scotia – this one confirmed in its existence though not in its boundaries by the Treaty of Utrecht, and continuing for more than forty years to have a colonial population that was primarily Acadian – but again with a governance structure that relied on royal direction rather than elite co-option.

What does the history of New Scotland, and the more general history of Acadia / Nova Scotia to 1670, reveal about the nature and significance of lost colonies? First, the recurrent patterns evident in this case confirm that European imperial outreach could be expressed in a variety of forms, of which intensive colonial activity was only one. This principle held in northeastern North America and the North Atlantic world just as it did in Africa and Asia. Colonization in the seventeenth century had its proponents, and for some promoters and potential migrants it had its merits. The arguments in its favour were strongest when there were 'push' factors at play such as displacement of population from rural areas of England, through a combination of rising numbers, succession practices that favoured elder sons, and tensions in traditional industries such as textile production.[44] The establishment of local economies in the Americas based on cash crops could also supply 'pull' factors, since colonial settlement was an obvious prerequisite for development of a plantation economy, even though non-European labour would also emerge in the creation of a variant on colonial society that had affinities with earlier and continuing Portuguese practices in Brazil. Migration itself could provide new 'pull' factors, not only in such a region as the Chesapeake but also in some areas of southern New England, where the thrusting aside of disease-stricken aboriginal populations and rapid environmental degradation combined to facilitate the growth of a non-aboriginal economy that soon extended into surplus agricultural production, urban development, and a proliferation of radial lines of trade. Thus, there were local areas of North America where colonization effectively generated its own logic.

These are the areas that have primarily attracted the attention of historians of the Atlantic world, even though in a more sophisticated context than that of the earlier historiographical preoccupation with the notional 'colonial America.' David Armitage's recent theoretical analysis of 'Three Concepts of Atlantic History,' for example, frames an important book of essays by taking full account of the complexities of Atlantic political economy, notably in the contexts of 'circum-Atlantic' and 'cis-Atlantic' approaches, while another leading collection begins with an introduction by Amy Turner Bushnell and Jack P. Greene that elaborates on 'the unevenness of actual [European] hegemony' in the Americas by distinguishing usefully between an '*ecumene*' and a '*sphere of influence*.'[45] Yet the elucidation of a full range of patterns of Atlantic outreach and exchange requires that more sustained attention than hitherto be given to those models that involved little or no migration, where the feasibility of migration was contested, or where limited migration took place only as long as aboriginal leaderships chose to tolerate it. The historical significance of European transatlantic migration and its consequences is, of course, beyond dispute. There is also, however, an alternate historical perspective, in which colonial settlement in a seventeenth-century region such as northeastern North America can be seen as essentially peripheral to aboriginal societies that continued to control all but a few coastal and riverine enclaves.[46] There was also an alternate contemporary perspective on transatlantic exchange that not only did not envisage mounting any effective challenge to this ascendancy but in which also – at least in the view of important metropolitan commercial interests – it was undesirable to do so.

In this wider context, within which New Scotland and its successors must be set, the rationale for colonization was highly controvertible and the state and mercantile energies devoted to it were correspondingly intermittent. Thus, the reasons for the weakness of colonization efforts in Acadia / Nova Scotia cannot be sought only in specific flaws that may have afflicted a given venture. Rather, the creation of lost colonies was a normal and even – to the contemporary sceptics – a predictable phenomenon. Yet it was so because there was a possible case that could be made for colonial activity. There were areas of North America,

Hudson's Bay offering a conspicuous example, where colonization per se was so clearly unfeasible that only commercial enterprises merited serious consideration. In Acadia / Nova Scotia – as in Canada and, to a lesser degree, Newfoundland – there were arguments for and against. The case in favour of colonization might rest in the early seventeenth century on such considerations as the aggrandizement of the state, either through conquests of territories and peoples to rival the attainments of the Iberian empires or in geographical advances such as the location of the Northwest passage. Pre-emption of the claims of competing states to possession or influence was also a possible justification, and one that by the later part of the seventeenth century had emerged into a more consciously strategic appreciation of the value of North American territory. At a commercial level, as well as the consideration that a colonial population might help to defend access to valuable resource commodities, settlers had the advantage of a year-round ability to guard favoured locations such as fishing harbours or maintain the health of essential relationships with aboriginal trading partners. On the contrary side, however, colonization was an expensive strategy for merchants who opted to position employees in commercially sensitive areas, just as it was for colonial promoters such as Alexander and d'Aulnay who attempted to recruit mixed groups of men, women, and children for their personal domains. Again from a commercial perspective, a colonial settlement (especially, though not exclusively, if accompanied by a trade monopoly) could be seen to represent an undue competitive advantage. Should the colonial population involved be self-perpetuating through natural increase, the problem was all the greater, and all the more worthy of the attention of the state as well as of commercial interests.

Doubts regarding the feasibility or desirability of colonization did not signify that northeastern North America and its resources were unimportant to the relevant western European states or mercantile interests. Indeed, the French state and interested merchants laboured long, though against the tide of traditional migration patterns, to recruit colonists for Canada, and this despite periodic metropolitan doubts as to the value of colonial settlement even in the St Lawrence valley.[47] Comparable expressions of state and merchant interest in Acadia / Nova Scotia, however, showed a lesser commitment to settlement and a greater preoccupation with the harvesting and trading of resource commodities. The fur trade was the outstanding commerce that was specific to the area. However, its coastline was also one of the perimeters of the

North Atlantic fishery. Always keenly contested in Anglo-French treaty negotiations during the seventeenth century, Acadia / Nova Scotia came strongly into play during those leading to the Treaty of Utrecht. Following intense discussion of fisheries in early April 1712, French negotiators reported to Versailles that their British counterparts 'nous ont protesté cent fois quils avoient ordre exprés de tout rompre' rather than make concessions on either Acadia / Nova Scotia or Newfoundland.[48] An accurate expression of the importance of these areas to the imperial outreach of the respective states, it was not necessarily – even in the early eighteenth century – an endorsement of colonization.

Hence the persistent ambiguities that attended the succession of lost colonies of which New Scotland was a conspicuous example. Sir William Alexander was initially well equipped to gain the support of the Scottish state for his colonial enterprise, but failed to mobilize significant merchant support and was powerless in its absence to prevent competing interests of the state from turning away from support for New Scotland. Alexander faced particular difficulties in the context of an eastern-oriented Scottish economy, but French and English counterparts were no more successful in harnessing state and mercantile connections together in the interests of colonial promotion. Together, these examples illustrate the way in which lost colonies represented, in seventeenth-century northeastern North America, not an aberration but a mainstream phenomenon. They were products of the debatability of colonization's value in the context of resource exploitation, and also of the many nuances of the spectrum of interactions among imperial, colonial, and aboriginal interests. In some locales, colonial settlements thrived. In others, they did not. The complexities of early modern empires could hardly have allowed it to be otherwise.

PART TWO

Imperial Exchange

5 'The best Conditioned Gentleman in the World'? Verbal and Physical Abuse in the Behaviour of Sir William Phips

WITH EMERSON W. BAKER

Sir William Phips, the first royal governor of Massachusetts, found a sympathetic biographer in Cotton Mather. Of the many laudable qualities Mather attributed to his subject, there was one that stood out: 'for which I must freely say, *I never saw Three Men in this World that Equall'd him*; this was his wonderfully *Forgiving Spirit*.' Mather admitted that Phips might respond angrily to a serious affront, and that over the course of his life there had been instances when he had even struck out physically when provoked. Yet, Mather assured his readers, 'in fine, our Sir *William* was a Person of so sweet a Temper, that they who were most intimately acquainted with him, would commonly pronounce him, *The best Conditioned Gentleman in the World!*'[1] Mather's judgment was based on a close relationship with Phips during the early 1690s. It was also influenced by self-justification, as Mather had been a supporter and adviser of Phips during the controversial years of his governorship of Massachusetts from 1692 to 1695. The biography was written in 1697, some two years after Phips's death. Later historians have treated

This essay, a product of the collaboration between Emerson W. Baker and myself on the life and career of Sir William Phips, was presented at the American Historical Association (Pacific Coast Branch) Conference, San Francisco, in August 1996. A valuable commentary was given by Charles L. Cohen. The paper argues that the roles of verbal and physical violence in Phips's behaviour were misunderstood by earlier historians, and that analysis of Phips's calculated use of both forms of aggression offers useful insights on the relationship between empire and social class. The theme of Phips's violence also became part of our full-length biography (Emerson W. Baker and John G. Reid, *The New England Knight: Sir William Phips, 1651–1695*, Toronto, University of Toronto Press, 1998), but it is explored in greater detail in this hitherto unpublished essay.

Mather's favourable portrayal with scepticism, preferring in most cases to see Phips as crudely aggressive in both word and deed. A close examination of the evidence, however, reveals this interpretation to be just as dubious as Mather's self-serving testimonials. The reality was more complex, and this essay will seek to advance both a historical and a historiographical explanation for the confusion that has pervaded existing accounts of Phips's behaviour.

Sir William Phips had an unusual career. Born in 1651 in a small English settlement in the Kennebec-Sheepscot area of northern New England, he was raised there as a member of a large extended family that lived by trading with Wabanaki native inhabitants and small-scale farming. The young William Phips apprenticed as a shipwright, before moving to Boston in 1673 and marrying the widow of a respectable though far-from-wealthy merchant. He suffered a setback in 1676, when a brief return to the Kennebec ended with his narrow escape from a hostile Wabanaki force with a newly completed ship and without its intended cargo of timber. Nevertheless, he continued to ply his trade in Boston and by approximately 1680 was a sea captain. Increasingly preoccupied by voyages in search of sunken Spanish treasure in the Caribbean, Phips had some success in attracting wealthy and influential patronage in London. Eventually, after several years of fruitless effort, he succeeded in raising treasure worth over £200,000 from the wreck of the *Nuestra Señora de la Conceptión* off the coast of Hispaniola in 1687. Rewarded by a share of some £11,000 and a knighthood, Phips returned to Boston and confirmed his nascent alliance with the political faction of Increase and Cotton Mather with a well-timed religious conversion in early 1690. He was thereupon appointed to command successive expeditions against the French at Port Royal and Quebec. Port Royal, the headquarters of Acadia, fell easily, while the Quebec expedition was a disastrous failure. Hastening to London to justify these military efforts, Phips was drawn into the discussions preceding the issue of the new Massachusetts charter of 1691 and gained appointment as the first royal governor of the colony. As governor, he claimed successes in ending the Salem witchcraft trials and in concluding a treaty with the Wabanaki in 1693. He also, however, had difficulty in gaining necessary political support in the factionalized General Court, aroused suspicion that he was profiting from illicit commercial transactions, and had damaging personal disputes with the collector of customs and with a naval captain stationed in Boston. Recalled to London in late

1694 to answer his critics, he died there of an acute fever in early 1695.[2]

Cotton Mather's biography of Phips quickly prompted criticism both of its subject's allegedly blameless life and of its author's motivations, notably by the Boston polemicist Robert Calef.[3] Even so, Mather's work continued to cast a long shadow over the conclusions reached by later biographers and by other authors who treated Phips's governorship as an aspect of the more general history of New England. Thomas Hutchinson was an exception. Avoiding moral judgments on Phips, either favourable or unfavourable, Hutchinson provided a balanced account of the political aspects of his governorship. Hutchinson did allude to Phips's quarrels with the customs collector Jahleel Brenton and the naval captain Richard Short, and declared that in these cases 'provocation ... caused him [Phips] to break out into some indecent sallies of passion and rage,' but he was circumspect in assessing the extent to which physical violence had resulted.[4] Nineteenth- and early-twentieth-century amateur historians hewed more closely to Mather's view of Phips's character and behaviour. William Goold's unremittingly laudatory account to the Maine Historical Society in 1879, praising a native son of Maine, drew extensively on Mather and took to task an earlier biographer, Francis Bowen, for raising doubts as to Phips's level of literacy and thus questioning his suitability for leadership. Bowen had indeed done so, but had still followed Mather in describing Phips as 'a kind husband, a sincere patriot, and an honest man.'[5] Henry O. Thayer's biography of 1927 also enumerated Phips's virtues, although Thayer took a more critical approach to Mather and was clearly troubled by what he considered to be Phips's 'irascible temper' and the 'inner malign force' that led him to acts of personal violence and ultimately 'cast the governor down among rough sea-dogs of the wharf and street.'[6]

Among professional historians, Phips's attributed characteristics of violence and irascibility were brought early to the fore by Herbert L. Osgood. In some passages, Osgood – another native son of Maine – seemed willing to excuse 'the extremely undiplomatic temper of the doughty old sea captain and governor,' but elsewhere he remarked on Phips's 'brutality' and the hindrances to effective governorship caused by his 'uncouth' behaviour.[7] Viola Florence Barnes, writing in 1928, also accepted the inseparability of Phips's 'ungovernable temper' from violent behaviour, although she set this in the context of violent actions by other governors and characterized Phips as a 'human, likeable, ... adventurer.'[8] It was left to Perry Miller in 1953 to take a more consistently severe approach. Miller wasted few words on Sir William Phips. To do so in a work entitled *The New England Mind* would no doubt have seemed to him to be a contradiction. Miller's Governor Phips was a creature of Increase Mather, 'bewildered in a dignity that was none of his choosing,' and personified the degeneration of the office once held by John Winthrop, whom Phips so little resembled.[9] By now, Mather's fulsome glorifications of Phips represented more of a provocation than a foundation for historians who associated intellectual sophistication with political competence and morality, and found in Phips a crudeness and violence thinly disguised by the self-serving glibness of his first biographer. For T.H. Breen, Phips was a 'weak, ineffective, and crude' governor, who 'seems to have believed that the best way to settle an argument was with his fists or cane.' For Michael G. Hall, he was 'a blunt, uneducated man ... [in whom] an ungoverned temper and a swashbuckling personality were fatal flaws.' Thus, in the space only of the early months of 1693, the governor – in his affrays with Short and Brenton – 'had bullied and beaten two officers of the crown.'[10] The harshest verdict was that of J.M. Sosin, for whom much of the responsibility for Phips's 'disastrous administration' could be placed on the governor's flaws in character. In one passage, Phips was 'a crude, outspoken man with a violent temper and poor judgment'; twenty pages later, he was described with admirable consistency as 'a coarse, uneducated man, ... possessed of a brutal temper.'[11]

Thus, a historical orthodoxy grew up, retaining Mather's emphasis on the importance of Phips's moral temper, but rejecting Mather's specific contentions and showing instead the influence of Miller's attribution to Phips of a crudeness that could not be excused in a governor. Violence in word and deed alike has emerged as a defining characteristic of both Phips the individual and Phips the governor. When the evidence of Phips's behaviour is specifically examined, however, a more ambiguous reality is revealed. Of the frequency of Phips's use of harsh and threatening language, there is no doubt. Instances pervade the written record of his life. Whether in street confrontations with Boston constables while Phips was a treasure-hunting sea captain, in taunting a visiting Spanish trader in Jamaica, in leading crowd actions originating in the north end of Boston, in berating (as governor) emissaries from other colonies, in his public altercations with Short and Brenton, or in other situations, Phips's displeasure was roundly and ribaldly expressed. Few exact citations of his words have survived, but those that do exist are consistent with the many more general descriptions of his harsh use of language. The evidence suggests, first, that his vocabulary was vulgar and obscene rather than profane. In November 1683, when Phips was briefly in Boston as captain of the borrowed naval frigate *Golden Rose,* en route to an unsuccessful voyage to a Spanish wreck off the Bahamas, he and his crew stirred up complaints by their unruliness and their demands that other vessels lower their flags in salute. In the course of the disputes that took place ashore, Phips was quoted as declaring on one occasion 'that he did not care a turd for the Governour for he had more power than he had.' A few days later, a deponent testified that on another occasion 'I heard him [Phips] bid the constables kiss his Arse and called him [*sic*] shit breech.'[12] Second, his language in such circumstances was overwhelmingly abusive, rather than adjurative or expletive.[13] Third, it was frequently combined with threats. 'He [Phips] would break his head or bones and send him to Gaol,' was the way a deponent – albeit one friendly to Jahleel Brenton – remembered Phips's words to the customs collector during their quarrel on a Boston wharf in the spring of 1693.[14]

Where the paradox enters into the evidence, however, is in the dearth of documented instances in which verbal abuse led to physical violence. The incident with Brenton provides, in a negative sense, a prime example. Originating in conflicting interpretations of the respective authorities of the governor and the collector over the entering and clearing of vessels – an ambiguity that would be resolved only with the passage of the *Navigation Act* of 1696 – the dispute between Brenton and Phips also had to do with their competing ambitions to control the profits and patronage opportunities that flowed from these powers. The altercation of 29 May 1693 was occasioned when Brenton seized a vessel and cargo that had been entered under Phips's personal authorization, and Brenton complained to London some weeks later that the governor had caned him into submission.[15] The complaint came at the end of a lengthier statement of other matters of dispute between Brenton and Phips, and may have been intended only as a vignette to support the collector's more general arguments. Be that as it may, imperial authorities quickly seized on the episode and linked it with reports also reaching London of Phips's dispute with Richard Short earlier in 1693. As a result, both matters came under the scrutiny of the Massachusetts council in 1694, as it collected evidence to be used in the hearing that was intended to follow Phips's recall to London to answer his critics.[16] Brenton undoubtedly had some justification in complaining that he had enemies on the council, and that the presence of Phips may have intimidated those testifying. Yet the case in support of his allegation of violence on the part of Phips was quickly revealed as insubstantial. Timothy Clarke, despite his attestation of the governor's threatening words, could remember no blow actually being struck. Brenton's supporter and brother-in-law, Nathaniel Byfield, had to admit that he had arrived on the wharf too late to see the confrontation itself. The customs 'waiters' William Hill and Henry Francklyn tried at first to support their employer's version of events, but under questioning they altered their testimony as to Phips's use of his cane by stating that 'by strikeing they did not intend downright blows.' In the end, not a single witness could be found to support Brenton's claims, and the majority of the deponents contradicted him explicitly.[17]

Thus, despite their acceptance by many historians, Brenton's allegations of personal violence by Phips do not stand up to scrutiny. Other instances are documented more convincingly, though they are few in number and each is explicable in terms that are rational even if not necessarily creditable to Phips. The first occurred in 1684, during the first of two mutinies on the *Golden Rose.* According to Mather, members of Phips's crew held him at sword-point as they demanded that the vessel should be turned to piracy. Although lacking a weapon, Phips 'rush'd in upon them, and with the blows of his bare Hands, *Fell'd* many of them, and *Quell'd* all the Rest.'[18] Although only Mather provides these details, which he presumably had from Phips himself, the account is plausible because it is supported by a later reference to the mutiny by the governor of Jamaica and by evidence that the lack of promised shares of treasure was causing disquiet among the crew.[19] A second instance occurred in May 1690, during the brief sojourn of Phips's invading force in Acadia. A French account described the capture at Port Royal of one La Roche, an employee of the French Compagnie de la Pêche Sédentaire who had escaped some days earlier with money belonging to the company and to the merchant François-Marie Perrot. Phips had had a rope put around La Roche's neck, and had forced him through 'la gesne' – torture – to reveal the whereabouts of the cash. Although also lacking specific corroboration, this too is believable enough in the context of the ongoing pillage of the fort and settlement of Port Royal.[20]

The most comprehensive documentation of a case of personal violence on Phips's part is in connection with his quarrel with Richard Short, captain of the frigate *Nonsuch*. Eyewitness accounts differ as to whether Phips was provoked by what one account described as Short's 'Insolent carriage and ill Language.' Short's son maintained, on the contrary, that Phips had called his father 'a Lay or whore' and had promptly set upon him with his cane. Phips himself claimed that he had at first intended only to give an aggressive Short 'a small blow' to warn him to keep his distance. For all that, there was no disagreement on the upshot: a severe caning for Short, followed by his imprisonment and eventual escape to seek redress in England.[21] The essential context of the incident, however, lay in the patron–client relationship that had existed between the governor and the captain. From the time of Phips's voyage to Boston on board *Nonsuch* in the spring of 1692, a contemporary observed, Short had been 'a perfect bigot to Sir William.'[22] The attachment is explicable in the context of arrangements by which Short, for his own financial gain, lent out seamen for merchant voyages recommended by Phips – who, no doubt, himself reaped benefits either in direct commercial profit or through the ability to dispense favours to other clients.[23] By late 1692, however, the relationship had become strained, partly because of Short's reluctance to sail *Nonsuch* to what he considered to be the dangerous waters of Pemaquid, where Phips was in the process of building a fort and also had trading interests, and partly because Short was beginning to find Phips's demands excessive and was increasingly inclined to regret the entire relationship. Nathaniel Byfield and others of Phips's critics had made it known to Short that they regarded his arrangements with the governor as 'amisse and more than the Capt. could well answer,' and it was apparently on the basis of their advice that Short had resolved that on the morning of 4 January 1693 he would refuse Phips's latest request to detach seamen for a merchant voyage to Pemaquid. Phips, in turn, was undoubtedly forewarned of Short's intention: Short had blurted it out the previous evening to John March, the Pemaquid commander, who was in Phips's company immediately before the confrontation began.[24] Thus, Phips's caning of Short – harsh as it was, and in all likelihood premeditated – was no random act of undisciplined violence, but represented for Phips the public chastisement of a disloyal client.

None of this is to endorse the portrait drawn by Cotton Mather of a generally placid and forgiving Sir William Phips. Phips was no stranger to violence of the military and naval variety, and it is entirely possible too that there were other incidents of more personal violence that have not survived on record. What is striking, however, is the contrast between the many extant accounts of his verbal abuse and the shortage of convincingly documented cases of physical violence. Also clear is the existence of rational – if not necessarily pleasant – grounds for his physical violence in the rare cases when it can be shown to have occurred: to retain control of his ship, to find a large amount of cash, and to discipline a client. For Phips, violence was a means to an end, rather than expressing the uncontrollable urge of a crude and irascible individual. Verbal abuse, conversely, was separable in Phips from actual violence. Insult and threat, normally, did not form a prelude to a physical attack. Thus, in turn, the question is raised as to how to assess, in itself, Phips's use of harsh language.

The necessary context lies, first, in Phips's ability to function in entirely different linguistic environments from those that might favour rough or abusive expression. 'So *proper* was his Behaviour,' wrote Cotton Mather of Phips's efforts in London to find patrons for his ultimately successful treasure-seeking voyage, 'that the best Noble Men in the Kingdom now admitted him into their Conversation.'[25] While all such statements of Mather must be treated cautiously, there is abundant evidence that Phips could readily make himself presentable to individuals of higher social rank than his own. Between 1683 and 1691 he met personally with four monarchs: with Charles II and James II regarding his treasure-seeking efforts, and with William III and Mary II on matters surrounding the Massachusetts charter. In the planning of the voyage of the *Golden Rose*, and then in the search for patronage for later voyages, he became closely associated with the admiral and naval administrator Sir John Narbrough. Narbrough, who was described by a contemporary as enjoying 'a great and well deserved Interest with the Court,' formed the essential link with well-connected patrons such as the Duke of Albemarle and the courtier Sir James Hayes.[26] Later, during the years immediately following the Revolution of 1688–9, Phips collaborated closely with Increase Mather in efforts in London to have the old Massachusetts charter restored or, eventually, to have a new one drafted along favourable lines. In this context, Phips met productively with leading Whig politicians and the occasional Tory. At the beginning he played only a supporting role, one necessitated chiefly by the need to excuse the failure of his New England force at Quebec. By the summer of 1691, however, he was a more important participant, working actively with

Mather and Sir Henry Ashurst, a prominent city merchant and one of the accredited Massachusetts agents in London. When Phips sat down on 6 August 1691 to dine with Mather, Ashurst, and the plantations secretary William Blathwayt, whatever sharpness may well have entered occasionally into the conversation certainly did not extend to crude or scatological terms of abuse.[27]

Phips's ability to participate successfully in such interactions had certain recognizable origins. First, his early association with Narbrough and the navy board put him in a social environment where rapid upward mobility was unremarkable. In the later Stuart era, social advancement could come just as readily to 'tarpaulin' naval officers of demonstrated ability as it eventually did to Phips.[28] Second, Phips's own social origins were not as humble in an English context as they were in that of New England. While his immediate branch of the family was distant from the Boston elite both geographically and in social status, its English connections were respectable enough to have a coat of arms, at least a technical mark of gentility. One of his cousins was Constantine Phipps, a young London lawyer at the time but soon to emerge as a prominent Tory and, later, lord chancellor of Ireland. Even though a poor cousin, William Phips did not arrive in London without some ability to muster the right introductions.[29] Nevertheless, Phips also required the personal ability to make his way. The ability to articulate his needs and goals persuasively, whether seeking investment in a voyage or advancing his aspirations to office and privilege, was indispensable. Harsh forms of expression constituted one of Phips's languages, but not the only one; and the manner of their use was far from the compulsive and indiscriminate crudity that has been attributed to Phips by historians.

Phips's ability to tailor his language to meet the demands of the moment was demonstrated with unique clarity at the time of the surrender of Port Royal in May 1690. His seven vessels and force of 446 New England militia were more than sufficient to overawe the courtly but demoralized governor of Acadia, Louis-Alexandre Des Friches de Meneval, who had at his disposal only a small and ill-supplied garrison in a partly demolished fort. After initial negotiations on the day of Phips's arrival in the Port Royal basin, Phips invited Meneval to meet him on board the flagship *Six Friends* to conclude the formalities while the New England troops were disembarked. A French officer described the meeting: 'When M. de Meneval had arrived on board the said commander's ship, he was brought to his cabin, at the back of which he was seated. On arrival, M. de Meneval made to him a deep bow, and this commander replied by inclining his head to the right and the left in the English way ... The conversation being opened, it proceeded with courtesies on both sides throughout the time it took to disembark 450 men and draw them up in battle line at Port Royal.'[30]

As soon as Phips and Meneval themselves reached shore, however, Phips's manner changed abruptly. Seizing upon the pretext that a few undisciplined soldiers of the garrison had broken into the supplies of the fort, Phips launched into a display of anger, ostentatiously demanded Meneval's sword, and imprisoned the French troops after relieving them of their arms and cash. The thorough plundering of Port Royal, in full contradiction of the verbally agreed terms of surrender – which Phips had refused to have put in writing – followed during the ensuing days.[31] Certain of the French observers were inclined to believe that Phips had become enraged because he had granted favourable terms of surrender to a fort he only now recognized as being indefensible. This explanation is unlikely, however, in view of the fact that Phips had had contact the previous day with a sympathetic Acadian inhabitant who had presumably advised him of the state of the fort and its garrison.[32] The evidence suggests instead, especially in view of Phips's reluctance to have the terms of capitulation set out in writing, that both the courteous conclusion of the terms and the subsequent accusation of misconduct by the French garrison were elements of a theatrical production designed to enable the New Englanders to plunder the settlement in spite of Meneval's inconvenient anxiety to surrender. As for Phips's behaviour and language, the significance of the episode was not that either the courtesy or the anger were exceptional, but rather that the two were so closely juxtaposed and so clearly calculated in their effects.

More generally, the evidence thus suggests the need for a reassessment of Phips's use of abusive language. There is no question that Phips knew his coarse vocabulary well, and that he used it with an assurance and effect that derived from long experience. He had no doubt learned it early in life, in the fishing harbours of the Kennebec and the Pemaquid Peninsula, and perfected its use at sea and on the Boston wharves during the 1670s. Over the years, however, it became for him an essentially political language. No matter how colourful the threats he might utter, harsh speech had no direct connection with personal violence except in the rare cases where specific circumstances intruded.

Phips's rough expression was not a form of discourse in the Foucaultian sense that implies a distinctive manner of organizing knowledge through language.[33] Nor was it a political language in the rhetorical and ideological form attributed by Gareth Stedman Jones to the Chartists, tying social class to the demands of a political movement.[34] It had some affinities with the notion of an antilanguage, especially in the context of Phips's efforts during the early months of the voyage of the *Golden Rose* to manage a crew in which a virtually equal distribution of shares was increasingly accompanied by an overt desire to adopt – in the words of Governor Hender Molesworth of Jamaica – the 'bewiching Trade' of piracy.[35] Language was certainly a major point of contention between, on the one hand, Phips and his crew and, on the other, the royal agent John Knepp, who sailed on the voyage to keep a watch on the borrowed frigate. When Knepp protested against drunkenness and swearing, crew members 'said god damn them they would Swear and be drunk as often as they pleased and they told me that their captain would not have said soe much to them which was very trew.'[36] Yet Phips's decisive and repeated rejection of the opportunity to become a pirate captain casts doubt on the usefulness of characterizing his speech as an antilanguage, with its connotation of embodying the exclusive speech of a self-consciously distinct society within a society.[37]

Rather, Phips's harsh language was used very much within the context of the wider society in which he sought advancement. It was used in the tradition of the '"rough talk" at sea' identified by Marcus Rediker, but with an additional element. Not only did Phips's expressions imply, in Rediker's words, 'defiance of middle-class society and its ideals of gentility, moderation, refinement, and industry,' but they were also typically employed in direct confrontations with social superiors – or with their minions, such as constables or gaolers – and frequently in a public setting calculated to gain for Phips the support of members of his own social class.[38] It was in this sense that Phips's speech was political. The management of the crew of the *Golden Rose* – which was organized on a basis on which the majority could, and on occasion did, overrule Phips's authority – was, among other things, a political task. Phips's coarse and contemptuous treatment of Boston constables, like his repeated 'affronts ..., with a Crowd of Rabble at his heeles,' to a Spanish merchant captain in Jamaica in 1684, had the implicit purpose of marking out Phips, for the benefit of his crew, as a captain who was not afraid to challenge the orthodoxies of the social order.[39]

Comparable episodes took place while Phips was back in Boston in 1690. Only days after his religious conversion and admission to membership of Cotton Mather's North Church, Phips headed a crowd that attempted to free two individuals from gaol. One was Phips's half-brother, the joiner John White, the other White's former business partner Daniel Turell. The two had been imprisoned for debt under a judgment dating from the time of the former Dominion of New England, which had been overthrown by the Boston revolt of April 1689 and was pointedly described by Turell as 'the Unjust and Arbitrary Government of Sir Edmund Andros.'[40] Phips's attempt at a rescue, according to the unsympathetic observer Benjamin Bullivant, was made in association with 'the Northend men' and was thwarted when the gaoler refused a bribe and then 'gives as hard language as he receives.'[41] It showed Phips again, however, resorting to verbal abuse in the face of authority, and striking a retrospective blow against the evils of the Andros regime to boot. Later in 1690, Phips orchestrated another crowd action on the Boston waterfront that temporarily restrained the unfortunate Governor Meneval – who had been imprisoned in Boston for several months – from taking ship for France to pursue a complaint against Phips for his actions at Port Royal.[42]

Phips, therefore, proved adept at selecting the targets of his insults so as to solidify his own support among members of his own social class, whether ship's crew or members of crowds who could intervene in situations in which he or a relative had a specific interest. Popular sentiments against the Dominion, Catholicism, the French, or (in Jamaica) the Spanish were grist to the mill. Not for nothing did Meneval bemoan the extent to which Phips's hold on 'la canaille' – the mob – had enabled him to obstruct the wishes of the colonial council with impunity.[43] Even as governor, Phips retained this affinity. 'Although,' commented the French commandant of Acadia in 1694 on the basis of intelligence reports, 'William Phips does not enjoy the friendship of the leading men of Boston owing to the jealousy caused by his elevation, for he was nothing more than a plain carpenter in 1685, it is nevertheless certain that he has the confidence of the people, because he had not forgotten his origin, and continues to treat them with the greatest familiarity.'[44] Phips's penchant for harsh language also remained, as Jahleel Brenton and Richard Short well knew. So did the lieutenant governor, William Stoughton, who in November 1694 found himself on the receiving end of Phips's 'very warm discourse' over the governor's threatening behaviour towards a sheriff who had arrested and imprisoned one of Phips's long-standing protégés, Thomas Dobbins.[45]

As governor, however, Phips faced certain dangers in his use of abusive and threatening language that had not existed before. It is a truism of sociolinguistics that the social meaning of insults varies according to the class identities of the insulter and the insulted.[46] Before his appointment as governor, Phips had made successful use of harsh speech in highly visible confrontations with social superiors and minor officials. During his years in office, at least in a superficial sense, the pattern continued in his various encounters on the Boston waterfront. The humiliation of Richard Short, as well as accomplishing Phips's primary purpose of chastisement, must have been enjoyed by those who relished the insulting of a naval captain in a town where, according to Short's fellow-captain Robert Fairfax, 'none that ever commands any of their Majesties Ships ... was ever used with common civility.'[47] While there is no reason to accept Jahleel Brenton's claim that Phips was abetted on 29 May 1693 by an actively participating crowd, it is likely that Nathaniel Byfield was generally justified in claiming that most of the fifty or so who gathered to observe the quarrel were sympathetic to the governor rather than the collector.[48] A more minor, but revealing incident came later in the year, when Phips intervened to prevent the seizure of a cargo imported by an Acadian and a Huguenot merchant, declaring loudly to the customs officials present that the two merchants were 'as good or better English men than the Collector is, and let him seize them if he dare. If he doth I will break his head.'[49] The differences now, however – as opposed to the confrontations of earlier years – were that Phips's social status in such situations had become highly ambiguous, and that the behaviour of a governor was liable to wider scrutiny than that of the immediate onlookers.

Consequently, although Phips's immediate purposes may frequently have been as well served by his use of harsh language after his appointment to office as before, there was also a serious price to be paid. It was most clearly seen in the case of Richard Short, partly because insult had been compounded in this instance by physical violence, but also because of the captain's effective resort to the admiralty for redress. As 'an old Servant in Their Majesties Navy,' first commissioned in 1678, Short protested that he should not have had to endure such 'Language and affronts against my person.' To make matters worse, Phips had not only dismissed Short from his command of *Nonsuch* but had also bypassed the normal channels of command by appointing his own nominee, the ship's gunner Thomas Dobbins, over the head of the lieutenant, Abraham Hoare. 'Tho the Left. is an Ancheant man,' Short continued, 'hee is a Seaman and an Old Left.' Short did complain about his physical wounds, and mentioned that an injured right hand had left him ill equipped to defend himself; but it was the humiliation of Phips's abuse, together with the governor's subversion of the customary chain of authority, that rankled the most.[50] Not only did these complaints contribute directly to Phips's recall in 1694, but also correspondence began to reach Boston from London indicating 'the great offence taken at your governor Phips ... [for] an act misbecoming his post.'[51] Phips's abusive language also caused consternation to Chidley Brooke, an emissary from New York whose request for military support prompted a tirade from the governor in early August 1693. 'He selects his company out of the mobb, for the most part,' commented Brooke the following day, 'amongst whom Noys and strutt, pass for witt, and prowis.'[52]

These two episodes together exemplified the political dangers for Phips of allowing his command of harsh language to become a prominent element of his speech as governor. Even though he might be addressing – in his own mind and in the perception of wharfside onlookers – representatives of authority, nevertheless by virtue of his office he himself could readily be seen by others as enjoying superior social status to those he abused. Thus, his treatment of Short was open to interpretation as a cruel humiliation far beyond what the partly disabled captain could possibly have deserved. When the chain of command was flouted at the same time, an arbitrary and personal flavour was added to an abuse that could not be understood as falling within the limits of any recognized disciplinary code. Thus, in the same sense as has been suggested by Greg Dening regarding Captain William Bligh, Phips stood open to the charge of 'bad language' even though he had used such words with impunity many times before and even though the physical violence with which he accompanied them on this occasion was not typical of his behaviour.[53]

Phips's language also blurred the distinctions of social class, as Chidley Brooke so clearly recognized. As historians such as Robert St George and Jane Kamensky have shown, aggressive speech could be seen in seventeenth-century Massachusetts as inherently disorderly even when class differences were not directly involved. Puritan preachers of the late seventeenth century – including, many years before he became Phips's lieutenant governor, William Stoughton – inveighed frequently against harsh language and those who used vocabularies that replicated Phips's more colourful phrases.[54] Phips's use of such language as governor, already subversive enough in this context of apprehended moral debasement, also introduced a further threat. At any time, though never more so than when declaimed on the waterfront before an appreciative audience, his rough speech was identifiably class-specific. When used to abuse and humiliate emissaries and officeholders, it introduced ambiguities into the exercise of power that were especially disturbing to those who preferred the more customarily modest and pious demeanour of a John Leverett or a Simon Bradstreet. To at least one councillor, Brooke reported, Phips's behaviour seemed compulsive: 'You must pardon him his dogg-days,' this unnamed individual had confided, 'he cannot help it.' In reality, Phips retained the control, for example, to interrupt an impromptu speech of 'great fury' to the house of representatives in May 1694 to express his personal regard for one of those he was taking to task for political opposition.[55] But 'bad language' was not easy to live down when it gave rise to an implicit challenge to established rules of class or command.

The contrast between Mather's '*best Conditioned Gentleman in the World*' and the brutally violent Sir William Phips of the historians is the difference between two constructions that equally fail to do justice to the complexities of Phips's behaviour. Mather, to be sure, told part of the truth: the part that best suited his purpose. Phips was fully capable of presenting himself with modesty and aplomb, and did so to good effect in a number of phases of his life. Physically powerful – according to Mather, he was '*Tall*, beyond the commen Set of Men, and *Thick* as well as *Tall*, and *Strong* as well as *Thick*' – he was also fully capable of personal violence, but confined it to rare occasions when a clear objective was in view. Verbal abuse was another matter. Although it too was largely a controlled and calculated element of behaviour, its use was frequent and insults were often delivered for theatrical effect. Phips spoke more than one political language, and for the most part he kept his vocabularies distinct and used them purposefully. After he became governor, however, the immediate net benefits attained through abusive language could carry a heavier and more complex price in the longer term. Had he survived to answer the charges of his critics in London, Phips might well have gained an opportunity to make new and more careful distinctions between his uses of language. As it was, his career finished untidily. Historians, meanwhile, have failed to distinguish either between verbal and physical abuse in Phips's behaviour or between his forms of speech.

This reflects in part the reality that Phips was an unorthodox figure, with his origins in northern New England and his career based – despite his relationship with the Mathers – in the acquisitive, expansionist, seaborne propensities of New England rather than those that were corporate, self-contained, and land-based. It also, however, signals the need to assess colonial governorship more explicitly in terms of social class, and to attend to the relationship between class and language in the behaviour through which governorship was expressed and experienced.

6 The Conquest of 'Nova Scotia': Cartographic Imperialism and the Echoes of a Scottish Past

The fifth of October 1710 (O.S.) witnessed an unusual military spectacle in the French colonial settlement of Port Royal, administrative centre of the colony of Acadia. The ill-fed and ill-clad soldiers who had made up the small Port Royal garrison marched out of their fort with colours flying and drums beating. Their governor, Daniel d'Auger de Subercase, handed over the keys of the fort to Samuel Vetch – designated to command it for the British – in the presence of Francis Nicholson, commander in chief of the British and New England expedition that had laid siege to Port Royal until its surrender had been agreed upon. Subercase gallantly informed Vetch that he hoped to pay him a visit in the following spring, and then the French troops departed to await their agreed passage to France. The British forces entered the fort, the Union flag was raised, and Nicholson 'gave the place the name of Annapolis Royal' in honour of Queen Anne.[1]

The meaning of these ceremonies was ambiguous. Obviously, control of the fort had changed hands. The articles of capitulation also provided for the immediate future of the Acadian colonial inhabitants within

---

This essay was presented at the Annual Conference Eighteenth Century Scottish Studies Society, held at Brown University in Providence, RI, in June 1994. I am grateful to Ned Landsman and Michael Vance for their valuable comments on the initial version. The essay was first published in Ned Landsman, *Nation and Province in the First British Empire: Scotland and the Americas, 1600–1800* (Lewisburg and London: Bucknell University Press and Associated University Presses, 2001). This piece was an early product of my interest in the British conquest of Port Royal in 1710. Although it explores some themes that are also discussed in John G. Reid et al., *The 'Conquest' of Acadia, 1710: Imperial, Colonial, and Aboriginal Constructions* (Toronto: University of Toronto Press, 2004), the essay is largely complementary to the book.

cannon shot of the fort: they were to be undisturbed in their lands and possessions for at least two years. Another provision hinted at what had been one of the major strategic reasons for the British and New England campaign. French West Indian privateers were to be provided with return passage to the Caribbean, bringing to an end the seagoing forays that had made Port Royal 'another Dunkirk' – a reference to that European port's notoriety as a privateer haven – in the estimation of worried New Englanders.[2] Beyond this point, the significance of the military conquest of 1710 was much less clear. How long would British possession of Port Royal endure? Whether or not Subercase proved personally able to carry out his chivalrously expressed threat, the immediate reaction of the French minister of marine to the news of the surrender was to think of counterattack.[3] If this proved impossible – which it did for the French, although Wabanaki and Mi'kmaq aboriginal forces came close to success during the ensuing months – there were ample seventeenth-century precedents for French re-establishment in Acadia by treaty, most recently by the Treaty of Ryswick in 1697.[4]

There was also a more fundamental issue. It was not clear exactly what the British had set out to capture in 1710. Even the official British documents surrounding the expedition were vague on this question. Nicholson's commission had defined the purpose of the mission as 'the reducing of Port Royal in Nova Scotia or any other place in those parts now in the possession of the enemy.' The only definition of the responsibilities of Vetch came in the penultimate paragraph of Nicholson's instructions: 'And if it shall please God to give such success to this Enterprise as that Port royal shall be reduced to our obedience. It is our pleasure that Coll: Vetch have the command of it, with such a number of fforces as shall be thought in a Council of war necessary for the security of the place from the designs of the enemy.' Nowhere in either document did the term 'Acadia' (or 'l'Acadie,' or any other variant) appear, and the term 'Nova Scotia' was used only in the single instance in the commission, and then only as an incidental qualifier to 'Port Royal.' The instructions preferred to cite only 'the reduction of Port royal and any of the Country and places adjacent belonging to the enemy.'[5]

Nicholson, Vetch, and the Council of War at Annapolis Royal were not so reticent. The term 'Nova Scotia,' frequently used in tandem with 'l'Acadie,' appeared often in their communications. A proclamation of 12 October 1710 formally announced the conquest to 'all the inhabitants of L'Accadie and Nova Scotia.' Both this and a further proclamation of the same date, directed to British colonists elsewhere in North America, referred to the 'dominions of L'Accadie and Nova Scotia,' although the latter proclamation also admitted that 'the season of the year will not allow the totall reduction of this large country of Nova Scotia.'[6] By January 1711 Vetch was ready to inform the Earl of Dartmouth, secretary of state, of an unorthodox personal initiative: 'I think fitt to acquaint your Lordship of my having taken the title of Governor for her Britannick Majesty of all the territorys of Accadie and Nova Scotia, though they are not yett wholly reduced, this I assure your Lordship I doe not out of the least vanity, but to assert Her Majesty's soveraignety to the same.'[7] This was not the first time Vetch had sought a new personal title from the conquest. As early as 14 October 1710 he had joined Nicholson and the seven other members of the Council of War in recalling to the queen a piece of Scottish history from the early part of the previous century. Noting that 'your royal predecessors ... to encourage the setlement of the said country instituted the Honourable order of Baronetts of Nova Scotia,' Vetch and the others advocated the order's revival and pressed their own case for membership.[8] The nine aspiring knights-baronets were not mistaken in their assertion of the purpose of the order created by James VI of Scotland in 1624, even though their ambition to join it would ultimately remain unrealized. Their letter provided an illustration of a process of historical and geographical reconstruction that was inseparable from the physical and strategic realities of the conquest.

The reinvention of 'Nova Scotia' has become familiar to historians as a recurring phenomenon, as characteristic of the twentieth century as of the seventeenth and eighteenth.[9] Yet the preservation of the concept depended at a critical moment on the conquest of 1710. The Scottish legacy of 'Nova Scotia' was in most respects a conspicuously empty one by that time. Its reappearance in the era of the conquest owed more to the imperial demands of the early eighteenth century, and to Scotland's increasing involvement in things British, than to any continuity from the Scottish colonization of the seventeenth, but the appearance of continuity was cultivated for both private and diplomatic purposes. During the intervening years, the concept of 'Nova Scotia' had been deployed in a variety of causes. It had been used as a front for commercial activity, as a tool in international negotiation, and as a pretext for the territorial expansion of an empire far removed from the Scottish efforts of the 1620s and 1630s. The Union of England and Scotland in 1707 gave renewed importance to 'Nova Scotia,' as it was subsumed into a context of increasing Scottish involvement in British imperial affairs.

In addition to reflecting shifting imperial spheres of influence, the changing roles of 'Nova Scotia' provide for the historian a revealing case study in the relationship between imperialism and the names that made their appearances from time to time on the map of colonial North America. As scholars such as Paul Carter and J.B. Harley have shown, the relationship between geographical names – with the spatial constructs they implied – and imperial possession was complex. Specific toponymies sought to determine, for example, whether the river eventually to be known as the St John should be designated as the Wulstukw (Wulstukwiuk), St-Jean (French), or Clyde (Scottish). Broader territorial divisions identified such overlapping areas as Mi'kma'ki (Mi'kmaq), Acadie (French), or New Scotland (Scottish). Both the specific and the broad designations represented competing cartographies that carried powerful implications regarding the maintenance of aboriginal possession or, alternatively, regarding imperial appropriation and the tension between imperial claims.[10] The evolution of the concept of 'Nova Scotia' provides a case in point. 'Nova Scotia,' and its imposition on the map of North America, would become a crucial element of the British effort to preserve the control over Annapolis Royal that had been asserted in 1710. There was nothing Scottish about the colony of Nova Scotia that was eventually to emerge from the peace negotiations that resulted in the Treaty of Utrecht in 1713. Yet the Scottish past, and its use as an instrument of cartographic imperialism, had become by that time a prerequisite for its existence.

The colony of New Scotland originated in the hopes of its promoter, Sir William Alexander, that 'as there was a New France, a New Spain and a New England, ... [my Countrimen] might likewise have a New Scotland.'[11] It originated in a more formal sense in the charter issued to Alexander by James VI on 10 September 1621, by which the Scottish claim encompassed all of the later Maritime region of Canada, along with the Gaspé Peninsula.[12] Despite repeated efforts by Alexander, it took until the summer of 1629 before colonists were established in two locations within the claimed territory. A settlement on the coast of Cape Breton Island, founded in August 1629, was destroyed in the following month by a French attack. The other settlement, at Port Royal, was more lasting. It too disappeared, however, when the colonists were evacuated in late 1632 in fulfilment of the terms of the Treaty of St-Germain-en-Laye. Thereupon, the French sphere of influence was re-established under the title of the colony of Acadia.[13]

Historically, the significance of the colony of New Scotland in the more general history of European colonization of North America during the first half of the seventeenth century is greater than the short duration of colonial settlement there might at first sight indicate. For a period of some three and a half years, the Scottish community at Port Royal represented a significant element in what was at the time a sporadic pattern of small European settlements on the Atlantic coast.[14] Once the colonists were removed, however, traces of their influence were erased with remarkable completeness. On the Mi'kmaq and Etchemin peoples, who remained the principal inhabitants of the region, the limited evidence suggests that the Scots made no significant impact beyond that already made by the French. Both the French and the Scottish claims to the territory had a flimsy and arcane quality in the face of the established occupancy and large numerical superiority of the aboriginal peoples. The influence of the fur trade on aboriginal cultures, to be sure, had not been negligible. Nevertheless, trade was no new experience for aboriginal peoples, and the arriving Scots found in 1629 that it was they, rather than potential aboriginal trading partners, who were in the position of responding to approaches by confident and established traders. The relationship being offered to the Scots was essentially a replica of that which had long existed vis-à-vis French and Basque sojourners.[15]

In other respects too, the Scottish presence was transitory. There is no evidence that the toponymy of New Scotland, as shown in Alexander's 1624 map, ever gained currency even while the Scottish settlement endured. Following the withdrawal of 1632, the notions of provinces of Alexandria (covering the modern New Brunswick and the Gaspé) and Caledonia (covering the modern peninsular Nova Scotia), or of the rivers Tweed (St Croix), Clyde (St John), and Forth (Miramichi) were permanently buried in obscurity.[16] With the eclipse of the nomenclature of New Scotland went the land allocations that had accompanied the knights-baronetcies. Titles continued to be conferred even after 1632 and carried grants of land, but the entitlement of a knight-baronet such as Sir James Skene of Curriehill to his 16,000 acres on the west side of 'that river now callit Clyde and formerlie St. John' was hardly convincing.[17] Nor, according to all surviving evidence, were there colonists who stayed to accommodate themselves to the aboriginal or French milieux. Later traditions that the brothers Melanson, founders of a large Acadian extended family, were Scots who had chosen not to depart in 1632 have been tested and found wanting. The Melansons, whose ancestry was English and French, were indeed survivors of a non-French immigration to a version of 'Nova Scotia,' but it was one that dated from the 1650s rather than the 1630s.[18] As a geographical entity, however, New Scotland tenuously survived. If Scottish references of the 1630s were to be believed, it could have been supposed to be a living colony even after 1632. A letter addressed by Charles I to the knights-baronets in August 1632 admitted that New Scotland 'hath not takin the root which was expected,' attributing the difficulty 'especially [to] the Colonie being forced of late to remove for a tyme by meanes of a treatie we have had with the French,' but promised continuing encouragement despite this temporary inconvenience.[19] Repeated royal assertions were made in 1633 that Alexander, by now ennobled as the Earl of Stirling, would 'prosecute the said work' of establishing New Scotland with the assistance of the knights-baronets. Also in 1633, the Scottish Parliament confirmed Stirling's grant of New Scotland, along with other royal concessions he had received in North America.[20] French consolidation in Acadia, however, and the chaotic state of Stirling's personal and political affairs before his death in 1640, prevented any real attempt at Scottish reassertion of New Scotland as a colonial presence.[21]

Significantly, it was as king of England that Charles I wrote to the English colonial promoter Sir Ferdinando Gorges in 1635 to charge Gorges with devising 'some good course ... for right prosecution of the work of the Plantation of New Scotland.' Gorges, however, accomplished as little with New Scotland as he did in his complementary role as designated future royal governor of New England.[22] When the notion of the Scottish colony reappeared in the 1640s, it was from a totally different direction. In late 1644 the younger John Winthrop wrote from Boston to Alexander, eleventh Lord Forbes, to inquire about 'Nova Scotia, called Acadia, where my Lord Starling once possessed a goodly harbor, and a fort in it called Port Royall.' Informing Forbes that New Englanders would be glad 'to have their brethren of Scotland to be their neighbors in enjoying that antient right is conceived they had of Nova Scotia,' Winthrop asked 'whether the State of Scotland hath wholy deserted that country ... and upon what ground, whether only upon my lord Sterling's surrender.'[23]

Surviving evidence does not make clear why Winthrop chose Forbes, then a prominent military leader of Covenanting forces in northeastern Scotland, as the correspondent to whom to address this enquiry, or whether he received any reply.[24] The circumstances that prompted Winthrop to raise the question of 'Nova Scotia,' however, are less obscure. His letter of 1644 began a period of some twenty-six years during which 'Nova Scotia,' no longer directly associated with Scotland, became a vehicle of French and English private interests and, more fleetingly, of Cromwellian imperialism. Earlier in 1644 Winthrop had entered into a commercial undertaking that involved him in an ongoing dispute between rival French governors of Acadia, Charles de Saint-Étienne de La Tour and Charles de Menou d'Aulnay. While the origins of this complex quarrel are not relevant to this essay, the result by 1644 was that La Tour was on the defensive following an unsuccessful attempt in the previous year to seize d'Aulnay's chief stronghold of Port Royal. La Tour had already entered into commercial arrangements with two Massachusetts merchants – Edward Gibbons and Thomas Hawkins – who had supplied him with munitions and other supplies, and in August 1644 Winthrop joined with Gibbons and Hawkins in acquiring the English-based rights to trade on the Penobscot River, where d'Aulnay was currently established.[25] Support for La Tour, in this context, represented an effort to dislodge d'Aulnay for private rather than public purposes, although even as a private goal it became more remote with the signing of an agreement between d'Aulnay and Massachusetts, promising coexistence and trade, in October 1644.[26]

La Tour also had a close connection with New Scotland. An attempt by Alexander to recruit the support of La Tour and his father, at the time the leaders of the few remaining French colonists in Acadia, had led to the conferral of knights-baronetcies upon father and son in 1629 and 1630 respectively. The effort to win over the La Tours to the Scottish interest had failed when Charles refused to follow his father's inclination to throw in his lot with Alexander. By the mid-1640s, however, the hard-pressed Charles de La Tour had found it convenient to rediscover his link with New Scotland. In May 1645, for example, he entered into a mortgage agreement with Gibbons as 'lord of La Tour in fraunce and Knight Barronet of Scotland.'[27] The inference is unavoidable that Winthrop's inquiry to Forbes resulted from La Tour's effort to make himself an attractive partner for his Massachusetts cohorts by holding out hopes of the eventual re-establishment of New Scotland as a strategic resolution of the problem of d'Aulnay's presence and as a lucrative trading ground for private interests.

For the time being, this effort was unsuccessful. La Tour suffered a decisive military defeat by d'Aulnay in a pitched battle at the mouth of the St John River. His personal survival ensured only by his absence in Boston at the time, La Tour soon took refuge in Quebec. Continued accommodation with d'Aulnay was inevitable for Massachusetts until d'Aulnay's accidental death by drowning in 1650. The subsequent period of strife among potential governors of Acadia – with La Tour among the contenders – came to an abrupt end in the summer of 1654. Robert Sedgwick, the leader of a small English naval force that had been cheated of its main purpose of attacking New Netherland when the First Anglo-Dutch War ended, resolved to occupy the waiting time in New England for a cargo of masts by 'rangeing the coast against the French, who use tradinge and fishinge hereaboute.'[28] Within a few weeks, French forts had fallen at Port Royal and on the St John and Penobscot Rivers. Small English garrisons had been deployed and La Tour – captured at his fort on the St John – dispatched to England as a prisoner.

By certain important measures, the significance of the episodes of the summer of 1654 was minor indeed. In terms of numbers, the European presence in the area defined by Sedgwick as 'hereaboute' – the territory from the Penobscot northeastward – was minimal. Port Royal had an Acadian population of some three hundred, and other locations may have added fifty or so more. Most remained, and coexisted with the English military and trading presence.[29] English rather than French trading networks were now developed, but their dependence on aboriginal cooperation was unchanged. In both France and England, reaction was restrained to the capture of what were described in official correspondence as, respectively, '[les] forts que les Anglois ont pris' and 'the fforts taken from the French in America.'[30] It was left to La Tour to associate the capture with the dormant Scottish claim to 'Nova Scotia.' In May 1656 the English Council of State reported approvingly on La Tour's claim to enjoy, by purchase from aboriginal people and by grant from Sir William Alexander, lands that included 'the country called Nova Scotia.' There were significant conditions attached, however. Most conspicuously, any formal patent that followed was to be granted not only to La Tour but also to two other partners: William Crowne and Sir Thomas Temple. Crowne, who had held minor civil and military offices in the Parliamentary cause during the English Civil War and in the early years of the Interregnum, was well connected in the City of London. Temple had attained the rank of colonel in the Parliamentary armies, and had family connections in the Council of State. The partners were supported by a powerful group of prominent London investors.[31]

The concept of 'Nova Scotia' had now been effectively cut off from its Scottish origins. What had begun thirty-five years previously as an enterprise directed at the private advantage of Sir William Alexander and his 'Countrimen' and at the public advantage of Scotland – even though, to be sure, both the private and the public purposes had English undertones – had bequeathed a Latin phrase that could be pressed into service for similar purposes that had no link with Scotland. The Cromwellian imperialism of the mid-1650s encompassed both the decision to retain Sedgwick's conquests and the capture of Jamaica in 1655. Initially, the English regime had to resort to vague generalities as it attempted to legitimate the retention of the Acadian forts during Anglo-French negotiations leading in 1655 to the Treaty of Westminster. The French ambassador in London, Antoine de Bordeaux, reported with ill-concealed contempt in February 1655 that the chief English negotiator 'a voulu justifier la prise des dits fortz par une pretension qu'ont les anglois sur toute cette Coste de l'amérique comme l'ayans les premiers descouverte.'[32] The treaty ultimately deferred the question to the later attention of special commissioners. However, the documented claim of La Tour – described by Bordeaux as making 'no great haste' to return to France even when freed to do so – gave a useful veneer of probity to the English refusal to surrender the forts.[33]

The personal involvements of La Tour, Temple, and Crowne with the English presence in what was described in their patent of 1656 as 'the Country and Territories called Lacadie and that parte of the Country called Nova Scotia' proved to be transitory.[34] La Tour quickly relinquished his interest to Temple and Crowne. Crowne took up residence in Boston and intermittently maintained trading interests in the Penobscot region. Temple took the most active role in attempting to maintain his own and the English claim throughout the 1650s and 1660s, in the face of political pressures arising from the Restoration and continuing French pressure for restitution. After the English Privy Council had ordered inquiries to be made in Scotland for relevant documentation, Temple apparently prevailed in his acquisition in 1662 of a new grant for 'the Countries and Territories called Laccadye and that part of the Country called Nova Scotia lately purchased by him of La Tour,' a commission as governor of the same area, and the title of knight-baronet. Five years later, however, the restitution of Acadia to France was embodied in the Treaty of Breda and in 1670 Temple reluctantly yielded to a new French governor, Hector d'Andigné de Grandfontaine.[35]

The events between 1654 and 1670 left certain significant legacies for Nova Scotia. One was the Temple claim itself, which survived into a later era through the efforts of his nephew, John Nelson. Nelson – whose activities in this and other contexts have been fully treated by Richard R. Johnson – was described in 1692 by Governor Frontenac of New France, his captor at the time, as 'un homme ... qui s'est mis dans la teste d'avoir de si justes prétentions sur le Port Royal et sur Laccadie, acause d'un oncle qu'il avoit et auquel il dit quelle appartenoit avant la restitution que les Anglois en firent an Consequence du traité de

Breda.'[36] A second legacy was the passing into common New England currency of 'Nova Scotia' as a geographical term denoting coastal territories northeastward of New England. Temple's ascendancy had produced no substantial English settlement, and no challenge to aboriginal territorial control, but in an economic sense had brought 'Nova Scotia' firmly into the trading and fishing hinterland of Massachusetts. Intermittent French efforts after 1670 to exclude New England fishers and traders brought responses such as the petition of William Vaughan and others to the English crown in 1684, in which 'Nova Scotia' was the term applied to the disputed coastline and the fact that it was 'now called Acadie' was a mere qualification.[37] A third legacy of the Sedgwick-Temple years, arising from the claims of La Tour and their facile acceptance by the Council of State, was lasting confusion over the boundaries of 'Nova Scotia.' The related notions that Alexander had conveyed to La Tour all of the colony of New Scotland, and that it had boundaries separate from those of 'Acadia,' had no historical justification but now created uncertainties for a century to come.[38]

In all of this, the Scottish past of the concept of 'Nova Scotia' had only peripheral significance. Scottish documentation might be seen as a useful quarrying ground in which to find support for an established position, and parties to the increasingly complex disputes of the Restoration era might find it convenient to make a declaration such as that made to Charles II by La Tour, Temple, and Crowne that 'the said fforts lye in New Scotland and the Sovereignety thereof doth as properly belong to your now Royall Majesty as old Scotland doth.'[39] Beyond that, Scotland was unconnected with either the private or the public roles in which 'Nova Scotia' was being cast. Events of the early 1690s confirmed the separation. In the spring of 1690, a New England expedition led by Sir William Phips captured Port Royal. Phips did not stay long, and in the absence of an English garrison his creation of a council of Acadian inhabitants to govern on behalf of King William and Queen Mary proved ineffective. In the planning and execution of Phips's assault, the term 'Nova Scotia' was continually used to define the expedition's destination. After Phips had prevailed at Port Royal, he ordered that submissions be demanded of French and aboriginal inhabitants in 'all places on the Coast of *Nova-Scotia.*'[40] Yet, when Phips demanded an oath of allegiance at Port Royal, the ambiguities of such terminology were fully evident in the addressing of the demand to '*the Inhabitants of* Port-Royal, L' Accadie, *or* Nova-scotia,' as well as in the confining of the supposed duties of the president of the newly created council to '*the Conservation of the Peace among the said Inhabitants.*'[41]

A footnote to the Phips expedition was written in the following year, beginning in June with the acceptance by the Massachusetts council of an offer by Nelson and a number of his merchant associates to send a garrison to 'the Country of Nova Scotia and L'accadie for the better securing of the said Country and Inhabitants thereof for and under the Obedience of the Crowne of England (whereto they have lately been subjected).' The expedition was also intended as a commercial venture, and it ended disastrously in September when a French naval vessel – in the acerbic words of a contemporary – 'tooke all the Pillgarlicks prisoners.'[42] Just over two weeks earlier, in London, the Lords of Trade had agreed – following representations from Phips and others – that Nova Scotia should be incorporated into Massachusetts. A new charter, passed on 7 October, accordingly provided for the uniting of 'the Territorie called Accadia or Nova Scotia' into the newly bounded colony of Massachusetts.[43] Nelson's response was long delayed by his captivity in Quebec and in France, but in April 1697 he offered to the English Lords Justices a detailed pedigree of his personal claims on Nova Scotia, derived from Alexander by way of La Tour and Temple. He maintained that Nova Scotia's incorporation into Massachusetts had been carried out 'by surprise' and also urged against any form of restitution to France in the negotiations at that time leading to the Treaty of Ryswick. The treaty, however, provided for the restoration of colonial boundaries to the *status quo ante bellum*, and thus for the continuation of the French in Acadia. To all appearances, 'Nova Scotia' had failed to survive the seventeenth century as anything more than a geographical term of arcane origin.[44]

That it did not remain as such was owing to the strategic needs of New England, the intervention of Samuel Vetch, the Union of 1707, and the changed imperial demands of Great Britain. When war was renewed between England and France in 1702, Port Royal came quickly to be seen by New Englanders as a lethal threat. Acadia was now governed by a hardened military veteran, Jacques-François de Mombeton de Brouillan, whose methods for inducing reluctant Wabanaki allies to participate in the war were as unorthodox as they were determined. Even after Brouillan's death in 1705, his successor – Subercase – compensated for shortage of troops and supplies at Port Royal by actively recruiting privateers from the French West Indies to disrupt New England fisheries and trade. The governor of Massachusetts, Joseph Dudley, joined with Vetch in October 1709 to warn the British government of the threat posed by 'another Dunkirk.'[45] The need to unseat the French regime in Port Royal had become, by then, a major strategic priority for Massachusetts and for all of New England.

Dudley and Vetch were collaborators in more than mere letter writing. Vetch, born in Edinburgh in 1668 as the son of a leading Covenanting minister, had removed to the Netherlands at the age of fifteen as his father sought to avoid persecution. Vetch had served with William III's invasion force of 1688, gained the rank of captain during the wars of the 1690s, sailed for Darien with the expedition of 1698 and served for a time as a councillor of the colony of Caledonia, removed to New York as a survivor of the withdrawal from Darien in 1699, and then moved again to Boston in 1705.[46] Dudley, older by some twenty-one years and a survivor of New England political wars spread over four decades, quickly came to regard Vetch as a 'particular friend.'[47] Whether it was particular friendship that then led Dudley to authorize Vetch to join with a number of Boston merchants for trading activities with French and aboriginal inhabitants along the Acadian coast, or the governor's desire for personal gain, was a question publicly debated in Boston in the summer of 1706. Dudley's governorship survived, but Vetch was convicted of illegal trade and fined. He paid his fine before setting out for England with the intention of clearing his name and then pursuing new colonial schemes.[48]

Vetch had already begun to urge the promotion of Scottish colonization in North America. In early 1706 he had used John Chamberlain – an influential London friend and patron of Dudley – as an intermediary in presenting a series of proposals to a leading Whig politician, the Earl of Halifax. Chamberlain, describing Vetch as 'an old Buccaneer, tho' a young man,' stopped short of endorsing the paper but commended it to Halifax's attention. The first passage, a forerunner of Vetch's more elaborate later tract entitled 'Canada Survey'd,' proposed 'that a Colony of Scotch Men may be permitted to take and settle the Territory of Canada.' Then Vetch turned to 'Nova Scotia and Le Acada,' in a passage that combined New England strategic concerns with an appeal to the era of Scottish colonization:

> Nova Scotia and Le Acada are in the possession of the French ... Port Royall is to the plantations here as Dunkirk to England, from whence they fitt out privateers, and infest our Coast, they also fitt out and send the Indian Enemies and Rebells upon our frontiers by land ... Nova Scotia was given by King James in 1621 to Sir William Alexander who in 1622 sent a Colony thither ... but it is said that Sir William Alexander sold it to the French, and supposing it once belonged to the Crown a subject could not dispose off the Royalty and Government, if he could the Soile.[49]

In this document, Vetch did not explicitly call for Scottish colonization of 'Nova Scotia' as he did in regard to Canada, referring only to 'a Colony of suitable people.' Within months, however, both he and Dudley were advocating Scottish settlement in both locations, and linking the matter to the question of Union. 'As to the business of Quebeck and Nova Scotia,' wrote Dudley to the Board of Trade in October 1706, 'upon the News of the union of the Kingdoms, I most humbly propose to your Lordships that a Scotch Colony there of five thousand men, would find their own Scotch Climate and health, and a Country farr Surpassing all Scotland, for all sorts of Provisions, flesh and Fish, Infinite Timber, and masts the first of the whole continent.' The Scots, he continued with easy assurance, 'would with the assistance of these Provinces very easily remove the french and put an end to the troubles upon the whole Shore of America, and they would be therefore very acceptable here.'[50] Vetch, presenting his case to be cleared of his conviction for illegal trading, went so far as to claim that even after his conviction the Massachusetts General Court had heard proposals 'to send him their Agent into this Kingdome, to Endeavor after an Union of England and Scotland, to procure a Body of Scotts to settle in Nova Scotia.'[51]

The Act of Union, with its creation of a political climate in which Scottish interests assumed a modestly increased significance for English politicians, combined with the limited but real Whig connections that Dudley and Vetch could muster between them to establish the candidacy of such a proposal at least for serious discussion. An obstacle, however, was the characteristic Whig priority on direct defeat of France on European battlefields, as opposed to colonial expeditions that could be seen as diversions from the central purpose of the war. In 'Canada Survey'd,' submitted in final form to the Board of Trade in July 1708, Vetch addressed this problem by focusing on the most dramatic of his earlier proposals, and the one that would arguably most affect the overall course of the war: the conquest of Canada. The 'Country of Accadia' – described as 'that which was formerly by us called Nova Scotia' – was mentioned, but only peripherally. On this basis Vetch's scheme gained the approval of the Board of Trade by late 1708, although the support of such powerful ministers as the senior secretary of state, the Earl of Sunderland, was always subject to the exigencies of higher military priorities. The cancellation of an assault on Canada that Vetch was to have led in 1709 was a product of this ambivalence.[52]

Dudley, directly concerned with the military and naval threat from Port Royal, had continued to advance plans specifically based on Scottish colonization of 'Nova Scotia.' In March 1709, while welcoming the projected attempt on Canada, he also stressed to the Board of Trade the strategic advantages of having 'the North Britains setled in Nova Scotia,' and went on pointedly to note that all legislation pertaining to the Union had been duly proclaimed in Boston.[53] Dudley had already launched a disastrous assault on Port Royal in 1707, in which a large force of New England militia had twice failed to translate landings on the surrounding marshes into any serious threat to the French fort. With the abandonment of the attack on Canada in 1709, Dudley and Vetch – assisted by Francis Nicholson, former lieutenant governor of Virginia and commander of land contingents for the abortive 1709 design on Canada – began to focus their arguments on gaining British military support for the more limited objective of taking Port Royal. They were rewarded with the arrival of Nicholson in Boston in July 1710 at the head of a force of some four hundred marines. The marines were combined with enough New England volunteers to bring the total to approach two thousand, and the fall of Port Royal followed in September.[54]

The Scottish overtones of the 1710 conquest, as they related either to private advancement or to immigration, now quickly faded. The aspirations of Vetch, Nicholson, and the others for knights-baronetcies were ignored. The notion of settlement by 'North Britains' had never been thought through by those who had advocated it, and in particular it overlooked the expanded possibilities brought to Scots by the Union of the Parliaments of settlement in more attractive colonial environments than that of 'Nova Scotia.' Vetch's own grandiosely announced assumption of the title of 'Governour ... of all the territorys of Accadie and Nova Scotia' in early 1711 rang empty in the following year, by which time the lack of supply from Britain, mutiny among unpaid and underfed troops, and pressure from aboriginal forces had reduced Vetch to reporting that he was 'allmost ... in Dispair.'[55] Yet there was one context in which 'Nova Scotia' and its Scottish antecedents continued to arouse interest. In a lengthy and wide-ranging account of British interests and claims in North America presented to Secretary of State Henry Boyle in June 1709, the Board of Trade commented extensively on the Scottish origins and historical evolution of the colonial entity it designated as 'Nova Scotia or Accadie.' The emphasis was laid on the need to preserve coastal New England fisheries and, if prospective treaty negotiations were to leave the French undisturbed in the region, to confirm boundaries that would confine them northeastward of the St Croix River.[56]

The Board of Trade's submission of June 1709 derived neither from the ambitions of Vetch nor even directly from the strategic admonitions of Dudley. Its provenance was from the representations that had been made by Nelson during the late 1690s. The wording came directly from a submission made by the Board of Trade to then-Secretary of State James Vernon on 17 February 1699, which had been based in turn on statements provided by Nelson on 12 April, 2 November, and 2 December 1697.[57] At the time, Nelson's evidence to the Board of Trade had a close connection with his private interest as a claimant on 'Nova Scotia' and a merchant with trading interests there. By 1709, however, Nelson had withdrawn into respectable private life in New England, and was no longer actively involved either in the eastern trade or in promoting the claims he had derived from Temple.[58]

The Board of Trade's revival of its earlier analysis had, in 1709, a simpler and more straightforwardly public purpose. Submitted at Boyle's request, it represented an early effort at preparation for the Anglo-French negotiations that would eventually lead to the Treaty of Utrecht in 1713. As such, it incorporated the characteristic seventeenth-century confusion as to the relative status of 'Acadia' and 'Nova Scotia.' Not until April 1712, in the midst of the Utrecht negotiations – and after the capture of Port Royal had created a direct British military interest to be protected, in addition to the safeguarding of New England's fisheries and northeastern boundary – did the Board of Trade finally establish a clearer position. It then urged upon Secretary of State Henry St John, without entering into any discussion of Scottish or seventeenth-century origins, the definition 'that Nova Scotia does comprehend all that the French call Accadie, and is bounded by the River St. Croix on the West, by the Sea on the South and East, and by Canada River on the North, and ought to be so described for avoiding future disputes.'[59]

Although the Utrecht negotiations resulted in a formula for defining Nova Scotia that was far less specific than that adopted by the Board of Trade – citing only 'ses anciennes limites,' and thus ensuring the persistence of seventeenth-century ambiguities – the Board of Trade's statement of 1712 marked an important stage in the transition of 'Nova Scotia' into a concept serviceable primarily for purposes of straightforward cartographic imperialism.[60] Whether expressed in explicitly cartographic form, as by Sir William Alexander in 1624, or – as by the Board of Trade in April 1712 – by a text based on cartographically derived geographical features, this was an approach that emphasized, in the words of J.B. Harley, 'boundaries rather than other features.'[61] The 'Nova Scotia' that the Board of Trade commended to British negotiators at Utrecht represented a boundary claim that could be used for effective negotiation with the French over fishing rights, as a tool for the sustaining of strategic interests that were common to New England and to Great Britain, and as a justification for holding on to territory seized in 1710.

'Nova Scotia' had been a settlement colony only between 1629 and 1632, and then with a numerical strength that made its single community tiny by comparison with aboriginal peoples. What fragile progress may have been made toward, the establishment of a Scottish toponymy had also been erased in 1632. The concept had been kept alive by an interlocking chain of private interests. The explanation of its survival lay not in any continuing connection either with Scotland or with the Alexanders and their aspirations. 'Nova Scotia' had been commodified, claimed by La Tour on specious grounds, sold to Temple and Crowne, and passed by Temple to his heirs. This process had culminated in the efforts of John Nelson during the 1690s.

'Nova Scotia,' to be sure, was no longer by that time the only serviceable vehicle for promoting private interests in the region. Sir William Phips, for example, was keen to advance his own and related private interests in the territory for which he frequently used 'Nova Scotia' as a geographical term, but sought its integration with Massachusetts rather than any continuing separate identity. Furthermore, when the era of the Act of Union seemed to Vetch and others to suggest new ways of using the Scottish past for current advantage, the reality proved disappointing. Consciousness of the Scottish origins of the concept of 'Nova Scotia' was still significant for some purposes. The echoes of the Scottish past reverberated in the Board of Trade's submission to Boyle in 1709. Yet the real sustenance for the reappearance of Nova Scotia on European maps and in formal colonial terminology after 1713 was a British imperialism for which the Scottish past, and its deployment as a support for boundary claims, was an inert prerequisite. Aboriginal inhabitants were properly sceptical, and some Mi'kmaq seized an apparent opportunity to counterattack in 1715 when early reports of Jacobite activities in the British Isles suggested the imminent outbreak of war between France and the Hanoverian regime.[62] That was as close as the current realities of Scotland, as opposed to the reinvention of the seventeenth-century past, would come to influencing the early development of the new 'Nova Scotia.'

7 Imperialism, Diplomacies, and the Conquest of Port Royal, 1710

In July 1720 Governor Richard Philipps of Nova Scotia reported to London that British authority was 'in a manner dispised and ridiculed' by both Acadian and native inhabitants. Two months later Philipps was even more blunt: 'This has been hitherto no more than a mock Government. Its Authority haveing never yet extended beyond cannon reach of this ffort.'[1] To prove the point, in the interim, Mi'kmaq raiders had seized fish and other goods from New England vessels at Canso, and a New England merchant had been similarly used in the Minas basin. Referring to both incidents, Antoine and Pierre Couaret, Mi'kmaq leaders from Minas, had remarked to Philipps that 'jamais Ceux de vostre Nation ayent eu aucune part avec nous pour les soufrir encore libres dans nostre Pays come vous le voulez.'[2] The governor's mortification – his own word to describe his frame of mind – contrasted with the expansiveness with which a British envoy to France had described seven-and-a-half years earlier the resolution of the few out-

---

Presented as a paper at the Annual Meeting of the Canadian Historical Association in St John's in 1997, but designed from the beginning to be a chapter in John G. Reid et al., *The 'Conquest' of Acadia, 1710: Imperial, Colonial, and Aboriginal Constructions* (Toronto: University of Toronto Press, 2004), this essay made what was for me an important statement regarding the negotiated character of imperialism in northeastern North America. The gap between imperial assertions and the realities of diplomacy was considerable, and implied that imperial officials often had little choice about going in directions that they found difficult or impossible to report fully to their metropolitan masters. Although I am the sole author of this particular essay, all of my thinking on the Conquest era was influenced by, and benefited greatly from, the collaboration with my co-authors on the book: Maurice Basque, Elizabeth Mancke, Barry Moody, Geoffrey Plank, and William Wicken.

standing matters delaying the British-French peace treaty at Utrecht. With a thirty-league fishing limit agreed to for French vessels off the coast of Nova Scotia and the Acadians (and French inhabitants of other ceded territories) denied the right to sell their lands but assured of freedom of religion if they chose not to move, Matthew Prior assured the Lord Treasurer of the day, the Earl of Oxford, that these final issues were 'so well adjusted, that ... I may congratulate Your Lordship upon the Peace made.'[3]

That the realities of native control had unmistakably caught up by 1720 with the fanciful British assumptions of 1713 is not surprising in historical retrospect, although the surprise and embarrassment caused to the Nova Scotia governor at the time were obviously real. The comments made by Antoine and Pierre Couaret, like those of Philipps and Prior, stemmed from the changes flowing from the British conquest of Port Royal in 1710, but more particularly from the role of diplomacy in defining the extent of those changes. Prior in 1713 believed that diplomacy had done its work, and that the imperial and economic consequences of the confirmation of British rule in Nova Scotia would now follow in logical and predictable sequence. Philipps in 1720 was aware that something had gone badly awry, but was torn between an enforced recognition of the need for a new round of British-Mi'kmaq negotiations based on native protocols of gift-giving and a desire for greater military force to be used to frustrate the French in Cape Breton, whom he assumed to be prompting 'the Savages ... to assert their Native Rights to this Country' and Acadians to show 'Marks of Contempt ... to my Authority.'[4] The Couarets certainly showed scant regard for British military force, and offered no hint that even a further diplomatic process would consolidate the full extent of British gains in Nova Scotia agreed to at Utrecht. Diplomacy, for all that, was envisaged by the chiefs as the key to British maintenance even of the limited ascendancy at Annapolis Royal: 'Nous disputerons à tous les hommes qui voudroient l'habiter [notre pays] sans notre consentement.'[5] Yet a serious problem was that all sides, in the wake of the 1710 conquest, had a status quo to defend through diplomatic channels – and it was only through diplomacy that the necessary negotiated relationships could be stabilized to facilitate future coexistence – but it was not the same status quo. Also promising future conflict was the existence of differing and multilayered approaches to diplomacy that were difficult or impossible to reconcile.

The conquest of 1710 first entered into British-French negotiations in the following year, though it was not mentioned explicitly. Early British proposals, in secret exchanges during the spring and summer of 1711, included cession by France of all its claims in Newfoundland and Hudson's Bay and the retention by either side of 'all such places in North America, as each shall be in possession of at the Publication of the Ratifications of the Treaty in that Part of the World.' The French response, embodied in preliminary articles signed by both sides in the early autumn, was to acknowledge the existence of the British demands, reserve specifically the fishing and drying rights of French vessels on the Newfoundland coast, and refer all other North American issues to the general peace conference that eventually opened in Utrecht in early 1712.[6] The reference to the peace conference was disingenuous. Although North American affairs were discussed at Utrecht, and some important details of the eventual treaty terms were hammered out there, the real negotiation was handled by special envoys whose dealings were not immediately known to the formal plenipotentiaries. At one crucial point in the discussions over Newfoundland, the British envoy Prior observed from Paris that at Utrecht 'the Plenipotentiaries on both sides are at this moment fighting in the Dark.'[7] As early as March 1712, just a few weeks after the conference had begun, the French plenipotentiaries had complained to Louis XIV that both sides had firm enough instructions to avoid concessions on the question of Acadia / Nova Scotia to ensure that the matter was generating only 'disputes perpetuelles entre les parties.'[8] Concessions would eventually follow, but they did not originate around the bargaining tables of Utrecht.

In reality, the issues surrounding the disputes over Acadia / Nova Scotia and the other North American questions were complex, by no means unimportant in the general scheme of the peace negotiations, and well known in advance of the Utrecht conference. Aside from the matter of Hudson's Bay – important to both sides for trade purposes, and also territorially significant to France because of the possibility of overland access to Canada, but only loosely connected with the east-coast questions – there were two pre-eminent issues. Both had been discussed by Prior and the French secretary for foreign affairs, the Marquis de Torcy, in July 1711. One, not surprisingly, was the control of the North Atlantic fisheries. 'Say whatever you please for Newfoundland,' Prior recalled Torcy informing him, 'we can say the same and more; it is the nursery for our seamen ... and for the fish we have more need of it than you.'[9] The fate of Acadia / Nova Scotia was relevant to this in two ways: as a bargaining counter for possible concessions in Newfoundland, and for the fisheries off its own shores now largely exploited by New England. The other major issue was strategic and territorial. Torcy, citing Louis XIV's personal reaction to the preliminary British demands, observed to Prior in 1711 that 'you ask in America all that which [with] our sweat and our blood we have been endeavouring for a hundred years to acquire.'[10] Should the British take control of Newfoundland, Acadia, and Cape Breton, observed a French briefing document in March 1712, 'ils seroient aussy les maistres de l'entrée de la Rivière de St Laurent' and Canada itself would be in jeopardy. The British, however, had the security of New England to consider, and the French plenipotentiaries at Utrecht were soon left in no doubt that Nova Scotia was seen in London as 'un ancien Domaine qui faisoit la communication de leurs principales Colonies d'Amerique.'[11]

The initial exchange of demands at Utrecht confirmed the areas of active dispute in North America between Great Britain and France. While the British claimed full territorial control of Newfoundland, 'comme aussi l'Acadie avec la ville de Port Royal, autrement appellée Annapolis Royale, et ce qui en depend du dit Pais,' the French offered only to cede Newfoundland if Plaisance were excluded from the cession and if French fisheries on the Newfoundland coast were left as they had been before the war. France did agree to other cessions demanded by the British, of the Caribbean island of St Christopher and of Hudson's Bay, but only on condition that Acadia should be restored.[12] In reality, the French position was the more flexible. A passage written in cipher in a French document of late March 1712 set out a series of fall-back positions, beginning with the possibility of agreeing to cede Acadia without Cape Breton, thus retaining for France some degree of control over the navigation routes to Canada. If the peace was still threatened by this issue, a more extreme concession would be to allow Great Britain to choose between Cape Breton and mainland Acadia. The last resort would be to cede both of these territories, along with Newfoundland, though this would buy peace at the expense of serious damage to French fisheries and the isolation of Canada.[13]

The limits of the French resolve, however, were never tested. Although the French plenipotentiaries were pessimistic by early April about any possibility of gaining restitution of Acadia, reporting that their British counterparts 'nous ont protesté cent fois quils avoient ordre exprés de tout rompre' sooner than to make concessions either there or on Newfoundland, a new British proposal in May offered some further basis for negotiation. While continuing to press for cession of both Acadia and Newfoundland, and seeking to limit French fishing on the Newfoundland coast to the *Petit Nord*, the British demand for Acadia 'selon ses Limites anciennes' was qualified by the proposal that the two powers should share Cape Breton on condition that neither should be allowed fortifications there.[14] The French response refused to concede or share Cape Breton in any circumstances, nor to give up the right to fortify the island, but did set out two alternatives for the balance of the Acadian and Newfoundland disputes. France would agree to relinquish any territorial claim in Newfoundland – including Placentia, but not adjacent islands and without any concession on fisheries – and would surrender mainland Acadia. Alternatively, France would additionally cede the islands adjacent to Newfoundland, as well as two others off St Christopher, and would agree to give up all of its fishing and drying rights on the Newfoundland coast – but only if Great Britain restored Acadia with the boundary (as, the French maintained, it had always been defined by the British) at the St George River.[15]

Although it was predictable enough that neither alternative would lead to immediate agreement, there was scope for future discussion. Here matters rested for several months. When the British secretary of state, Viscount Bolingbroke, visited France in August 1712 to renew a temporary armistice, he professed chagrin to find that the North American issues – along with contentious aspects of the commercial treaty concurrently being negotiated – were not even under active consideration.[16] A month later, under political pressure to show results from the Tory ministry's peace strategy, Bolingbroke wrote privately to Prior on the need now to cut short any further idle debate, and instead to find 'a Scheme of the lowest Expedient which we can admit of on the Subject of North America.' What this meant was to make as many concessions as British trade interests could bear, and then issue an ultimatum accordingly.[17] By mid-December, another special British envoy was en route to the French court, and one politically and socially more prestigious than Matthew Prior. The instructions issued to the Duke of Shrewsbury noted that 'the most essential dispute that remains between Us and the French Court in the Project for a Treaty of Peace ... consists in fixing the Bounds of their fishing and drying their Fish on the Coast of Newfoundland, and in the Possession of Cape Breton.' Shrewsbury's task, at least as set out in the instructions, was simple. The French must choose between their Newfoundland fishing rights and the possession of Cape Breton. If they insisted on continuing their Newfoundland fishery, Shrewsbury was to 'show them, that we likewise look'd upon

Cape Breton to belong to Us, and reckoned that Island as part of our Ancient Territory of Nova Scotia which is by this Treaty restored to us.'[18]

As a contribution to the reaching of a settlement, Shrewsbury's mission had an uncertain beginning. Torcy – who, reported Prior, was 'in the last concern to find the Duke's instructions so strict' – declared that France would never accept having to relinquish either Cape Breton or a fishery that was 'absolutely necessary' for the French economy.[19] According to Bolingbroke some days later, however, the real British aim was not so drastic. 'What we see we may obtain when we shall please to come to it,' wrote the secretary of state to Prior, was the limitation of the French fishery to the Petit Nord in exchange for sole French possession of Cape Breton. In a more private letter, Bolingbroke impressed on Prior the political dangers to the Tory ministry that would accompany a breakdown in the negotiations: 'We stand indeed on the brink of a precipice, but the French stand there too.' To Torcy, he urged that 'nos contestations a l'egard de Terreneuve ne seront point la pierre d'achopement.'[20] In reality, a solution to the apparent impasse on Cape Breton and Newfoundland was already available, although not yet fully acknowledged by either side. In late December, Prior – who considered the French claim to Cape Breton to be only 'too well founded' – had reached agreement with Torcy to recommend a proposal by which France would retain Cape Breton while Great Britain would be ceded Acadia 'avec tous les Droits et prerogatives dont les Francois ont jouy.' The French fishery in Newfoundland, meanwhile, would extend from Bonavista to Pointe Riche, taking in the Petit Nord and more besides – though not as much as the French had originally claimed.[21]

For the time being, Bolingbroke held out on Newfoundland in order to exert pressure for compromise on the commercial treaty, while Louis XIV instructed the French plenipotentiaries to hold Prior's proposal in reserve as a minimum demand pending efforts to wring further concessions from the British at Utrecht.[22] By the second week in February, however, both the king and Shrewsbury had agreed to accept Prior's article, while Torcy busied himself writing to the French plenipotentiaries on the need to accommodate Tory political interests by bringing the peace negotiations to a rapid and successful conclusion.[23] There were flurries of disagreement still to come over the thirty-league limit on French fishing off Nova Scotia and over whether departing Acadians (or French colonists in Newfoundland or the Hudson's Bay settlements) would have the right to sell their lands. In early March, France conceded on these matters – although British royal orders were unilaterally given some weeks later to allow Acadians and French Newfoundland residents to sell or retain their lands – and the treaty was signed in April. The text concerning Acadia / Nova Scotia in Article XII was by no means free of ambiguities, notably over just what were the 'anciennes limites' by which the colony was vaguely defined. Nevertheless, to all appearances the diplomacy surrounding the treaty negotiations had transformed the seizure of Port Royal in 1710 into a genuine advance for Great Britain in North America.[24]

Acadia / Nova Scotia had been no mere pawn in the hands of the Utrecht negotiators, to be moved around or traded away as expediency dictated. While North American considerations did not head the list of *casus belli* in the same sense as did the Spanish succession or other major western European issues, neither control of the Gulf of St Lawrence nor what Torcy defined as 'the Subsistance of the Maritime Provinces of West France where thousands of Family's would be reduced to Beggary in case ... [the Newfoundland] Fishery be taken from them' was apt to be taken lightly by either France or Great Britain.[25] Thus the removal of negotiation on these issues away from Utrecht and into the hands of the ministers and their direct envoys, and thus also the ability of these issues to delay and at times to imperil the conclusion of the peace. Seriously as North America was taken in these respects, however, the negotiations were also characterized by crucially untested assumptions. The most significant of these was, quite simply, the existence of defensible colonial empires in northeastern North America. When French-British discussion centred on the Newfoundland fisheries or those in offshore reaches elsewhere in the North Atlantic, it was (to use an inappropriate metaphor) on firm enough ground. Those fisheries had long been integrated into western European economies, and by 1713 it was well within the power of France and Great Britain, subject only to environmental constraints, to agree or disagree on the allocation of fishing grounds and the manner of their exploitation. The New England inshore fishery on the coasts of Acadia / Nova Scotia, though, was a different case, and for reasons that also cast doubt on the entire treatment of strategic and territorial issues in the negotiations leading to the treaty of Utrecht. Control of the territory of Acadia / Nova Scotia – whether for the tangential needs of fishing vessels, for other economic uses, or for settlement – was far beyond the reach of either European power. Thus, while claims of sovereignty were easy to make, the Treaty of Utrecht offered scant prospect of their legitimation in the face of aboriginal scepticism.

With some modification, this principle could be extended even to

Canada or New England. While extensive settlement of those areas gave an air of solidity, worthwhile questions could be raised about their military defensibility and whether, in the light of those questions, the solidity was real or apparent. Even prominent imperial officials, such as the Earl of Bellomont in 1700, governor of both Massachusetts and New York, and in 1718 the intendant of New France, Michel Bégon, expressed pessimism regarding the ability of their colonies to withstand sustained aboriginal attack.[26] If these insecurities were current in the more heavily settled colonial areas of northeastern North America, the ability of French and British negotiators to arbitrate the strategic or imperial status of Acadia / Nova Scotia, where the carving out even of European spheres of influence had been a notoriously arduous and fickle business, was doubtful indeed. Not that the existence of limits to imperial sway had gone entirely unnoticed at Utrecht. Article XV of the treaty sought to safeguard the security of the native 'Sujets ou amis' of either European power, as well as to open up mutual trading arrangements, but it had little effect in view of the absence in future years of the planned consideration by commissioners as to exactly 'quels sont ceux qui seront ou devront être censez Sujets & amis de la France, ou de la G.B.'[27]

There was, however, another framework for the recognition and partial resolution of such dilemmas. It was the practice of a double diplomacy, by which territorial dispositions arrived at in western Europe would inform the exchanges between colonial administrators and imperial authorities, while a secondary and largely oral form of diplomacy would characterize the relations between the administrators and indigenous peoples. The era of the treaty of Utrecht, in which the independent power of aboriginal peoples had been necessarily identified by colonial officials during a quarter-century of intermittent warfare, created a fertile environment for this approach. Precedents existed: both immediate and chronologically or geographically distant from Acadia / Nova Scotia in this period. The image of the Janus-faced relationships of the French with Algonkian allies, invoked by such historians as W.J. Eccles and Richard White, stemmed from similar imperatives further north and west.[28] In Acadia itself a temporarily successful double approach, though not one involving aboriginal inhabitants, had been practised during the 1640s by Governor Charles de Menou d'Aulnay Charnisay. While maintaining a negotiated peace with New England from 1644 until his death six years later, d'Aulnay had reported consistently to France on the vigour of his efforts to displace the 'Religionnayres estrangers' whose settlements in Massachusetts encroached within

Acadia's claimed boundaries.[29] The most recent examples in a neighbouring territory to Acadia / Nova Scotia, however, came from the New England relationship with the Wabanaki.

On 13 July 1713 Governor Joseph Dudley of Massachusetts and New Hampshire summarized for the benefit of assembled Wabanaki and Mi'kmaq representatives at Portsmouth, New Hampshire, the North American provisions of the Treaty of Utrecht:

> In fformer Warrs twenty or thirty years ago what Lands and ffortifications wee then took from the ffrench King wee returned them againe, but now all that wee have got from him, wee hold it, And alsoe some things wee demanded of Him which wee had not taken And those he has surrendered to Her Majestie. We have taken Port Royal and we keep it. Wee demanded Menis [Minas] and Senectica [Chignecto] and all Cape Sables and he hath given it us, and all the Settlements of Placentia and St Peters on New ffound Land is ours and our Soldjers are now Entring in and takeing possession thereof. Noe more ffrench are to live in those places unles they becom Subjects to the Crown of Great Brittaine.[30]

The tone of Dudley's pronouncement, as reflected in the official record of the proceedings that led eventually to the Wabanaki-British treaty of 1713, was uncompromising. So, the record also indicated, was the governor's blame for the Wabanaki as the aggressors in the recent warfare, and insistence that they must submit to the authority of the British crown. The nature of his description of the treaty of Utrecht is corroborated in the criticisms levelled at it during a further meeting held immediately afterwards at Casco Bay, at which a larger native gathering met with New England commissioners to receive and comment on the news of the Portsmouth conference. Wabanaki and Wulstukwiuk leaders followed a polite expression of pleasure at the conclusion of peace between France and Great Britain with a seemingly innocuous question as to how it came about that so much territory had been surrendered from one crown to the other. Receiving a patronizing answer about the superiority of British arms, Moxus of the Kennebec Wabanaki and the other sagamores came to the nub of their concern: 'The French never said any Thing to us about it and wee wonder how they could give it away without asking us, God having att first placed us there and They having nothing to do to give it away.'[31] Both native and British views of the treaty of Utrecht were stated, therefore, without agreement between them.

When it came to other salient elements of the Wabanaki-British treaty, the evidence reveals further differences of understanding between the two sides. By contrast with Dudley's portrayal of the treaty as a submission, the Wabanaki leaders at Casco Bay made clear that they took it to be an agreement that was both reciprocal and conditional. 'If the Queen att home makes this Peace contained in these Articles as strong and durable as the Earth,' remarked Moxus and his colleagues, 'Wee for our Parts shall endeavour to make it as strong and firm here.'[32] Where the text of the treaty asserted the right of English colonists to repossess the areas of the old province of Maine where settlements had been displaced, another Wabanaki account of the discussions – summarized by the Jesuit missionary Sébastien Rale – recalled the Wabanaki view of this matter to have been prefaced by yet another expression of scepticism regarding the ability of the French to give away native territory. This document is ambiguous as to whether the statement was made at Portsmouth or at Casco. It can be read to imply a direct response to Dudley, which would have been necessarily at Portsmouth, but its citation of the presence of 358 assembled natives (including 40 Wulstukwiuk and 20 Mi'kmaq) is more consistent with the meeting at Casco. The statement itself was not ambiguous in the least: 'J'ay ma terre que je n'ai donnée a personne et que je ne donnerai pas. Je en veux tousjours etre le maistre, j'en courrois les limites et quand quelqu'un y voudra habiter il payera.'[33]

That there would be different understandings of the treaty and related discussions is not surprising, given the complexities of cross-cultural negotiation. The Wabanaki accounts, however, indicate a marked discrepancy between the tone and the substance of the remarks made by Dudley for, respectively, British and native consumption. The preceding forty years had seen a number of agreements made between English and Wabanaki. All of them had reflected the English need for a negotiated relationship, and the treaty of 1678 that had ended the northeastern hostilities associated with the so-called King Philip's War had explicitly provided for English payment of a tribute in recognition of their use of Wabanaki land, the principle to which the Wabanaki speaker in 1713 had returned.[34] The treaty of 1693 negotiated by Sir William Phips, governor of Massachusetts at the time, had introduced the language of sovereignty and submission, but in a context that cast doubt on any likelihood that any common understanding of such terminology had been reached.[35] At the beginning of the eighteenth century, however, New England negotiators – including the newly appointed Joseph Dudley – dropped the language of submission in favour of that of friendship and coexistence, and adopted such protocols of native diplomacy as reciprocal gift-giving.[36] The resumption of hostilities in 1703 led to English condemnation of the Wabanaki as 'bloody Rebells,' and public statements by Dudley up until the early stages of the Portsmouth conference reflected this view.[37] More privately, according to reports of Dudley's intermittent efforts to neutralize the Wabanaki, the governor's statements were altogether different. Governor Vaudreuil of New France reported in 1710 that 'Monsieur dudley ... na rien negligé cette année' to win over the Wabanaki; the effort had even extended to an offer of gifts to a group that had recently raided a New England settlement, 'leurs temoignant le chagrin quils [the British] avoient d'estre en guerre avec ceux' and offering trade on favourable terms.[38] The Wabanaki account of the 1713 discussions, as relayed by Rale, was consistent with this form of approach. It had Dudley allowing for Wabanaki wishes as to whether the English settlements should be resettled and again offering a favourable trade.[39] The double style of diplomacy, at least in the short term, had prevailed.

The inherent tendency of this diplomatic technique was for it to collapse under the weight of its own contradictions. Though outright duplicity was likely the exception rather than the rule, it was identified by one Boston merchant in 1715. 'I have been present,' observed Thomas Bannister to the Board of Trade, 'when an Article of the Peace has run in one Sence in the English, and quite contrarie in the Indian, by the Governours express order.'[40] In 1717, at a further major British-Wabanaki conference held on Arrowsic Island, the Kennebec speaker Wiwurna clashed repeatedly with a new Massachusetts governor, Samuel Shute, on matters that ranged from Wiwurna's insistence that 'other Governours have said to us that we are under no other Government than our own' to the existence of a guarantee orally made by the New England commissioners at the Casco meeting of 1713 that no more British forts would be built in Wabanaki territory.[41] Such tensions, focusing notably on continuing colonial encroachments in the Kennebec and Androscoggin valley, led eventually to the re-igniting of hostilities in 1722. Nevertheless, it was diplomacy of this nature that framed initially the relationship between native peoples of the area claimed by Great Britain as its colony of Nova Scotia and the Annapolis Royal regime following the treaty of Utrecht. Earlier exchanges had been inconclusive, despite the Mi'kmaq initiatives of early 1711, and had been eclipsed by the intermittent hostilities that had subsequently persisted. Governor Samuel Vetch, optimistic over the arrival of a Mohawk company at Annapolis Royal in 1712, signalled to London his expectation that the new force would 'in a litle time ... Either wholly Banish our Troublesome Indians, or Oblidge them to submitt themselves to her Majesties Government.'[42] The weak and isolated military status of the Annapolis Royal garrison, however, hardly justified his hopes. More consistent with reality was the letter sent by the missionary Antoine Gaulin to Dudley in July 1713 to warn in a matter-of-fact way that failure to release Cape Sable Mi'kmaq captives who had been held in Boston – and who were now, unknown as yet to Gaulin, in the process of being returned – would result in ship seizures and the capture of officers from the Annapolis Royal garrison, to be used as bargaining counters.[43]

The presence of Mi'kmaq representatives at the Portsmouth-Casco meetings in August 1713, and Dudley's announcement of the release of the prisoners – some twenty-one 'men of your Tribes' – put matters on a different trajectory.[44] Also by this time, Francis Nicholson had succeeded in wresting the governorship of Nova Scotia from Samuel Vetch after a period of deteriorating relations between the two. For the next year, until the roles were reversed following the death of Queen Anne and the Hanoverian succession, Nicholson was a regular attender at conferences held between Dudley and the Wabanaki. His presence reflected the location of the Penobscot Wabanaki within the claimed boundaries of Nova Scotia, and also the more general recognition of Dudley that – as the Massachusetts governor commented to the colony's general court in February 1714 – the government of Nova Scotia 'must be equally concerned [as Massachusetts] in the Trade with the Indians.'[45] No doubt Thomas Caulfeild, the British officer who commanded at Annapolis Royal during the frequent absences of both Nicholson and Vetch, would have agreed with Dudley's principle. In practice, Caulfeild was not optimistic: 'The chiefest trade with the Indians,' he reported to Nicholson, 'is upon the Coast and most partly followed by those from Boston who affording their Commoditys att much Cheaper rates than our Merchants here Cann ... and unless there be a method found to put a stop to that way of management wee never shall have any Correspondence with them [natives], who seldom or never Come here but when Necessity or Want of provisions drives them.'[46]

The ensuing nine years saw a series of wary and largely unproductive initiatives on both sides. At Annapolis Royal, Caulfeild received instructions from Nicholson in the summer of 1714 to draw the attention of neighbouring native leaders to the recent British-Wabanaki conferences inaugurated through the treaty of Portsmouth as examples of imperial benevolence.[47] Consistently enough with the British text of that treaty, though not with the native side of the diplomacies that had surrounded it, Caulfeild seized on the news of the accession of King George I to send commissioners to both Aboriginal and Acadian inhabitants of the territory claimed as Nova Scotia to demand an oath of allegiance. From a British viewpoint, little success was achieved. The visitors to the Penobscot, for example, were informed politely but firmly that, while trade would be acceptable, 'je ne proclame point de roy Etranger dans mon pays.'[48] A few weeks later came a complementary Mi'kmaq statement, in the context of a brief though intense period of ship seizures off Cape Sable that were apparently prompted by rumours of renewed war between France and Great Britain over the claims of James Stuart as a rival to George I.[49] On at least one occasion, the Mi'kmaq captors had asserted their right to apprehend a vessel and its crew pending the payment of £30 for its release by declaring – as quoted by aggrieved Boston merchants – that 'the Lands are theirs and they can make Warr and peace when they please.'[50]

A further result of the seizures was for Caulfeild to appoint Peter Capon, commissary at Annapolis Royal, to sail around the coast to Louisbourg, visiting ports en route to enquire into the causes of the outbreaks. On three occasions during his return voyage, Capon became the intermediary for overtures made by Mi'kmaq groups to Annapolis Royal. At Port Maltais (Port Medway), he reported, 'I went ashoar to theire Wigwamms, and told them the dammage the Indians had done to the English, which they seemed sorry for, and desired me to meet them in the Spring on the Coast, being sent by theire Chiefe to tell me, that all theire Chiefs and Indians would meet me, and desired Articles then to be drawn relating to trade and other affairs at that Conference, and the Articles then agreed upon, they would signe and faithfully perform, and pressed me hard to promise to meet them, I answered them if I had the Governors orders soe to doe, I should willingly obey them.'[51] While there is no evidence that further meetings arose out of the invitations extended to Capon, his discussions of 1715 illustrated both the Mi'kmaq receptiveness to a diplomatic approach and the concurrent native concerns regarding the activities of irregular and unscrupulous New England traders on the coast. 'The Indians are very Cross,' a letter from Annapolis Royal had noted earlier in 1715: 'They say the English Cheats them.'[52] Increasingly, the stability of the market for furs at Louisbourg, and the regular gift-giving of French officials, became a potent attraction. As a member of the Nova Scotia council, William Shirreff, informed the Board of Trade, the avarice of Boston traders in the region 'hath Caused the Indeans ... [to] Complain and Retire from Thence with their furrs and other Marchandize to Cape Breton, where all manner of Necessarys are furnished them att reasonable Rates (if not by the Marchants) out of the King's Magazine keept There for supplying both Officers and Soldiers, and for the Encouragement of the Savages and others to Trade to that Place.'[53]

Shirreff's suggestion was to establish a similar magazine at Annapolis Royal, and it was endorsed by Caulfeild in a lengthy report to the Board of Trade in November 1715, advocating an effort to win over the Aboriginal inhabitants by favourable terms of trade and 'by kindly using of them, on which foundation their friendshipp is wholy founded.'[54] This, along with Shirreff's assertion earlier in 1715 of the successful results for the French of intermarriage between colonists and Aboriginal inhabitants, proved intriguing to the British Board of Trade as it grappled with North American questions.[55] Its instructions of 1719 to Richard Philipps as the new governor of Nova Scotia contained a strong endorsement of a gradual and diplomatic approach. Philipps was instructed to 'cultivate and maintain a strict friendship and good Correspondence with the Indian Nations inhabiting within the precincts of Your Government, that they may be reduc'd by Degrees not only to be good Neighbours to His Majesty's Subjects, but likewise themselves become good Subjects to His Majesty.' The means specified were through the distribution of presents, and through financial incentives for intermarriage. Any British man or woman who married a native spouse would receive £10 in cash and a land grant of fifty acres.[56] A more general statement followed from the Board of Trade some two years later, in a lengthy report on the trade and government of all the British colonies in North America. It identified three general areas that were essential to British interests in America: to curb French expansion, to improve colonial governance, and to cultivate 'a good understanding with the Native Indians.' On British–Aboriginal relations, the Board skirted the question of subjection by concentrating on ways of establishing and solidifying relationships with Aboriginal peoples on what it supposed to be the French model. The Nova Scotia instruction regarding intermarriage 'should be extended to all the other British Colonies.' Presents should be regularly distributed and put on a secure budgetary footing. British missionaries should be dispatched among 'those poor Infidels.' Trade should be developed as an instrument of state policy. Finally, the report argued, 'the Several Governors of Your Majesty's Plantations should endeavor to make Treaties and Alliances of Friendship with as many Indian Nations as they can,' and the unity of British colonies and native allies should be promoted at all times.[57]

As the British imperial approach to native diplomacy evolved, however, Mi'kmaq and Wulstukwiuk leaders had more immediate concerns. One of them was the failure of the Annapolis Royal regime to follow due diplomatic protocols. A new lieutenant governor, John Doucett, reported in early 1718 that 'some of the Cheifs of the Indian's have been with me to tell me, that if wee Expected them to continue our Freind's, they Expected Presents Yearly from His Majesty, as they allway's receiv'd when this country was in the hand's of the French King.' Doucett's recommendation was that gifts be given, and he repeated it in a more urgent context four months later. Blaming the incitement of the missionaries, he observed that 'Some of the Indian's ... pretend that the Country belongs only to them, and that neither the English or French have any thing to doe here, and have Insulted and used the Like Argument's to some of our Traders on the Coast, but yett are very Civill when they are in reach of our Country.'[58] Richard Philipps, as governor, arrived convinced of the need for gifts to be distributed but with slender resources for doing so. 'I heare nothing of the presents,' Philipps complained from Boston, while on his way to Annapolis in 1720, 'that were ordered for the Indians, and would be very apropos at my arrival among them.'[59] During the following spring and summer, Philipps finally met formally with both Mi'kmaq and Wulstukwiuk chiefs. 'The Chiefe of this [Annapolis] River Indians ...,' he reported in May, 'has been with me with half a Score others, and desired me to resolve him if the French were to leave the country whether the Two Crownes, were in Allyance, whether I intended to debarr them of their Religion, or disturb them in their Traffick, to all which Querys, I answered to sattisfaction, and sent them away in good Humour, promising they would be very peaceable while the Union lasted between the two Crownes.' Philipps admitted that he was delaying meeting with the Wulstukwiuk because of his lack of presents. Eventually, he issued an invitation to a conference in late July, at which he apologized for having no better gifts to offer than those provided from funds voted the previous day by the council at Annapolis Royal. For all that, the meeting was friendly, with the Wulstukwiuk representatives addressing Philipps respectfully though not submissively as 'Notre Perre,' while complaining that British governors and merchants had reneged on promises of trade.[60]

Then came the raids of August 1720, at Canso and at Minas, and tensions on the coastline that increased with the concurrent deterioration of Wabanaki–British relations further to the southwest.[61] Philipps's perplexity at the obvious inability of his Annapolis Royal garrison to deter such events was deepened rather than relieved when in November he received messages from Wulstukwiuk groups in the Wulstukw valley and on Passamaquoddy Bay, disavowing the Mi'kmaq actions at Canso and Minas. 'Nous sommes vos amis,' read the Wulstukw letter, 'et ... nous esperons pareilment de vous.' Philipps's mystification showed in his assurance to the British Board of Ordnance of his good relations with most native inhabitants of the region and immediate confession that even those most friendly to him would commit themselves only so long as peace was maintained between Britain and France.[62] Although poorly understood by Philipps, there were two related processes at work. First, the effective confinement of the British regime to Annapolis Royal was clearly recognized by those native leaders who wished for whatever reason to enter into diplomatic contacts. Diplomacy meant that respect, formality, and protocol must be maintained, but it did not demand that native representatives be drawn into the fiction that 'Nova Scotia' was British territory. The more absurd of British pretensions could thus be politely ignored. Where outright denials of British authority were made, they came from a somewhat different source.

For an extended period, going far back into the previous century, New England fishing and trading vessels had enjoyed an informal Mi'kmaq tolerance, except at times when – because of war, trade irregularities, or other sources of tension – it was withheld and ship seizures resulted. The British claim to 'Nova Scotia,' however, had combined with Massachusetts trade deregulation to bring more New England vessels to the coasts than ever before. Mi'kmaq chiefs had expressed their disquiet to the French governor of Île Royale – the French designation now used for Cape Breton Island, and also including for administrative purposes Île Saint-Jean (later known as Prince Edward Island) – both in 1715 and in 1720, and the conspicuous New England fishing presence at Canso and equally noticeable trading activities at Minas were obvious examples of what was taking place.[63] One Mi'kmaq option was to demand a tribute; another was to attempt by force to loosen the New England grip. Such tensions, combined with those affecting the British-Wabanaki relationship, were fully capable of undermining whatever rudimentary diplomatic relationship might be emerging, and even the report in a Boston newspaper in late 1722 of a treaty signed at Annapolis with local Mi'kmaq residents ended with the telling observation that 'all the English inhabitants are fortifying their Houses, resolving never to trust such perfidious, blood-thirsty Enemies.'[64] Armed conflict followed and diplomacy, for the time being at least, had failed.

Throughout the earliest years of the Annapolis Royal regime, however, there was a further relationship that was essentially diplomatic in nature, though not formally so. Superior Acadian numbers, and the ability of Acadians to withhold necessary supplies or labour from the fort, had been sources of frustration for the British garrison from the time of the conquest. The treaty of Utrecht removed some elements of uncertainty by determining that, however the boundaries of Nova Scotia might be defined or controverted, the British province would include most of the existing Acadian settlements. Whether Acadians would still be occupying those areas, however, remained to be clarified. Early British talk of deporting the Acadians had subsided in the absence of a settler population to replace them. Samuel Vetch, in January 1711, had been eager for imperial permission to dispatch the Acadians – except for those who might become Protestants – to Martinique and Plaisance. By November, with the notion of expulsion unencouraged from London and contradicted by the efforts of the commanders of the Canada expedition to induce Acadians to stay and swear allegiance to the British crown, Vetch's pleas for Protestant settlers and dire warnings on the presence of 'no Inhabitants in the Country save Roman Catholicks and savages yett more biggott than they' were offered – however reluctantly – in a different context.[65] Vetch claimed to have succeeded in persuading some Acadians to take an oath of allegiance, although the accounts of others invariably portrayed his relationship with them as sour and troubled. An officer of the garrison, George Vane, reported in May 1712 that Vetch's absence in Boston had improved matters noticeably and that 'the [Acadian] people dread him to that degree that now he talkes of comming back ... theres a perfect cloud in Every face, and Ime informed severall of the Inhabitants, talke of abandoning ther habitations; if he be not changed before next winter.'[66]

The prospect of Acadians' quitting their settlements was an issue that went far beyond the personal failings of Vetch. Following from the terms of the treaty of Utrecht, two French officers arrived from Cape Breton in August 1714 to supervise the arrangements for those Acadians who wished to remove to the new colony of Île Royale, consisting of both Île Royale itself and Île Saint-Jean. A series of meetings followed, at which Acadians were invited to declare their intentions in the presence of the two envoys and of Nicholson and Caulfeild. The sessions were eventful, and at Annapolis Royal saw demands from Acadians for compensation for their hardships under the earlier British regime. Here and in the other major settlements, most of the assembled Acadians opted to move to Cape Breton. Any thought that this would be straightforwardly accomplished was soon disproved, however, when Nicholson made difficulties both regarding the treaty provision for the Acadians to take with them their movable effects and the later royal order to permit them to sell their lands. Both of these, Nicholson ruled with the support of the Nova Scotia council, must be referred to London.[67] Later allegations had Nicholson not only putting obstacles in the way of Acadian removal, but also harassing any who seemed determined to leave by cutting them off from trade with the Annapolis Royal garrison. The net result, according to two officers of the garrison, was to incline Acadian inhabitants further towards leaving. Nicholson himself cited reports during the summer of 1715 that 'the ffrench here [at Annapolis Royal] and at Minas have built ... forty or fifty sloops in order to carry them to Cape Breton. Severall of them Slips away dayly.'[68] Yet there was also evidence of Acadian reluctance to depart and, by the fall of 1715, of some who had returned from Cape Breton disillusioned by poor lands and shortage of supplies. In all, during the twenty-one years following the treaty of Utrecht, only some sixty-seven Acadian families moved there to stay.[69] Even a few who had moved to Île Saint-Jean as early as in the fall of 1710 were returning by that time, refused land grants by a French absentee proprietor.[70] That the large majority of Acadians elected to remain in their existing communities prevented an immediate economic crisis for the British regime to contend with, but also represented a source of renewed frustration for British officials. Philipps and his officers complained in 1720 that 'the ffrench Inhabitants unanimously refuse to sweare Allegiance to the Crowne of Great Brittain ... That notwithstanding this, they do not seeme to entertain much thoughts of quitting their Habitations.'[71] Some months earlier, the lieutenant governor, John Doucett, had rightly noted that French colonial officials had urged Acadians not to take the oath. An exasperated Doucett had speculated that soon the French 'will Claim every thing to within Cannon Shott of this Fort, which has been often the Topick of the Inhabitants discourse.'[72]

The reality was more complex. By the time Doucett wrote, the British regime was well embarked on the lengthy and tortuous process of establishing a negotiated relationship with Acadian inhabitants, even though the uncompromising terminology of the British claims that proceeded from the treaty of Utrecht prevented the discussions from being recognized as the diplomatic exchanges that they essentially were. It was true that Acadians had generally refused to take an oath of allegiance to the British crown. Nevertheless, a number of more circumscribed commitments had been offered. Acadian declarations in early 1715 – the subscribers including the influential Prudent Robichaud of Annapolis Royal – had promised peaceable conduct, and even a temporary form of allegiance to the British crown, until the expected removal to Cape Breton.[73] Later communications to Doucett put the often-repeated argument that swearing the oath would jeopardize both the Catholicism of the jurors and their relationship with Mi'kmaq neighbours, but that a less formal understanding or even an oath not to take up arms for either France or Great Britain would surely suffice.[74] By the spring of 1720, declarations carrying substantial numbers of signatures – 136 from Annapolis River Acadians, and 179 from those of Minas – refused again the oath of allegiance, renewed the question of migration to Île Royale, but also promised to keep the peace in the meantime and hinted at the possibility of a longer-term understanding.[75]

While such declarations must be interpreted in the context of the existence of other Acadian factions that took a more thoroughly pro-British or pro-French position, the repeated promises of limited cooperation with the Annapolis Royal regime revealed an approach to negotiation that was accurately informed by the weakness of the British bargaining position. In the absence of other colonists, as Samuel Vetch reflected in 1715, a general removal of Acadians 'will wholly Strip and Ruine Nova Scotia so it will att once make Cape Brittoun a populous and well stocked Colony which many years, and great Expence Could not have done directly from france.'[76] Variations on this theme ranged from Caulfeild's fear later in 1715 that the loss of Acadian settlement would remove a buffer against the hostility of the Mi'kmaq, 'the worst of Enemys,' to the argument advanced by a group of Annapolis Royal merchants in 1718 that employment of Acadian fishers was indispensable to their operations.[77] More generally, the lack of an institutional framework for Acadian governance that was recognizable to British civil or military officials forced on the new authorities an unwelcome need to improvise. Their only option in the existing circumstances was to work uneasily with Acadian leaders such as Robichaud or the seigneurial landholder Agathe de Saint-Étienne de La Tour, and otherwise to govern, as Thomas G. Barnes has argued, '"by rule of thumb."'[78]

While Philipps and his officers might argue from time to time for a military solution to their dilemma regarding the Acadian presence – additional troops to expel or subdue the Acadians, followed by British settlement – expense and the lack of an obvious source of new immigration were decisive obstacles.[79] The British Board of Trade, however, had another expedient to prescribe, in the form of a double diplomacy originating – unlike that practised vis-à-vis the Wabanaki by governors who found it unnecessary to report their approach to London – in imperial directives. In a submission to the Crown dated 30 May 1718, the Board of Trade reviewed the difficulties facing the Annapolis Royal regime. One of its less likely solutions was to encourage British residents of Newfoundland to move to Nova Scotia. The recalcitrance of Acadians regarding the oath of allegiance, however, would have to be dealt with in the context of the precarious British hold on Nova Scotia: 'It might be adviseable at least, till more British Inhabitants shall be settled there, and the Indians brought over intirely to Your Majesty's Interest, that the French should not be treated in the manner they deserve for so undutiful a behaviour.' At the governor's discretion, efforts might be made to impose economic penalties for refusal to take the oath, such as exclusion from fisheries, but the starker ultimatum of a choice between the oath and departure would have to await the strengthening of the British regime.[80] Soon after Philipps's arrival at Annapolis Royal, he summoned Acadians to send deputies 'de traiter entre moy, ou ceux que je deputerai et les ... Habitans,' and signalled in a report to London his intention 'for the sake of gaining time and keeping all things quiet ... to send home the Deputys, with smooth Words, and promise of enlargement of time, whilst I transmitt their Case home and receive his Majestys farther direction therein.'[81]

The Board of Trade approved. 'As to the French Inhabitants of Nova Scotia,' it informed Philipps, 'who appear so Wavering in their Inclinations, We are apprehensive they will never become good Subjects to His Majesty whilst the French Governors and their Priests retain so great an Influence over them: For which reason we are of Opinion they ought to be removed so soon as the Forces which We have proposed to be sent to you shall arrive in Nova Scotia ..., but as you are not to attempt their removal without His Majesty's possitive Orders for that purpose, you will do well in the mean while to continue the same prudent and cautious conduct towards them.'[82] British actions were not always so cautious. When naval force could be brought effectively to bear, as in the disputed fishing ports of the Canso area from which French inhabitants were 'dislodged' by force in September 1718, the opportunity would be taken. Reviewing this action, the Board of Trade admitted that 'a gentler method might possibly have been more adviseable,' but held that any criticism on this ground was outweighed by the 'very laudable Zeal' that had been shown.[83] Where French or Acadians were concerned, the implication went, the question was one of tactics only. The treaty of Utrecht had established the legitimacy of the British position. What remained was to ensure that principle was carried satisfactorily into practice. Viewed in that deceptive light, the British–Acadian relationship was not a diplomatic one at all.

The unstated imperial context, however, argued otherwise. Even within the areas of established British settlement in North America, imperial authority was a matter for negotiation between colonists and the inherently unsystematic institutions of the early modern state.[84] In an eighteenth-century empire that increasingly sought to bring non-British peoples within its geographical and economic bounds, but lacked the theoretical or institutional infrastructure to do so, the complexities were greater and ambivalence became a recurring characteristic of the resulting relationships. In some cases, quasi-autonomous corporations such as the Hudson's Bay Company and the East India Company could act as intermediaries for the state. Existing non-British institutional frameworks also had an established role, even in English law, in providing a clothing of legitimacy for imperial claims.[85] Yet Nova Scotia presented unusual complications that were resolved by none of the obvious available parallels. In Jamaica in 1655, English settlers in substantial numbers soon erased the Spanish character of the population. English settlement of New York had also followed the conquest of 1664, and the Protestants of the former New Netherland quickly assimilated in an institutional context even while remaining linguistically distinct. Minorca, taken by the British in 1708, had a highly systematized institutional structure that was left virtually intact despite the misgivings of the first British governor.[86] Indigenous structures for the ordering of native and Acadian affairs already existed in Nova Scotia, but in forms largely unrecognizable to the incoming British. Meanwhile, the independence and pragmatism of Acadian leaders combined with the economic dependence of the colony upon their continuing presence to ensure that the need for a negotiated relationship could not be ignored even by the most reluctant of imperial officials. Similarly, the military potency of the Mi'kmaq and Wulstukwiuk, and the articulacy with which excessive colonial demands were rebuffed by native diplomats, demanded that negotiation be a continuing process even though it had not proved successful by 1722.

Nova Scotia after the conquest of 1710 was characterized by tensions that, in the broadest imperial sense, were normal results of the attempt to incorporate and accommodate non-British peoples. Nova Scotia also presented, in the forms these tensions assumed, complexities that at the time were unique. Far from ending the diplomatic history of the conquest of Port Royal, the treaty of Utrecht had been only the launching-point for the diplomatic activity that involved those whose lack of representation at Utrecht was an inaccurate reflection of their power to influence events in the world of reality that underlay the notional extensions of empire. Not that the French-British agreements at Utrecht were unimportant. They too exerted an influence after 1713, for they created the status quo of putative control of Nova Scotia that British officials were obliged henceforth to defend as best they could, as well as the status quo of continuing strength in the Gulf of St Lawrence and in the North Atlantic fisheries that was more solidly asserted by France. The status quo defended by native diplomats, however, was one in which any imperial presence was peripheral, while that of Acadians was framed by the majority rejection of removal to Île Royale and the continuing existence of communities that now faced both imperial and native pressures.

If the existence of these competing understandings endangered the ability to resolve future disputes without resort to violence, matters were further confounded by the uneasy coexistence of diverse and inherently unstable diplomacies. The ambiguities of the treaty of Utrecht on the boundaries of the British and French claims to Acadia / Nova Scotia had remained unresolved after futile attempts at negotiation in 1714 and 1719–20.[87] Mi'kmaq-British negotiation had ended for the time being in 1722, as had Wabanaki-British contacts further southwest, and the prospect for resumption after hostilities ended was in the context of the double diplomacy that had produced agreement on certain issues at Portsmouth in 1713 but also carried significant risks of contradictory understandings. Double diplomacy in a somewhat different form had emerged as the favoured British approach towards the Acadians. While the notion that the British-Acadian relationship was a diplomatic one would have been denied by British officials, it had been carried on as such. That the aim was ultimately to replace negotiation with coercion was not disclosed for the time being. The future of a long-term alternative to violent conflict rested, therefore, on diplomacies of which none was yet conclusively discredited but each in its own way was compromised. What would result from their interaction was ominously unclear by the early 1720s. Richard Philipps, however, had clearly grasped the essence of what little was obvious as he remarked to the Board of Trade in September 1720, '[I] tell you plainely that I find this Countrey in no likelyhood of being setled under the King's Obedience upon the footing it is.'[88]

PART THREE

Aboriginal Engagement

8 Amerindian Power in the Early Modern Northeast: A Reappraisal

WITH EMERSON W. BAKER

On 20 April 1700 the governor of New England and New York, the Earl of Bellomont, informed the English Board of Trade that, 'if ... there should be a generall defection of the Indians, the English in a moneth's time would be forced on all the Continent of America to take refuge in their Towns, where I am most certain they could not subsist two moneths, for the Indians would not leave 'em any sort of cattle or corne.' While this warning was based on concurrent apprehensions of a Houdenasaunee-Wabanaki alliance – a feared union that would never in fact occur – it was a striking estimation of the dangers posed to the English imperial presence by aboriginal coercive power. For Bellomont, the simple result would be that the native forces 'would in a short time drive us quite out of this Continent.'[1] Some thirteen years later, the intendant of New France, Michel Bégon, echoed Bellomont by express-

Like chapter 5, this essay is a product of my collaboration with Emerson W. Baker. Unlike the earlier piece, however, this one was written some time after the publication of the Phips biography. Taking its inspiration partly from the chapter on Phips's frontier activities vis-à-vis the Wabanaki, the essay reflected the belief – common to Baker and myself – that the significance of colonization in New England during the late seventeenth and early eighteenth centuries had been exaggerated by historians who concentrated their efforts narrowly on the more heavily settled enclaves. Aboriginal control of most territory outside of the colonial pales conditioned both military and diplomatic exchanges, with the Wabanaki providing an especially clear example. The essay was originally presented as a paper at the seventh Annual Conference of the Omohundro Institute of Early American History and Culture, held at the University of Glasgow in July 2001, with a valuable commentary by Huw V. Bowen. It was published in the *William and Mary Quarterly*, 3rd series, 61 (2004), 77–106, and subsequently received the 2004 Harryman Dorsey Award of the Society for Colonial Wars in the District of Columbia.

ing his own fears of Wabanaki military force. Bégon envisaged circumstances in which the Wabanaki might be persuaded by the British 'piller et détruire les habitations de la costé du sud du fleuve de St. Laurent et même de tout le canada.' This, he continued, 'leur soit facile, ces sauvages connoissant parfaitement toutes les habitations de la nouvelle France.'[2]

Both of these statements were made at times of critical change. Bellomont's belonged to the era leading up to the Houdenasaunee-French reconciliation known as the 'Grand Settlement of 1701,' while Bégon was reacting to the concessions made by France in the Treaty of Utrecht earlier in 1713. Each statement betrayed elements of fear and consternation. Yet neither was made as a rhetorical exaggeration. While both Bellomont and Bégon were recent appointees to their positions when their statements were made, each could expect to carry weight with imperial authorities: Bellomont as an experienced Whig politician, Bégon as a well-schooled marine administrator whose father had also been an intendant.[3] Neither had any need to impress by making extravagant statements, and each had a strategy to recommend. Bellomont had come to North America in 1698 unconvinced of the seriousness of the Wabanaki threat that had preoccupied his Massachusetts predecessors Sir William Phips and William Stoughton, but now urged that the shoring up of English relations with both Houdenasaunee and Wabanaki demanded a high priority. Bégon, in the wake of the French surrenders at Utrecht, counselled a narrow interpretation of the French cession of Acadia/Nova Scotia, to exclude most of the Wabanaki territory. Thus, both statements were rational assessments of the situation. Bellomont further substantiated his concerns with a brief analysis of the tactical effectiveness of native warfare. Using the terminology familiar to historians through the work of Patrick M. Malone and others, he described the native manner of 'sculking in the woods behind bushes, and flat on their bellies.'[4] The governor confessed that 'I us'd to ridicule the people here for suffering 3 or 400 Indians to cut off five times their number, of them: but I was soon convinced that it was not altogether the want of Courage and Conduct in the English that gave the advantage to the Indians this Last warr, but chiefly the Indians manner of ... using the advantage of the woods.'[5]

Bellomont and Bégon expressed views that could reasonably be held, not only regarding native tactics but more importantly with respect to the broader implications of native military power. They were not alone among contemporary imperial and colonial officials in taking native coercive power seriously in a strategic sense. Historians should do likewise – rather than, as hitherto, concentrating largely on tactical matters.[6] It is undoubtedly true that Wabanaki and other native fighters derived their effectiveness in battle from their tactical use of aimed fire from covert positions – 'the Indians manner of birding (as I may call it) the English,' was how Bellomont defined it[7] – followed by concentrated assault with edged weapons. It was also true that fear of these methods was a weapon in itself, in the panic it could sow among colonists encroaching on aboriginal land. But there was much more to native power in northeastern North America than tactical effectiveness in battle. Native control of large tracts of territory, and the potential for native incursions into the far more limited areas of non-native settlement, had wider implications that were strategic in two senses. First, from an imperial perspective, the unwelcome strategic reality was that native forces were capable of doing irreparable harm to outlying colonial settlements, either English or French, and of striking even inside core areas. Second, aboriginal nations themselves consistently pursued strategic objectives (broadly defined goals approached through conscious and consistent methods), such as protecting borders and promoting favourable trade agreements. Warfare, for the Wabanaki, was not the preferred method to achieve these goals.[8] Yet repeatedly between 1675 and 1725 it became a counterpart to and an underpinning of diplomatic activity with the European powers.

The relationship between the Wabanaki and New England, from King Philip's War to Dummer's War, together with the associated roles of the Houdenasaunee, Wulstukwiuk, and Mi'kmaq, demonstrates that these northeastern nations exercised strategic power, both diplomatic and military.[9] The Wabanaki compelled New Englanders to apprehend a profound and wide-ranging threat. The colonists could foresee not only calamitous circumstances envisaged by Bellomont in 1700, but also attacks causing economic and social hardships to spread from devastated rural towns to areas protected from the initial assault. Non-native observers did not necessarily recognize Wabanaki strategic objectives. As for any group, their military and diplomatic strategies were related to and constructed by their particular cultural concerns and imperatives. However, while tactics continued to be those normally associated by military historians with non-state warfare, the safeguarding of boundaries – stemming originally from expectations based on environmental considerations and resource harvesting – increasingly influenced Wabanaki demands on New England. The wielding of aboriginal power had diplomatic implications also, as hostilities framed treaty negotiations. More generally, and in historical perspective, colonial settlement in northeastern North America had a fragile and provisional quality in this period. Even in the relatively small areas where colonial population was densely established – southern New England, the lower Hudson valley, and the St Lawrence valley between Québec and Montréal – French and English colonists necessarily feared that native forces could reclaim settled land. Until 1725 in New England – much later in some areas, as in Acadia / Nova Scotia – the northeast remained what it had been since the early seventeenth century: an area where colonial inroads into Amerindian territory were severely limited, and where colonial populations could readily become pawns of the imperial–Amerindian relationships that were central and integral to the shaping of the North Atlantic world.

The concentration of historians on the supposedly transient impact of native tactical success on colonial activities in North America has been long-standing. Most works published in the 1950s and 1960s allowed little military sophistication to native forces. Although invariably portrayed as fierce fighters, native warriors in this view had few skills beyond the ability to set an ambush, and were quite innocent of strategic calculation.[10] More serious attention to native warfare, at least in its tactical elements, gradually emerged. Peter Paret's 1964 analysis of the impact of colonial conflict on eighteenth-century European warfare noted that the uses of aimed fire – as opposed to lines of soldiers firing high volumes of shot into the equally massed ranks of the enemy – had been established in North America by 'decades of fighting the elusive Indian.'[11] Adam J. Hirsch coined in 1988 the useful term 'military acculturation' in defining the explosive results of the removal of cultural restraints from both native and New England modes of warfare through the encounter of each with the tactics of the other.[12] In 1997 Colin Calloway further developed this theme by focusing on the societal effects for both natives and non-natives of tactical melding: 'Indians experienced new weapons and tactics of mass destruction; Europeans learned to emulate Indian hit-and-run tactics.'[13] The most comprehensive discussion of native tactics, and the effects on them of firearms technology, remains that of Malone, for whom native tactics were adaptive and innovative. Ultimately, however, Malone concluded that as early as in the era of King Philip's War the New Englanders had an inevitable and decisive strategic advantage deriving from 'their overwhelming numbers, their fortifications, and their vast network of technological and logistical support, extending from New England villages to manufacturing centers abroad.'[14]

This connection of strategic issues with logistical networks created by the transatlantic reach of the early modern European state was reinforced in turn by a British historiography that, by its linkage of state formation with military power, implicitly defined 'non-state' warfare as random and disorganized hostility. In 1955 Michael Roberts launched the influential concept of the 'military revolution, 1560-1660,' arguing that in this period the greater effectiveness of European infantry firepower led to a new manoeuvrability of land forces, and then in turn to the expansion of professional armies and greater coercive power for monarchies. Although scholars would challenge Roberts's periodization, the notions that use of disciplined infantry with concentrated firepower revolutionized European warfare and that state formation influenced this development have proved durable.[15] At a dangerously broad level of generalization, these developments in military technology and tactics could be taken to establish the essential invincibility of European arms when deployed against non-European peoples. Geoffrey Parker argued that by as early as 1650 the West had achieved 'military mastery' in several major non-European territories, including northeastern North America – he admitted that in tactical terms, even in the later seventeenth century, 'the Indians of New England were ... learning fast,' but demographic decline sealed their fate.[16] Nevertheless, this was not the only possible inference. Jeremy Black pointed out that Amerindians, including those on the eastern seaboard, 'were able to fight "European" Americans to a standstill almost to the end of the eighteenth century.'[17] Ultimately, the distinction between state and non-state warfare remains useful, but only if shorn of the notions that non-state warfare was 'primitive,' and thus irrational, and that it was inherently less effective than state warfare.[18]

This recasting of the notion of non-state warfare has been a key element of the work of those few scholars who have addressed seriously and in detail the strategic dimensions of native warfare in northeastern North America. In 1983 Daniel K. Richter broached the possibility 'that the non-state societies of aboriginal North America may have waged war for different – but no less rational and no more savage – purposes than did the nation-states of Europe.'[19] Emphasizing the traditional role of the mourning war in Houdenasaunee society, in which deaths within the community would be expiated through a war to gain captives for adoption or ritual execution, Richter traced the entry during the seventeenth century of other motivations – economic conflict based on the fur trade and redress of the demographic crises brought about by European disease through taking captives in much greater numbers than before. Eventually, after these pressures had created a destructive spiral, the Houdenasaunee succeeded in restoring a more limited and traditional level of warfare, to which their neutrality in French-English conflicts after 1701 was crucial. A 'growing independence' was thus re-established.[20] In the larger study published by Richter in 1992, the importance of 'the Six Nations' commitment to a strategy of balance, peace, and neutrality' was reaffirmed, although Richter added a rider attributing strict limits to their residual military power: the first two decades of the eighteenth century had revealed a northeastern North America in which 'Europeans, rather than native Americans, now substantially controlled the destinies of all the peoples.'[21] Be that as it may, Richter's insight regarding the rationality of non-state warfare was an essential one. It can be applied equally to the Wabanaki, even though – as Evan Haefali and Kevin Sweeney have observed – the taking of captives was a lesser motivation for the Wabanaki than for the Houdenasaunee.[22]

The effectiveness of non-state warfare has been appraised by a number of recent authors. Commenting on native-English clashes at Deerfield, Richard I. Melvoin observed: 'The Indian threat was huge; the problems were frightening; the future of the continent was hardly preordained.'[23] Ian K. Steele, while giving limited attention to the late-seventeenth and early-eighteenth-century eras, argued that Pontiac's War demonstrated the effectiveness of 'multitribal war.'[24] Armstrong Starkey's *European and Native American Warfare, 1675–1815* argued that European military methods and technologies 'by 1675 had provoked a military revolution of a sort among Native Americans, a revolution that for 140 years gave them a tactical advantage over their more numerous and wealthier opponents.'[25] Nevertheless, for Starkey, this advantage was offset by the vulnerability of native combatants to economic exhaustion from extended warfare, by political divisions that prevented the building of stable coalitions among aboriginal nations, and by demographic decline. Native warfare, therefore, could significantly slow down imperial expansion but could never bring it to a halt, and in southern New England even this capacity was eliminated by defeat in King Philip's War.[26]

Northeastern North America as a whole, however, offers to the historian a wider arena in which the experiences of southern New England

and the other areas of dense colonial settlement were peripheral rather than central. Northern New England was geographically central and historically crucial. Here historians concur that while economic vulnerability and political division limited Wabanaki effectiveness, the scattered line of English settlement and a rugged, forested landscape gave the Wabanaki strong tactical advantages. These factors, combined with English and Native populations that were of roughly similar size, meant that the Wabanaki effectively won the northern extension of King Philip's War, and would remain a serious military threat for decades afterwards.[27]

The narrative of Wabanaki interactions with English/British officials during the fifty years beginning in 1675 is well known in general outline, and requires only brief recapitulation here.[28] Initially unwilling to become involved in the conflicts that were breaking out in southern New England, some Eastern Wabanaki groups were drawn into hostilities by clumsy colonial attempts to disarm them. In the Wabanaki territory there was no native defeat, total or otherwise. Instead, the English were expelled from all areas northeast of Falmouth, and in May 1677 even the substantial town of York was described by leading inhabitants as being brought to 'a low ebb' by repeated raids.[29] Matters were then settled for the time being by the treaty of 1678, which obliged English colonists to pay a tribute to the Wabanaki in return for the privilege of resettlement.[30]

Cumulative tensions arose during the 1680s from English resettlement of the region, culminating in violent incidents and the resumption of hostilities in 1688. With French support from 1690 onwards, Wabanaki forces again went on the attack. The fall of York in January 1692 marked the destruction of virtually every English settlement northeast of Kittery, and brought Wabanaki territorial control within seventy miles of Boston. English counter-attacks, led by the new royal governor Sir William Phips and the irregular fighter Benjamin Church, brought no territorial reversal but prevented further inroads and allowed the construction of a fort at Pemaquid. There, in August 1693, Phips and Wabanaki leaders concluded a new treaty.[31] Far different in tone and content from the treaty of 1678, the text of this treaty was couched as a submission by the Wabanaki. Later Wabanaki statements indicated, however, that on the native side it was intended as a non-submissive treaty of peace and friendship.[32] Hostilities re-ignited in 1694 despite the treaty, and only in 1699 – three years after the fall of Pemaquid to Wabanaki and French forces – was it renewed.[33] A four-year period of peace ensued, during which the Wabanaki economy had an opportunity to regenerate and some modest English resettlement took place. Regular diplomatic exchanges took place between Massachusetts officials and Wabanaki delegates, held for the most part according to Wabanaki protocols. In 1703 hostilities began once again, fuelled by mutual mistrust and French encouragement. The resulting damage was severe on both sides, as many Wabanaki made their way to mission villages in Canada to escape economic dislocation, while English pretensions to Wabanaki territory were again reduced drastically. This time, little remained northeast of Wells beyond a small and fragile fort at Falmouth.

A new era of Wabanaki–British relations seemed to open in the summer of 1713. The treaty of Portsmouth was again worded in its written form according to the language of submission. Related discussions at Casco Bay a few days later had an entirely different tenor, as Wabanaki spokespersons emphasized the reciprocal nature of the Portsmouth accord, and responded sceptically to British claims to Wabanaki territory based on French concessions at Utrecht: 'The French never said anything to us about it and wee wonder how they would give it away without asking us, God having first placed us there and They having nothing to do to give it away.'[34] Following four more years of regular diplomatic communication, it was land – the unnegotiated expansion of British settlement, and the related construction of forts – that brought relations to a further crisis. A major conference on Arrowsic Island brought an apparent agreement on trade but none on the land questions.[35] British advances and Wabanaki cattle-killing by way of response then set matters on a downward path to the resumption of hostilities in 1722. The so-called 'Dummer's War' was a confused series of episodes in which British settlement advances in the Androscoggin and Kennebec valleys were decisively reversed, while the burning of the Wabanaki village of Norridgewock and the killing of its Jesuit missionary Sébastien Rale represented a damaging setback for the Wabanaki. British efforts to have the Houdenasaunee intervene to tip the balance were fruitless, but talks in Boston in late 1725 between Penobscot Wabanaki negotiators and officials of Massachusetts, New Hampshire, and Nova Scotia produced a treaty that was gradually ratified by Wabanaki groups and their allies over the following three years.[36] Again the written terms read as a submission, but again the surrounding evidence indicates something more complex. As one of the Penobscot negotiators remarked some two years later, in rejecting the notion of Wabanaki subjection to Great Britain, 'I know not what I am made to say in another language, but I know well what I say in my own.'[37]

All these developments obviously figure prominently in the history of Maine. The existing literature, notably the analysis of Kenneth Morrison, has also established the importance of the Wabanaki experience in demonstrating the centrality of aboriginal law and diplomatic practices in shaping native–English and native–French relations.[38] But why should the Wabanaki case have significance for the wider history of northeastern North America? It does so because it attests to crucial weaknesses in the non-native hold on the northeast that have not hitherto been admitted by historians, even though they were evident to contemporaries. For northeastern North America as a whole, at least until 1725 – and in the most northeasterly areas, much later still – it is misleading to conceive of a 'colonial period.' Where colonies existed, they were confined within restricted geographical areas and their permanence was far from assured in the event of any determined aboriginal effort to dislodge them. While assembling substantial populations and bringing about crucial environmental change in some localities, colonies were not a defining phenomenon of the northeast. They were as yet only scant manifestations of the greater and ongoing dialogue between native and imperial worlds.

Wabanaki leaders knew this, and shaped their strategic thinking accordingly. Containment of English settlement became a crucial goal. Throughout the 1675–1725 period Wabanaki speakers took pains to make clear that they had no objection to English settlement in their territory, provided that proper diplomatic protocols were observed and provided that settlers did not stray into areas where they were unwelcome. As the Kennebec *sakamow* Wiwurna informed Governor Samuel Shute in 1717, 'we now return Thanks that the English are come to Settle here, and will Imbrace them in our Bosoms that come to Settle on our Lands ... [but] we desire there may be no further Settlements made. We shan't be able to hold them all in our Bosoms.'[39] When these provisions were violated, Wabanaki leaders made it equally clear from the beginning of the 1675–1725 period that their displeasure was with all New England, not just with local settlers or officials. The Saco *sakamow* Squando was quoted by an escaped English prisoner in early 1677 as declaring to Wabanaki audiences 'that god doth speak to him and doth tell him that god hath left our nacion to them to destroy and the indenys do tak it for a truth.' The prominent Wabanaki diplomat

Mogg, meanwhile, 'saith that he hath found the way to burn boston.'[40] Later that year, the succinct statement of a group of Kennebec *sakamows* to the governor of Massachusetts was that 'we are owners of the country and it is wide and full of enjons [Indians] and we can drive you out.'[41] Repeated Wabanaki assertions – both diplomatic and military – of control over their own territories followed. The council of New Hampshire took note in 1699 of a report from the commander of the fort at Saco, Maine, that 'those Eastern Indians carry themselves verry Surly and insolently and do say that the English shall not repossess and enjoy the lands in the Province of Maine otherwise then by agreement with them.'[42] Wabanaki speakers at the Casco conference fourteen years later, as quoted by the missionary Rale, declared, 'J'ai ma terre que je n'ai donné à personne et que je ne donnerai pas. J'en veux toujours être le maitre. Je connois les limites et quand quelqu'un voudra y habiter, il payera.'[43] By 1721 the implications for southern New England were again being made explicit. A letter to Governor Shute threatened reprisals on behalf of 'Toute la Nation Abnaquise repandu dans le Continent est [*sic* for 'et'] au Canada est de tous les Sauvages Catholiques hurons Iroquois Mikemaks est Autre Alliez des Abnaquis,' if the English failed to withdraw from Wabanaki lands.[44]

Wabanaki statements regarding territory were not only based on the assertion that, as the commander of the fort at St George was informed by Wabanaki besiegers during a truce in July 1724, 'it is not your Land.'[45] They reflected too a simple geographical reality. When Wabanaki delegates had informed Massachusetts and New Hampshire officials and councillors in January 1714 – in the context of an enquiry concerning any remaining English prisoners – that 'our Country is large,' they had expressed a crucial truth. The Wabanaki's vast domains along the northern frontier gave them effective control of most of the land in what the English knew as New England, by comparison with the smaller area that could seriously be considered as populated by colonists. The imbalance became even greater with northeastern North America as a whole taken into consideration. While the English occupied coastal regions they had little control of interior areas, save for the Connecticut and Hudson River valleys. The traveller proceeding northwards from Albany on the Hudson River, or Deerfield on the Connecticut River, would encounter only a sparse colonial presence before entering territory claimed by the French as the colony of Canada. There, settlement proceeded along the St Lawrence River from the Island of Montréal eastwards to Québec and the Île d'Orléans (somewhat further on the south shore) with southward extensions in the valleys of the Richelieu and Chaudière rivers. Moving further east, occasional coastal settlements supervened until Acadia / Nova Scotia was reached, where a small British headquarters had been established at Annapolis Royal in 1710 but with most of the non-native population was gathered in four clusters of Acadian settlement around the Bay of Fundy.[46]

While it would be facile to ignore the large population numbers that were represented by densely populated colonists in southern New England, the lower Hudson valley and its surrounds, and to a lesser degree on the St Lawrence, the configuration was clear. Territories of colonial settlement were greatly exceeded in area by the massive central core of northeastern North America that remained in the early eighteenth century under native control. And this does not even include the areas to the west – compellingly designated by Richard White 'the middle ground'[47] – or to the north, through the boreal forests of the subarctic. Most important to both Native Americans and Europeans was Native control of most of the rivers of the region. These waterways were of immense strategic importance, for they controlled access to the interior. Large in numbers, colonial population was superficial in extent. In this context, the Wabanaki threat in 1721 to bring a wide alliance to bear on New England had necessarily to be taken seriously. Governor Samuel Shute described the Wabanaki letter's terms to the Board of Trade as 'haughty and menacing.' He was confident, he wrote, that serious damage to New England could be avoided, but noted – in an unconscious affirmation of Bellomont's earlier concern – that measures had been taken 'to cover our harvest.'[48] Even more striking was Shute's choice of terminology in early 1722 when he referred, in a letter to Governor Vaudreuil of New France, to 'the English Pale or Territory.'[49]

The notion of British settlement within a pale, analogous to that of Ireland and perhaps also to later British enclaves in India, owed much to recurrent New England fears of a native 'combination' or 'conspiracy.' These apprehensions reached a peak at the turn of the eighteenth century, when Bellomont became certain of the reality of an aggressive Wabanaki-Houdenasaunee alliance. After returning to New York in the late summer of 1700 from a conference with the Houdenasaunee, Bellomont remained convinced of the threat that had existed earlier in the year.[50] While such assertions were frequently bracketed with suspicions – sometimes justified, sometimes not – of French incitement, it was native military force that was primarily feared. Other expressions of the same anxiety were scattered liberally through the late seventeenth and early eighteenth centuries. The former royal agent Edward Randolph wrote to London from Boston in 1689 that 'severall nations' had joined with the Wabanaki against New England.[51] A report reached Boston in July 1694 that 'the Maquas' had united with the Wabanaki – a reference, presumably, to the Mohawks of Kahnawake and La Montagne.[52] Governor Joseph Dudley, in 1703, harboured continuing doubts regarding the Houdenasaunee; eleven years later, the Treaty of Portsmouth notwithstanding, he warned Massachusetts and New Hampshire councillors that 'wee are in some danger of a General Combination of the Indians throughout the Continent against us.'[53] Hearing of Mi'kmaq seizures of New England fishing vessels during the summer of 1715, Dudley stressed to London the strategic dangers that might follow: 'Upon the whole, I am very doubtfull [i.e., apprehensive] these Beginnings will poyson the Indians all along the Coast, as They have done Thrice within these Thirty years past, to the great Disadvantage of his Majesty's Governments in North America.'[54]

Combined with these apprehensions was a healthy respect for the military capacities of both the Houdenasaunee and the Wabanaki. The Wabanaki, commented a correspondent of the Lords of Trade in 1689, were 'an intelligent Enemie.'[55] Some New Englanders were inclined to believe that the Wabanaki had good reasons for hostility. In 1715 the Boston merchant Thomas Bannister cited treachery, land seizure, and diplomacy in bad faith on the British side; another New England correspondent, eight years later, provided a long list of examples of 'barbarous dealing with the Indians,' and argued that southern New England might soon share the fate of 'the country of Maine' in being 'entirely taken.'[56] Governor Samuel Shute did not share in any sympathy for Wabanaki motivations, but in 1720 his professional opinion as a former colonel of dragoon guards was that 'during the Late Warrs they [the Penobscot and Kennebec Wabanaki] have been bloody Enemys to the English.'[57] Some years earlier, the Massachusetts General Court had summarized the matter in even greater agitation: the Wabanaki were 'Enemys and Rebells within our very Bowells.' Not for nothing had the General Court resorted in 1708 to terminology more closely associated with earlier Puritan generations to convey the geographical vulnerability of New England: 'They have the Advantage of Retiring for Shelter to the Obscure Recesses of a vast rude Wilderness, full of Woods, Lakes, rivers, ponds, Swamps Rocks and Mountains, whereto they make an Easy and quick passage by means of their Wherries, or Birch Canoes of great swiftness and light of Carriage.'[58] Four years before, the General

Court had similarly referred to the Wabanakis' operating 'under Covert of a vast hideous wildernesse,' and described the fruitless efforts of Governor Dudley in sending 'greater and lesser parties into the Desart in places almost inaccessible.'[59] Dudley himself, in 1705, put a more positive gloss on the futility of this pursuit, by claiming that a seaborne attack on Acadian settlements on the Bay of Fundy had prompted both French and Wabanaki to retreat further and further inland; but his chosen metaphor for overland expeditions was 'my marching partyes in the desert.'[60]

French colonial officials agreed wholeheartedly that the active military role of the Wabanaki had importance beyond the Wabanaki lands themselves. French-British correspondence in North America dealt frequently with the Wabanaki's strategic role, and from 1713 onwards it often focused on rival interpretations of two articles of the Treaty of Utrecht. In article XII France undertook to cede to Great Britain 'la nouvelle Ecosse autrement dite Acadie, en son entier, conformement à ses anciennes limites, comme aussi ... la Ville de Port-Royal, maintenant appellée Annapolis Royale, et généralement ... toutce qui dépend desdites Terres et Isles de ce Païs-là.' Article XV, as well as defining the Houdenasaunee (without their consent) as 'soûmis à la Grande Bretagne,' committed the French to behave peacefully towards these or any other 'Nations de l'Amérique' who were friends of Great Britain – and likewise the British towards 'les Américains Sujets ou Amis de la France.' Freedom of trade with all aboriginal nations was guaranteed, while the enumeration of the nations friendly to either France or Great Britain was left to commissioners, and was never completed.[61]

Following the signing of the treaty, the clash of conflicting interpretations quickly began. What were the 'ancient boundaries' of Acadia/Nova Scotia? British interpretations, naturally enough, favoured a wide definition, so that Acadia/Nova Scotia extended far enough down the eastern seaboard to reach a land boundary with New England and ensure that the entire coastline was British-controlled. French interpretations varied somewhat, but were characterized by a narrow definition of Acadia/Nova Scotia that ruled out any land connection between that colony and New England. For Intendant Bégon – representing a mainstream French position – it was perverse to argue that the British had a claim to 'les terres habitées par les sauvages depuis le premier fort anglois nommé Kaskebey jusqu'a la baye Françoise ou est Beaubassin.' Everything from Casco Bay to the Isthmus of Chignecto, therefore, should be known as the lands of the Wabanaki and their Wulstukwiuk allies, who Bégon did not doubt would be adjudged friends of France under the terms of article XV.[62] For New England governors such as Dudley and Shute, the Wabanaki were subjects and friends of Great Britain, by virtue both of the treaties and of territorial location under the Treaty of Utrecht. For the French, and notably for Philippe de Rigaud de Vaudreuil – governor of New France from 1703 until his death in 1725 – this was a fraudulent claim. Thus the sharp-edged French-British disagreements on the issue, even at a time when France and Great Britain were in an unusual phase of diplomatic harmony.[63] Thus too the broadly strategic context in which Vaudreuil consistently threatened reprisal. Writing to Shute in late 1723, Vaudreuil sketched his position in broad outline:

> I know not what you now think of the War with the Abanakeys which you have drawn upon your selves, in Taking and possessing (against all right) their Land; you may see that it is not so Easy a thing as you thought at first to reduce these Indians; I can likewise Assure you, that you will find more difficulty in the pursuit than Ever for that besides their Resolution of Defending their Countrey as long as any of them remain and not to hearken to any Accommodation until you entirely abandon all their Rivers, and order that things be set on the same foot as they were before the Treaty of Utrecht, all the Indians of other Nations to whom they have reported the Evil Treatment which they have received from you, have taken up the hatchet for their help or succour, and are ready to strike the blow on all sides, to Revenge the Abanakeys their Countreys and Friends, and to Deliver them from the Yoke and Oppression which you would reduce them unto; have they not in Effect reason, what new right have you acquired upon the Abanakeys and their Lands; I know not of any, the Treaty of Utrecht do's Conceed to you L'Accadie, Conformable to its Ancient limits; the Lands of the Abanakeys are they Comprehended? if so wherefore do's the same Treaty add in the 15th Article that there shall be named on each part Commissioners for the Regulation of the limits between the two Crowns and to determine the Indians that are Subjects or Friends to either one or the other?[64]

Vaudreuil returned to these themes frequently as long as 'Dummer's War' continued, informing Lieutenant Governor Dummer in late 1724: 'If you had had Imitated the Governours of Boston your predecessors, Contented yourselves to Trade with the Abenakey Indians and had built no fforts on their Lands, all this Continent would have been in peace.'[65]

New England commissioners who travelled to Canada to meet with Vaudreuil in 1725 heard further dire predictions:

> Monsieur Vaudreuil told us ffrankly and plainly that he could at any time sett the ffive Nations of Iroquois ... on the English and Cause them to Kill and Captivate the Subjects of the King. Monsieur Vaudreuil has ... so far Instigated the Abenaques to make demands on the Government of the Massachusetts of Thirty leagues on the Sea Coast all within the Grant of that Province from the Crown of Great Britain and in which has been settled severall Towns and many hundred Inhabitants and fforts built by Order from home and some of it possessed upwards of ffour score years ... On our asking those Indians how far their demands were Eastward, their Answer was in the presence of Governour Vaudreuil the whole Country of Lacadie or Nova Scotia Excepting only the ffort of Annapolis Royall notwithstanding the said country of Lacadie belongs to the British Crown and these unreasonable Indians were countenanced by the said Governour and a numerous company of French.[66]

When shorn of bombast and empty threats – Vaudreuil lacked either power or the influence to pit the Houdenasaunee against the British, and the position stated regarding Annapolis Royal was indeed that favoured by Mi'kmaq leaders but was not that of France – these statements confirmed that the situation of the Wabanaki was of profound strategic concern to the French. It was also clear to Vaudreuil that the Wabanaki strategic objectives of containing British settlement by diplomacy if possible, while undermining it by military means if necessary, were central to that aboriginal nation's search for allies.

Yet how far can a nation waging non-state warfare accurately be said to have a strategy? The Wabanaki did so, first, by virtue of the nature of their political organization. Not a state in the European sense, with hierarchical and coercive structures, the Wabanaki did form a polity, and one that was demonstrably gaining in coherence during the second half of the seventeenth century. Scholars have traditionally pointed to the riverine orientation of the Wabanaki and cited this as in impediment to their unity. There is no denying that the Wabanaki usually pledged their principal political loyalty at the local level. However, marriage alliances tended to develop wider alliance patterns, and gave many Wabanaki leaders a growing appreciation for a more regional perspective. For example, during King William's War, the ruling families of the Androscoggin, Merrimac, and Kennebunk drainages were all related by marriage. Indeed, in 1690 Benjamin Church ran into members of all three families on his expedition up the Androscoggin River. The Androscoggin leadership also had ties to the Piscataqua, for Hope Hood, the son of the late sachem Robin Hood, was a Native leader on the Salmon Falls River in the 1680s. In King William's War, he fought in both areas, until he was killed while fighting near the Salmon Falls River.[67]

The fluidity of movement among leaders like Hope Hood facilitated alliances and a concern for the larger diplomatic picture. The specific reasons for individual movement is not always clear, but the possible explanations include matrifocal marriage, migration, and adoption. The matrifocal tendency in marriages meant that the sons of many sachems would ascend to positions of leadership among other Wabanaki bands. Documents suggest that even the great Penobscot sachem Madockawando originally came from Wulstukwiuk territory. A contemporary also noted that Madockawando was the adopted son of Assiminisqua, a principal Kennebec sachem. A matrifocal marriage would also explain why Mogg, the son of the chief sachem of the Saco, signed a peace treaty as an Androscoggin, and negotiated another for Madockawando. Alternatively, it may be that Mogg was among those many natives from southern Maine who moved north and east to escape the devastation of disease and warfare. This mass migration effectively led to the reconstitution of the Kennebecs and Penobscots in the latter seventeenth century. Regardless of the specific reasons for his movements, Mogg's various political allegiances and diplomatic powers show that the Wabanaki were evolving an increasing sense of commonality and polity during the seventeenth century.[68]

As in other non-coercive polities, the reaching of consensus was frequently complicated by the existence of opposed groups or factions. Some Wabanaki favoured the English, others the French, and a third group argued for neutrality. This factionalism and its membership was fluid, often changing with the circumstances, and shifts in equilibrium could bring apparently sudden changes and reversals. The outbreak of new Wabanaki-English hostilities less than a year after the treaty of 1693, for example, followed the abrupt loss of prestige by the *sakamows* most closely associated with the treaty – Madockawando and Egeremet – when they became entangled in a questionable land transaction with Governor Sir William Phips. Francophile leaders quickly came to the fore, forging a new consensus in favour of attacks on New England.[69] Nevertheless, certain broad currents of agreement within the Wabanaki polity were consistently evident. The English/British presence in Wabanaki territory was generally welcomed insofar as it promoted the trading of English goods for beaver at favourable rates. Even more than discussions of war and peace, trade matters frequently took pride of place in conferences between Wabanaki and New England leaders. Massachusetts legislation on the management of Wabanaki trade followed closely not only after the treaty of 1693 but also after its renewal in 1699.[70] The *sakamow* Querabenawit expressed a characteristic and repeated concern to New England officials at Portsmouth in July 1714 in the statement 'Wee desire that the Truck may now be settled Effectually and the prices of Goods that wee may not be at a loss again.'[71]

Nevertheless, support among the Wabanaki for the British colonial presence was far from unconditional. Convenient trade at favourable rates, or at least the conviction that a reasonable level of fairness was being observed, was essential. Governor Dudley had good reason for his opinion, expressed when commenting to the Massachusetts General Court on the treaty of 1713, that 'the Principal Article ... [of the treaty] is The Restoring those Indians to a true and certain Friendship and Confederacy with us, By establishing an easy and just Trade with them for all Things necessary for Humane Life.'[72] The Wabanaki frequently asked the English to place trading posts in places that would be convenient for the Natives to trade. A second essential was the maintenance of diplomatic protocols. Again addressing the general court in 1714, Dudley emphasized the urgency of his meeting with Wabanaki delegates: 'They seem to be impatient that they are not visited at Casco Bay or else where by Generall Nicholson [governor of Nova Scotia] and my self.'[73] Third, harmonious relations depended too on the absence of British encroachment on Wabanaki territory without due negotiation. Despite British claims that large areas of Wabanaki land had been purchased during the mid-seventeenth century, this issue was a persistent source of tension. For example, encroachment in the Kennebec and Androscoggin valleys, accompanied by the building of forts in those areas, was the key cause of the renewal of hostilities in 1722.[74]

Accordingly, exclusion of English/British settlers from unauthorized areas was one consistent Wabanaki aim. The more encroachment was taking place at any given time, the less the ability (and the inclination) of Wabanaki anglophiles to argue against an armed solution. Once hostilities had begun, however, Wabanaki aims were never restricted to their own territory. Although war leaders focused their attacks on driving the English out of their tribal lands, sometimes Wabanaki diplomats made explicit the threat to the centre of Massachusetts's power and population to the southwest. This threat could come either in words, such as Mogg's speech in 1676, or in deeds, such as the burning of York and the raids to the south in 1692. New England, of course, was far from static in population. The approximately 52,000 colonists of 1670 had more than tripled fifty years later, with more than half residing in Massachusetts in each case.[75] Hence, Mogg's threats gave way to the patient efforts of Wiwurna and others in 1720 and 1721 to solidify alliances, encompassing not only Eastern and Western Wabanaki groups but ranging from the Mi'kmaq in the east to Algonquins in the west and taking in both the Mohawks of Kahnawake and La Montagne and the Loretteville Hurons. All of these were signatories to a declaration in 1721 that British settlement must be confined according to Wabanaki requirements. 'Au reste ce n'ai pas ne la parole,' the letter asserted, 'de 4 ou de 5 Sauvages que par tes presens tes mensonges et te ruse tu pense faire facilement tomber dans tes Sentiment ces la parole de toute la Nation abnaquise rependu dans ce Continent et en Canada est de tous les autres sauvages chretiens leurs Allies.'[76] Thus, as Kenneth Morrison has pointed out, Wabanaki strategy increasingly involved the use of alliance to counteract the growth of New England. Also a developing aim was the creation of a boundary between the Wabanaki and the British. This approach had been hinted at in the provision of the treaty of 1693 that the English were to be undisturbed in 'former Settlements and Possessions,' a principle that was reaffirmed in a Wabanaki letter of welcome addressed to Bellomont in 1699, and it reached its most explicit form eighteen years later in the proposals of Wiwurna.[77]

At the Arrowsic Conference of 1717, while denying the assertions of Governor Shute regarding the extent of earlier Wabanaki land sales, Wiwurna introduced the offer of a specific boundary: 'We are willing to cut off our Lands as far as the Mills, and the Coasts to *Pemaquid*.' The response from Shute was a vague: 'We desire only what is our own, and that we will have.'[78] In reality, the governor was never going to agree to the proposal, both because of New England claims to land deeds further north and east, and because of the more general implication of a limit on the territory to which Great Britain could claim dominion regardless of specific sales. The exchange well illustrated, however, Wabanaki aims that translated into diplomatic strategies until hostilities became inevitable, and military strategies thereafter: to safeguard essential lands, but to do so through wider approaches to or (when necessary) attacks on New England, in alliance with other aboriginal nations.

Given the tactical limitations of Wabanaki warfare, however – notably the difficulty of sustaining raiding warfare over an extended period – the question arises as to whether the corresponding tactical strengths of mobility and surprise were sufficient to give substance to threats on New England. French logistical support offered a possible answer to problems associated with extended warfare, but it was neither consistent nor invariably acceptable to the Wabanaki. Over the 1675–1725 period, French–Wabanaki military relations experienced frequent and profound variations. On the Wabanaki side, although French supplies and the occasional military adviser were accepted sporadically as early as during King Philip's War, more consistent military collaboration began in 1690. By late 1692 almost all Wabanaki leaders had become disillusioned with what they regarded as French unreliability, and the treaty with the English in 1693 followed. Collaboration with the French resumed in 1694, and lasted for three years that encompassed, among other military successes, the fall of Pemaquid. A further phase of Wabanaki-French military accord began in 1703, but soon lost momentum as Wabanaki forces were unwilling to fight just to further French war aims, so cooperation had dwindled long before the Treaty of Utrecht.[79] French supply of the Wabanaki resumed after that treaty; however, the continuing influence of anglophile *sakamows* such as Bomoseen – as well as the willingness even of francophiles such as Wiwurna to entertain both formal and informal contacts with New England[80] – demonstrated that the Wabanaki were never content simply to serve the turn of French interests. The French, meanwhile, had their own constraints. For only approximately nineteen of the fifty years from 1675 to 1725 France and Great Britain were at war, while nine years were spent in uneasy peace and twenty-two in peace and alliance. In times of peace, and within the frameworks of the Treaty of Westminster (1686) and the Treaty of Utrecht, the scope for French military cooperation with the Wabanaki was limited. Even though Vaudreuil might declare in 1724 to Dummer, 'I can't help taking their [the Wabanaki's] parts in this, to let you know you are in the wrong to fall out with 'em as you have,'[81] all support for the Wabanaki had to be justified under article XV of the Treaty of Utrecht, and even the French interpretation of the treaty's terms could not justify underwriting an offensive Wabanaki campaign against southern New England.

For all that, New England's fear of the Wabanaki, even to the extent articulated by Bellomont in 1700, was not unreasonable up until the era of the treaty of 1725. With or without French collaboration, the

Wabanaki never did attack Boston, or launch any seriously damaging raids anywhere else south of Essex County. The alliances that had been nurtured diplomatically in 1720-1 proved to be of limited assistance, especially since Houdenasaunee diplomacy kept the Mohawks of Kahnasake and La Montagne out of the conflicts of 1722–5.[82] Although Western Wabanaki forces led by Grey Lock enjoyed repeated success in raids on western Massachusetts and the Connecticut valley, Grey Lock's efforts too were restricted by Houdenasaunee diplomacy. Cooperation between Eastern Wabanaki and Mi'kmaq forces was more direct, but conflict in Mi'kmaq and Wulstukwiuk territories remained sporadic.[83] Nevertheless, before 1725, New England lacked a proven capacity to resist effectively a determined campaign by native assailants. Whether any circumstances existed in which a Boston observer's prediction of 1723, that Massachusetts itself stood 'in great danger,'[84] could have been sustained in reality is a matter for counterfactual speculation. Only eight years earlier native inhabitants of the Carolinas had risen up in the bloody and destructive Yamasee War against the English. This recent example, together with the Wabanaki threats of alliance, ensured that the apprehension itself was not extravagant. Even if this level of defeat were avoided, Wabanaki raiding warfare was demonstrably capable of causing serious and unpredictable levels of economic and social dislocation.

Perhaps the best example of the financial and social chaos caused by Wabanaki warfare took place during King William's War. The virtual collapse of all Maine settlements in the face of Wabanaki raids did not just affect frontier residents. A substantial amount of Maine land and many sawmills were owned by Massachusetts merchants, and the war made these investments worthless. Massachusetts had to support the hundreds of impoverished and homeless war refugees who fled the frontier. At the same time, the government expended huge sums in its largely unsuccessful efforts to fight the war. Despite a substantial rise in taxes, the government of Massachusetts was forced to issue paper currency to fend off financial collapse. The massive inflation that resulted only increased the distress of the citizenry. Scholars now recognize that war hysteria was essential to the causation even of the Salem witchcraft outbreak.[85]

This hysteria was well founded, for it drew upon the recent experiences of New Englanders during King Philip's War. To many modern observers the defeat of King Philip and his allies is seen as a historical inevitability, part of a continent-wide conquest of Native Americans by Europeans. Those who lived through the war knew English victory was by no means assured. In the first months of the war the English reeled from a string of defeats. The situation became so gloomy that at one point the General Court considered erecting a huge palisade around core settlements in the greater Boston area, and abandoning frontier settlements to the Native Americans. While the strenuous objections of inhabitants who lived outside this proposed English pale led to the defeat of the idea, Salem Town so feared attack that it did construct a lengthy palisade around its urban core. Though the English would ultimately win this costly war, the Native threat was still very real to residents of Salem and all of Massachusetts in 1692. Some scholars have suggested that King Philip's War was so devastating and long lasting a trauma to the psyche of New Englanders that it changed the very nature of Anglo–Amerindian relations and helped to forge regional and national senses of identity in New England and the United States.[86]

A further illustration of the power of the Wabanaki strategic threat was its influence on New England diplomacy. From 1701 to 1703 New England diplomatic discussions with the Wabanaki were conducted using Wabanaki protocols and adopting Wabanaki values of friendship and alliance to the total exclusion of claims to sovereignty and submission. In June 1701, during the period between the death of Bellomont and the arrival in New England of Dudley as his successor, four New England commissioners met with Moxus and other leading *sakamows* at Casco Bay. The commissioners defined their mission as reaffirming the Wabanaki's 'mutual and publick League of amity with us,' and – among other topics of discussion – guaranteed that in the event of a further breach with France, 'you may be assured, of perfect peace and quiet from us, and unto all those Indians who shall not take any part or assist the French.' In neither of these contexts was there any effort to invoke the terminology of the written text of the treaty of 1693, and the meeting closed with the ceremonial raising of two cairns at the point 'now mutually agreed for ever hereafter to be called the two Brothers point, from the two Pillars.'[87] Among the first remarks of Dudley as governor to *sakamows* – again led by Moxus – whom he met at Sagadahoc in July 1702 was an explicit acceptance of this form of diplomacy: 'I have seen the Two Brothers, the Record of your friendship, and I am content that they Continue there, and I shall Add one stone in the Governours name as I return, if you shew your Respect to the Queen, and her subjects here.'[88]

While the abandonment of language of sovereignty and submission was a testimony to the urgency of the English need for conciliation with the militarily powerful Wabanaki, the language of peace and friendship understandably disappeared after the re-igniting of hostilities in 1703. It was resumed at the time of the treaty of 1713, though in a less public manner. The official British record of the Portsmouth conference had Dudley reprimanding the Wabanaki for their past aggression and the treaty text itself not only blamed them for beginning the war but also contained a submission article.[89] French sources, however, conveyed an entirely different perspective on the discussions leading to the treaty. According to Vaudreuil, as early as in 1710 Dudley had been assiduously offering gifts to Wabanaki groups and promising trade on favourable terms.[90] An account of the 1713 exchanges relayed by the missionary Rale from Norridgewock had Dudley promising British resettlement in Wabanaki territory, 'si tu veux,' and requesting – 'je te prie' – that the settlers should be allowed to hunt and gather wood to fulfil their needs.[91] This double form of diplomacy had evident ambiguities, and it did not survive the advent as governor of the less supple-minded and more militaristic Samuel Shute. While it lasted, it was a perhaps-grudging but nonetheless sincere tribute to Wabanaki coercive power.

The Wabanaki's tactical effectiveness could be devastating, as New Englanders well knew between 1675 and 1725, and as historians have traditionally recognized. The Wabanaki also, however, presented a profound strategic threat to New England, as imperial officials acknowledged both explicitly in their statements and implicitly in their behaviour. The Boston treaty of 1725, as David L. Ghere has shown, did not bring an end to Eastern Wabanaki involvement – reluctant as it now frequently was – in the French-British quarrels of the eighteenth century.[92] Following the stresses and defeats of 'Dummer's War,' however, it did mark the end of any reasonable shred of Mogg's hope that Wabanaki warriors would one day burn Boston. Southern New England, by now, was secure from assault by aboriginal neighbours. Not that this new degree of colonial insulation applied all through northeastern North America. From Halifax as late as 1768, Lord William Campbell reported as governor of Nova Scotia that the Mi'kmaq retained the capacity to 'bring fire and Destruction to the very entrance of this Town.'[93] Further west, as Fred Anderson has recently noted, Pontiac's War had shown graphically that 'the sufferance of the supposedly conquered ... had limits that were all too easy to exceed.'[94] Further west still, as Richard White has shown, strategically based expansion remained open to the Sioux.[95] But while these authors rightly attributed strategic awareness to aboriginal nations, the issues had changed by the mid-eighteenth century. Aboriginal autonomy was still attainable throughout much of North America, but the persistence of non-aboriginal settlement in the east was no longer in doubt.

In September 1721 the Board of Trade completed an extensive review of the state of British colonization in North America. It lamented the failure of article XV of the Treaty of Utrecht to stabilize British–native relationships, putting the blame on French refusal to cooperate in the article's implementation. A pessimistic view followed of the British failure to nurture native alliances as successfully as the French: 'By one view of the Map of North America, your Majesty will see the danger your subjects are in, surrounded by the French who have robbed them of great part of the trade they formerly drove with the Indians, have in great measure cut off their prospect of further improvements that way; and in case of a rupture may greatly incommode if not absolutely destroy them by their Indian allies.'[96] While the Board's analysis was on firm enough ground in identifying British weakness vis-à-vis native forces, it subtly misrepresented the role of France. As Catherine M. Desbarats has pointed out, New France had few troops and relatively few settlers with which to make good on French territorial claims: 'The resulting military weakness – sometimes depicted as imperial benignity – compelled Canada's leaders to enter into alliances on Indian terms.'[97] The same could be said (even though in these cases friendship and non-aggression were at stake, rather than alliance per se) of the raising of the Two Brothers, or the double diplomacy of Joseph Dudley. And two weaknesses, those of the French and the British, did not add up to a strength in the overall European imperial influence in northeastern North America. Because the terminology of European state formation – resting on its three-legged stool of sovereign institutions, defined territory, and coercive force – had been imported to North America along with imperialism, historians have all too often mistaken for the real thing the halting efforts of imperial officials to create a workable facsimile of these characteristics. Historians have also too often failed to recognize the strategic acumen of native polities; not allowing for divergent cultural constructions of strategy, they have fallen into the same logical trap as the early missionaries who concluded that their native hosts had no religion. Contemporaries, especially the imperial officers who had the responsibility of defending vulnerable settlements, knew better. Like Bellomont and Bégon – and Samuel Shute in his recognition in 1722 that the British in northeastern North America inhabited a 'Pale' – they had no choice but to perceive and grapple with dire possibilities.[98] The Wabanaki were among those aboriginal nations who proved, through military and diplomatic strategizing, all too adept at demonstrating how closely the empires' terminological coverings resembled the emperor's new clothes.

9 The Sakamow's Discourtesy and the Governor's Anger: Negotiated Imperialism and the Arrowsic Conference, 1717

On the morning of 9 August 1717, the sixth-rate naval vessel *Squirrel* made its way cautiously up the Kennebec River, in the territory known to the British as northern New England. The frigate carried the governor of Massachusetts and New Hampshire, Samuel Shute, and a retinue including councillors from both colonies, to a meeting with Wabanaki leaders at Georgetown on the island of Arrowsic. Although a sloop carrying others of the governor's party had already arrived safely, the *Squirrel*'s captain, Thomas Smart, had not been anxious to risk his ship by venturing this far up the Kennebec. When Shute and the councillors pressed him to continue, on the ground that the vessel was needed 'to keep the Indians in more Subjection at the Place of Conference,' Smart – who had arrived with his ship on the New England station only in late June – referred them to the experienced pilot Cyprian Southack. Smart's report to the Admiralty implied that Southack too had doubts,

---

Originally written for an edited collection that did not reach publication, this essay explores the significance of a Wabanaki-British conference held in 1717 that provides – largely because of the unusually detailed transcript that was published soon afterwards – unique insights into the texture of the relationship that the conference reflected. Although it was not the first time that I had made use of this evidence, I became especially aware of its significance when testifying in treaty-rights legal cases during the late 1990s. When testifying that British and aboriginal understandings of treaty relationships could differ in key respects, this above all was the document that provided the clearest examples. The conference of 1717 also represented a dramatic exchange, and on many occasions I have invited my students in seminar classes to take the parts of the several participants and read the transcript aloud as a play. I hope the students have learned as much from the experience as I have from hearing their varying interpretations. This essay is hitherto unpublished.

but 'they prevaild with him to carry her higher.'[1] It was a decision that all of them soon regretted. The *Squirrel* reached the harbour at Arrowsic safely, but only to be caught by an unexpected current close to land. As the captain's log recorded laconically, '[the] ship drove a Shoar.'[2]

The consequences for Smart and his vessel proved less damaging than at first seemed likely. The *Squirrel* could not have run aground at a worse time, just as the high tide was beginning to turn. However, feverish efforts succeeded in shoring it upright, while the guns, anchors, and any other heavy or combustible items were removed. Thus lightened, the ship was floated off at the next tide. Smart reported that the damage was 'not mutch,' and it was true that the return voyage to Boston was accomplished safely after the vessel's departure on 13 August. Nevertheless, a twenty-foot section of keel and several deck beams had to be replaced, along with more minor repairs.[3]

The consequences for Samuel Shute were subtly different. Although there is no evidence that the governor and his party were ever in physical danger, it was a disappointing and undignified arrival. For officials such as Shute, it was axiomatic that a warship represented the most effective show of imperial might that could be used to overawe aboriginal opponents in either diplomatic or military contexts. Not only was this explicitly the reason for bringing the *Squirrel* upriver, but already en route on 5 August the vessel's log had recorded the firing of five guns 'to give Notice to the Indians of His Excellency being in Casco Bay.'[4] When the vessel had been refloated on the 10th, and the guns replaced on board, Captain Smart 'saluted the Indian king with 19 Guns.' The salute was repeated on each subsequent day – except for the 11th, a Sunday – during the frigate's short stay at Arrowsic.[5]

Yet the smoke and noise of the *Squirrel*'s cannons could hardly camouflage the reality that the British diplomatic position was as uncertain as the circumstances of the governor's appearance at Arrowsic. Samuel Shute was only the latest of a series of New England governors who had travelled to Wabanaki territory to be interviewed by aboriginal *sakamows* (or chiefs). Like his predecessors Sir William Phips and Joseph Dudley, Shute came armed with the knowledge that his responsibility was to maintain the British claim to Wabanaki lands and Wabanaki subjection to the British crown. Unlike either Phips or Dudley, however, Shute seemed unaware that Wabanaki military power made it inadvisable to make either position unduly explicit. While Phips had initiated in the 1690s the practice of embodying English-Wabanaki treaty agreements in written texts, specifying submission, that stood at variance with verbal understandings, it was Dudley (governor from 1702 to 1715) who refined this tactic into a full-blown system of parallel diplomacies. Shute in 1717 had been in North America less than a year, by contrast with the New England–born Phips and Dudley. He had had a successful military career during the War of the Spanish Succession, reaching the rank of Lieutenant Colonel of Dragoon Guards.[6] Although this background provided Shute with a robust determination to defend British territorial rights, and notably the right to build forts regardless of aboriginal opposition, it had not endowed him with the intellectual plasticity with which his immediate predecessor had approached diplomatic dealings with the Wabanaki. Given that the Wabanaki came to Arrowsic in 1717 with serious complaints about the encroachment of New England settlers and a British-built fort on their lands, the potential for confrontation was greater than at any such conference within recent memory.

It was this tension that made the Arrowsic conference of 1717 not only a dramatic event that was recognizable as such to contemporaries, but also for the historian a revealing illustration of the nature of imperial-aboriginal diplomacy in northeastern North America. Although the conference itself lasted only four days, the issues that it brought to the fore were long-standing. As well as the questions of settler encroachment and the building of forts without Wabanaki permission, they extended to the interpretation of earlier treaties and the terms under which trade would be carried on. Most important for the historian, and owing much to the unusually detailed recording of the exchanges that took place, the Arrowsic conference provides a window into the negotiating process that was essential to the expansion of British imperialism in eighteenth-century northeastern North America. An area such as northern New England could be brought within the British sphere of influence only through the tolerance of aboriginal peoples who wielded both military force and diplomatic skill. It was the role of the Wabanaki negotiators at Arrowsic to attempt, though with limited success, to alert the new governor to this unpalatable state of affairs. Detailed consideration of the conference, and its longer-term context, can provide an effective insight into the nature of the negotiated imperialism it exemplified.

Despite the treaties in which the English/British and the Wabanaki had previously joined – the major ones in 1678, 1693, 1699, and 1713 – the history of their relationship was a troubled one. During the first half of the seventeenth century, English settlement in Wabanaki territory was sparse. Some local disputes arose between settlers and natives, notably over the environmental impact of cattle, but in general settlement remained at a tolerable level and had advantages for the Wabanaki in promoting the fur trade. During the 1650s, however, the active assertion of a claim by the Massachusetts colony to jurisdiction over Maine led to increasing English migration to the northeast. Encroachments, occasional violent incidents, and the more general tensions that brought about King Philip's War in southern New England, led to the outbreak of hostilities in 1675. By the time the intermittent conflicts were brought to an end by the treaty of 1678, the English had been almost completely expelled from Wabanaki lands. The treaty obliged the colonists to pay a tribute to the Wabanaki if they wished permission to resettle.[7] The tribute quickly came to be ignored, however, and the pattern soon repeated itself. Hostilities broke out again in 1688, and by 1692 the result was the same. Even the substantial town of York, some fifty miles northeast of Boston, was sacked by Wabanaki forces in January of that year. The threat was all the more menacing in English eyes because of the close collaboration between Wabanaki and French that had begun in 1690, and the English-Wabanaki treaty of 1693 represented an attempt by Governor Phips to forestall further moves in this direction. It failed to do so. Within a year, new conflicts had arisen. Only in 1699, with the conclusion of a further treaty effectively repeating the terms of 1693, was peace restored.[8]

An interlude followed that had direct influence on the expectations the Wabanaki would take into later dealings with British officials. Although the treaty of 1699 included in its written text the language of British sovereignty and Wabanaki submission, as the treaty of 1693 had also done, this language was altogether absent from the ensuing diplomatic exchanges. Following a brief period of English alarm at reports that the Wabanaki might join together with the Houdenasaunee in an alliance aimed at dislodging the English altogether from North America – a goal, according to the governor of Massachusetts and New York (the Earl of Bellomont), that was well within their reach should they have chosen to attempt it[9] – Massachusetts commissioners met with Wabanaki *sakamows* at Casco Bay in June 1701. Far from asserting either sovereignty over the Wabanaki or ownership of their lands, the commissioners endorsed the notion of 'a mutuall and publick League of amity,' and at the close of the conference this was symbolized by the raising of two large cairns at a place now to be known as 'the two Brothers point, from the two Pillars.'[10] Subsequent conferences, involving Governor Dudley after his taking office in 1702, also adopted Wabanaki protocols, while issues such as trade and settlement were discussed. In

1703, however, the ascendancy of francophile *sakamows* led to Wabanaki participation with the French in hostilities arising out of the War of the Spanish Succession, which had begun in the previous year. Although many Wabanaki took no part in the intermittent hostilities that followed, and some withdrew to mission villages near the French settlements in Canada, once again little remained of English settlement in Wabanaki territory.

When formal negotiations resumed between British and Wabanaki at Portsmouth, New Hampshire, in the summer of 1713, the result was another treaty of which the written text purported to give effect to Wabanaki acceptance of blame for the breach of their earlier treaties and to their renewed submission to the crown of Great Britain.[11] Surrounding evidence, however, gave a different impression. An account of the discussions written by the French Jesuit missionary Sébastien Rale, who was living among the Wabanaki at the time, had Governor Dudley undertaking that British resettlement on Wabanaki land would be contingent on Wabanaki approval – 'si tu veux' – and requesting – 'je te prie' – that any colonists who needed to hunt or cut wood should be allowed to do so.[12] Both in this account and in the British accounts of the negotiations, agreement on favourable rates of trade for the Wabanaki was a central issue. Several months later, Dudley urged the Massachusetts General Court to speed the passage of necessary measures to foster the trade, the alternative being 'a Rupture and the Indians deserting us and Going entirely over to the French.' The governor underlined the urgency of the matter by noting that the Wabanaki 'seem to be impatient that they are not visited at Casco Bay or else where' by himself and his Nova Scotia counterpart, Francis Nicholson.[13] That the Wabanaki were able to exert pressure of this kind on two colonial governors eloquently belied the notion that they were a subservient population.

Pressure of a different kind, however, was soon felt by the Wabanaki themselves. In 1714 a group of politically and socially well-connected New England merchants, known henceforth as the Pejepscot Proprietors, bought out an extensive claim to lands on the lower Kennebec and Androscoggin Rivers. The genealogy of the claim was long and tortuous, deriving originally from a grant of the Council for New England in 1632 to Thomas Purchas and George Way, and later enlarged through deeds purportedly obtained from Wabanaki vendors.[14] With available land in increasingly short supply in southern New England, the proprietors saw an opportunity for profit through settlement and development of their tract. Once the General Court had given its approval in 1715, they began to lay out the town of Brunswick, on the lower Androscoggin, built and garrisoned a stone fort nearby, and commenced surveying in the Kennebec valley.[15] For the proprietors, whose political connections assured them the ear of Governor Shute from the time of his arrival in October 1716, these activities represented nothing more than the exercise of long-standing entitlements within British territory. For the Wabanaki, notably those of the Kennebec and Androscoggin valleys, they could only be seen as a violation of the treaty relationship and ultimately as a provocation.

Despite the travails of the *Squirrel* earlier in the day, the Arrowsic conference opened ceremonially on the afternoon of 9 August. The Wabanaki delegates had established themselves on nearby Puddlestone's Island, and arrived for the first session bearing a Union flag sent to them by Shute, 'in token of their Subjection to His Majesty King GEORGE.' Shute himself was 'seated under a large Tent (Erected for the occasion),' and was flanked by councillors of Massachusetts and New Hampshire.[16] The Wabanaki representatives numbered eight *sakamows*, five of them from the Kennebec and one each from the Androscoggin, Penobscot, and Saco regions. Although not all of the eight can be conclusively identified, it is clear that collectively they had much diplomatic experience at their disposal. Moxus and Bomoseen, of the Kennebec, were long-standing anglophiles and had conferred with previous governors. So had Atecouando of the Saco. Querebenawit of the Penobscot was a signatory (as was Bomoseen) of the Portsmouth treaty of 1713, while Sabbadis of the Androscoggin had participated (as had Atecouando, Bomoseen, and Querebenawit) in a further major conference in Portsmouth in July 1714. Wiwurna, of the Kennebec, may have been younger than those whose names were more familiar to the New Englanders, and was just beginning on what would be a long period of diplomatic and military involvement. Wiwurna emerged in later years as a leading francophile, although the sparse evidence suggests that he had not yet adopted this position in August 1717.[17]

There were two other participants of major importance to the Arrowsic conference: the interpreters John Gyles and Samuel Jordan. Gyles was a frequent interpreter at conferences and during parleys under flag of truce at times of conflict. He was also the commander of the newly built Fort George at Brunswick. Born at Pemaquid, a short distance northeast of the mouth of the Kennebec, Gyles had been captured by Wulstukwiuk raiders in 1689, when aged nine years. He spent the next six years among the Wulstukwiuk – whose language was closely related to Eastern Wabanaki – before becoming a servant to a nearby French *seigneur* and then being liberated by an English expedition on the Wulstukw (St John) River in 1696.[18] Jordan, the son of a fur trader on the Maine coast, was also a former captive and had traded with the Wabanaki for some years.[19] The role of the interpreters was, of course, crucial to the unfolding of the conference. Wiwurna apparently had some facility in English, but this was uncommon. Most eastern Wabanaki leaders would have understood some French, but communicated primarily in Eastern Wabanaki. With the exception of the interpreters, it is unlikely that any of the British present would have had any command of that or any other Algonkian language.[20]

There is no evidence that the interpreters were anything but honest and faithful translators of what they heard. Certainly, the Wabanaki indicated confidence in them. Gyles, despite his military position at Fort George, was repeatedly accepted by them as an interpreter, while towards the close of the Arrowsic conference Querebenawit made the request 'that Interpreter *Jordan* may be near us, to Represent to your Excellency any thing that may happen.'[21] This is not to say that fraudulent translation was unknown in British-Wabanaki conferences. One Boston merchant, Thomas Bannister, stated in 1715 that 'I have been present when an Article of the Peace has run in one Sence in the English, and quite contrarie in the Indians, by the Governours express order.'[22] However, this was likely more the exception than the rule, and perhaps characterized the double diplomacy of Dudley more than the abrupt but straightforward style of Shute. A more complex question concerned the extent to which even the most honest interpreter could successfully make abstract concepts comprehensible across the deep cultural gulf that existed between British and Wabanaki. An especially fertile source of misunderstanding in earlier conferences had been the use of familial analogies such as references to English/British kings – or French, for that matter, in Wabanaki conversations with French imperial officials – as 'father.' While western Europeans took a father to be a figure of authority, for the Wabanaki a father was characterized primarily by obligations to his children and not by any entitlement to obedience. At Arrowsic, similar confusion would arise over the term 'obedience' itself.

A record of the Arrowsic conference was published in Boston later in 1717, and has remained the principal source for historians' knowledge of the deliberations. As a source, it has certain weaknesses. First, it was based on the written record kept by the British side, and it was published by order of Governor Shute and by his printer. Thus, it must be approached with a presumption that it incorporated the presuppositions, the cultural perspective, and the editorial hand of one side of the dialogue. The account of the four days of discussion, while phrased in the style of direct quotation, is compressed into the space of thirteen printed pages. Clearly, more was said that was lost as the document was edited down. Nevertheless, this source also has important strengths. As conference records go, it contains much valuable detail both of the speeches made and of surrounding circumstances. Most important, whether intentionally or not, it conveys a sense of interaction and of the conflicts of will and opinion that took place. It uncovers, with unusual clarity, difficulties in the translation of abstractions. Thus, while the record of the Arrowsic conference is far from a perfect source – as if such a thing existed – it is substantial and revealing.[23]

The Arrowsic conference opened at three o'clock in the afternoon of 9 August with a speech by Governor Shute. He began with an effort to turn the manner of his arrival into a strength rather than a weakness by referring to 'the great Fatigue and Danger of this Expedition,' notwithstanding which he had fulfilled his promise to visit the Wabanaki. Reaffirming the validity of the treaty signed at Portsmouth in 1713, Shute reviewed the Protestant succession of George I and the 'very good agreement' that now existed between Great Britain and France. The Wabanaki, he admonished, 'must ... remember at all times that they are KING GEORGE's Subjects ... [and] that they will always find themselves safest under the Government of *Great Britain*.' A Protestant missionary – he introduced the Reverend Joseph Baxter formally to those present – had been appointed to the Wabanaki, and a schoolmaster would soon follow. The colonial settlements recently made were intended, Shute continued, 'partly on their [the Wabanaki's] accounts, and ... they will find the benefit of them in having Trade brought so near them, besides the advantage of the Neighbourhood and Conversation of the English, to whom I have given strict Orders, that they be very just and kind to the Indians, upon all accounts.' The speech concluded with the governor's promise to be 'their great and safe Shelter,' and was followed by ceremonial handshakes, a gift to the *sakamows* of bibles in English and Algonkian, and the drinking of toasts to George I. The designated Wabanaki speaker was Wiwurna, who now took the opportunity – as did Captain Smart more prosaically in his logbook – to comment on the clearing of the morning's clouds so that 'the Sun shines so bright upon us; and [we] Hope the Angels in Heaven rejoyce with us.' As for any more substantive response to Shute's speech, Wiwurna proposed that this should wait until the next day, and the session came to an end with the governor's gift of an ox to be roasted for dinner.[24]

The next morning the real diplomatic fencing match began. Wiwurna opened with the statement, 'We have done with the Treaty at *Piscataqua* [Portsmouth]; and now proceed to a new one.' Perhaps taken aback by this apparent disavowal of the 1713 treaty, Shute questioned whether the Wabanaki confirmed their previous treaties. 'Yes, we do,' was Wiwurna's reply, and after the 1713 treaty had been read and translated, it was reaffirmed by all the Wabanaki present. In reality, there was no contradiction. An essential principle of Wabanaki diplomacy, and the reason why the *sakamows* insisted on reciprocal visiting – their own visits to Boston and Portsmouth balanced by the governors' visits to Casco Bay and Arrowsic – was the need for a relationship to be nurtured if it was to survive. A treaty, no matter how sincerely endorsed, could not be left to stand by itself without further conversations. This, for Wiwurna and those he spoke for, was a major purpose of the conference, and he went on to praise Shute's promise the previous day of 'Love and Unity' and to voice the hope that 'all hard thoughts will now be laid aside, between the English and Us, and that the Amity will be hearty.' Shute was willing to agree, but with the significant riders that the Wabanaki must 'carry themselves suitably, with Duty and Allegiance to KING GEORGE' and 'behave themselves well.'[25] Love, unity, and amity were unexceptionable enough in themselves, but they smacked of reciprocity – and of the diplomatic style of the conferences between 1701 and 1703, which Atecouando, Bomoseen, and Moxus could remember from direct experience.

The governor's implied suspicion that Wiwurna's comments represented more than mere courtesies was borne out in a discussion that soon became testy, at least on Shute's part. 'We have had the same Discourse from other Governours, as from your Excellency,' Wiwurna continued, 'and we have said the same to them; Other Governours have said to us that we are under no other Government but our own.' After Shute had interjected a question as to what this statement meant, a revealing exchange followed:

> *Wi.* We Pray leave to Speak out. Your Excellency was pleased to say that we must be Obedient to KING GEORGE, which we shall if we like the Offers made us.

> *Gov.* They must be Obedient to KING GEORGE, and all just Offers and Usage shall be given them.
> *Wi.* We will be very Obedient to the KING, if we are not Molested in the Improvement of our Lands.
> *Gov.* They shall not be Interrupted in the Improvement of their Lands; and the English must not be Molested by them in theirs.[26]

In this passage, the essential division between British and Wabanaki notions of the treaty relationship became evident. While Shute took the basis of the relationship to be submission, along the lines enshrined in the written texts of the treaties, Wiwurna took it to be a relationship of mutual obligation, as had been discussed during conferences while Dudley had been governor. The gap evidently could not be closed by translation, for the interpreters used the word 'Obedient' to define the statements of both protagonists. It was clear, however, that Shute and Wiwurna were following entirely different lines of thought. Their discord became greater now that the matter of land had been raised, and the exchanges were increasingly punctuated by terse questions or statements from Shute, and requests by Wiwurna along the lines of 'we pray leave to go on in order with our Answer.' The question of land led on to the question of settlement, which Wiwurna broached with an endorsement of British resettlement in places that had formerly been colonized – including Arrowsic itself: 'We now return Thanks that the English are come to Settle here, and will Imbrace them in our Bosoms that come to Settle on our Lands.' This latter thrust was too much for Shute to let pass. 'They must not call it their Land,' the governor admonished, 'for the English have bought it from them and their Ancestors.' Wiwurna's response was to ask that no new settlements be made, for 'we shan't be able to hold them all in our Bosoms.'[27]

Wiwurna, still claiming the initiative in the morning session because it was devoted to the Wabanaki answer to Shute, moved the discussion briefly on to a polite rejection of the proffered bibles, on the ground that other teaching – he did not mention the Jesuits by name – was already available. He was less dismissive of the Protestant missionary, and in fact visited Baxter to discuss religious matters on at least three occasions spaced throughout the balance of 1717.[28] Publicly, however, he observed: 'We are not capable to make any Judgment about Religion.' Wiwurna then raised the matter of the *Squirrel*'s mishap the previous day, speaking of the profound distress of the Wabanaki delegates to see the ship aground, the willingness of their 'Young Men' to help, and the relief they would feel to see Shute 'get safe down this River, and home.' What Shute thought of this excursion into the vulnerabilities of the warship was not recorded, but it effectively ended the Wabanaki response to his opening address and opened the way for the governor to steer the discussion back to the land question, and to broach some complaints. Referring by implication to the Wabanaki deeds held by the Pejepscot Proprietors, Shute informed the aboriginal representatives that 'they must be sensible and satisfied that the *English* own this land, and have Deeds that shew, and set forth their Purchase from their Ancestors.' He charged that British settlers had been subjected, on their own lands, to theft, threats, and killing of cattle at the hands of the natives. This brought a rapid end to the morning session, as Wiwurna requested time for consultation. The two sides parted with admonitions: Shute that he expected the natives to return 'with a positive Answer about the Lands,' and Wiwurna that 'it is not a jesting matter we are now upon.'[29]

The afternoon session began with a fresh and clearcut proposal from the Wabanaki, but ended in confusion. 'We are willing,' proposed Wiwurna in his opening statement, 'to cut off our Lands as far as the Mills, and the Coasts to *Pemaquid*.' The notion of a fixed boundary between British and Wabanaki lands was new, although the proposed British territory was broadly equivalent to the former areas of colonization that Wiwurna had already approved for resettlement. Pemaquid represented the northeastern limit of substantial English settlement at any earlier time, going back to its first emergence as a fishing and fur-trading centre during the 1620s, while 'the Mills' were the upriver sawmills that produced pine boards for export.[30] The Wabanaki initiative received no direct answer from Shute, but his statement that 'what is our own we will be Masters of' was rejection enough. Wiwurna then moved on to the matter of forts, raising a promise that he asserted had been verbally given during discussions with New England commissioners at Casco Bay immediately after the treaty signing at Portsmouth in 1713: 'It was said at *Casco* Treaty, that no more Forts should be made.'[31]

This was too much for Shute. Forts, he declared, were built freely by kings and their governors, and were for the protection of all subjects. He professed surprise that the Wabanaki, as subjects, would have any objections to forts built for their own security. At any rate, 'King GEORGE builds what Forts he pleases in his own Dominions.' Wiwurna's response was to question again whether land on the Kennebec had ever been sold to English purchasers. To Shute, this may well have seemed to be a non sequitur. The right of kings to build forts where they held dominion, for him, was a separate matter from the specific ownership of lands by purchase from aboriginal vendors. Nevertheless, he responded by ordering the Pejepscot Proprietors' principal Wabanaki land deed to be read and interpreted.[32] Wiwurna was noncommittal regarding the southwestern side of the Kennebec, while denying absolutely any land sales on the northeastern side, but now returned several times to the construction of forts. 'We should be pleased with King GEORGE if there was never a Fort in the Eastern Parts,' he ventured, to be met with Shute's renewed pledge that 'wherever there is a new Settlement, I shall always order a Fort, if I think it proper.' A hint of conciliation followed, as Shute assured the Wabanaki representatives that he would uphold their traditional practice of hunting and fishing wherever they wished, but it was not enough to save the session: 'The Indians rose up at once & withdrew, in a hasty abrupt manner without taking leave, and left behind their English Colours, returning to their Head quarters at *Puddlestones-Island*.'[33] The missionary Joseph Baxter confirmed in his journal that 'the Indians broke away disorderly and in an ill humour.[34]

If there was any doubt that the conference had reached a critical point, it was dispelled when Wabanaki delegates – the record did not specify who they were, or how many – brought a letter to Shute that evening. Written a few days before, it was signed by the Jesuit Sébastien Rale. The letter relayed from the governor of New France, Philippe de Rigaud de Vaudreuil, the French position on the Wabanaki lands. Briefly summarized, the French held that the Wabanaki lands, at least from Casco Bay eastward, had not been conveyed to Great Britain under the Treaty of Utrecht (1713) or in any other way, that the Wabanaki retained legitimate ownership, and that because the Wabanaki were friends and allies of France (within the terms of article XV of the Utrecht treaty) they would have French support if they needed it.[35] Shute read the letter 'and rejected it as not worthy of his Regard. And the Indians return'd.' The next day, the 11th, loading of firewood aboard the *Squirrel* began at 5.00 a.m.[36] Later, Shute made a display of boarding the frigate and ordering its fore topsail to be unfurled. The governor, recorded Joseph Baxter, 'acted as if he were going away.'[37] He was rewarded by the appearance of two Wabanaki in a canoe, who 'acknowledged the rudeness & ill manners they were guilty of Yesterday, and Pray'd that they might see his Excellency again.' At 6.00 p.m., the time appointed by Shute, the native delegates returned under the

Union flag, 'leaving behind them *Wiwurna*, because (as was said) he had behaved himself so improperly Yesterday.' The new speaker was Querebenawit.[38]

Matters now proceeded more cordially, with Querebenawit opening by apologizing again for the previous day's 'rude Carriage.' The formalities observed conformed more closely to Wabanaki diplomatic protocols, with wampum belts presented to Shute to underline each important point. Querebenawit undertook that the provision of the Portsmouth treaty allowing British resettlement would be observed, and promised peace and benevolence towards the colonists. Shute, on Querebenawit's request, promised in turn that trading houses would be established close to Wabanaki villages and that 'the Traders shall have order to supply them with what they want, at reasonable Rates.' He also agreed to attempt to find a smith to serve the Wabanaki by repairing their firearms. At the end of the day, the articles contained in the Portsmouth treaty were read and interpreted to the Wabanaki present, and reaffirmed by them. The following day, the last of the conference, 'twenty of the Sachems, and Principal Men' signed a written instrument again endorsing the Portsmouth articles, and undertaking that British settlers would be allowed peacefully to 'Cohabit with us.' When a few final matters had been settled, ceremonial handshakes were exchanged, Shute distributed gifts of 'Provisions & Ammunition,' and a group of young Wabanaki men came in return to 'give his Excellency a Dance.' The next morning at 10.00, the *Squirrel* weighed anchor and started downriver. Frigate and governor found safe harbour in Boston five days later.[39]

Governor Samuel Shute deemed the Arrowsic conference a success. 'I met,' he reported to the Board of Trade, 'a great Number of the Eastern Indians who have ratified and Confirmed all former Treatys and Entred into some new on's, which I hope will tend to the Honour of the King my Master and the Quiet and Peace of these Provinces.'[40] In a lengthy response to Sébastien Rale, written some six months after the conference, Shute specifically reviewed the Wabanaki land question:

> You will find, notwithstanding some little difficulty and dispute at first, it was finally agreed on [at Arrowsic] that the English should have, enjoy, and settle, if they saw good, where their predecessors had done, and be looked upon as the just and rightful owners or proprietors of such places and lands, as at any time heretofore have been under the English improvement; nor would I put it wholly on the foot of possession, but a just and

> good title by purchase from the natives, the original Indian sachems or proprietors of those eastern lands; for we not only had it in command anciently from the kings of England, but it was one of the fundamental laws of this government, not to enter upon any of the lands belonging to the aborigines without a fair, honest purchase; and accordingly the gentlemen claiming lands about Kennebeck river, and those parts, have their Indian deeds to show for the same.[41]

In reality, however, the governor was seriously mistaken about what had taken place at Arrowsic, at least from a Wabanaki perspective. Central to the misunderstanding was the Wabanaki apology for Wiwurna's rudeness. According to Wabanaki diplomatic protocols, Wiwurna had indeed behaved discourteously. However, the offence leading to his exclusion from the discussions was not, as Shute supposed, an obstinate or unreasonable refusal to recognize the validity of British claims on the Wabanaki. Rather, Wiwurna had allowed himself to be drawn too far away from the protocols of diplomacy. Although, to judge from the written record, his words had never varied from a scrupulous politeness, their effect had been to draw an irate reaction from Governor Shute. No matter how calmly they had been phrased and presented, Wiwurna's pointed questions and remarks had thus caused the governor to embarrass himself and his listeners by giving way to the emotion of anger. The role of Querebenawit had been to allow Shute to regain his gravity and thus to hold on to what was left of his fragile dignity. This the new speaker had accomplished by the ceremonial presentation of wampum to punctuate the exchanges, and by avoiding direct disputes.

What Querebenawit had not done was to retrench on the principal positions already established by Wiwurna. Of the major issues that had divided Shute and Wiwurna, two – the questions of obedience and fort-building – were not raised again in the discussions between Shute and Querebenawit. Nor, although Joseph Baxter interpreted the Wabanaki position as showing acceptance of the construction of forts, was there any trace of such a concession in the formal record of the agreement reached.[42] On the land question, Querebenawit noted that, in conformity with the terms of the 1713 treaty, the Wabanaki 'desire the English may settle as far as ever they had done.' This was no more than the restatement of a long-standing agreement, and did nothing to endorse the establishment of new settlements or the recognition of specific land sales. Querabenawit had gone on to praise the values of 'Peace and Unity' before raising the final important issue of trade, and receiving satisfactory promises from Shute. Even in the document signed on the final day, which stated consent to British resettlement and in general to settlement of 'all [lands] which they have obtained a Right & Title unto,' the guiding principle was that of 'mutual & reciprocal Benefit and Advantage to them [the settlers] & us, that they Cohabit with us.' The Wabanaki had agreed, therefore, to limited resettlement and in return had received guarantees of trade on favourable terms. They had not agreed to be subservient to British interests, nor had they given consent to the building of forts or to expansion of settlement in the Kennebec or Androscoggin valleys or further northeast. When Sébastien Rale informed Shute that the Wabanaki regarded the Arrowsic agreement as having been almost immediately violated by the activities of the Pejepscot Proprietors in the Kennebec valley, the Massachusetts governor responded with surprise and disbelief. What was chiefly illustrated by the complaint and by Shute's reaction, however, was the discrepancy between understandings of what the agreement itself had been.[43]

Shute also responded harshly to what he described as the 'harangue' in which Rale's letter had 'set before me the warlike and terrible genius of the Indians, and the strong alliances they have with some other Indian tribes.'[44] However, the warning was not as extravagant as the governor supposed. Further encroachments up the Kennebec valley by the Pejepscot Proprietors saw a fort, named Fort Richmond, built in 1719 opposite Swan Island – an island that had strong religious significance for the Kennebec Wabanaki. In the following year another group of proprietors, the Muscongus Company, launched its plans to develop its claim in the St George River valley, some distance northeast of the Kennebec, with an accompanying blockhouse.[45] The Wabanaki response was swift, and in the wintry weather of early January 1720 three Massachusetts commissioners met with Kennebec chiefs at Casco Bay to ascertain the reasons for 'the many Insults and abuses the Indians have Offered to His Majestys Subjects in the Eastern parts.' The difficulties arose, the commissioners concluded, 'from the English being Setled & Setling above or northwestward of Merry-meeting Bay ...[,] All which the Indians utterly deny to have disposed of.'[46] By summer, reports were reaching Boston of 'the Malancholly State of the eastern parts, who being so frequently alarm'd by the repeated insults of the Indians, are all entering into garrison even from Arowsick to Newchawanock [York] ... by which means several of their cornfields are destroyed, by the swine, and others Through fear are drawing of their Cattle in great numbers, insomuch That unless they are Speedily covered, The new Settlements will be totally overthrown.'[47]

In November 1720 discussions returned to Arrowsic, where a new group of commissioners took an aggressive approach and surprised the Kennebec chiefs (who on this occasion included Wiwurna) by surrounding the meeting place with militia. Under duress, the *sakamows* agreed to pay reparations of two hundred beaver skins and were informed that in the event of any further violent incidents the British 'will not leave you till we have cut you off Root and Brach from the Face of the Earth.'[48] The Wabanaki had an ultimatum of their own to deliver the next summer, after several months of diplomatic communication with native allies. Led by Wiwurna, accompanied by two Jesuits, and carrying a French flag, some two hundred warriors landed at Arrowsic to pay the promised beaver skins but also to warn, in the name of eleven Wabanaki groups and seven allied peoples, that the British must either respect Wabanaki territorial ownership or withdraw from the lands they had usurped and from all Wabanaki lands, on pain of violent expulsion.[49] Samuel Shute observed to London that 'the Indians have broken the Treaty concluded at Arowsick,' and blamed Sébastien Rale for inciting them to resistance, while Philippe de Rigaud de Vaudreuil professed to Rale that he was 'charmed' at the role taken by Wiwurna.[50] In the following year, hostilities broke out in earnest. The so-called Dummer's War was an intermittent and indecisive affair, and was ended by a further treaty in 1725. Yet it was destructive for both sides. The principal Kennebec village at Norridgewock was sacked by New England forces, and Sébastien Rale killed and scalped. Conversely, raids led by Wiwurna and others ensured the expulsion of settlers yet again from the Kennebec and Androscoggin valleys and from other settlements further southwest. To be sure, the setback proved not to be permanent, with the flow of colonists ultimately becoming too great for the Wabanaki effectively to resist. This imbalance, however, was a product of the circumstances of the period after 1725, and had not characterized the earlier era.

In sum, the Arrowsic conference of 1717 proved to have been a success for none of the participants, despite the apparent harmony of its last two days. Neither the mental agility of Wiwurna nor the more conventional diplomacy of Querebenawit had succeeded in persuading the British to relax their settlement efforts in the most crucial contested areas, or to stop them from building new forts. On the other hand, the

British hopes of inducing the Wabanaki to accept imperial and colonial claims had been equally ineffective. The failure had two principal causes. The first was the sheer intractability of the dispute between the two sides. British claims to dominion and to the allegiance of the Wabanaki were altogether at variance with the aboriginal intention to retain autonomy and territorial control even while tolerating settlement within specified limits.

Secondly, however, the failure had also been one of diplomacy. There had been periods over the preceding century, since the start of continuous English overwintering on the Wabanaki coast, when conflicts had been kept within manageable bounds. To be sure, the activities of the Pejepscot Proprietors had added a new and dangerous dynamic. Yet the exchange between Shute and Wiwurna created instabilities of its own. Samuel Shute was no fool, but his inexperience in native-imperial diplomacy was laid bare as the Arrowsic conference unfolded. Just as the grounding of the *Squirrel* had dashed his hopes of an making an impressive entrance, so his outspoken assertions of British claims had the effect of complicating rather than simplifying the discussions. Wiwurna, conversely, had the advantage of experience with the outstanding issues – perhaps his own experience, but certainly that of colleagues such as Moxus, Bomoseen, and Atecouando – but allowed himself to be drawn into the argument so far as to compromise the governor's dignity and thus also to compromise his own essential courtesy. The return under Querebenawit to more conventional diplomacy had the immediate result of salvaging the conference, but left a dangerous ambiguity. As British settlement and fort-building activities proceeded, and as Wiwurna continued his journey towards emerging as a fully fledged and powerful francophile, armed conflict became increasingly unavoidable. Undermined at the same time was the position of an anglophile such as Bomoseen, considered by John Gyles to be 'as onnest a fellow as hany of em,' who as late as August 1720 was attempting to find common ground with Boston and counteract the influence of Rale and Wiwurna.[51]

Ultimately, of course, the Arrowsic conference was an incident in a larger process. While the Wabanaki ability to resist British encroachment did not disappear quickly or conspicuously after 1725, the weight of increasing settlement made the task steadily more onerous. The Arrowsic conference, however, belonged squarely to the era when the outcome of the contest for the Wabanaki lands was undetermined, and when it was not unreasonable to suppose that Wabanaki hostility could have an important impact on New England even beyond those specific territories. Detailed study of the Arrowsic conference provides an opportunity to observe diplomacy at work in this context. Historiographically, a persuasive case can be made for applying to native–imperial relationships the established techniques of diplomatic history. Historically, it is important to recognize too the reality of the Wabanaki military power that underlay the diplomatic process. This determined that a workable relationship was, by necessity, a negotiated relationship. Much as Samuel Shute may have arrived at Arrowsic intending to assert imperial prerogatives, it proved impossible to do so. Wiwurna, even though he undoubtedly had the better of Shute in their exchanges, was no more successful in inducing British retrenchment. The *sakamow*'s discourtesy and the governor's anger combined to create a dangerous deadlock, which was only superficially resolved in the later stages of the conference. The Arrowsic dialogue also exemplified, however, the wider reality that outside of the few areas of dense colonial population in northeastern New England, imperialism remained a negotiated process, and colonization, accordingly, a fragile and provisional one.

10 *Pax Britannica* or *Pax Indigena*? Planter Nova Scotia (1760–1782) and Competing Strategies of Pacification

Planter Nova Scotia spanned the years from the start of the New England migration into the province in 1760 to the Loyalist influx that began on a large scale in 1782. For many years, historians of this era concentrated their efforts on two principal questions, Why did the New England Planters fail, in significant numbers, to join the American Revolution? What differentiated the Planters from the later Loyalist migrants?[1] These remain significant issues, and yet the historiographical context for considering them has shifted markedly in recent years. The change is owed in part to the publication since 1987 of four major collections of essays bearing specifically on the Planter era. The Planter Studies Conferences at Acadia University, and the published volumes drawn from them, have accomplished much more than their original modest aim of rescuing the Planters from historical obscurity.[2] The series has provided the motive power for a fundamental re-engineering of our understanding of the Maritime colonies in the eighteenth century. Planter Studies, from the beginning, was broadly and inclu-

---

This essay was originally presented as the Charles H. Read Family Lecture in Planter Studies at Acadia University on 20 March 2003, with the title 'Planter Nova Scotia: Before the Flood.' I am grateful to all those who provided comments and discussion at that time, especially Barry Moody and the late Jim Snowdon. I am much indebted to Elizabeth Mancke and Bill Wicken for their valuable comments on the written text, and to the four anonymous readers who reviewed it for the *Canadian Historical Review*. My interest in the issues discussed in this essay was prompted in part by the experience of testifying in *Regina v. Marshall* and other legal cases, and this is one of the reasons I am grateful to have been afforded that opportunity. The essay was originally published in *Canadian Historical Review* 85:4 (December 2004), 669–92.

sively designed so that not only could a wide variety of disciplinary approaches be accommodated but also studies of Acadians, Mi'kmaq and Wulstukwiuk, Halifax and Lunenberg settlers, and even Loyalists were included along with those dealing more strictly with New England Planters. Taking the four Planter Studies volumes together, the result has been to underline the socio-ethnic diversity of Planter Nova Scotia.

Yet one area considered only peripherally in the Planter Studies volumes is the interaction of Planters with aboriginal inhabitants. While the Mi'kmaq and the Wulstukwiuk, as noted above, are far from being ignored, the only essay dealing centrally with aboriginal history is William Wicken's 'Mi'kmaq Land in Southwestern Nova Scotia, 1771–1823,' which explores a specific aspect of the Mi'kmaq experience over a period that goes chronologically far beyond the Planter era.[3] The absence of other essays on aboriginal themes reflects a broader historiographical reality: that the role of aboriginal nations in the region during the 1760s and 1770s has hitherto lacked comprehensive study (especially by comparison with the attention historians have given to earlier decades) and that the integration of the aboriginal with the non-aboriginal history of the era has been hindered accordingly. Especially important, since this was an era not only of British-Mi'kmaq and British-Wulstukwiuk treaty-making, in 1760–1, but also of the longer-term working through of the ensuing relationships, is the question of the relative diplomatic and military weight wielded by either side. Was British hegemony characteristic of Planter Nova Scotia, or did Mi'kma'ki and Wulstukwik persist autonomously despite British imperial claims?

The earlier eighteenth-century context for addressing this question has been elaborated significantly in recent studies. Historians such as Elizabeth Mancke and William Wicken have added, respectively, new imperial and aboriginal dimensions to the existing historiography. My own work has emphasized the limitations on imperial endeavours in the region in the seventeenth and early eighteenth centuries, while Geoffrey Plank has demonstrated the British inability to erase Acadian and Mi'kmaq distinctness even by harsh military actions. Naomi Griffiths and Maurice Basque (although presenting divergent views of Acadian political economy) have shown the sophistication of Acadian responses to imperial and aboriginal neighbours, while Barry Moody has exposed the delicate balances that kept the pre-1749 British regime intact at Annapolis Royal. For all these authors, imperial–colonial–aboriginal relations were invariably complex rather than simple, and it was in response to these very complexities and balances that the possibility of coexistence could be lost or found.[4]

Yet the recent studies, for the most part, make their central contributions in periods that do not extend significantly beyond the treaty-making years 1760–1. L.F.S. Upton's older and groundbreaking work, meanwhile, covers the Mi'kmaq experience of the 1760s and 1770s in greater detail but takes an ambivalent position as to the aboriginal role at this time. Upton recognized that the Mi'kmaq 'refused to admit defeat' when concluding the treaties of 1760–1, but saw this manifested in their having 'kept the past alive' through cultural retention rather than in any remaining control over events.[5] Indeed, the long-ago assertion of J.B. Brebner that 'the conquests of Louisbourg and Canada had left the Indians absolutely at the mercy of the British,'[6] with its implication that aboriginal relations had little further significance for the non-native settlement history of the region, has retained a tenacious currency among historians. Stephen E. Patterson, though in a more nuanced manner than Brebner, has argued similarly that the defeat of France in 1758 prompted 'the Native collapse as a fighting force' and that as a result the treaties of 1760–1 were made in a context where the end of the French-aboriginal alliance represented for the British 'both the fulfilment of their strategy and a vindication of their "total war" approach.'[7] Daniel N. Paul, while taking a totally different view of the British military role as brutal and repressive, has also argued that by the treaty-making era of 1760–1 the Mi'kmaq posed 'no real threat' to the security of the British regime.[8]

The point is a critical one. If British hegemony had indeed been consolidated conclusively by the early 1760s, whether in ways that could be characterized as crudely oppressive or strategically expedient, there are profound interpretive implications for our understanding of the treaties themselves and of the Planter era more generally. If the treaties of 1760–1 were made between a victorious empire and disempowered aboriginal nations, then their provisions must be interpreted in the light of this imbalance. Logic could even extend to regarding them as surrenders in which any British concessions were made in a spirit of mercy towards conquered peoples. If, by contrast, the treaties were negotiated by two sides that shared a strong need to reach agreement, and to hammer out a relationship accordingly, then the articles must be understood as commitments made for that urgent and highly practical purpose.[9] If the Planters moved in during the 1760s to take over a territory pacified by British hegemony, then Nova Scotia as a colonial entity had decisively taken the place of Mi'kma'ki and Wulstukwik. If, by contrast, this was still debatable territory, the Planter era must be seen as one in which colonial settlement was far from central in its historical significance, and in which the process of pacification initiated by the treaties could yet take different and unpredictable directions. At a more general level still, the argument is between the notion that British imperial advance (with its twin engines of military power and colonial settlement) was ineluctable and the competing view that the aboriginal role remained diplomatically and militarily powerful far beyond the chronological point at which most historians have been willing to write it off.

This essay takes the latter position. Offering a re-examination of certain key elements of the evidence regarding the aboriginal role vis-à-vis the Planters and the British imperial authorities in Nova Scotia, it seeks also to draw out the imperial implications of the aboriginal–colonial relationship in Planter Nova Scotia. Whereas Brebner's celebrated *The Neutral Yankees of Nova Scotia* (1937) attributed Nova Scotia's non-involvement in the American Revolution partly to the unscrupulous self-interest of Halifax merchants but mainly to the essential apathy of most Planters, isolated as they were from the political and ideological mainstream of North America, it is argued here that the Planters were part of a different and larger mainstream of imperial experience.[10] Far from accomplishing a pacification of Nova Scotia under British rule, the events of the 1750s and early 1760s – the expulsion of the Acadians, the British military victories of 1758–60, and the treaties of 1760–1 – set the stage for a ten-year era during which aboriginal and British pacification strategies competed, followed by a partial reconciliation which was finally swept away only by the sudden force of numbers brought by the Loyalist migration.

Revisiting the significance of the Loyalist influx that overtook Nova Scotia during the early 1780s, in an effort to evaluate the societal conjuncture that existed in Nova Scotia before the onset of this flood of migrants, also implies a challenge to the long-established consensus that eighteenth-century northeastern North America, until 1775, was experiencing a colonial era, and that the American Revolution then established a new and dramatic demarcation between British North America and the United States. Rather, the Loyalist migration extended into Nova Scotia a weight of settlement that, as in many parts of what was now the northeastern United States, was incompatible with aboriginal economies. It was not, however, the culmination of a linear or inescapable process. Before 1782 – whether imperial officials sought to advance their cause in ways that were brutally oppressive, strategically astute, or both – colonization was limited to defined areas and there was no inexorable advance of British power. Rather, the earlier era must be understood by identifying more complex historical patterns, and through a historiographical triumvirate in which aboriginal, imperial, and colonial history continuously interact.[11]

The British conquest of Acadia in 1710, closely followed by the Treaty of Utrecht in 1713, was an ambiguous affair. The British established their headquarters at Annapolis Royal, and attempted with intermittent success to establish British economic interests in such forms as the Canso fisheries and merchant activities around the Bay of Fundy. However, the majority of the settler population was Acadian, and the bulk of territorial control continued to rest where it always had: in the hands of the aboriginal nations. Environmentally, the British presence in what was now defined as Nova Scotia remained fragile. Meanwhile, the non-British peoples were environmentally well established. The Acadians, numbering some two thousand at the time of the conquest and rapidly increasing, primarily occupied the Fundy marshlands, while the aboriginal nations utilized the much larger expanses of territory that continued to support a hunting, gathering, and fishing economy. The aboriginal population of perhaps four thousand at the time of the conquest was numerically overtaken by the Acadians about 1720. The four hundred or so British, by contrast, were confined to an enclave in Annapolis Royal, the site of European enclaves of various nationalities (French, Scottish, English) that had existed with only brief intermissions since 1605.[12]

From a global perspective, the presence of a British enclave in which a small body of military and mercantile leaders – accompanied by an only slightly larger number of their military and civilian followers – conducted their dealings with more numerous and spatially unrestrained indigenous civilizations was familiar enough, especially in Africa and Asia. In northeastern North America, however, there were other models. In southern Massachusetts and along stretches of the Connecticut, Hudson, and St Lawrence valleys, clusters of agricultural settlement had brought about fundamental environmental alterations, even though certain qualifications must be made. Massachusetts, Connecticut, New York, or Canada: none was an exclusively agricultural colony. Commerce was fundamental to each, whether through the internal market economy or external trade connections with aboriginal suppliers or overseas merchants. In New York and Canada, more so than in New England, imperial military expenditure was also a vital invisible export. A second caution is that, even as late as the mid-eighteenth century, it is important not to exaggerate the extent of agricultural development, which remained localized not only in juxtaposition with the aboriginal lands further west but also with the large heartland associated with the Appalachian spine of northeastern North America itself.

These qualifications made, however, European-style agriculture had long been the engine of environmental change in the areas of colonial settlement, and by the mid-eighteenth century it had combined with commerce to support large, dense, and partly urbanized non-aboriginal populations in some parts of northeastern North America. Agricultural development had led in these areas to what Daniel Richter has rightly described as 'an inexorable demand for new agricultural land – land that in one way or another had to be expropriated from its aboriginal owners.'[13] Agriculture, with its land clearances and its demands for the pasturing of livestock, was a potentially lethal threat to aboriginal hunting-gathering economies.[14] Although eighteenth-century Europeans would have seen agricultural development at one level as a natural and beneficial use of the soil, imperial strategists were aware that it also represented an efficient means of undermining aboriginal societies where they had become obstacles to strategic or economic ambitions. Thus, the deliberate unleashing of an agriculturally based population on aboriginal territory was an act of profound aggression, in which environmental destruction became a tool of empire.

Yet there was at least one instance in northeastern North America where non-aboriginal agriculture had proved compatible with an immediately neighbouring aboriginal economy. Acadians and Mi'kmaq were different and separate peoples, between whom tensions existed. As William Wicken has shown, environmentally generated disputes tended to become more frequent over time, as the Acadian population increased.[15] Nevertheless, the confinement of Acadian environmental alterations largely to coastal marshlands meant that mutual forbearance could generally prevail. Accordingly, for more than three decades after the conquest of 1710, Nova Scotia was characterized by an internal equilibrium by which disputes among Mi'kmaq, Acadians, and British could be accommodated with only sporadic violence. 'Until 1744,' one recent study has concluded, 'coexistence was largely though not continuously peaceful, and negotiation the favoured safeguard against destructive frictions.'[16]

Warfare between 1744 and 1748, while ultimately inconclusive, revealed both British and French imperial weaknesses in the region. Each suffered a humiliating defeat – the French with the capture of Louisbourg in 1745, the British with the crushing of a New England force at Grand Pré in 1747 – and each determined to assert a more powerful imperial grip following the Treaty of Aix-la-Chapelle in 1748. The building of military installations at strategic points proceeded rapidly. While the French repossessed Louisbourg under the terms of the treaty, and set about re-fortifying it, the British established the heavily defended town of Halifax on Chebucto Bay in 1749. In seeking to counteract their chief imperial rival and mend the weaknesses that had appeared in wartime, the British envisaged an approach that would be both military and environmental. With the protection of available forces, concentrated in forts and outposts that now overlooked the principal areas of Acadian settlement, British and 'Foreign Protestant' colonists would begin to clear and cultivate adjoining lands. As Elizabeth Mancke has observed, it was far from unusual in eighteenth-century British colonies in North America, outside of the older settlement colonies that ranged southward from Massachusetts, for settlement to follow the state and its military forces.[17] Yet during the ensuing years this strategy for pacification of Nova Scotia would have to compete with a treaty-based aboriginal strategy for a different form of pacification in which colonial settlement would be rigorously confined.

The strategic linkage between imperial objectives and Protestant European settlement in Nova Scotia was made explicit in the instructions issued to Governor Edward Cornwallis in 1749. They included a series of instructions relating to settlement that had not been issued to previous governors, in Nova Scotia or elsewhere. Cornwallis was enjoined to lay out townships not only for the convenience of settlement but also for 'security ... against the insults and incursions of neighboring Indians or other enemies.' Land was to be set aside for military installations, and the governor was explicitly instructed to ensure that Acadian settlements were included within township boundaries, 'to the end that ... French inhabitants may be subjected to such rules and orders as may hereafter be made for the better ordering and governing the said townships.'[18] In the short term, it was hoped, the new settlers would quickly outnumber the Acadians. In the longer term, they would not only assimilate the Acadians into a larger British and Protestant society, but would also extend into strategically selected localities of Nova Scotia the agriculturally based settlement that had proved so durable in certain other portions of northeastern North America.

The British initiative of 1749 proved successful in some respects, unsuccessful in others. Halifax itself endured, despite three years of containment by Mi'kmaq forces. Annapolis Royal remained a significant settlement, though no longer the colony's headquarters. From 1753 onwards, the Foreign Protestant settlement at Lunenburg formed the third area of British-sponsored colonization in Nova Scotia. An additional though localized military presence was effectively established in such locations as Fort Lawrence (on the isthmus of Chignecto) and Fort Edward (at Pisiquid). Most important, after the outbreak of renewed hostilities between British and French in 1754, Nova Scotia–based British forces played a significant role in the defeat of France in key battles for Fort Beauséjour (1755) and Louisbourg (1758), and thus in the campaigns that led to the eventual withdrawal of France as an imperial power from continental North America by the Treaty of Paris in 1763.

Even by 1758, however, the other side of the balance sheet weighed heavily against British interests in the region. Settlement efforts fell far short of expectations. Even the hastily improvised establishment of Lunenburg highlighted the absence of the planned pattern of Protestant-settled townships elsewhere. The Acadians had not been assimilated. Instead, most Acadians had been deported, starting in 1755. Although Nova Scotian military authorities put a bold face on the deportation, portraying it as an unfortunate necessity, it was in reality a defeat. As aptly characterized by Julian Gwyn, it was 'an act of econocide ... unparalleled in pre-1815 British colonial history,' and produced 'such economic devastation that it set Nova Scotia behind for perhaps at least a generation.'[19] Also, despite the specific affronts offered to the Mi'kmaq by the foundation of Halifax and Lunenburg, and the destructive irregular campaigns waged by companies such as that headed by the brothers John and Joseph Gorham, there was no generalized encroachment on aboriginal lands.[20] While years of hostilities, and the loss of French gifts and supplies after 1758, brought severe economic strain to both Mi'kmaq and Wulstukwiuk villages, the territorial basis for regeneration remained intact. Thus, the supreme irony of the 1750s for the British in Nova Scotia lay in the reality that at the same time as British arms had succeeded against the French, all of the plans for what the Halifax regime had chiefly attempted to accomplish within the region – the assimilation of the Acadians and the environmental change of selected aboriginal territories – lay in ruins.

These circumstances formed the basis for a realignment in the region that took effect between 1758 and 1761. Its two central departures lay respectively in the conclusion of the British-aboriginal treaties of 1760-1, and the renewal of efforts to recruit settlers for Nova Scotia. The treaties, while not unprecedented – previous treaties of lasting historical importance had been concluded in 1725–6, 1749, and 1752 – had their origins in the consequences attending the fall of Louisbourg. For the aboriginal leaders of the region, the withdrawal of the French enhanced the importance of the treaty relationship with the only remaining imperial presence. Trade required especial attention, and this was prominently reflected in British negotiations in Halifax in early 1760 with Wulstukwiuk and Passamaquoddy representatives, at which the establishment of a system of provincially operated truckhouses was negotiated, and a specific tariff of prices for trade goods was agreed upon.[21] The truckhouse trade became an integral part of the Wulstukwiuk-Passamaquoddy treaty dated 23 February 1760, and similar provisions characterized each of the known texts of the several agreements made with Mi'kmaq villages later in 1760 and in the following year.[22] On the British side, the necessities were to take stock after the setbacks of the 1750s and to seek colonists in an effort to breathe new life into the endeavours of that decade. Gaining an accommodation with aboriginal inhabitants was a prerequisite for both. The written texts of the treaties contained expressions of aboriginal submission to the British crown that, as ever with such formulae, were open to varying interpretations. Nearer the mark was Governor Charles Lawrence, who observed to the British Board of Trade in May 1760 – regarding both the Wulstukwiuk-Passamaquoddy treaty and those Mi'kmaq treaties that had been signed to that point – that 'One of the Chief Articles in these treaties is that of Commerce,' and that 'the greatest advantage from this Article ... is the friendship of these Indians.'[23]

A major issue that was not directly addressed in the treaties was that of land. Although the texts of the Mi'kmaq treaties contained an aboriginal undertaking not to 'molest any of His Majesty's Subjects or their dependants in their settlements already made or to be hereafter made,' no boundaries were specified and there was no mention of aboriginal land surrender.[24] The extent to which Nova Scotia authorities would seek to extend colonial settlement remained to be determined. As William Wicken has argued, it was undoubtedly restricted in part by the assumption that the Mi'kmaq hunting-gathering economy would remain in existence sufficiently to provide for a continuing fur trade.[25] Nevertheless, the tenor of concurrent recruitment efforts for New England settlers made it clear that colonization on the southern New England pattern was sought, at least in some places. The proclamations inviting settlement, issued by Lawrence on 12 October 1758 and 11 January 1759, noted that settlement would not be confined to former Acadian areas, promised that where possible each individual land grant would comprise upland as well as marsh and meadow, and took pains to portray the institutional framework as closely resembling the governance structures of New England towns and provinces.[26] Accordingly, the establishment of townships went beyond the boundaries of the former Acadian settlements both by encompassing upland acreages in township grants in former Acadian areas and by creating townships in additional areas – though, with the exception of Maugerville, these were for fishing rather than primarily agricultural settlements – that had not seen large-scale Acadian settlement.[27]

An expansion to non-aboriginal settlement was in prospect, therefore, despite the absence of land surrender in the treaties of 1760–1. Planters who arrived in the expectation that tensions with aboriginal inhabitants had been laid to rest would soon find out otherwise. Treaty-making continued apace until the summer of 1761, when an elaborate signing ceremony at the Governor's Farm in Halifax – attended by Mi'kmaq chiefs from the Miramichi, Shediac, Pokemouche, and Cape Breton – brought the acting governor, Jonathan Belcher, to declare that 'a covenant of peace' now existed.[28] Like any covenant, however, this one had two sides. Time would tell that peace would prevail to a remarkable degree over the ensuing two decades. However, it was neither an easy peace nor one that was passively sustained by aboriginal leaders, who proved ready and willing to use the threat of coercion to reinforce their interpretation of a treaty relationship that, in their estimation, precluded undue Planter encroachments. Apprehension of the application of Mi'kmaq and Wulstukwiuk force thereupon became a central theme of the Planter experience during the 1760s, and a central concern of successive governors of Nova Scotia.

As late as the summer of 1759, a year after the fall of Louisbourg, the ability of aboriginal forces to inflict damage on British settlements and outposts had been graphically demonstrated. In April of that year, Governor Lawrence had reported to London on raids taking place at Lunenburg and on the Isthmus of Chignecto. Although he hoped to be able 'to cover the inhabitants against these mortifying and very discouraging incursions upon them,' by September he was forced to admit that matters had become even worse as a result of aboriginal raids on land and the sea-borne activities of armed Acadian fugitives.[29] Not only did these circumstances lead to the postponement of the first Planter migrations for a year,[30] but also Lawrence ensured that initial Planter settlements were planned with defence in mind. In Horton, Cornwallis, and Falmouth townships, reported his successor Jonathan Belcher, 'Pallisadoed Forts were erected in each ..., by order of the late Governor, with room sufficient to receive all the Inhabitants, who were formed into a Militia to join what Troops could be spar'd to oppose any attempts that might be formed against them.'[31] Even so, and even after the treaty-making process was well under way, there were serious doubts as to whether the protection would be adequate. The surveyor Charles Morris wrote to the Nova Scotia council from Pisiquid in June 1760: 'The want of a sufficient number of Troops at this Juncture where so many Settlements are carrying on, is not a little discouraging to the new Settlers. I am in hopes no accident will happen to make a greater number necessary.'[32] Henry Alline would have agreed with Morris in every respect. The young Falmouth settler and future evangelist declared that within a short time of his family's arrival in mid-1760, 'it was frequently reported, that the Indians were about rising to destroy us; and many came out among us with their faces painted, and declared that the English should not settle this country.'[33]

The treaty relationship offered to the Planters a realistic possibility that aboriginal military capacity would not be exercised, even though the limited evidence suggests that Planters themselves had little if any sense of their aboriginal neighbours as treaty partners. Certainly Bartholomew Nocvut, a Mi'kmaw from Porcupine Cove who was severely beaten by Planters in successive incidents at Horton and Cornwallis during the summer of 1763, had no reason to think that they did.[34] Yet responsible British officials were fully conscious that aboriginal restraint could not be taken for granted. Even though British understandings tended over time to depend on narrowing interpretations of the written texts,[35] no textual readings could obscure the necessity of reaching a stable understanding in two crucial respects: first, on the extent to which the British could be judged by their aboriginal treaty partners to be living up to their own commitments; second, on somehow reaching a modus vivendi on the territorial questions with which the treaties had not dealt explicitly.

Jonathan Belcher, acting as governor after Lawrence's death in late 1760, was acutely aware of these imperatives. To the council and assembly of Nova Scotia in March 1762, Belcher praised the role of favourable trade terms in consolidating the treaty relationship, and urged that 'every reasonable Method ought to be pursued for preserving this Peace inviolate, and fixing their Affections and Attachments, from the Sense and experience of Protection, Integrity and Friendship.'[36] Six weeks later, he turned his attention to the land question, issuing a proclamation that reserved for the use of aboriginal inhabitants, pending confirmation or otherwise by the Crown, lands adjoining the entire coastline from Musquodoboit to the Bay of Chaleur. Justifying the proclamation to the Board of Trade, Belcher made it clear that it stemmed from 'the Pretensions of the Indians' and from his recognition that aboriginal discontent could have 'disagreeable consequences in the present Situation of Affairs.'[37] The Board of Trade eventually wrote to the incoming governor, Montagu Wilmot, to disavow the proclamation, although even so it emphasized that 'giving disgust or dissatisfaction to the Indians' must scrupulously be avoided.[38] The proclamation belonged to an era in which the crown itself extended far-reaching, though more general, recognition to aboriginal territories throughout eastern North America in the Royal Proclamation of 1763, to which successive governors of Nova Scotia professed their adherence.[39] Even though the concessions specifically made in the Nova Scotia proclamation were too extensive to be received favourably in London, they offer persuasive testimony as to the crucial importance attached by Belcher in the spring of 1762 to the placation of aboriginal interests.

The summer of 1762 brought more direct evidence to bear, as perceived aboriginal threats brought desertions from Planter settlements and disaffection in the militia. British officials were inclined to blame the crisis partly on the incitement of fugitive Acadians and partly too on the hope of French intervention in Nova Scotia following the capture of St John's, Newfoundland, by French forces at the end of June. But it was 'the threatnings of the Indians' that made the situation critical.[40] From Lunenburg in mid-July came news that 'the Indians which Surround us are Certainly very Numerous, and by their Motion and Insults for the last Twenty four Hours, its more than doubtfull they are meditating an Attack.'[41] Belcher took the threat seriously, cancelling orders for Lunenburg militia to march to the defence of Halifax against a possible French assault. The acting governor also observed, accurately, that 'it must be presum'd that in other parts of the Weak settlements the inhabitants might be alarmed.'[42] Planters from the King's County settlements of Horton, Cornwallis, Falmouth, and Newport protested the removal of their militia for duties at Fort Edward and Fort Sackville at a time when 'a Considerable Body of Indians were assembled together menacing the Inhabitants with Destruction,' and the Halifax council of war responded by allowing the King's County men to return home, 'but to hold Themselves in Readiness to March hither at a Moments Warning.'[43] By August, both Belcher and the council of war were taking note of desertions from the King's County settlements. Belcher also reported to General Jeffery Amherst that by that time the threat had been extended to Halifax, where in his view the nearby assembly of an aboriginal force estimated at six hundred strong, along with the presence in the town of several hundred captive male Acadians of military age, 'should make the people in the New Settlements fear the fate of this Town [Halifax], and their own.'[44]

The crisis of 1762 ended as suddenly as it had begun. By early September, Belcher believed the threat had subsided and credited 'the Measures ... taken for checking and dispersing the Indians.'[45] The question remains as to whether aboriginal forces had ever intended more than a show of force. Certainly, the lessening of the tension before the French evacuation of St John's in mid-September, and well before news of that development could have reached Nova Scotia, casts doubt on any direct connection of the summer's various events. The vulnerability of the settlers and the continuing insecurity of the British presence had, however, been clearly demonstrated. During the ensuing years, successive governors of Nova Scotia used blunt language in their efforts to make this lesson clear in London. The specific causes of concern varied from year to year. In 1763 it was the fear that reports of the exploits of Pontiac's followers might prompt 'the Indians of this Province to follow their Example from the present weak condition of the several Posts.'[46] In 1766 it was the possibility that the Mi'kmaq were maintaining contact with the last remaining French outpost in North America, on the island of St Pierre.[47] On some occasions specific incidents between aboriginal and non-aboriginal individuals prompted urgent efforts from Halifax to mollify aggrieved Wulstukwiuk or Mi'kmaq. The aboriginal nations, thought the Nova Scotia provincial secretary in the context of a case in the St John valley in 1766, were 'ever ready to revenge injuries in the Severest Manner.'[48]

Maintenance of the peace, therefore, conferred responsibilities on both sides. If responsibilities were not fulfilled, then courtesy and the credible threat of coercive force could prove to be two sides of the same coin. This explained the eagerness of Nova Scotia officials to respond positively to requests made of them in the name of the treaty relationship, whether for gifts and supplies or for the support of a Roman Catholic priest.[49] It also underlay the warnings the same officials repeatedly transmitted to the Board of Trade. Governor Wilmot argued in 1764 that 'the custom of giving them provisions and cloathing, has been too long established to be broke through with Safety, particularly at a time when the Settlement of this Country, and the further increase of its inhabitants depend so much on their [the aboriginal] temper and disposition.' The alternative, for Wilmot, was unthinkable: 'The Indians exceed six hundred fighting Men in number, of whom a small party might carry terror and devastation thro' a Country before the Troops cou'd have sufficient Notice to prevent the Mischief; which is always secretly concerted, and suddenly executed.'[50]

Acting governor Benjamin Green warned similarly in August 1766 that 'the humour and disposition of the Indians have always merited a particular attention of the Government here as the safety and Success of the Settlements depend in a great measure on the turn they shall take.'[51] Green's successor as acting governor, Michael Francklin, confirmed a few weeks later that 'a rupture with the Indians ... would throw the Settlements into the utmost Confusion, if not totally break up the greatest part of them.'[52] But it was left to the next fully appointed governor, Lord William Campbell, to use the bluntest language of all. In mid-1768, as British troops began to leave Halifax to meet the revolutionary crisis in New England, the Nova Scotia council expressed concern about the weakening of military outposts in the region, notably Fort Cumberland.[53] When Campbell arrived back in Nova Scotia in September after travels in England and New England, he wasted no time in writing to senior imperial administrators to warn that troop withdrawals would provide 'cause of most uneasy Allarmes for the safety of the yet thinly Inhabited Settlements in the Interior parts of the Province,' and that Nova Scotia was an 'infant struggling Province' and vulnerable to aboriginal attack.[54] Some six weeks later, he reported further to the colonial secretary, Lord Hillsborough, that 'I have daily advices from ... [the interior settlements] which seem to confirm my apprehensions are not groundless.' Campbell then went on to set out the military balance of power succinctly: 'The outposts of this Province fixt, as a Shelter and retreat for the Inhabitants settled upon the Frontiers, left destitute of Garrisons, to protect them, may be either destroyed or possessed by the

Savages, a very small Number of which, would be able at this juncture to bring fire and Destruction to the very entrance of this Town [Halifax].'[55]

By early 1769, Campbell was still reaffirming to Hillsborough the vulnerability of Nova Scotia. 'They are daily coming in here,' he wrote of the Mi'kmaq, 'and demanding provisions in such terms, as indicates their being sensible of the weak State of the Interior parts of the Province, deprived of all Military protection.'[56] Yet it was noteworthy that what the governor was describing was not an attack but a request for supplies. No doubt, to judge from Campbell's description, it was made as a request that could not reasonably – or, from a British standpoint, safely – be refused. It was, however, an indication of the persistence of the treaty relationship rather than a threat to end it. From the time of the treaties' conclusion at the beginning of the 1760s, there had been a peaceful undercurrent in aboriginal–British relationships despite the tensions that had repeatedly arisen during the initial phases of Planter settlement. It was seen in a series of episodes that can be glimpsed in the evidence. Following the assaults at Horton and Cornwallis in the summer of 1763, according to the Nova Scotia council, Mi'kmaq leaders at Cape Porcupine were 'very civil and courteous,' and when a prompt investigation uncovered the Planter culprits the chiefs took the opportunity to confirm that 'they would inviolably observe the Peace which they had made.'[57] A military settler in the St John valley described in 1764 how 'an Indian made me a present of a Pair of horns of a small Moose.'[58] Some four years later, Wulstukwiuk chiefs travelled to Halifax to meet formally with the Nova Scotia council, receiving assurances regarding the colony's continuing support of a priest in the St John valley, the removal of specific non-native land encroachments, and the lack of any 'Restriction on your Trade.'[59] Two days later, the acting governor Michael Francklin wrote to Hillsborough noting that the supply of the services of the priest, Charles-François Bailly de Messein, had been seen as an unavoidable obligation, 'Conformable to the provisions made them at their first making Peace.'[60] The fulfilment of another promise, this one made at the Halifax meeting in 1768, was presaged in early 1769 when the Nova Scotia provincial secretary Richard Bulkeley told a St John valley Planter that agricultural tools would be sent to the Wulstukwiuk 'by the first Opportunity.'[61] By late 1770, even Campbell was inclined to praise the work of Bailly and hoped that the priest might persuade a substantial number of Mi'kmaq to settle in one place near Halifax, so that 'their Motions may be watched and prevented if ill designed, and in time [they may] become peaceable and Usefull Subjects.'[62]

The idea of settling aboriginal inhabitants in one consolidated village was an ancient preoccupation of imperial administrators in the region, and it came no closer to fulfilment now than when promoted by French officials and missionaries at the turn of the eighteenth century. Nevertheless, its contemplation by Campbell was yet another indication that aboriginal–British relationships had become less troubled as the pace of Planter settlement had slackened. A report reaching London in 1773 declared, even though with some oversimplification, that 'the Indians ..., since the French have been expell'd from the Neighbourhood of this Province ... have become quiet and at present are well disposed.'[63] A year later the Yorkshire travellers John Robinson and Thomas Rispin portrayed the aboriginal population of the region as 'very expert in hunting, and excellent marksmen with the gun,' but to the settlers 'friendly, harmless, well-behaved.'[64] In effect, the Planters – from being the *provocateurs* of the 1760s – had become the new Acadians of the 1770s. The number of non-aboriginals in the region remained, even at the end of that decade, many fewer than on the eve of the Acadian deportation. Although population figures for this period are necessarily estimates based on imperfect sources, Julian Gwyn has put the population of mainland Nova Scotia (including the modern New Brunswick) at 18,000 in early 1755, including Acadians, British and British-sponsored, and aboriginal inhabitants. The corresponding figure for 1781 was 14,000.[65] As a number of scholars have observed, the rural settlements of Planter Nova Scotia were scattered and lacked effective interconnecting routes.[66] Furthermore, Planter incursions into cleared uplands had been limited in scope, and Planter marshland agriculture retained many affinities in technique with the old Acadian forms of cultivation.[67] The settlement of Planter communities had lasting results in a number of localities. Yet, insofar as the migration had represented a coordinated, military-inspired intervention into aboriginal territory, and one that had intended substantial environmental change in key locations, it had met with no greater success than had the British efforts of the 1750s. Despite the persistence of occasional tensions between settlers and aboriginal inhabitants,[68] and of debates among aboriginal leaders during the mid-1770s over the merits of support for the revolutionaries,[69] the Halifax regime had settled into a pattern that made it only the latest of the many imperial intrusions that the aboriginal nations had been able to domesticate since the early seventeenth century.

The Loyalist migration, beginning in earnest in 1782, was different. Most important, the Loyalists arrived with crude force of numbers. At least thirty thousand Loyalist refugees flooded into Nova Scotia, which from 1784 onwards was divided into the three provinces of Nova Scotia, New Brunswick, and Cape Breton. Although they met aboriginal resistance in some areas, ranging from Antigonish to Fredericton, this was a migration that was fully capable of filling in the valleys and the interstices of the region.[70] The Loyalists did not lack for military support, either from forces deployed to Nova Scotia for the purpose or from the presence among the settlers of disbanded Loyalist troops.[71] Yet the primary force of their transformative effect was environmental. No longer were either lack of settlement numbers or an enforceable treaty relationship containing forces. Instead, the chief constraint now was simply the limited quantity of productive agricultural land in the region. Even this was insufficient to prevent substantial encroachment on aboriginal lands, and the severing of aboriginal communication routes by settlement. Although in places some versions of the hunting-gathering-fishing economy were able to persist for a time, the aboriginal nations now faced a defensive struggle that had little likelihood of success in the foreseeable future. Even the fur trade – which, as Julian Gwyn has shown, expanded greatly during the Loyalist era – became largely the preserve of poor Loyalists rather than aboriginal hunters and trappers.[72]

Examination of settler–aboriginal relations in Planter Nova Scotia, therefore, reveals that the Planter migration represented, in one sense, a failed military intervention. There was, of course, more to the Planter communities than just that, as there had been to the Acadian communities before them. Yet the existence of Planter Nova Scotia as an arena in which imperial outreach came into direct interplay with indigenous nations, with settlement on a scale insufficient either to conflict with imperial objectives or to undermine the environmental basis of aboriginal society, casts the role of the Planters as being entirely distinct from the role and the experience of colonial populations in the more populous areas of the Thirteen Colonies. This does not mean that the Planter experience was less significant either historically or historiographically. Rather, the Planters participated in a pattern of interactions that was more global than conventionally North American. They were members, as Elizabeth Mancke has aptly put it, of 'Another British America.'[73] The imperial state was present and visible. P.J. Marshall has observed of the East India Company in the same era that, although far from establishing any imperial ascendancy in India, it had emerged as 'a regional power of some consequence.'[74] While events in the subcontinent were unfolding on a much larger scale, it was true in the same sense that in Nova Scotia the British state also had established itself as a regional power of some consequence. Its base was secure in Halifax, it had a lesser capacity to influence developments in the areas of rural settlement, and it had little ability to do so at all in the larger swaths of territory that lay beyond. It was unthinkable that aboriginal inhabitants should ignore the British presence, and vice versa. Yet it was not at all clear what if any kind of ascendancy might eventually separate the two sides, and whether *Pax Britannica* or *Pax Indigena* would prevail. Ultimately, the Loyalist migration settled the question. In the process it eclipsed the treaty relationship for some two hundred years, during which any active recollection of the eighteenth-century treaties persisted primarily in the aboriginal record. The Loyalist migration also removed Nova Scotia from a globalized pattern of imperial–aboriginal relations, and placed it in the more limited context of more closely resembling an eastern North American settlement colony.

In this context, the older questions regarding Planter settlement re-emerge in a newer context. Or, rather, the two traditional questions – why the Planters did not give substantial support to the American Revolution and what made the Planters distinct from the Loyalists – coalesce into the same question. What were the characteristics of Planter Nova Scotia that distinguished it and its colonists from the rebelling colonies and from those of their inhabitants who were protagonists on one side or the other? The overarching answer to the question, however, can best be approached by posing a newer one that can and should be applied by historians to any and all areas of early modern northeastern North America: what were the prevailing balances among aboriginal, imperial, and colonial interests? In Planter Nova Scotia, the simple reality was (though its implications were far from simple) that the relationship between colonists and the imperial state was not a compelling issue. More urgent was the relationship between colonists and aboriginal neighbours. Most pressing of all, here and in other areas of the world where the increasingly rambling – and, at home, ideologically disputed – empire came in contact with a seemingly infinite variety of indigenous peoples, the real question concerned the future shape of relations between the imperial state and the aboriginal societies.[75]

That Nova Scotia should be, in a sense, a laboratory for the application of such a significant global question to British North America was not new in the Planter era. The same comment can be made regarding the earlier part of the eighteenth century, as the consequences of the Conquest of 1710 unfolded.[76] The Planter era, however, was distinct in that the imperial–aboriginal relationship was more direct than had been true as long as the Acadians and the French imperial state had been important factors in the region. On the other hand, Nova Scotia in this period had a lesser claim to uniqueness in this regard. There were now comparable conjunctures in the southern part of the continent, and the British acquisition of Florida in the 1763 Peace of Paris raised questions there that related closely to those current in Nova Scotia.[77] Affinities with more westerly cross-cultural meeting places, as examined by Richard White and others, were less marked because of the largely non-state character of encroachments in these areas to this point.[78] Planter Nova Scotia, however, belonged to a world that did not include the heavily settled colonies of what was to become the eastern United States. As Ernest Clarke has most recently shown, the origins of some Planter settlers inclined them, in combination with controversies during the winter of 1775–6 over the removal of local militias to Halifax, to create a small revolutionary movement.[79] In reality, however, by joining the Planter migration the settlers had crossed into a different sphere from that which had spawned the rebellion. It was one in which loyalism was a possible and relevant choice, because of the crucial significance here of the imperial state as well as the more pragmatic influence of the economic and military power of Halifax, but where the revolutionary crisis further south could reasonably be seen as a local difficulty that impinged but little on the wider world of which Planter Nova Scotia formed a part.

As regards the settlers themselves, the crucial historiographical flaw in so much of the analysis that flowed from the work of Brebner and his successors was that it posited a symmetrical choice for the Planters – they could be revolutionaries, they could be loyalists, or they could avoid the choice altogether by being apathetic. In reality, however, the symmetry was absent. Active loyalism was indeed an option, but even that choice would not excuse the Planters from their more urgent involvement in working through the relationship between the state and the aboriginal nations as embodied in the treaties and lived out in the region every day. Ironically, of course, it was the revolution that brought an end to this phase in the region's experience by prompting the flood of Loyalist refugees. This inundation swept away the characteristic patterns of Planter Nova Scotia. Now, as Loyalist scholars have shown, the imperial state had to define itself in relation to colonial rather than aboriginal interests.[80] Colonial interests, in turn, could define themselves in isolation from increasingly marginalized aboriginal neighbours and in a relationship with the imperial state that would shift over time until in the mid-nineteenth century the initiative in state-building lay with colonial rather than imperial elites. None of this, however, should overshadow either the distinctness of the historical experience, or the historiographical importance, of those who lived in Mi'kma'ki/Wulstukwik or in Nova Scotia during the preceding era, when *Pax Britannica* and *Pax Indigena* hung in the balance.

PART FOUR

Commemoration

11 Chronologies, Counterfactuals, Trajectories, and Encounter 1604

The failure of the French settlement at St Croix Island during the winter of 1604–5, coming hard on the heels of the disasters encountered by the earlier French colony on Sable Island, had profound consequences. It was a crucial setback, in that it was instrumental in persuading the French state that commercial interests must be pursued without colonial settlement. The commitment of the state to the colonizing plans of the de Monts expedition had always been insecure, with the powerful minister the duc de Sully the leading sceptic. Severe critics of the enterprise were also found among competing merchants whose interests had been infringed upon by de Monts's fur-trade monopoly.[1] When word reached France in the summer of 1605 that the St Croix venture had resulted in substantial loss of life without significant commercial success, de Monts's merchant opponents were quick to renew

---

This essay derives from a paper presented at the Encounter 2004 Conference, Saint John, NB, on 30 September 2004. I am grateful to Greg Marquis, Jacques Mathieu, and Nicole Neatby for valuable comments on earlier versions of the text. I am also greatly indebted to my Saint Mary's University colleague Andrew Seaman, whose guest presentations to my graduate seminar formed my introduction to chaos theory. Although this was the last of the papers I delivered in connection with the 2004–5 anniversaries, its chronological scope makes it logically the first to be included here. One of the difficulties of marking anniversaries is that they tend to reinforce the instinctive sense that the past could only have unfolded in one pattern – the one represented by the anniversary. While there was a playful element in this essay – I enjoyed the opportunity to have a creative freedom beyond what is normally allowed to historians – the serious point is that even slightly different contingencies could have altered considerably the processes that flowed from the events of 1604–5. The essay was first published in *Port Acadie: Revue interdisciplinaire en études acadiennes* 6–7 (Autumn 2004–Spring 2005), 163–75.

their protests against the monopoly. It was damaging to legitimate commerce long pursued through transatlantic sojourns confined to the summer trading season, they argued, while promising no counterbalancing benefits to the state. De Monts himself arrived in France during the autumn of 1605 to make the case for the monopoly's continuation, but matters had proceeded too far. The best he could secure was a one-year continuation to cover the 1606 trading season, but only on condition that all colonial settlement would be dismantled by September of that year. Even the newly constructed habitation at Port Royal would have to be burned or demolished, to set the seal on the abandonment of settlement as a strategy for French resource exploitation on the east coast of North America. Seasonal voyages would now prevail as the basis for the fur trade.

There were some among the would-be colonists who were reluctant to accept that settlement in the Americas, which had proved to be a successful strategy for the Iberian powers in Central and South America, had been so conclusively discredited as an approach to be followed by France in northeastern North America. Jean de Biencourt de Poutrincourt, who was personally close to Henri IV and had received the king's explicit permission to participate in the 1604 expedition, had been promised a seigneurial grant at Port Royal by de Monts.[2] During the autumn of 1605, Poutrincourt not only gave forceful support to de Monts's lobbying efforts, but also advanced his own claim to royal confirmation of his land grant. Unsuccessful on both counts, he sailed for Port Royal again in 1606, but never revisited North America after returning to France at the end of the trading season. De Monts himself entertained hopes of gaining a further extension of the trade monopoly by promising to move to an alternate location that was geographically further removed from the seasonal operations of rival merchants. In close association with Samuel de Champlain, a cartographer who had sailed in a junior capacity with the expedition of 1604 and had stayed at Port Royal during the winter of 1605–6, de Monts proposed to set up a fur-trading settlement at a site known as Quebec. When merchant opposition to the monopoly and Sully's scepticism proved to be an insurmountable combination, however, de Monts resigned himself to remaining in France to cultivate his access to royal patronage in other areas. Champlain, who had visited the Caribbean during a partly documented absence from France at the turn of the seventeenth century,[3] turned to promotion of French settlement efforts in that region, with noticeably more success than in northeastern North America.

There was a certain irony in the timing of the French retreat from North America, for the potential had existed for another major argument in favour of colonial settlement, which might have tipped the balance differently. In 1604 Henri IV had requested that the Jesuit order send two of its members to accompany the French fishing fleet in the North Atlantic. Although at that time the principal purpose had been to serve the spiritual needs of French fishers, the correspondence also mentioned the possibility of missionary activity among North American aboriginal inhabitants.[4] Negotiations were still in progress when the issue became moot because of the final withdrawal from Port Royal in 1606. This did not quite mark the end of the discussion of missionary activity among the aboriginal nations of northeastern North America, for the writings of Marc Lescarbot set off a brief revival of interest in 1609. Lescarbot, a French lawyer and writer who spent the summer of 1606 at Port Royal, is best known for his *Théâtre de Neptune*, an elegiac pageant written to commemorate the French departure from Port Royal and first performed there in the autumn of 1606. Added to the written version of the piece as a postscript was a translated version of the speech given on the same day by the Mi'kmaq *sakamow* Membertou, who had expressed his frustration that the French habitation was to be abandoned despite the lengths to which neighbouring Mi'kmaq had gone to extend to it their toleration and their willingness to trade. Lescarbot, on his return to France, began work on a history of French involvements in North America. Angry in tone, it was entitled *L'échec de la France en Amérique septentrionale*. Among other themes, the book lamented the loss of opportunities to convert such amenable aboriginal inhabitants to Christianity, which Lescarbot attributed to the decision to withdraw the trade monopoly and thus undercut the settlement of Port Royal. Probably deliberately, as Lescarbot was closely associated with Poutrincourt, the book gave a temporary momentum to Poutrincourt's intermittent efforts to revive the notion of colonial settlement. Discussions took place in 1610 with a potential patron – Antoinette de Pons, marquise de Guercheville – on the possibility of combining the fur trade with a missionary effort at Port Royal, but ultimately went nowhere in the absence of convincing evidence that colonization could ever be a workable approach in northeastern North America. In later years, missionaries did travel with some seasonal fur-trading voyages, just as they continued to do on fishing vessels. A few overwintered in aboriginal villages, but there was no serious attempt to reproduce the settled missions that characterized the Spanish colonies in Mexico and elsewhere.

More generally, the clear lack of interest shown by the French state in promoting or even facilitating settlement activity after the St Croix failure had further, longer-term consequences. Among merchants in such ports as Rouen, St-Malo, and La Rochelle, scepticism of the commercial returns to be derived from colonial settlement was powerfully reinforced by the attitude of the state. Even the level of investment gathered by de Monts in 1604, inadequate as it had been, would have been unthinkable five years later. Instead, the fisheries and the fur trade began to operate along increasingly similar and interrelated lines. Although French offshore fisheries on the Grand Banks continued to follow the existing pattern of the green fishery, with fish salted wet in barrels on board ship and brought to France directly from the fishing grounds, the dry fishery on the mainland coast of North America developed significantly. Pursued initially by French Basques, the dry fishery now became a common technique for vessels from all the major Atlantic ports of France. In the operations of some merchants, it was combined with the fur trade, either through parallel voyages by different vessels with the same ownership or – increasingly by the mid-seventeenth century – in larger vessels that would set sail with both a fishing crew and a fur-trading crew. While the fishing crew would set up its installations on the shore, or simply reoccupy those that had been used in previous years, the trading crew would disperse to a variety of inland locations that had been identified as agreed trading points with aboriginal inhabitants. At the close of the season, all would foregather at the original harbour to load the vessel with dry salt cod and accumulated furs, and would depart for France by mid-October.

The French state had a clear interest in advancing and protecting these commercial patterns. Together, the North Atlantic fisheries and the fur trade made up a large proportion of France's resource trades, with substantial investors in Paris as well as in the western port cities. The French navy expanded during the middle decades of the seventeenth century – especially after the Newfoundland War of 1661–2, in which English naval forces succeeded in fending off French efforts to establish a dry fishery on the south coast of the island – to support the marine-based strategy of excluding all foreign competitors from an area of coastal North America stretching from the western tip of Long Island to the north shore of the Gulf of St Lawrence. Within that northeastern zone, French merchants plied their vessels seasonally, and aboriginal trade networks converged on trading sites located at the mouths of major rivers. The dry fishery flourished, on a scale ultimately exceeding the similar English fishery in Newfoundland. English and Dutch efforts to encroach on the French sphere of influence were effectively rebuffed, although a rival English sphere of influence emerged out of the colonial settlement of Virginia. Because the Virginian economy was based on tobacco as a cash crop, the rapid expansion of colonial settlement was a logical progression, accompanied as it was by increasing reliance on the forced labour of enslaved Africans. English energies were increasingly preoccupied with developing the plantation economy and with managing an ongoing series of conflicts between Spanish Florida and the Puritan settlements that had been established along its borders during the 1630s. Thus, Greater Virginia, extending from the Savannah River to the Delaware, marked in effect the northern limit of European colonization of the Americas. All territory further north saw extensive trade, but remained firmly under the control of aboriginal nations until the mid-eighteenth century. Then, in a manner analagous to the operation of the English East India Company, the French *Compagnie de l'Amérique du Nord* began to assert its hegemony over a gradually expanding area of the northern interior of the continent. Trade had finally led to colonization, though the numbers of the colonizers always remained small in relation to the aboriginal population.

The foregoing, of course, outlines a course of historical development that never took place in linear historical reality. Yet it is more than just an imaginative work of fiction. Rather, consideration of possible courses of development that would have flowed from alternatives anticipated by contemporaries can offer a useful corrective to teleological or even deterministic orthodoxies, such as the notion that seventeenth-century colonization of northeastern North America was somehow inevitable. Counterfactuality, it is true, has never been fashionable as a form of historical enquiry. It has frequently been dismissed contemptuously and associated with the notion, in the words of the historiographer E.H. Carr, 'that history is, by and large, a chapter of accidents.' Carr cited in particular 'the famous crux of Cleopatra's nose.'[5] The reference was to the contention that if Queen Cleopatra's nose had been differently shaped, Mark Antony might not have found her personally attractive. In that case, Mark Antony's quarrel with Octavius Caesar (later Caesar Augustus) would never have taken place, the Second Triumvirate would have endured, and the Roman Republic would never have given way to the Roman Empire. This argument was endorsed in summary form in a famous essay by J.B. Bury, a British historian of the early twentieth century whose impeccable academic credentials as an exponent of 'scientific history' included a lengthy term as Regius professor of modern history at Cambridge.[6] Bury's purpose was to explore the role of contingency in history, and notably the results of 'the valuable [i.e., consequential] collision of two or more independent chains of causes,'[7] without necessarily going on to speculate about what might have taken place had the intersection somehow failed to take place. Nevertheless, in later twentieth-century historiography, even Bury's cautious formulation was ridiculed by historians who saw chance as, at best, a neutral factor in the unfolding of broadly based and long-term forces of historical causation.[8]

The essential criticism, that an over-concentration on the role of chance and contingency in history would tend logically to reduce historical interpretation to a farcical confection of meaningless narratives, carried force and continues to do so. The point has been reinforced by Ged Martin's recent admonition that any consideration of alternative courses of historical development 'should not be an invitation to fantasize about what might have come about, but a device to help us reinforce the significance of what actually did happen.'[9] Yet historians cannot properly ignore the reality of unpredictability. As Martin also pointed out, 'events become historically significant if we can reasonably assume that a markedly different outcome was plausible.'[10] Moreover, the diversity of possible outcomes is and has been a basic influence on human thought and action. How, therefore, to take account of unpredictability without reducing the past to chaos?

Ironically, historians wrestling with this conundrum can find assistance in a body of scientific argument known as 'chaos theory.' Although having its origins in a larger body of non-linear approaches to natural science going back to the turn of the twentieth century, chaos theory in its modern form was a product of the 1960s and 1970s. It continues to develop, of course, doubtless in non-linear directions. The meteorologist Edward N. Lorenz began in the early 1960s to publish a series of studies of global atmospheric patterns, and some thirty years later wrote more generally on *The Essence of Chaos*.[11] His most striking and most celebrated contention was contained in a paper delivered in 1972, though unpublished until 1993, entitled 'Predictability: Does the Flap of a Butterfly's Wings in Brazil Set off a Tornado in Texas?' The most minuscule of atmospheric disturbances, Lorenz argued, can have enormous results. Furthermore, the complex combinations of stable and unstable air are beyond human power to define or fully understand, rendering weather patterns unpredictable at any given time and place.[12]

The implications of carrying this logic into historical study are far-reaching and, at first sight, can be taken to justify all the fears of the harshest critics of contingency-based interpretation. However, the nuances of Lorenz's contentions and of chaos theory in general argue otherwise. Significantly, Lorenz's 1972 paper was not a dismissal but an affirmation of the possibilities of weather forecasting. Like all studies in chaos theory, it had not one but two essential elements. It was characterized first by relying on the principle of 'sensitive dependence on initial conditions,' implying that any active phenomenon can set subsequent events on a trajectory that may start as being only subtly different from other possible trajectories, but will vary more widely from their assumed path as time goes by and may well be affected also by subsequent unstable influences. Thus the unpredictability. Secondly, however, chaos theory asserts that there is an underlying order to such events. Their unpredictability lies not in any fundamentally random pattern, but in the complexity of detail that makes the unfolding of processes undefinable in any all-encompassing sense. Chaos, in this context, is not the anarchic chaos of the popular definition of the word, but a way of recognizing the limits of human explanatory power when causation is complex. As defined by Peter Smith, this paradigm of chaos theory is characterized by the 'combination of large-scale order with small-scale disorder, of macro-predictability with the micro-unpredictability due to sensitive dependence.'[13]

Transferred to historical analysis, therefore, chaos theory does not threaten to reduce the human experience to a random collection of chance occurrences. Rather, it leaves untouched the need for historians to wrestle with questions of causation and relate them to broad currents of historical change. At the same time, it allows the inherent complexity of any and all series of events to be recognized. Together with the unavoidable incompleteness of evidence, with which historians have always laboured, this complexity accounts for the existence of – and the necessity for – different and competing historical interpretations of the human past. Furthermore, by affirming the importance of trajectories and the unpredictability of their emergence, chaos theory also points the way to a cautious and limited use of counterfactuality by the historian.

Counterfactuality has been explored by many historians, but frequently in ways that, at least implicitly, trivialize its significance: as speculative asides (what, for example, would have happened had Montcalm not ordered a precipitous advance on the Plains of Abraham?), as whimsical attempts at humour or entertainment, or as computerized projections based on questionable statistical premises.[14] The most significant recent effort to provide counterfactuality with a serious theoretical justification was contained in a collection of essays edited by Niall Ferguson in 1997. In *Virtual History: Alternatives and Counterfactuals,* Ferguson's introduction reviewed earlier objections to counterfactuality and the implications of chaos theory. For Ferguson, counterfactual investigation could be justified only if an essential condition were fulfilled. Namely, counterfactual alternatives to actual historical developments had to be plausible in the specific sense that consideration should only be given to 'those alternatives which we can show on the basis of contemporary evidence that contemporaries actually considered.'[15] This criterion established, counterfactuality could be seen as a logical way of testing interpretive assertions on historical causation. It could also be an essential step towards comprehending the different possibilities that contemporaries envisaged as they contended with the unpredictability of their own experience, and towards a historical recognition that what actually took place was often not what contemporaries had anticipated and planned for. Historiographically, Ferguson also argued, counterfactual arguments could take a useful role in exposing determinist tendencies – acknowledged or, more often, unacknowledged and even unconscious – in interpretive orthodoxies.[16]

The essays in *Virtual History* dealt primarily with major events in Western history since the seventeenth century, and what would have happened had they turned out differently or been avoided altogether: the English Civil War, the American Revolution, the two world wars, the defeat of Nazism, the collapse of the Soviet Union, and others. Ferguson added a synthesis, linking the events and non-events together.[17] However, a similar logic can be applied to counterfactual analysis of historical processes, and no historical process has suffered more from unacknowledged deterministic tendencies as the European colonization of the Americas. Historians have debated vigorously the reasons for the time lapse between colonization of Central and South America and that of North America, for the different forms that colonization took in various localities and among European national groups, for the varying impacts of colonization on aboriginal inhabitants, for the political processes that separated some colonies from their imperial origins, and a host of other issues. On the supposed ineluctability of the settlement process and its assumed primacy as an expression of imperialism, however, there has been much less questioning. Seen in this context, consideration of the 1604–5 experience of the St Croix Island venture has much to tell us, for it represented an effort to establish a colonial settlement in an area far removed from where any such attempt had enjoyed success. At the same time, St Croix Island was situated squarely in a region of established economic interest to Western European merchants. The results were highly uncertain, and were clearly perceived as such by contemporaries, but one way or the other would equally clearly have considerable consequence.

The St Croix Island settlement existed within not one but a series of chronologies, each of which had its own trajectory. In terms of western European exploitation of the natural resources of northeastern North America, 1604 was not the beginning or even close to the beginning. Fishing vessels of varying nationality had harvested cod from the offshore banks for more than a century. For fifty years or more, French Basque fishers had frequented inshore areas of the Gulf of St Lawrence and the coasts of what was to become known as Nova Scotia. Basque whalers had also been active on the Strait of Belle-Isle, while the English dry fishery on the coast of Newfoundland was also well established. Wherever fishers came into close proximity with aboriginal inhabitants, trade took place, frequently involving the exchange of furs for European manufactured goods. The 1580s, however, brought a marked acceleration of trade activity, as expansion of European markets for beaver fur coincided with environmental and political disruptions of the traditional supply routes from eastern Europe. For the first time, the fur trade could be pursued profitably as a venture distinct from the fishery. While the number of voyages to the Gulf of St Lawrence, and to the mouth of the Saguenay River in particular, showed the most rapid increase, the enterprise of de Monts was also inseparably linked to this quickening of trade, which was also beginning at this time to extend the reach of European fishing and trade into the Gulf of Maine. As a commercial venture, therefore, St Croix was only the latest point in a long existing chronology, but it was a chronology characterized by a strong and recent upward push in its trajectory.[18]

As an episode in state involvement in the Americas, 1604 was also a point in an extended chronology, although one that had significant complexities and interruptions. At the most general level, the Iberian powers had exerted state authority since the early sixteenth century in efforts to extend their realms into the Caribbean, Central and South America, and Florida. For Spain the political and fiscal rewards had been spectacular, notably in Mexico and Peru, while Portugal had established a plantation-based economy in Brazil that drew on the larger variety of Portuguese state-encouraged ventures in Africa and the Atlantic islands. For the emerging nation states of northern Europe, these were attractive models. The French state gave its sponsorship on a number of sixteenth-century occasions to voyages that sought to rival the Iberian achievements, whether on the St Lawrence in the 1530s and 1540s, or later in the century in Florida. The English state made its own attempts in Newfoundland and Virginia.[19] All of them, French and English, failed quickly and abjectly. The early seventeenth century offered the promise of new state involvements overseas, as state security increased in France, England, and soon afterwards the Netherlands. The end of the French Wars of Religion, sealed in 1598 by the extension of a measure of religious toleration to Huguenots through the Edict of Nantes, brought a stability that the French state had not enjoyed for half a century. The Treaty of London, signed with Spain in 1604, freed the English state from its most pressing external threat. The truce of 1609 between Spain and its rebellious Dutch provinces essentially ensured the independent existence of the Netherlands. Given that all three states faced pressures from merchant communities with important overseas interests, and depended in turn on the merchants for fiscal stability, there was no option for each state but to respond. The form of the response, however, was much less certain, especially in the context of depleted treasuries. As Elizabeth Mancke has pointed out, the large areas within which European states attempted to carve out spheres of interest – or even of domination – included oceans as well as lands. By 1604 there was no clear answer to the question of whether the northern European states would countenance territorial claims overseas or only seek to protect the routes that crossed oceanic expanses with commercially significant coastal peripheries.[20] Thus, although there was a lengthy chronology of state engagement overseas, its trajectory was passing through unstable space.[21]

As for the chronology of attempts at European colonial settlement of North America outside of Florida, it barely existed by 1604. It was true that attempts had been made in locations ranging from Florida to Quebec by would-be settlers from England, France, and Portugal. It was true also that settlement could take a variety of forms. Although there had been sixteenth-century colonizing efforts that brought women to North America, as did the Roberval expedition to Quebec in 1542–3, male predominance was the norm. Thus, the transplantation of a non-aboriginal society to North America was not necessarily the implication of a colonial expedition. As was the case with the St Croix and Port Royal endeavours, the immediate goal was rather to facilitate extended or permanent overwintering for commercial purposes. What bound together all preceding efforts, however, was their failure. Whether through Spanish intervention, miscalculation of environmental constraints, or fatal ignorance of the need for aboriginal toleration, every venture had ended in withdrawal or collapse. Colonization in any form remained a highly questionable notion, perhaps worth pursuing for commercial reasons but still without a hint of a proven likelihood of success. Thus, for all essential purposes there was no chronology and no trajectory. Instead, for North American colonization in 1604, there was only a profoundly sensitive dependence on initial conditions. What took place at St Croix Island would have consequences for the French outreach to North America, but further colonization was only one of the possible results.

The longest chronology of all was that of the aboriginal nations of northeastern North America. Continuous human occupation had existed for at least 11,000 years. While linear change through time was not a preoccupation of northeastern aboriginal cultures, material evidence documents a lengthy evolutionary process, with the emergence of the direct cultural ancestors of such Algonkian-speaking peoples as the Mi'kmaq and Wulstukwiuk at least 2500 years before the opening of the sixteenth century. Starting around 1500, give or take a decade, intermittent contacts with European fishers began, with its accompanying small-scale trade. Although the contacts became more frequent over time, it was only as the seventeenth century approached that the fur trade assumed an existence independent of incidental encounters through the fishery. For aboriginal inhabitants, European contact and trade brought certain changes. Trade goods such as knives and kettles made for greater speed and efficiency in discharging existing tasks, but at the same time European disease made its appearance. Historians debate the dates and the severity of epidemics, just as they also deliberate over the extent of cultural and environmental change brought about by the fur trade. Recent scholarship, however, counsels caution in attributing disruption and decline to aboriginal societies. David S. Jones has cast doubt on the notion of epidemics caused solely by an alleged lack of immunity to European disease. The late Ralph Pastore found no evidence of major epidemics anywhere in northeastern North America during the sixteenth century. William Wicken has emphasized the adeptness with which aboriginal societies were able to domesticate non-aboriginal intrusions of any kind, through the seventeenth and far into the eighteenth century. The trajectory of aboriginal northeastern North America was long and steady. European contact did promise some instability, but it could just as easily lead – as Membertou for one clearly anticipated – to a florescence of traditional culture through trade as to the more historiographically conventional process of weakening and dislocation.[22]

Thus, at St Croix Island in 1604–5, a number of historical processes intersected. The longest and steadiest of existing chronologies were those of aboriginal societies and European mercantile outreach. The St Croix venture, whether a success or a failure, was unlikely to be anything but incidental to those two, although it could conceivably nudge their interactions on to a subtly different trajectory. The involvement of the state in North American affairs was also likely to continue, but its mutability in 1604 meant that – at least as far as France was concerned – de Monts's enterprise might well have consequences leading in any one of a number of directions. Colonial settlement, however, was a doubtful proposition. Even the limited attempt made by the de Monts colonists to set up a permanent overwintering base invited scepticism from those who questioned its value to the state or saw it as an infringement of their own commercial interests. The failure at St Croix and the retreat to Port Royal gave renewed force to the critics, with unpredictable results. The counterfactual narrative that began this chapter would have portrayed a fully plausible sequence of future developments. I have argued elsewhere that, as matters turned out, the events of 1604–5 led over time to an unusual coexistence of colonial and aboriginal societies in Mi'kma'ki/Acadie, and that the importance of this development offers a legitimate basis for commemorating the anniversaries of 2004–5.[23] It is important to remember too, however, that those who lived through the events of four hundred years ago did not know that they were creating grist for the mill of later commemorators. For them, there were many possible outcomes. It was clear that trade contacts between aboriginal inhabitants and non-aboriginal sojourners were going to continue for the foreseeable future. But what would be the nature of state involvement, to what extent if at all colonization would be pursued, and what would be the longer-term results? The ultimate answers to these questions would depend upon sensitive dependence on initial conditions and trajectories passing through unstable space.

12 Champlain: Longevity and Commemoration

In Canadian popular memory, Samuel de Champlain is often remembered as a colonizer and a leader of colonization in what is now Canada. Many books have been written about Champlain, and their subtitles are often revealing. 'Father of New France' was the sobriquet chosen by Samuel Eliot Morison for the subtitle of his biography of Champlain published in 1972, and it echoed a phrase used many years before by N.E. Dionne.[1] 'Founder of New France' had been the designation selected by both Charles W. Colby and Ralph Flenley for early-twentieth-century biographies published respectively in 1915 and 1924.[2] Morris Bishop's classic work of 1948 was entitled simply *Champlain: The Life of Fortitude.*[3] But what does it mean to cast Champlain in the role of colonial leader? What *was* a colony in northeastern North America in the early part of the seventeenth century? What did it take to establish one and perpetuate it? Was fortitude enough, or was there a particular com-

---

This essay originated as a public lecture delivered in August 2004 in Petite Riviere, Lunenburg County, Nova Scotia. It was one of a series presented there during a single weekend, commemorating Samuel de Champlain's visit to Petite Riviere – the name first appeared on the map he drew on the basis of this visit – in 1604. The other presentations in the series were by Joan Dawson, Elizabeth Jones, and Jean de Saint Sardos. I do not claim any particular expertise on Champlain's career, and certainly not by comparison with others who have written extensively about him and whose works are cited in the essay's endnotes. What I set out to do, however, was to assess the reasons that might prompt us to remember such a person as a significant historical figure as opposed to an iconic creation. I am grateful to Thomas Peace for his valuable comments on the initial draft of the essay, and to Christopher Gill for organizing the lecture series. The essay was printed for limited circulation in Christopher Gill, ed., *The Champlain Lectures* ([Bridgewater, NS: Lighthouse Publishing, 2005]), 28–39.

bination of skill and luck that was also needed? At first sight, questions such as these may seem deceptively simple, or even simplistic. I hope to establish, however, that they need to be asked and that answers need to be found if we are to be able to assess satisfactorily the career of a colonizer such as Champlain.

The study of Champlain's life has lost some of its attraction for historians in recent years. The last major biography was published by Joe Armstrong in 1987.[4] The works of Marcel Trudel published or initiated during the 1960s, meanwhile, still retain their primacy as analyses of the colonial contexts of Champlain's career. Trudel's studies range from a concise but indispensable biography in the *Dictionary of Canadian Biography* to the relevant passages of his series on the origins and seventeenth-century development of New France.[5] This is not to say that there is an absence of more recent work bearing on Champlain's role in New France. The focus, however, has been different. Reflecting the increased importance attached by both anthropologists and historians to the aboriginal history of the early modern period, authors such as Bruce Trigger and Denys Delâge have set Champlain's career in this context. While a number of Trigger's works do so, the 1985 study *Natives and Newcomers: Canada's 'Heroic Age' Reconsidered* is especially effective in demonstrating the limitations of Champlain's understanding of aboriginal protocols and the resulting difficulties that attended his interactions with aboriginal nations in both peaceful and hostile situations. Delâge, meanwhile, offered in the same year a different emphasis, attributing to Champlain an ability to gain sophistication in matters of trade and gift-giving that involved aboriginal allies.[6] Most recently of all, a number of essays in *Decentring the Renaissance,* edited in 2001 by Germaine Warkentin and Carolyn Podruchny, have explored the French response to the indigenous nations and physical environment of northeastern North America, with the personal role of Champlain receiving attention notably in the context of his ability to obtain and interpret aboriginal historical and geographical knowledge.[7]

This essay will attempt to sort out these issues in such a way as to offer a modest reassessment of how we might look at Champlain during this four hundredth anniversary of the expedition that led him to the south shore of what is now Nova Scotia, on to St Croix Island, and then to Port Royal. Beginning with a summary account of Champlain's various experiences as a colonizer, I will then broach the question of what colonization really meant in this time and place – that is, in the northeastern North America of the early decades of the seventeenth century. I will then explore what Champlain himself thought about the colonization of New France, and go on to assess the outcomes of his efforts in the context of the predominantly aboriginal character of the territories in which he sought to colonize.

Champlain's colonizing experience, considering that almost all of it unfolded in northeastern North America, was remarkably varied.[8] His one major experience outside northeastern North America came at the turn of the sixteenth century. Following the end of the French Wars of Religion in 1598, Champlain travelled to Spain and then on a voyage to the Spanish West Indies. How and why he travelled there, and what conclusions he may have drawn from what he saw, are questions that have no well-defined answers. Although an account of such a voyage was described in a 'Brief discours' later attributed to Champlain, doubts about the provenance of this work are sufficient to make it unreliable as a historical source. By his own repeated statement, however, Champlain did visit the West Indies at about this time and would have observed at first hand the Spanish efforts to base colonization here on mining of precious metals and increasingly – though with mixed success – on the production of sugar. He would also have had cause to reflect on the complex effects of colonization on the aboriginal inhabitants of the islands, as wholesale depopulation during the earliest years of Spanish colonization had given way in some places to the successful resistance of the Island Caribs to Spanish domination. This resistance was still active, notably on islands such as Guadeloupe, at the time of Champlain's visit, which took place more than a century after Spanish colonization had begun. Thus, Champlain's sojourn in the Caribbean likely added significantly to his understanding of the results of European overseas expansion and, as David Quinn has suggested, he may have refined it further by relaying his assessments to King Henri IV in the capacity of 'Henry's principal overseas intelligence agent.'[9]

Returning to France in 1601, Champlain waited two years to have the opportunity to expand his first-hand perspective on colonial possibilities – and to communicate it again to the Crown and to metropolitan merchants. In 1603, he sailed with the large-scale commercial expedition of François Gravé Du Pont to the St Lawrence valley, and spent a good part of the summer observing trade between the French and aboriginal inhabitants, notably at Tadoussac, and probing the river valleys of the region. He gathered geographical knowledge from aboriginal informants, both regarding the Great Lakes and the existence of a large salt-water bay to the north that would later bear the name Hudson Bay.

Although this expedition was not intended to leave behind a colonial establishment, Champlain did observe what he regarded as an ideal site for a habitation at Trois-Rivières:

> There is [an island] in the middle of the said river [St Maurice], opposite the channel of the river of Canada, and commanding the others which lie four or five hundred paces distant from the shore on either side. It is high on the south side, and falls somewhat toward the north side. In my judgment this would be a place suitable for settlement, and might be quickly fortified; for the situation is strong of itself, and near a large lake, not more than some four leagues distant. It almost connects with the Saguenay river, according to the report of the Indians, who travel nearly a hundred leagues northward, and pass many rapids, then go by land some five or six leagues, and enter a lake, whence the said Saguenay takes the best part of its source; and from the said lake the Indians come to Tadoussac. Moreover a settlement at Three Rivers would be a boon for the freedom of some tribes who dare not come that way for fear of their enemies, the ... Iroquois, who infest the banks all along the said river of Canada; but if this river were inhabited we might make friends with the Iroquois and with the other [natives], or at the very least under protection of the said settlement the said [natives] might come freely without fear or danger, inasmuch as the said Three Rivers is a place of passage.[10]

This account of Trois-Rivières is worth not only quoting at length but also pondering for a moment, as it embodies a number of ideas about colonization that would influence Champlain in later years. The importance of fortification and the defensibility of an island site were prime considerations. But also essential was proximity to aboriginal travel routes and trading networks. Finally, Champlain explicitly saw one of the roles of colonization as being intervention in inter-aboriginal relationships in whatever way would benefit the commercial interests of the French. The nuances of such an undertaking were as yet far beyond Champlain's range of understanding, but the intent was clear.

In the following year, 1604, Champlain sailed again for northeastern North America. Although he was not formally among the leaders of the expedition of Pierre Du Gua, Sieur de Monts, in his role as a geographer Champlain exerted considerable influence, especially over the choice of sites for settlement. The expedition was explicitly commissioned by the French crown to make a colonial establishment, although it was also a commercial enterprise. De Monts had assembled a group of merchants from four major ports and signed them on to the ten-year fur-trade monopoly he had received from the Crown. Experience would show that the solicitation of private subscriptions had serious deficiencies as a means of raising capital in the amounts necessary to launch a serious colonial expedition, by comparison with later alternatives such as the Crown-sponsored trading company, but just four hundred years ago the would-be colonists set up their habitation on St Croix Island. Following a disastrous winter of cold and scurvy, the remains of the group set up the habitation at Port Royal in 1605. Here, a close relationship with Mi'kmaq neighbours was quickly formed and fur-trading activities began, no doubt assisted by the existence of an already-lengthy history of earlier trade relationships that had led to the development of a *lingua franca* based on Mi'kmaq, Basque, and French. However, protests from competing merchants prompted the Crown to cancel the de Monts monopoly, and Port Royal was abandoned in 1607. For Champlain, the affair offered a graphic demonstration of why an island was not a good site for colonization – despite the defensibility of St Croix Island, it had proved to have few resources and in winter the ice made the mainland inaccessible. In this situation, its proximity to an aboriginal travel route was of no help until the spring. Port Royal, however, had proved much more workable, and the value of a harmonious diplomatic relationship with the powerful Mi'kmaq *sakamow* Membertou was also evident. Thus, of the criteria for settlement that Champlain had brought from Trois-Rivières, some had been discredited and others vindicated.

Although the French presence at Port Royal would be re-established in 1610, by this time Champlain had struck out in a new direction. Returning to North America in 1608, he had an official position as lieutenant to de Monts. Having managed to obtain a one-year extension to his trade monopoly, de Monts instructed Champlain to return to the St Lawrence region, where he established a habitation at Quebec. Although the purpose remained primarily commercial, from 1608 to 1611 Champlain also immersed himself in diplomatic and warlike pursuits among the aboriginal inhabitants not only of the St Lawrence valley itself but also of the Houdenasaunee territory. In doing so, Champlain carried out one part of the program he had set out in 1603 at Trois-Rivières by allying with aboriginal trading partners – Montagnais Innu, Algonquin, and Huron – to push the Mohawk back from the St Lawrence region. Two major victories for the French-allied forces, one in 1609 and one in 1610, were assisted by Champlain and his use of firearms. Along with the availability of Dutch trading goods to the Mohawk (either directly or through Mahican intermediaries) after the Dutch voyage up the Hudson River in 1609, these actions effectively eliminated the Mohawk influence for a number of years from the St Lawrence region. Colonization and trade were henceforth linked to French involvement in the larger complex of interrelationships among aboriginal nations, and although Champlain had not entirely created this dynamic – French-Houdenasaunee tensions predated 1608 – his actions had undoubtedly reinforced and perpetuated it. For the French, there would be a price for Houdenasaunee enmity, although given the tenuous position of French colonization there arguably would have been a greater price for attempting to stand aloof from the clash of more powerful forces. Further extensions of the same principle came during the years up until 1618, when Champlain increasingly moved the French commercial sphere of influence westwards. Although making regular voyages to France to look after commercial and political business, he also frequented the countries of the Algonquins and Hurons and even wintered among the Hurons in 1615–16. He was also drawn again into conflict with the Houdenasaunee.

Soon, however, Champlain reached a crisis. The security of his colonial role already lessened by the death of his royal patron, Henri IV, in 1610, the withdrawal of royal favour from his subsequent patron and the viceroy of New France, the prince de Condé, led in 1617 to Champlain's loss of his position as lieutenant at Quebec. Active on his own behalf in France, he made strenuous efforts to find new sources of patronage both in the imperial state and among metropolitan merchants. On the basis of detailed proposals he advanced in 1618 to the Crown and to the Paris chamber of commerce – which will be discussed in greater detail below – Champlain won restitution of his official position although with only a tenuous and ultimately ineffective royal commitment to reinforce the settlement of the colony. The 1620s did see, however, continuing efforts under Champlain's leadership to reinforce and partially rebuild the habitation at Quebec, to initiate Recollect and Jesuit missionary activity (which had important patronage implications in France) throughout the territories of aboriginal allies, and to consolidate trade networks through ongoing diplomatic activity. A further crisis intervened, however, in 1628. During the Anglo-French war of 1627–9, an English force led by the brothers Kirke – whose personal origins included French Huguenot – launched a seaborne attack on the St Lawrence. Champlain put off defeat by refusing the Kirkes' demand for surrender in July 1628 and exaggerating for effect the defensive capacity of Quebec. However, a year later there was no room for bluff, and the habitation was surrendered to the Kirkes in July 1629. The timing was devastating for French interests in North America, as only in 1627 the French crown had signalled a new degree of involvement in imperial schemes through the creation of the *Compagnie des Cent-associés*. Not only did the Kirke conquest – along with the concurrent occupation of Port Royal by a Scottish colonial effort under the name of New Scotland, or Nova Scotia – throw the plans of the *Cent-associés* into confusion, but also, worse still, the Kirkes succeeded in capturing a major supply fleet sent by the company to New France. For his part, Champlain left Quebec soon after the conquest and did not return for almost four years.

Yet this experience of the vulnerability of tiny colonial habitations to external force did not prove to be the end of New France or of Champlain's career there. The conquest of 1629 had taken place after the signing between France and England of the interim peace treaty of Suza. When negotiations began for the final Treaty of Saint-Germain-en-Laye (signed in 1632), French diplomats demanded the restitution of Quebec and their English counterparts made no objection. In July 1632 the English departed from Quebec, and some ten months later Champlain landed there to command in the name of Cardinal Richelieu. By this time Champlain was ageing, and although he was apparently in good health it was only two and a half years before he was incapacitated by a stroke. He died in December 1635.[11] The Canada over which he exercised command during the early to mid-1630s had changed in subtle but telling ways. Although the *Cent-associés* had been severely weakened by the setbacks of earlier years, and the company fell far short of its initial goals of expanding the fur trade while sending four thousand colonists in its first fifteen years, the year 1634 did bring the first new colonists since 1617. The immigrant groups of this era included not only skilled artisans but also family groups. Champlain responded by speeding the rebuilding and refortification of the damaged habitation at Quebec, and also initiating new ones at Trois-Rivières and at the confluence of the Richelieu and St Lawrence Rivers. Plans to start another at Montreal were put off for the time being. Westward extension of the French fur-trading network was another priority, and in 1634 Champlain dispatched Jean Nicollet, a minor official of the *Cent-associés*, on a diplomatic mission to aboriginal nations in the Great Lakes region. Nicollet was also charged with finding the elusive route to China, which still figured prominently in Champlain's thinking about the ultimate commercial significance of New France. While Nicollet never got to deliver the elaborate Chinese-style robe that he brought along as a gift for the Asians he hoped to encounter, he did add substantially to French geographical knowledge.

The Canada of the 1630s also had a profoundly ecclesiastical character. Jesuit missionaries were prominent at Quebec, and undertook lengthy voyages of evangelization as far afield as the Huron country and beyond. Champlain appears to have given personal encouragement to this renewal of the religious purpose of colonization – in the context, of course, of the potential commercial benefits that could also flow from missionary activity – at least according to the Jesuit superior Paul Le Jeune:

> The wise conduct and prudence of Monsieur de Champlain, Governor of Kebec of the River Saint Lawrence, who honours us with his good will ..., has caused our word and preaching to be well received ... The fort has seemed like a well-ordered Academy. Monsieur de Champlain has some one read at his table, in the morning from some good historian, and in the evening from the lives of the Saints.[12]

Samuel de Champlain's colonial career, therefore, encompassed a variety of forms of colonization even though from 1608 onwards it was pursued exclusively in Quebec and Canada. That this was the case raises the more general question of the nature of colonization in the period of Champlain's active career. Colonization had no single accepted meaning in this era, except the very general criterion that it involved the residency of colonizers – in this case, European colonizers in the western hemisphere – for a period of more than a single season. In this era, much of the European commercial contact with northeastern North America came in the form of seasonal voyages. Although these commercial enterprises might leave lasting traces in North America, whether in the form of wooden fishing installations that were reoccupied from year to year or in the form of local trade networks with which given European traders would make contact annually, by no definition did these voyages involve colonization. As soon as employees overwintered, however, the historian's task of definition becomes more complex. Many of the habitations that contemporaries referred to as colonies contained not a single individual who expected to spend the rest of his life there – and the masculine pronoun is deliberate, since such sites were disproportionately populated by young males. The goal of those who overwintered, even if they did so for four or five consecutive years, was typically to have enough capital from accumulated wages to be able to pursue a trade or some other ambition back in the home country. Some of these individuals, of course, might ultimately choose not to return and would become colonists in the more permanent sense of the word. When women and children were present, whether as a result of European–aboriginal interrelationships or family-based immigration, the dynamic became different again. Then, the possibility of permanence through self-generated population growth could become real, although there were many obstacles to such a development. For one thing, there had to be an economic basis. The Spanish colonies observed by Champlain in his youth depended on mines and the raising of cash crops, both of which demanded populations on the ground. When the economic resources were fish and furs, the case for colonization of any kind – and especially of the kind that involved substantial permanent populations – was not only much weaker but also was likely to be contested by merchants whose business depended on seasonal voyages and who saw colonial installations as unfair competition. As Champlain was well aware, other rationales for colonization could be advanced, but they invariably depended on considerations that went outside the realm of colonization itself and involved imperial and/or aboriginal interests.

The phenomenon of colonization was not the only logical form of imperial outreach. Commercial considerations were always prominent, especially as the financial foundation of the nation state depended to a significant degree on the state's relationships with merchant communities in major port and commercial towns and cities. The state typically also had other interests that could prompt imperial outreach, including a further one that related to public finance, namely, the possibility of mining precious metals. The Spanish example, some elements of which Champlain had observed at first hand, was influential in prompting the states of northern Europe to aspire to similar gains. Strategic considerations were also potentially important, especially insofar as imperial activity could deny resources or important spheres of influence to competing states. Religious activity too was of direct significance to the state, through the prestige that could be claimed on the basis of successful conversion of aboriginal inhabitants to Christianity. Thus, if a case were to be made for colonization in an imperial context, it was never one that was self-evident but had to be linked to other key factors. Colonization also had to be related to the reality of the aboriginal presence. In some areas of the western hemisphere, aboriginal societies were quickly undermined by epidemic disease and systematic violence on the part of the colonizers. Even in some local areas of northeastern North America, notably in the vicinity of Massachusetts Bay, large-scale immigration combined with these factors to create a densely populated non-aboriginal society and a drastically altered physical environment. This situation, however, was the exception rather than the rule in the seventeenth century and especially in the lifetime of Champlain. In most of northeastern North America, any European presence had to gain the tolerance and, if possible, the support of aboriginal neighbours in order to have any chance of survival. Diplomacy was the key, along with trade on favourable terms. Underlying both was the recognition, informal as it might be by comparison with the large territorial claims made by nation states, that northeastern North America remained aboriginal territory despite the existence in some places of colonial establishments of one kind or another.

Knitting together the elements that made for sustainable colonial enterprises demanded certain forms of leadership. A colonial promoter of the early decades of the seventeenth century was characterized by definable skills and abilities, of which one was the ability to relate colonization to wider matters of state and to articulate the case for a particular colonial enterprise to receive state endorsement – though not usually, in this period, state investment. Access to patronage networks was also essential to the enlistment of state support. A further necessity was the ability to mobilize capital, or at least to ensure the existence of merchant networks that were willing and able to do so. Colonial promoters who actually moved to North America required the ability to administer a colonial community large or small, with its inevitably diverse interests, and to coordinate defence against competing European states. Most of all, in northeastern North America, they had to be able to conduct an effective aboriginal diplomacy in a region where the small non-aboriginal settlements existed purely on aboriginal sufferance. In assessing the career of Champlain, there is no doubt of his effectiveness as an officeholder responsible for the continuing operation of the habitation at Quebec, and the regulation of its short-term and longer-term inhabitants. Champlain was also an astute defender of Quebec from actual and potential attack by water, despite the defeat of 1629. Learning from the disaster at St Croix Island that defensive positions could not be maintained at the expense of sustainability in other respects, Champlain henceforth selected river locations that were both defensible and close to aboriginal travel routes that offered not only trade but also the information that aboriginal allies could provide regarding the approach of a hostile fleet. Yet in many respects, for Champlain and for other colonial promoters of whatever European nationality, the principal measures of effectiveness lay in the advocacy of colonization to state and merchants and in the positioning of a colony among aboriginal nations. Champlain, necessarily, was active in both areas.

Throughout his colonial career, Champlain made repeated voyages between France and northeastern North America. At the outset of his career, his travels were undertaken without any official leadership position but likely with an informal mandate from the Crown, and from at least 1603 he was staking out through his publications a growing area of influence on French understandings of northeastern North America and the possible reasons for colonization. By the time he took command at Quebec in 1608, he was an experienced advocate of colonization as a form of imperial outreach. Working at first with de Monts, and then in a more individual manner – though always mindful of the need to attract and retain powerful patrons – Champlain repeatedly articulated the controvertible but sustainable argument that colonization could simultaneously advance the interests both of the state and of the merchants. The high point of these efforts, although they continued to the end of his life, was represented by the proposals he advanced in 1618 to the Crown and to the Paris chamber of commerce.

Champlain's two *mémoires* of 1618 presented sophisticated arguments designed to justify North American colonization – and thus, of course, the interests of Champlain himself and his patrons – and to persuade both leading metropolitan merchants and the state itself to underwrite colonial activities. The first of the two went to the Paris chamber of commerce. Champlain was well aware that he and his commercial associates had aroused controversy through the eleven-year trade monopoly that had been granted in 1613 to Champlain and a company composed primarily of merchants from Rouen and St-Malo. The chamber of commerce itself took note of the complaint of excluded merchants that 'Champlain and his associates in the trade in beaver and other furs ... have not had a single family taken there to settle in the said country, although by charter of their association they were bound to do so, in view of the fact that the freedom of trade is denied and forbidden to all other merchants in favour of them.'[13] Champlain's response was to promise commercial benefit from the colonization of New France on a scale that could not fail to enrich metropolitan merchants as a group. New fisheries (including the hunt for sea mammals), over and above the existing migratory fisheries, would yield the enormous annual sum of 2,000,000 livres. Half of this would arise from cod fisheries, from which an export trade in dry salt cod would compete with English products from Newfoundland, while whale and other sea-mammal products would yield most of the balance, along with salmon, sturgeon, and other species of fish. Timber, masts, and other wood products would produce another 1,300,000 livres, while mines and quarries would add 1,000,000. Cultivation – including raising hemp as a cash crop and as a base for naval supplies – and cattle-ranching would be worth another 1,700,000. This was a key point, as these were the pursuits that most clearly demanded a colonial population. The fur trade, meanwhile, would make up only a modest 400,000 livres from the overall annual total of 6,400,000. And, of course, Champlain pointed out in conclusion, all of this was in addition to the rich profits that would flow once the route to China had been found.[14]

While historical hindsight enables most of this to be dismissed as fantasy, it proved persuasive to the chamber of commerce, which endorsed Champlain's case for colonization and called upon the Crown to offer practical support. Champlain promptly presented his second *mémoire*, this one addressed to the Crown. Emphasizing his own labours in northeastern North America and his success in drawing from aboriginal informants 'such and so faithful a report of the north and south seas that one cannot doubt that this would be the means of reaching easily to the Kingdom of China and the East Indies, whence great riches could be drawn,' Champlain set about relating the supposed benefits of colonization to the interests of the state.[15] Commercial benefits were promised, though not elaborated to the same degree as to the chamber of commerce. Missionary activity would reach 'an infinite number of souls.' Urban development at Quebec (to be renamed 'Ludovica'), and fortification there and elsewhere, would be a complement to agricultural settlement. Together with 'three hundred good men well armed and disciplined,' these colonial establishments would guarantee continuing French control of a vast and resource-rich territory. Moreover, the commercial and tax benefits of the trade with China and the East Indies, which would flow once the water connection between Asia and the St Lawrence had been fully explored, would also be assured to France. The dismal alternative was for France to be pre-empted by the

English and the Dutch, who had already taken over substantial areas of North America and would always be on the lookout for new acquisitions to feed their economies at the expense of France. All these benefits, Champlain concluded, could be attained by the allocation to him and his merchant associates of trade privileges and tax revenues from the resources of New France. It would be, he avowed, 'a holy and glorious enterprise.'[16]

The practical results of Champlain's appeal to the Crown were severely limited. Financial support from the Crown was not forthcoming, and merchant investment remained sparing and subject to the shifting of political as well as commercial calculations. Nevertheless, Champlain did receive the formal endorsement of the Crown, which invited merchant support for his ventures, while the chamber of commerce likewise declared itself in favour. The significance of his effort can be measured not so much in terms of its actual accomplishment in New France (colonial development was far from an exact science, and there were many intractable obstacles beyond the control of any colonial promoter) as by considering its merits as a work of advocacy. Champlain was not himself a merchant, and – by contrast with comparable advocates of colonization such as Sir William Alexander in Scotland, Sir Ferdinando Gorges in England, and Isaac de Razilly in France – he had little independent access to the highest levels of the state. Lacking high state office, or even kinship or feudal ties to those who did hold office, Champlain had to rely on his own exertions from year to year to hold on to his place in key patronage networks. To win the endorsements that he gained in 1618, regardless of what happened next in Canada itself, was a remarkable testimony to his effectiveness in the metropolis.

As for what did take place in the colony itself, much depended not only on French endorsements and investments but also crucially on relationships with aboriginal nations. In this area too, Champlain (like most other European colonial leaders of the time) faced many situations that were beyond his control, given the enormous imbalance of power between tiny European colonial outposts and the much more substantial indigenous societies with which they had to deal. Insofar as Champlain did have the ability to influence events, it was through diplomacy and occasionally through warfare. In both he started with profound disadvantages that arose from his own inexperience and lack of cultural understanding. These difficulties were entrenched rather than alleviated when he enjoyed military success in supporting aboriginal allies against the Houdenasaunee in 1609 and 1610. While it was true that the use of French firearms had provided a surprising and temporarily effective ascendancy for the allied forces, Champlain appears also to have exaggerated the prestige that his role had generated. His efforts in subsequent years to intervene in disputes involving aboriginal allies, and to influence their selection of leaders, were invariably clumsy and ill conceived. When not actually counterproductive, they received bare toleration. In handling military alliances too, Champlain had serious limitations. Not initially understanding the linkages between diplomacy and warfare among the Hurons, Champlain allowed himself to be manoeuvred into closer alliances against the Houdenasaunee in 1615 than he had anticipated, while during the late 1620s he abandoned the notion of seeking peace with the Houdenasaunee in favour of attacks on them whenever possible despite their presenting little immediate danger to French interests. To the killing of a French envoy in a Houdenasaunee village, Champlain responded by observing: 'I have noticed in these nations that, unless you resent offences committed against you ... they will some day come and try to cut your throat, if they can manage it, by a sudden surprise, as their custom is.'[17] When combined with an absence of cultural understanding that enabled Champlain, for example, to condemn the 'uncivilized ways' of the Huron and to declare that even in matters of religion they 'recognize no divinity, and believe in no God nor in anything whatever, but live like brute beasts,' such crude generalizations betrayed little trace of an appreciation of the subtleties of either hostility or alliance.[18]

Yet there is an additional context within which to assess Champlain's dealings with aboriginal inhabitants and nations. While his cultural assumptions and political misjudgments set the limits, there remained an area within which Champlain was able to operate in a more realistic manner. First, Champlain consistently recognized the importance of aboriginal knowledge in matters of geography and technology. In matters of transportation, and in formulating plans to reach geographical areas that were potentially important for resources or trade routes – and in his dogged pursuit of the route to China – Champlain had no hesitation in drawing on aboriginal assistance to make up for his own lack of comprehension.[19] In diplomacy Champlain did have a firm grasp on at least one of the essential principles: the demonstration of respect and friendship through gift-giving.[20] It was an understanding that could go a long way towards solidifying alliances that, in other respects, Champlain had only an uncertain ability to sustain. More generally, Champlain – for all the bluster and the ethnocentricity of so many of the observations that he put in writing – recognized that the French in northeastern North America were too weak to survive without aboriginal cooperation and alliance, much less be able to pursue expansionist goals. About to travel westwards in 1615 from the future site of Montreal, he reflected on Huron requests for military assistance: 'It was very necessary to assist them, both to engage them the more to love us, and also to provide the means of furthering my enterprises and explorations which apparently could only be carried out with their help.'[21] Whatever the inadequacies of Champlain's conduct of aboriginal relationships in their nuances and details, there was a certain pragmatic humility in his actions that was not always reflected in his words. As an elementary recognition of what it took for an exotic venture to exist in an overwhelmingly aboriginal milieu, it was better than nothing at all.

In conclusion, to characterize Samuel de Champlain as the father, or founder, of New France seems overly facile in the light of the evidence as we currently understand it. The establishment and perpetuation of the French presence in North America depended on many others beyond just Champlain, and those others came from many backgrounds. They did not only include other colonial promoters such as de Monts, Gravé Du Pont, and Razilly, but also extended to key decision-makers in the imperial and aboriginal realms. French colonization itself came in many forms, and it is questionable whether one individual can properly be made emblematic of them all. Yet it remains true that Champlain was an important, even a remarkable figure. His long career as a colonizer, much of it spent in leadership roles, spanned many diverse kinds of colonial experience: colonization as a marginal extension of commerce, colonization aimed at carving out a resource-rich territorial sphere of influence, colonization by family groups with a view to population growth, colonization as a basis for religious conversion. If variety was one hallmark of his colonial career, longevity as a colonial leader was another. In an era when most European colonial attempts in northeastern North America were short-lived, colonial promoters and officials came and went with breathtaking speed. Champlain, by comparison, went on forever – or at least until he died while still at Quebec. Other than Charles de Saint-Étienne de La Tour in Acadia and William Bradford of Plymouth, it is difficult to think of a contemporary who came close to matching him. No doubt luck took a role in Champlain's persistence through so many years of intermittent setbacks, but there were also important respects in which he set his own course through skill and persistence. In the standard tasks of the colonial official –

including administration of the colony and its population, and defence – Champlain showed a steady competence. As an advocate of North American colonization to the imperial state and to metropolitan merchants, he was diligent and sophisticated even though the actual results were always mixed. In his aboriginal diplomacy, Champlain often showed his limitations, but did not – as counterparts elsewhere sometimes did to their cost – allow his lack of cultural understanding to lead him into the trap of neglecting the central importance of aboriginal relations. Thus, in an era when imperial outreach did not necessarily imply support for colonization itself, and when aboriginal nations could and did expel colonizers if they so chose, Champlain's form of colonial enterprise not only survived but also evolved over time. Survival represented in itself a significant level of success. The luxury of an evolving vision of what colonization meant and what it could accomplish was a bonus to which few other colonial leaders were able to aspire. In this sense, Samuel de Champlain is indeed a figure worth commemorating.

13 Reflections on Seventeenth-Century Acadia

One hundred years ago, when those who were so inclined commemorated the anniversaries of events such as the de Monts / Champlain landings of 1604 and the foundation of Port Royal in 1605, they did so with every apparent sign that they were confident in what they were commemorating and why they were doing so. What could be more beneficial in its results, for those who were staging commemorations in the early twentieth century, than the arrival in this part of the world of the bearers of European civilization? And who could be more daring and intrepid than transatlantic voyagers such as Pierre Du Gua de Monts and Samuel de Champlain? Nowadays, in the early twenty-first century, we are much more cautious in what we celebrate. We are acutely conscious, and properly so, that there is no single story of 1604–5, any more than there is any single story of the entire seventeenth century as it unfolded in what is today the Maritime region. Rather, there were and are various narratives, and what sense we make of this time period

This essay was first presented to a conference on 'Anniversaries That Work / Des anniversaires réussis,' held in Amherst, NS, in May 2003. An innovative and proactive joint venture of the Federation of Nova Scotia Heritage and the History Section of the Nova Scotia Museum, the conference set out to provide a forum where members of the heritage, museum, university, and tourism communities could exchange ideas in connection with the approaching 2004–5 anniversaries. The event was generally agreed to have succeeded remarkably in bringing together a diverse group and in prompting productive conversations. My contribution was intended to underline some historiographical developments that had a bearing on how we might understand the anniversaries. Hitherto unpublished in English, the essay first appeared as 'Réflexions actuelles sur l'Acadie du XVIIe siècle,' *Port Acadie: Revue interdisciplinaire en études acadiennes* 5 (Spring 2004), 11–24.

depends essentially – as all history does – on what questions we choose to ask about the past.

It is only fair, of course, that we bear in mind that those who commemorated the anniversaries a hundred years ago were living through, as we are today, times of rapid and potentially destructive change. The novelist Hugh MacLennan reflected late in life on his early-twentieth-century upbringing in Glace Bay and Halifax by recalling: 'I ... grew up with the feeling that we were very much a part of the world – of the terrible world of the 20th century.'[1] There is no doubt that anyone who was old enough in 1904–5 to have anything to do with the de Monts / Champlain celebrations would find plenty to worry about in the world around them. The major powers were already embroiled in the arms race that would lead a few years later to the slaughter of the First World War. The fatal attack on U.S. President William McKinley, shot by an anarchist in Buffalo, New York, in September 1901, was only the latest in a series of recent assassinations of major heads of state. Soon afterwards the young Albert Einstein put forward his special theory of relativity. Although it would take time for Einstein's insights of 1905 to have their full effect, as human beings our understanding of the universe around us would never be the same again. Another young European scientist, Sigmund Freud, was already in the process of showing that human beings themselves were much more complex and sinister creatures than anyone had hitherto believed. Closer to home, Maritimers were leaving the region in large numbers to find employment in the United States, while those who remained had to try and come to terms with the complex legacy of late-nineteenth-century industrialization. Class conflict was acute in factories and coal mines, while at the same time Maritime entrepreneurs were increasingly selling out or being taken over by interests based elsewhere in Canada. Those of us who live in the current era of emerging electronic technologies are often fond of congratulating ourselves about what we may see as the unprecedentedly rapid pace of change in the world around us. No doubt in some respects we are justified in that perception, but I have a strong feeling that we would be hard pressed to sustain the point if those who lived one hundred years ago could somehow miraculously be here to debate it with us.

What connects all this with current thoughts about northeastern North America in the seventeenth century is that there was a strong sense in the commemorations that took place in the early 1900s that the past provided an escape to a time when life was simpler and better. De

Monts and Champlain – although, as Ronald Rudin has pointed out, the Protestant de Monts at times received noticeably greater acclaim than the Catholic Champlain, the latter increasingly gained celebrity[2] – could be seen as heroic adventurers whose efforts led over time to the many achievements of European settlement in the region. For the distinguished New Brunswick scholar W.F. Ganong, for example, there was an almost dream-like quality about the ceremonies in Saint John, especially when de Monts and his cohorts came ashore to mingle with volunteers who simulated a welcoming aboriginal delegation. 'They took possession of the land,' wrote Ganong, 'with formal ceremony in the name of the King of France, and their new [native] friends danced the war dance about them. All this part of the ceremony was extremely effective. In fact so well was it done that I quite forgot for a time that it was a show.'[3] Ganong and others were well aware, of course, that the colonizing process had its tensions and conflicts, but these could be seen as incidental to a process that was ultimately constructive and benign. The same could be said more generally about the seventeenth century as a whole, and indeed about the entire development of non-native society in the region up to the time of the Loyalists and beyond. Today, this formulation would be inconsistent enough with prevailing sensibilities to be unacceptable in either a heritage or a historical context. We are well aware, and again rightly so in my view, that the past is complex and contested. Yet, in certain respects, recent developments in historical analysis may be helpful in enabling us to make sense of a past that we can no longer view through the lens that provided an image so apt and so engaging to our predecessors.

What has changed, then, over the past hundred years and during more recent years, in our historical understanding of the seventeenth century in the territory we now know as the Maritimes? First of all, we have had a hundred years' worth of research by professional historians. A century ago, Canadian history as a disciplined area of study was in its infancy. We are better equipped now to understand the past in all its complexity. But it is not only Canadian history that has evolved. Particularly as a result of research directions over the past twenty or so years, we are also in a better position to understand the anatomy of western European empires and how they encroached on northeastern North America. Historians had already established a long time ago that commerce and colonization were the main results of European outreach in the sixteenth and seventeenth centuries, and that the relationship between the two was variable depending on time and place. Historians today are demonstrating that when empires are examined globally, colonization formed only one manifestation – and often a relatively minor one when compared with commercial interactions – of the imperial exchanges taking place, and that we need to adjust accordingly our perceptions of what people like de Monts and Champlain were really all about. More of this in a few moments. But by far the most important change in recent years, at least in my view, is the belated recognition by professional historians that aboriginal history is *central* to any realistic understanding of seventeenth-century North America, or of any other place in the world where Europeans interacted with powerful indigenous civilizations.

This is not the time or place to consider at length why such a seemingly obvious insight escaped so many otherwise able historians for so long. It undoubtedly had to do with what was until the late 1960s the small size and narrow social base of the historical profession in this country. Certainly the evidence was there, and aboriginal voices such as that of Grand Chief Gabriel Sylliboy in his courtroom evidence on the treaty relationship in 1928 could have been heard if the historians had cared to listen.[4] In the ranks of professional historians, there was also a dissenting voice, that of Alfred Goldsworthy Bailey of the University of New Brunswick, who was politely ignored by most of his colleagues across the country.[5] Real change began three to four decades ago. Aboriginal leaders themselves began to probe more vigorously the realities of the historical process by which the First Nations had been deprived of access to land and resources. This was a North American–wide renewal, but in this region it was represented notably by the efforts of Mi'kmaq leaders such as Alex Denny and Joe B. Marshall to reactivate the treaty relationship that had been eclipsed but never erased over time. Their efforts were rebuffed at first, but later vindicated by the Supreme Court of Canada. At the same time, young historians of the late 1960s and early 1970s rebelled against what they saw as the failure of their elders to ask the right questions about the aboriginal role during the so-called colonial period of North American history. The result of these parallel developments has been that our historical understanding of the relationship between native and non-native people in the seventeenth century (and in the two adjacent centuries also) has changed in ways that are fundamental and, I think, irreversible.

Accordingly, I would suggest that we need to re-evaluate the older-established interpretations both of the de Monts/Champlain expedition and its anniversaries and of the seventeenth century as a whole. Let us come first to the era of de Monts and Champlain. The expedition of 1604, and the resulting efforts between 1604 and 1607 to establish French settlements first on St Croix Island and then at Port Royal, represented at most an incident in the aboriginal history of the region. These developments had been preceded by the better part of a century of trade and cultural dialogue between, on the one hand, the Mi'kmaq and the Etchemin and, on the other hand, western European fishers and traders. When the contacts began is impossible to say, but we do know that by the time of Jacques Cartier's first voyage in 1534 the Europeans' strange interest in old pieces of beaver fur was well known to Mi'kmaq inhabitants of what is now northern New Brunswick. Although the fur trade did not become a large-scale or systematic form of commerce until the 1580s, Basques and others had been returning regularly to the same fishing harbours year after year long before that time. They came repeatedly in contact with aboriginal people, and trade took place on an incidental but ongoing basis.

When actual fur-trading expeditions began to reach the shores of the region in the late 1500s, the relationship changed in some respects. Furs, notably beaver furs, assumed unprecedented importance as a medium of exchange, and for the aboriginal peoples of the region the hunt for beaver came to assume ever-greater significance as a means of gaining access to European technologies and to products such as copper kettles and edged weapons. Yet the depth of the change can all too easily be exaggerated. Aboriginal traders were highly selective in the commodities they traded for, and suggestions by earlier generations of historians that dependence on the fur trade came to undermine the spiritual and political bases of aboriginal society are belied by the ability of peoples such as the Mi'kmaq to retain cultural and political coherence through centuries of contact with non-native societies. The regular seasonal return of French, Basque, and other fishers and traders, therefore, was a resource for aboriginal inhabitants. Like natural resources, it could be managed and harvested in a controlled manner. The de Monts/Champlain voyage was not generically different in this regard. Certainly, it turned out to involve the precarious placement of small numbers of French on the fringe of aboriginal territory, but this too could readily be seen as a resource, and one that involved no surrender of control, territorial or otherwise. The idea that these tiny settlements might one day lead to significant encroachment could quite reasonably be seen as ridiculous. In the meantime, the French presence at Port Royal had solid advantages, especially for those Mi'kmaq who lived in the immediate vicinity, in ensuring the ready and ongoing availability of trade goods.

From the French perspective too, the efforts of 1604–7 had important elements of continuity with previous voyages. Although de Monts was equipped with a colonial claim made by the Crown of France to an area of North America stretching from today's Pennsylvania to Cape Breton Island, the venture was also a commercial effort. Its monopoly of the fur trade in the region was underwritten by the investments of merchants from a number of the major French ports. The mercantile calculations that prompted this investment did not differ greatly from those that soon thereafter would prompt English settlement attempts in Newfoundland. Both stemmed from the pursuit by merchant entrepreneurs of the most effective and profitable ways to exploit North American resources. To have employees on duty year-round to ensure that the best opportunities to acquire fish and/or furs were taken quickly and efficiently made good business sense as far as it went. More sceptical merchants, however, claimed that it would never work because the cost of supporting colonial communities would be too high. Another difficult issue would be the question of whether the placing of resident employees in North America by some merchants but not others would lead to unfair competition. This was the controversy that would eventually destroy de Monts's fur-trade monopoly in 1607, while in Newfoundland it would smoulder on for the better part of two centuries as English merchants tried to combat the growth of colonial residency on the island. Be that as it may, in Acadia the sharp disputes that pitted de Monts and his fellow-monopolists against competing French merchants showed clearly the extent to which the entire venture of 1604–7 was a commercial one, aimed not so much at establishing something new as at conducting an existing trade more profitably.

Thus, we have to be very careful before we start claiming that the de Monts/Champlain expedition represented a dramatically new departure in the history of the region. In many respects it simply enabled both the dominant aboriginal nations and the handful of French would-be colonizers to do in a slightly different way what they had already been doing for many years. Does this mean, then, that there is little or nothing to commemorate in 2004 and 2005? Far from it, in my view. As well as adding significantly, for better or worse, to the western European store of geographical and knowledge of northeastern North America – in ways that were reflected, for example, in Champlain's remarkable map-making – the de Monts/Champlain expedition did set the course of aboriginal–French relationships on a subtly different trajectory. I say *subtly* different, because the significance of what had taken place was not necessarily clear at the time. But like every alteration in trajectory, its importance became more and more evident as time went on. Several years ago, I wrote of the decade of the 1600s as one of the most crucial in all of the history of the Maritime region.[6] What made it so pivotal, I still believe, was that it saw the decision of aboriginal peoples in the region to tolerate and interact with small settlements of non-natives.

As I have indicated, this was not an altogether revolutionary decision, given the earlier history of trading relationships. Nevertheless, it was a decision that could have gone the other way, as similar decisions did in neighbouring areas. In Newfoundland, by 1612, the Beothuk had reached the conclusion that the best approach to English settlement was to stay away and have no direct interaction. This was, arguably, a decision that served the Beothuk well for a century and a half, despite the disasters that afflicted them in later years. In Maine in 1608, meanwhile, Wabanaki forces effectively expelled the English from their tiny settlement at Sagadahoc. It was true that the colonists were already weakened by disease and internal disputes, but the reality there and elsewhere was that it was the aboriginal nations who decided whether any given settlement would survive or not. They had all the power they needed to tolerate the non-native presence or not, as they thought best.

In Mi'kma'ki, and in the neighbouring territory of the Etchemin – among whose descendants would be the Wulstukwiuk and Passamaquoddy – the decision was to tolerate and even encourage European settlement. No doubt, like all decisions in a consensually governed society, this one was controversial, though in ways of which surviving evidence does not allow us any precise knowledge. But it was a crucially important decision, and one that was reaffirmed in varying forms in later years. Despite the temporary removal of the French from Port Royal in 1607, the French presence in the region was continuous from 1610 onwards. This included a period of several years after Port Royal was burned by an English expedition in 1613, when the French contingent numbered only a dozen or two (including the famous father and son Claude and Charles de La Tour) who lived by fishing and trading on the southwest coast of what is today peninsular Nova Scotia. That Mi'kmaq approval was essential to their survival is not only self-evident from their circumstances, but is also indicated by the alliance represented by the younger La Tour's marriage to a Mi'kmaq woman whose name is unknown to us but who with La Tour had three daughters whose legitimacy was acknowledged even in France.[7] The Mi'kmaq toleration was not extended only to the French. When Scottish settlers established themselves at Port Royal in 1629, they were soon visited by two native delegations who made it clear that the same trading relationship that had been long established with the French was equally open to the Scots. A further important development came about during the following decade. Scottish settlement at Port Royal lasted only until 1632, and when the French re-established themselves in that year it was not at Port Royal but at La Hève. Only in 1636 did the French return in any substantial numbers to Port Royal, although even yet the Acadian population took until mid-century to reach a level of some 350.[8]

The major change that had taken place in the 1630s involved the presence of women and children. The colonies established by the French in earlier years had been largely or completely male. Thus, they were not colonial settlements at all in the sense that people expected to live out their lives there. Like comparable English settlements in Newfoundland, they were places disproportionately occupied by young males whose goal was to stay for a few years and then return home with a small amount of accumulated capital. The colonial promoter Charles d'Aulnay, however, began in the 1630s to recruit family groups for his renewed settlement at Port Royal. In association with this change, marshland agriculture began to assume the central role within the Acadian economy that it would occupy well into the eighteenth century. Still essential, however, was aboriginal forbearance. The question was whether Mi'kmaq tolerance would continue to be extended to a non-native group that no longer represented just a trading and fishing enclave, but instead might give rise over time to significant population growth based on an agricultural economy. That coexistence did continue was owed in part to an important environmental factor. Acadian agriculture, as is well known, was carried on largely by draining and cultivating the marshlands of the Bay of Fundy. This was true in the Port Royal region, and it continued as subsequent generations of Acadians moved to Beaubassin in the 1670s (that is, the area where we now are) and to the shores of the Minas Basin in the 1680s. The marshes had limited importance to the Mi'kmaq economy, and seventeenth-century Acadian agriculture was not yet sufficiently extensive to compromise Mi'kmaq access to coastal resources such as waterfowl. Therefore, Acadian marshland cultivation did not present the same kind of direct challenge that was offered, for example, by English agricultural settlement to the Wabanaki in what is today the state of Maine.

Yet this environmental consideration does not explain completely the toleration that was extended by aboriginal inhabitants to the Acadian population. Also required was an ongoing commitment on the part of Mi'kmaq and Etchemin leaders to refrain from using the military power which they unmistakably possessed and could have used at the expense of the much weaker non-native presence. This is where the experiences of 1604–7 again become relevant. The decisions made at that time by aboriginal leaders had rested on the possibilities of trade and the likelihood of being able to establish a diplomatic relationship with the newcomers, thereby gaining the economic and military advantages that came with access to trade goods. These remained important considerations, and over time they coalesced into an attitude and an approach to non-native settlements that was largely consistent among aboriginal leaders in the region throughout the seventeenth century. A non-native presence at Port Royal proved consistently acceptable. For much of the century this implied a French presence, but at times it was either Scottish or English. The Scottish experience in 1629, as already indicated, was one in which Mi'kmaq diplomatic overtures followed quickly after initial settlement. From 1654 to 1670 Port Royal was loosely occupied by English forces, and New England traders were active on the major rivers of the region. While evidence of their activities is sparse, the fact that they were trading at all is an indication that they had established a working relationship with Mi'kmaq and Etchemin inhabitants. By the end of the century, intensified imperial disputes between England and France were introducing new complications, and Mi'kmaq and Etchemin/Wulstukwiuk forces participated intermittently in raiding warfare on the English settlements in northern New England. Yet when the British completed what would be their final conquest of Port Royal in 1710 – an inter-European squabble from which Mi'kmaq forces largely stood aloof – it took only a few weeks for Mi'kmaq representatives to initiate diplomatic discussions aimed at extending to the British occupants privileges similar to those previously enjoyed by the French.

Thus, the encounter between the French expedition of 1604–5 and the aboriginal leaders of the region had profound consequences. Although the events of 1604–5 can hardly have seemed all that extraordinary to those who experienced them, the trajectory then followed by later events was one that brought a century and more of remarkable coexistence. Nevertheless, it is important also to define what kind of a coexistence this was. The relationship between French settlement and the aboriginal nations was not always an easy one, any more than was the eighteenth-century treaty relationship between those nations and the British. We are not talking here about relationships that were comfortable or always congenial. Rather, we are examining something more complex and more dramatic. These were relationships between two sides, native and non-native, composed of peoples who differed widely from one another in cultural terms. They were peoples who often misunderstood each other, who often mistrusted each other and who at times had good reason to do so. Nevertheless, warily and fully conscious of what they were doing, they chose to live side-by-side. The non-natives did so primarily because they had no choice. For the Mi'kmaq and the Etchemin, trade was always an important consideration. Also crucial was the extent to which the non-native presence continued to fulfil certain criteria. First, it had to be restricted in scope: to Port Royal, the Fundy marshlands, and a few trading sites around the region. Second, there must be a respectful diplomatic relationship. European colonizers of any nationality would contravene these restraints at their peril. Intermittent frictions were common enough. Certain sources of tension were more apt to arise from the actions of French traders or officials than from those of Acadians themselves: a French trader might be presumptuous enough to show up uninvited in an aboriginal village rather than staying in the accepted trading location, or there might be disputes over the weights and measures used for trade goods, or a French officer might expect aboriginal military cooperation when it had not been offered. More generally, there might be any one of many reasons for incidents between native and non-native individuals. Nevertheless, both sides would generally abide by the rules.

But how unusual was all this in seventeenth-century northeastern North America? One answer is that it was not as unusual as older-style historical interpretations might have us believe. For a variety of reasons, historians have given enormous attention over the years to the seventeenth-century experience of southern New England, and notably to the colony of Massachusetts Bay. There, the arrival of large numbers of English settlers during the 1630s coincided with the reduction of aboriginal populations by epidemic disease. Clearance of forest on a large scale, and English military force that was highly effective on a localized basis, did the rest. Environmental change was drastic, and aboriginal resistance was fatally undermined by the defeat of the Wampanoag leader Metacom in 1676. Yet the Massachusetts Bay experience was essentially a local phenomenon. If northeastern North America is considered as a whole, European colonization made a much lesser impact everywhere else, other than in small areas of the Connecticut, Hudson, and St Lawrence valleys. Northeastern North America remained overwhelmingly aboriginal territory, and in that sense Mi'kma'ki and Wulstukwik were not exceptions to the general rule.

In another sense, though, this region *was* unusual. What made it exceptional was the combination of the role of the aboriginal nations and the role of the Acadians. I emphasized at the beginning the importance of the commercial causes of European imperial expansion. Had it not been for the commercial ambitions of Pierre Du Gua de Monts, the events of 1604–5 would never have taken place. Acadia, however, was never a successful venture from the point of view of imperial trade. Its resources of fish and furs could be exploited by seasonal voyages without either private merchants or the French state having to go to the expense of supporting colonization. Insofar as colonial settlement did take place, it was on a scale that was too small to justify the merchants in involving themselves in commercial interactions with the Acadians themselves. Any merchants who tried to do so during the first half of the seventeenth century ended up losing large amounts of money. As a result, Acadian communities quickly lost any immediate sense of day-to-day contact with France. For their economic needs, they had no option but to rely upon neighbouring peoples: specifically, on aboriginal neighbours for supplies of furs and other goods, and on visiting New England traders for certain essential imports such as spices and textile goods. This pattern led in turn to the emergence of a political pragmatism that enabled the Acadians to adapt to the occupation of the fort at Port Royal by a variety of regimes both French and British. It was a pragmatism that prompted efforts of many (though not all) Acadians to remain neutral in the face of imperial conflicts, and one that, as Maurice Basque has shown, owed much to the example of aboriginal nations and their ability to maintain diplomatic relations with diverse European nationalities.

In conclusion, I would re-emphasize that the seventeenth-century history of the territory we now know as Nova Scotia, and of the larger territory we know as the Maritimes, is *primarily* aboriginal history. This is so not only because most of the people living here were aboriginal people, but also because it was aboriginal leaders who had the power (though always within a consensual framework) to make most of the really important and fateful decisions of that era. The seventeenth-century history of the region is not, of course, *only* aboriginal history. The de Monts/Champlain expedition had important results for both aboriginal and non-aboriginal peoples, in that it generated an ability to coexist that continued throughout the ensuing century and beyond. The patterns of that coexistence, I would suggest, have major historical importance because although they reflect in part the wider reality of northeastern North America, they are also unique in the sense that in this region aboriginal toleration was complemented by Acadian pragmatism in a way that led to a unique form of wary but healthy mutual regard. This is surely an attainment that fully justifies commemoration of the events of 1604–5 and of other developments as the century went on. The key to the most effective commemoration, though, has to depend on our ability to avoid any sense of the past as quaint or of its people as simple folk. The people who lived in this region during the seventeenth century, be they native or non-native, lived lives that were just as important to them as are yours and mine to us. They laughed, they cried, they celebrated, they struggled. Most of all, their lives were just as complex and just as unpredictable as ours, and they lived with these realities as best they could, as all human beings must. Insofar – and only insofar – as we can recognize these people of the past as being just as fully human as we ourselves are, thus far we will be well placed to recognize and commemorate what they said and did in 1604, in 1605, and at other times.

14 Epilogue

The processes that flowed throughout northeastern North America following the era of the establishment of French colonization at the beginning of the seventeenth century were complex, unpredictable, and full of contingencies. The development of colonial habitation, except in geographically restricted enclaves, was never a linear phenomenon. Imperial exchanges were characterized by fluid social relations, and a continuing process of negotiation and renegotiation. Aboriginal engagement proceeded from extensive territorial control and a military capacity that was tenaciously applied to the underwriting of diplomatic activity. Of course, across the seventeenth and eighteenth centuries, broad changes took place. Colonial populations increased, and they expanded spatially. Empires gained in coordination and in aggression towards both aboriginal and imperial competitors. Aboriginal leaderships faced territorial erosion and economic pressures. Yet the continuous interaction of colonial, imperial, and aboriginal influences in a contested northeastern North America admitted of no simple or ineluctable patterns of change.

Nowhere were these complexities more evident than in those areas of northeastern North America most directly concerned with the four hundredth anniversaries of 2004 and 2005. In 1978, the noted Mi'kmaq poet Rita Joe had delivered an admonition to researchers in an untitled

This epilogue is based on thoughts presented in a paper to the Society for the History of the Early American Republic at the Université de Montréal in July 2006, and developed in more mature and extended form in an address to the 'History Across the Disciplines' graduate student conference at Dalhousie University in March 2007. I am very grateful for the valuable responses of both audiences.

poem published in both Mi'kmaq and English: 'Let them find/Land names, / Titles of seas, / Rivers; / Wipe them not from memory. / These are our monuments. / Breathtaking views– / Waterfalls on a mountain, / Fast flowing rivers. / These are our sketches / Committed to our memory. / Scholars, you will find our art / In names and scenery, / Betrothed to the Indian since time began.'[1] While the poem affirmed the continuing existence of Mi'kma'ki in a cultural sense, the long eclipse of the treaty relationship between the Mi'kmaq and the Crown continued at that time to restrict the degree to which Mi'kma'ki could function in legal and political contexts. Meanwhile, a new generation of Acadian poets during the 1970s – such as Guy Arsenault, Herménégilde Chiasson, and Raymond LeBlanc – captured the urgency of an era when critical struggles over language rights had cast doubt on the effectiveness of the progressivist national vision that in 1955 had suffused the marking of the two hundredth anniversary of the *Grand dérangement.* 'Ta maison / çé ton ché vous,' wrote Arsenault in 1973: 'Shédiac by the sea / Bouctouche sur mer / J'ai faim de l'Acadie / et j'ai soif de la Parole.'[2]

By the early twenty-first century, much had changed. Notably in New Brunswick, where the provincial official languages act and such departures as the establishment of an autonomous francophone education system had lost their controversial edge, linguistic tensions had given way to a broadly based recognition that the persistence of Acadie was not only essential for Acadians – and recognized in the royal proclamation of 2003 – but was also integral to the overall cultural and political fabric. The persistence of Mi'kma'ki, and of Wulstukwik, had gained constitutional momentum from the enshrinement of aboriginal and treaty rights in the 1982 Constitution of Canada through the *Charter of Rights and Freedoms.* In this context, the eighteenth-century framework of negotiated relationships had already bequeathed a formal matrix of treaty obligations, which had been forgotten only on one side. Memory of the treaties remained continuous in the oral record-keeping of Mi'kmaq and Wulstukwiuk, and surfaced from time to time in written form, in reported conversations, petitions, and in occasional legal proceedings.[3] From the mid-1980s a new series of legal cases reached a crucial point with the decision of the Supreme Court of Canada in favour of Donald Marshall in 1999. The cases continued beyond the turn of the century, but also – this time notably in Nova Scotia – increasingly coexisted with a negotiation process that now proceeded from an established recognition that the treaty relationship was legally valid but also in need of renewal.

What had not changed was the centrality of historical understanding to any effort to make sense of the continuing coexistence of the long-established entities of Mi'kma'ki, Wulstukwik, and Acadie within a northeastern North America where conventional cartography did not include them. Nor did an ingrained historiography. The emergence in an academic context of new historiographical frameworks, within which the observation could readily be advanced that aboriginal, imperial, and colonial influences had intermeshed in complex and long-lasting processes, was insufficient in itself to erase entrenched understandings that still enjoyed wide currency in society at large. For too long, in the study of early modern North America, there existed a kind of Robert's Rules of Order by which the principal expression of empire was taken invariably to be colonial settlement, and the ability of colonial settlement to extend spatially to the point of marginalizing indigenous groups was held to be unassailable. Aboriginal societies, colonies, and emergent North American nation states chased each other across the historical stage but always in their strictly appointed chronological order. That the reality was layered rather than linear, and that the layers did not disappear with time, was not reconcilable with such a resolutely teleological construct. Yet the construct itself continued to live out its tenacious half-life, not so much any more in textbooks but certainly in the imaginations of those who had learned it from the textbooks and the teaching of not so long before.

Anniversary commemorations, such as those of 2004 and 2005, could offer unique opportunities for conventional understandings to be held up to challenge and scrutiny, and for historians to engage in this process. Not that their analysis could hope to predominate in such societal perceptions, for the reality remained that it would seldom if ever prevail entirely. Nevertheless, the opening was there for the historians to be represented at the table, to take up the responsibility defined by J.R. Miller as that of becoming 'more assertive and innovative in putting our discipline once more at the centre of the citizenry's consideration of history.'[4] The prerequisite for doing so in regard to any area of the early modern period of northeastern North American history lay in the more extended process of historiographical rebalancing. Thus, colonization was an uncertain business. Empire was complex, and negotiable at many levels. Aboriginal centrality – both geographical and transactional – was long able to survive the numerical exceeding of aboriginal populations by those inhabiting the pockets where settlers congregated.

In contexts such as these, the anniversaries of 2004 and 2005 offered scope not only for taking stock of recent societal changes – such as renewed treaty-related negotiations, and evolutions in relationships among linguistic groups – but also for setting them in a reflective historical context.[5] As with all such occasions, the anniversaries were negotiated events and at times contested ones. Since they proceeded from historical processes and historiographical understandings that were also negotiated and contested, it could hardly have been otherwise. The intertwining of colonial habitation, imperial exchange, and aboriginal engagement was so fundamental to northeastern North America in the formative era spanning the seventeenth and eighteenth centuries that the consequences are with us still.

Notes

This volume uses a shortened form of note citation. Full details of sources cited are provided only in the bibliography. In all references to dates, the appropriate calendar style has been retained: the Julian calendar where the citation is from an English, Scottish, or British source until 1752, the Gregorian calendar from that time onward or when the source is French. However, the years have been modernized in all cases to begin on 1 January. Quotations have been rendered exactly as written, with the following exceptions for clarity: standard abbreviations have been expanded; the thorn has been changed to 'th' and the ampersand to 'and' or 'et' as appropriate; where they are interchangeable, the letters 'v' and 'j' have been changed to 'u' and 'I'; superscript letters have been lowered. English translations of French-language quotations have been provided in the notes.

Abbreviations

AAS	American Antiquarian Society
AC	Archives nationales, Archives des colonies, France
BL	British Library
BN	Bibliothèque nationale, France
BODL	Bodleian Library, University of Oxford
CPA	Correspondance politique, Angleterre, Archives du ministère des Affaires étrangères, France
CWBP	Colonial Williamsburg, Blathwayt Papers
DCB	*Dictionary of Canadian Biography*
DHSM	*Documentary History of the State of Maine*
HMC	Historical Manuscripts Commission, Great Britain
LAC	Library and Archives Canada

MA	Massachusetts State Archives
MEHS	Maine Historical Society
MHS	Massachusetts Historical Society
NAS	National Archives of Scotland
NHARM	New Hampshire Archives and Records Management
NSARM	Nova Scotia Archives and Records Management
ODNB	*Oxford Dictionary of National Biography*
OED	*Oxford English Dictionary*
UKNA	United Kingdom, National Archives

1. Introduction

1 Trudel, *The Beginnings of New France*, 82–117, remains a useful summary of this well-known story.

2 Griffiths, *From Migrant to Acadian*; LeBlanc, ed., *Du Grand Dérangement à la Déportation*; Faragher, *A Great and Noble Scheme*.

3 Details of the commemoration can be found at http://www.commemoration250.ca.

4 See Hautecoeur, *L'Acadie du discours*, 92–123 and passim; Basque, with the collaboration of Snow, *La Société Nationale de l'Acadie*, 110–18.

5 Basque/Snow, ibid., 196; the full text of the proclamation can be found at http://laws.justice.gc.ca/en/otherreg/SI-2003-188/188971.html.

6 On the more complex status of the Passamaquoddy, see Wicken, 'Passamaquoddy Identity and the Marshall Decision.' As a matter of terminology regarding the identification of aboriginal nations, I have adopted in general the same practice as outlined in Baker and Reid, *The New England Knight*, xxii, viz:. 'to use the generalized term Wabanaki as a broad definition of ethnic identity among the groups from the Saco to the Penobscot Rivers, adding specific geographical descriptors wherever possible, and to refer separately to the Wulstukwiuk (Maliseet) and Mi'kmaq peoples who lived further to the northeast.' However, there are two variations. First, where the Passamaquoddy are distinguishable from the closely related Wulstukwiuk (as in regard, for example, to the discussion in Wicken, 'Passamaquoddy Identity and the Marshall Decision'), I have identified them specifically. Second, as Bruce Bourque has shown, the evidence suggests that until the later years of the seventeenth century the cultural ancestors of both Wulstukwiuk and Passamaquoddy had formed part of a wider entity known as the Etchemin, dwelling as far southwest as the Penobscot, and I have recognized this grouping when writing about the earlier era.

See Bourque, 'Ethnicity on the Maritime Peninsula,' 257–84. Also, the Five (later the Six) Nations are referred to as the Houdenasaunee.

7 The ruling in the Donald Marshall case can be found at http://scc.lexum.umontreal.ca/en/1999/1999rcs3-456/1999rcs3-456.html, while the ruling in the Stephen Marshall and Bernard cases is found at http://scc.lexum.umontreal.ca/en/2005/2005scc43/2005scc43.html. Discussions of the significance of the Donald Marshall ruling in a variety of contexts include Coates, *The Marshall Decision and Native Rights*; Isaac, *Aboriginal and Treaty Rights in the Maritimes*; and Wicken, *Mi'kmaq Treaties on Trial*. For the Port Royal commemoration, see http://www.portroyal400.com/eng/events.htm.

8 See the summaries at http://www.mikmaqrights.com/negotiations.php and http://www.ainc-inac.gc.ca/nr/prs/j-a2007/2-2847-bk_e.html. Texts of the agreements can be found at http://www.mikmaqrights.com/resources.php.

9 Axtell, 'Columbian Encounters'; quotation from 696. See also Axtell, 'Beyond 1992.'

10 See Christmas, 'Foreword.'

11 O'Neill, *At the Great Harbour*; Fingard, Guildford, and Sutherland, *Halifax: The First 250 Years*.

12 Nelles, *The Art of Nation-Building*, 319.

13 Ibid., 181, 196–7, and passim.

14 Rudin, *Founding Fathers*, 175–9 and passim.

15 Rudin, 'The Champlain–De Monts Tercentenary'; quotation from E.M. Slader is from 17.

16 Marquis, 'Celebrating Champlain in the Loyalist City,' 43. See also Pichette, *Le pays appelé l'Acadie*, 86–100.

17 Marquis, 'Celebrating Champlain in the Loyalist City.'

18 Nelles, *The Art of Nation-Building*, 194–7.

19 Berger, *The Writing of Canadian History*, 1. See also M.B. Taylor, *Promoters, Patriots, and Partisans*; and Rudin, *Making History in Twentieth-Century Quebec*.

20 For the plan of events, see http://www.pc.gc.ca/lhn-nhs/nb/stcroix/ne/ne2_e.asp. For background and commentaries, http://www.cbc.ca/news/background/champlainanniversary.

21 See http://www.portroyal400.com.

22 Rudin, in collaboration with Aristimuño, *Life After Ile Ste.-Croix*.

23 LeBlanc, 'Critique du film documentaire *Life After Île Ste-Croix*'; see also Huskins and Boudreau, 'Life After Île Ste-Croix' (review).

24 Doyle-Bedwell, 'How French Settlement Affected Mi'kmaq People.'

25 The crowning achievement of Andrews's work was the publication of his four-volume *The Colonial Period of American History*. On the 'imperial school' as a whole, and Andrews's role in it, see Johnson, 'Charles McLean Andrews and the Invention of American Colonial History.'

26 Clark, *The Eastern Frontier.*

27 Leach, *Flintlock and Tomahawk*; Leach, *The Northern Colonial Frontier*; Vaughan, *New England Frontier.*

28 See, among other works by these historians, Axtell, 'The Ethnohistory of Early America'; Jennings, *The Invasion of America*; and Washburn, *The Indian in America.*

29 Cronon, *Changes in the Land*; Demos, *The Unredeemed Captive*; Salisbury, *Manitou and Providence.* See also Axtell, 'The White Indians of Colonial America.'

30 Bayly, *Imperial Meridian*; Brewer, *The Sinews of Power*; Cain and Hopkins, *British Imperialism*; Marshall, 'Empire and Authority in the Later Eighteenth Century.'

31 Louis, editor-in-chief, *The Oxford History of the British Empire.* See also Shammas, 'Introduction'; and Wilson, 'Introduction: Histories, Empires, Modernities.'

32 See Armitage, 'Three Concepts of Atlantic History.'

33 While the literature generated by the Atlantic-world approach has attained dimensions that thwart any effort to summarize it effectively, one way to gauge its scope is to access the list of working papers presented since 1996 to the Harvard-based International Seminar on the History of the Atlantic World: http://www.fas.harvard.edu/~atlantic/compwp.html.

34 See Hornsby, *British Atlantic, American Frontier*; Mancke, 'Early Modern Expansion and the Politicization of Oceanic Space'; Pope, *Fish into Wine.*

35 Richter, *Facing East from Indian Country*, 8.

36 See Salisbury, 'The Indians' Old World'; also Richter, *Facing East from Indian Country*, 2–10.

37 For discussion of British colonies and their military vulnerabilities, see Baker and Reid, 'Amerindian Power in the Early Modern Northeast: A Reappraisal' (chap. 8 in this volume); and Reid, '*Pax Britannica* or *Pax Indigena*?' (chap. 10 in this volume).

38 Le Blant, *Une figure légendaire de l'histoire acadienne*; Le Blant, *Un colonial sous Louis XIV.* For Le Blant's article-length studies, see MacDonald, *Robert Le Blant, historien et chef de file de la recherche sur les débuts de la Nouvelle-France.*

39 Eccles, *Frontenac*; Eccles, 'Sovereignty-Association, 1500–1783.' See also Eccles, *Essays on New France.*

40 Trigger, *The Children of Aataentsic*; Trigger, *Natives and Newcomers.*

41 Banks, *Chasing Empire across the Sea.*
42 White, *The Middle Ground*; see also the relevant essays in Hornsby and Reid, eds., *New England and the Maritime Provinces.*
43 Kupperman, *Indians and English*; Haefeli and Sweeney, *Captors and Captives.* See also the essays in Daunton and Halpern, eds., *Empire and Others.*
44 Taylor, *American Colonies*, xiv; Taylor, *The Divided Ground.*
45 Havard and Vidal, *Histoire de l'Amérique française*; Pritchard, *In Search of Empire.*
46 Havard, *Empire et métissages*; quotation from 783: 'The *Pays d'en Haut* was not a dead weight on the French empire, or its downfall: it was its good fortune. The small size of the French population, far from being a handicap, formed in effect one of the preconditions for the alliances that sustained New France.' Other important explorations of related issues include Delâge, *Le pays renversé*; Desbarats, 'The Cost of Early Canada's Native Alliances: Reality and Scarcity's Rhetoric'; and Turgeon, *Patrimoines métissés.*
47 See, for example, Donovan, 'Slaves and Their Owners in Ile Royale.'
48 Griffiths, *From Migrant to Acadian*; Basque, 'Family and Political Culture in Pre-Conquest Acadia'; Basque, 'The Third Acadia.'
49 Pope, *Fish into Wine*, 438.
50 Pritchard, *In Search of Empire*, 230–63.
51 See Mancke and Reid, 'Elites, States, and the Imperial Contest for Acadia.'
52 Dechêne, *Habitants and Merchants in Seventeenth-Century Montreal*, 280; Miquelon, *Dugard of Rouen*, 155.
53 While many such studies could be cited from this currently productive area of Atlantic-world scholarship, those collected in Mancke and Shammas, eds., *The Creation of the British Atlantic World* offer a revealing range of examples.
54 On the term 'shadow empire,' see Winius, 'The "Shadow Empire" of Goa in the Bay of Bengal.'
55 See Cronon, *Changes in the Land*, passim; and Chet, *Conquering the American Wilderness*, 13–37.
56 See Baker and Reid, 'Amerindian Power in the Early Modern Northeast,' esp. the map on 81 Map 6.
57 Reid, 'How Wide Is the Atlantic Ocean?'

2. Sir William Alexander and North American Colonization

1 McGrail, *Sir William Alexander, First Earl of Stirling*, 185.
2 Ibid., 185–8; D.C. Harvey, 'Sir William Alexander,' DCB, 1: 50–4; Innes et al., eds., *The Acts of the Parliament of Scotland*, 5: 358, 672.

3 Urquhart, ed., *Tracts of the Learned and Celebrated Antiquarian Sir Thomas Urquhart of Cromarty,* 129; McGrail, *Sir William Alexander*; Harvey, 'Sir William Alexander,' DCB, 1: 50–4.
4 DCB 1: 50; John Callow, 'Archibald Campbell,' ODNB, entry 4471.
5 Harvey, 'Sir William Alexander,' DCB, 1: 50; Julian Goodare, 'John Erskine,' ODNB, entry 8867. On the importance of kinship connections in late-sixteenth-century Scotland, see Wormald, *Court, Kirk, and Community,* 154–5.
6 Ibid., 151–6, 184–5.
7 MacQueen and Scott, eds., *The Oxford Book of Scottish Verse,* 258–9.
8 See Quennell, *Shakespeare,* 327–8.
9 Harvey, 'Sir William Alexander,' DCB, 1: 51; McGrail, *Sir William Alexander,* 49–51.
10 Harvey, 'Sir William Alexander,' DCB, 1: 51.
11 Ibid., 53–4.
12 Cell, *English Enterprise in Newfoundland,* 95.
13 Alexander, *An Encouragement to Colonies,* 26.
14 Burton et al., eds., *The Register of the Privy Council of Scotland,* ser. I, 12: 774.
15 Alexander, *An Encouragement to Colonies,* 32.
16 Ibid., 31–2.
17 See Reid, 'The Scots Crown and the Restitution of Port Royal,' 39–42.
18 Alexander, *An Encouragement to Colonies,* 33.
19 Ibid, 33–6.
20 Burton et al., eds., *The Register of the Privy Council of Scotland,* 13: 616.
21 Ibid., 650–1.
22 Charles I to the Lard of Wemyss, 24 March 1626, in Rogers, ed., *Stirling's Register,* 30.
23 See Reid, 'The Scots Crown and the Restitution of Port Royal,' 44.
24 Alexander to William, Earl of Menteith, 18 November 1628, in Fraser, ed., *The Red Book of Menteith,* 2: 98.
25. William Maxwell to Sir John Maxwell, 23 November 1628, in Fraser, ed., *Memoirs of the Maxwells of Pollok,* 2: 199.
26 Reid, 'The Scots Crown and the Restitution of Port Royal,' 44.
27 See Insh, *Scottish Colonial Schemes,* 214–26; and Reid, *Acadia, Maine, and New Scotland,* 31.
28 Richard Guthry, 'A Relation of the Voyage and Plantation of the Scots Colony in New Scotland Under the Conduct of Sir William Alexander Younger, 1629,' NAS, Yule Collection, GD90/SEC3/23, 3. For a published text of this document, see Griffiths and Reid, eds., 'New Evidence on New Scotland.'

29 On the English and Scottish Company, see Propositions of accommodation for the settling of the trade and plantation in Canada or New France, 1628, HMC, *Twelfth Report, Appendix,* part I, *The Manuscripts of the Earl Cowper,* 376–7; McGrail, *Sir William Alexander,* 110–12.
30 Alexander to William, Earl of Menteith, 18 November 1628, in Fraser, *The Red Book of Menteith,* 2: 98.
31 Sir William Alexander's information touching his plantation at Cape Breton and Port Reall, [c. 1630], BL, Egerton MSS, 2395, f. 23; Guthry, 'A Relation,' 4–5. On the role of Ochiltree and the significance of the Cape Breton settlement, see Nicholls, '"The purpois is honorabill, and may conduce to the good of our service."'
32 Guthry, 'A Relation,' 4–5.
33 See Reid, *Acadia, Maine, and New Scotland,* 31–2.
34 'Out of seventy Scotchmen wintering there, thirty had died of hardship.' Biggar, ed., *The Works of Samuel de Champlain,* 6: 176.
35 Alexander to William, Earl of Menteith, 9 February 1630, in Fraser, *The Red Book of Menteith,* 2: 111.
36 Guthry, 'A Relation,' 9–11, 13; D.C. Harvey, 'Segipt,' DCB, 1: 605. That one group of native visitors was identified by Guthry as coming from the St John River does not conclusively identify them as Etchemin, as there were also Mi'kmaq dwelling in that area at the time. See Bourque, 'Ethnicity on the Maritime Peninsula,' 262.
37 Reid, *Acadia, Maine, and New Scotland,* 82.
38 'The Scotch were not disposed to leave Port Royal, but were making themselves more at home there from day to day; and had brought in some families and cattle, with the intention of peopling this place, which does not belong to them except by their illegal seizure of it.' Biggar, ed., *Works of Champlain,* 6: 199.
39 Henry De Vic and René Augier to Sir Dudley Carleton, Viscount Dorchester, 28 January 1631 [NS], UKNA, SP78/88, ff. 50–1.
40 Rogers, ed., *Stirling's Register,* 575–6. For more detailed discussion of the treaty negotiations, see Reid, 'The Scots Crown and the Restitution of Port Royal,' 49–56.
41 Innes et al., eds., *Acts of the Parliament of Scotland,* 5: 43. On the copper coinage scheme, see McGrail, *Sir William Alexander,* chap. 8; and Stevenson, 'The "Stirling" Turners of Charles I, 1632–9.'
42 See Dawson, 'Colonists or Birds of Passage?'; George MacBeath, 'Isaac de Razilly,' DCB, 1: 568.
43 Resolutions of the Committee of the Council of War, 11 November 1638, UKNA, SP16/401, no. 59; Edmund Rossington to Viscount Conway and

Killultagh, 23 April 1639, UKNA, SP16/418, no. 41. For lists of knights-baronetcies, see NAS, Privy Seal Register, PS5/1; also Laing, ed., *Royal Letters, Charters, and Tracts,* 120–3.

44 Trade Patent, 11 May 1633, UKNA, CO1/1, no. 13; Grant of the Council for New England, 22 April 1635, UKNA, CO1/8, no. 56.

45 Confirmation of Sales, 20 August 1639, UKNA, CO1/10, no. 34.

46 Alexander to Secretary Windebank, 1 April 1639, UKNA, SP16/417, no. 2.

47 UKNA, CO1/8, no. 44; Minutes of the Council for New England, 1 November 1638, UKNA, CO1/6, no. 29, 38–9.

48 Reid, *Acadia, Maine, and New Scotland,* 53.

49 See McGrail, *Sir William Alexander,* 144, 165–8, 174–85.

50 Urquhart, ed., *Tracts of Sir Thomas Urquhart of Cromarty,* 129.

51 Edmund F. Slafter, 'Memoir of Sir William Alexander, Kt., Earl of Stirling,' in Slafter, ed., *Sir William Alexander and American Colonization,* 117.

52 Insh, *Scottish Colonial Schemes,* 91; McGrail, *Sir William Alexander,* 188; Lythe, *The Economy of Scotland in Its European Setting,* 71; Harvey, 'Sir William Alexander,' DCB, 1: 51, 54.

53 For one treatment of the problems afflicting early colonial ventures, see Reid, 'European Expectations of Acadia and the Bermudas.'

54 Alexander, *An Encouragement to Colonies,* 38–9.

55 This argument is further elaborated in Reid, *Acadia, Maine, and New Scotland,* 22–8.

56 Alexander, *An Encouragement to Colonies,* 38–9.

57 See Hill, *An Historical Account of the Plantation of Ulster at the Commencement of the Seventeenth Century, 1608–1630,* 546–8; Lythe, *The Economy of Scotland in Its European Setting,* 64–9; and Reid, *Acadia, Maine, and New Scotland,* 13–14.

58 For an example of colonization within Scotland, see Mackenzie, *History of the Outer Hebrides,* 174. More generally, see Macinnes, 'Scottish Gaeldom.'

59 Rogers, ed., *Stirling's Register,* 386.

60 For an example of the religious argument, see Alexander, *An Encouragement to Colonies,* 44.

61 See Deschamps, *Un colonisateur du temps de Richelieu,* 5; Massignon, 'La seigneurie de Charles de Menou d'Aulnay, gouverneur de l'Acadie,' 471.

62 Allan M. Fraser, 'Sir George Calvert,' DCB, 1: 162–3; see also Codignola, *The Coldest Harbour of the Land,* 10–11; and Lahey, 'Avalon.'

63 'Charter in Favour of Sir William Alexander,' 10 September 1621, in Slafter, *Sir William Alexander and American Colonization,* 127–48; on Alexander's earlier schemes, see Insh, *Scottish Colonial Schemes,* 46–7.

64 On mercantile expansion in Scotland under James VI, see Devine and Lythe, 'The Economy of Scotland under James VI: A Revision Article,' 105; Lythe, *The Economy of Scotland in Its European Setting*, 248–52; and Wormald, *Court, Kirk, and Community*, 172–4.
65 Alexander to William, Earl of Menteith, 21 January 1630, in Fraser, *The Red Book of Menteith*, 2: 110.
66 On d'Aulnay and his debts, see Reid, *Acadia, Maine and New Scotland*, 47–9.

3. Environment and Colonization Styles in Early Acadia and Maine

1 'Our governor and lieutenant general, representing our person, in the entire country, territory, coast and confines of Acadia' (author's translation). Louis XIII to d'Aulnay, 10 February 1638, AC, C11D, I, 63; Letters Patent, February 1647, AC, E, Dossier 12.
2 Le Blant, 'Les Compagnies du Cap-Breton' 92–3; Trudel, *The Beginnings of New France*, 203–5; see also Baudry, 'Charles d'Aulnay et la Compagnie de la Nouvelle France,' 232–3.
3 Maine Charter, 3 April 1639, DHSM, 7: 223–43.
4 Gorges, 'A Brief Narration,' 54–7; see also Preston, *Gorges of Plymouth Fort*, 339–43.
5 George Cleeve to John Winthrop, 18 February 1646, *Winthrop Papers*, 7: 371–3.
6 Determination of Parliamentary Commissioners for Foreign Plantations, 27 March 1647, DHSM, 7: 136. See also Burrage, *The Beginnings of Colonial Maine*, 339–40.
7 *Province and Court Records of Maine*, 1: 171. See also Moody, 'The Maine Frontier,' 71.
8 See Reid, 'Maine and the Royal Commission,' chap. 2.
9 See Rawlyk, *Nova Scotia's Massachusetts*, chap. 2.
10 'Some small seigneurial dues to which they are entitled for lands of which they have ceded the possession to several individuals, so that their habitants can become well established and so that they will not abandon the French cause for that of the English' (author's translation). Declaration of the Le Borgne Heirs, n.d., AC, C11D, I, 68. Regarding the migration, Nicolas Denys recorded that 'depuis que les Anglois ont esté maistres du pays, les habitans qui s'estoient logez proche le Fort, ont la pluspart abandonné leurs logemens, et se sont allez establir au haut de la riviere' ('The residents who were lodged near the fort have for the most part abandoned

their houses and have gone to settle on the upper part of the river') Denys, *Description and Natural History*, 474; translation 123.

11 See Deschamps, *Un colonisateur du temps de Richelieu*; Preston, *Gorges of Plymouth Fort*.

12 See Charles McLean Andrews, 'Introduction,' in Bond, *The Quit-Rent System in the American Colonies*, 14–15.

13 Articles Granted to Company of New France, 29 April 1627, AC, C11A, I, f. 81.

14 Maine Charter, 3 April 1639, DHSM, 7: 223–43.

15 See, for example, Rutman, *Winthrop's Boston*, 141–3, 222–3.

16 'Although it has been believed that my principal object in all my enterprises in these parts has always been the trading in furs with the Indians, I have never considered that as anything other than an accessory which could serve in some measure to make capital for that which might be done in the country, which is the settlement fishery and the cultivation of the land.' Denys, *Description and Natural History*, 481–2; translation 146. For population numbers, see A.H. Clark, *Acadia*, 99–101; and Reid, *Maine, Charles II, and Massachusetts*, 256.

17 'There is a great extent of meadows which the sea used to cover, and which the Sieur d'Aunay had drained.' Denys, *Description and Natural History*, 474; translation 123. On d'Aulnay's relocation to the former Scottish fort, see Dunn, *A History of Port Royal/Annapolis Royal*, 16–17; Wallace, 'An Archaeologist Discovers Early Acadia,' 14–15.

18 Clark, *Acadia*, 95–8.

19 Rameau de Saint-Père, *Une colonie féodale en Amérique*, 80–1.

20 See, for example, Bernard, *Le drame acadien depuis 1604*, 73.

21 Certification, 27 December 1687, AC, C11D, II, 85–6.

22 'Two hundred men, including soldiers, labourers, and craftsmen, without counting the women and children, the Capuchin fathers, or the little native children who have to be maintained in the seminary established for that purpose. There are also twenty French married couples who came over with their families to start peopling these lands, to which the sieur d'Aulnay would have brought over many more if he had had the means' (author's translation). Memorandum, c. 1643, BN, Fonds français, 18593, 386–9. See also Massignon, *Les parlers français d'Acadie*, 18–20.

23 'From the time when the sieur de Menou became sole proprietor of Acadia, he caused to be built at Port Royal the existing fort, a church, a convent, some mills, and many dwellings; he also caused the clearing of a considerable number of *arpents* of land, so as to make up three large

farms, which cost him more than 150,000 *livres*' (author's translation). Declaration of the Le Borgne Heirs, n.d., AC, C11D, I, 68.

24 See Séguin, *La civilisation traditionnelle de l'"habitant' aux 17e et 18e siècles,* 221–7; Delâge, *Bitter Feast,* 27.

25 'As serfs, without allowing them to make any gain.' Denys, *Description and Natural History,* 483; translation 151.

26 See Massignon, 'La Seigneurie de Charles de Menou D'Aulnay,' 477.

27 See Preston, 'The Laconia Company of 1629,' 25–44.

28 Banks, *History of York, Maine,* 1: 48–9. See also C.E. Clark, *The Eastern Frontier,* 18.

29 Minutes of the Council for New England, 22 March 1638, UKNA, CO1/6, no. 29, p. 38; Grant to Thomas Waye, 16 February 1651, *York Deeds,* I, Part 1: f. 13.

30 Josselyn, *An Account of Two Voyages to New-England,* 248–9.

31 Reid, 'Maine and the Royal Commission,' 42–4.

32 Winthrop, *Winthrop's Journal,* 1: 129.

33 Ibid., 1: 190.

34 Thomas Gorges to Henry Gorges, 19 July 1640, in Moody, ed., *The Letters of Thomas Gorges,* 2.

35 See Van Deventer, 'The Emergence of Provincial New Hampshire,' 62.

36 Grant of Thomas Gorges to John Wheelwright, Henry Boade, and Edward Rishworth, 14 July 1643, *York Deeds,* 1: Part II, f. 9. See also C.E. Clark, *The Eastern Frontier,* 37–9, 46–7.

37 Edward Godfrey to Robert Trelawny, 22 September 1640, DHSM, 3: 240–1.

38 Deposition of Oliver Weekes, 20 November 1640, ibid., 265.

39 Robert Jordan to Robert Trelawny, 31 July 1642, ibid., 314.

40 Godfrey to Winthrop, 20 July 1647, *Winthrop Papers,* 7: 379.

41 Baxter, *George Cleeve of Casco Bay,* 253.

42 *York Deeds,* 1: part I, part l, f. 8; agreement between Paul White and Francis Champernown, 14 October 1652, MEHS, Champernowne/Gerrish/Pepperrell Papers, 67-2342-14; receipt of Thomas Kelland, 11 August 1662, ibid., 67-2342-32. See also Bailyn, *The New England Merchants in the Seventeenth Century,* 102.

43 See Reid, *Acadia, Maine, and New Scotland,* 62–70; Wicken, 'Encounters with Tall Sails and Tall Tales,' 228–34; and Wicken, *Mi'kmaq Treaties on Trial,* 129–30.

44 'That I have done nothing in the country ... For I built two forts and he burned one of them, and if he built nothing himself nor cleared more than seven or eight *arpents* of land, he also burned the church and the

monastery contrary to his instructions, which had enjoined him to install men in these establishments who would be responsible for them and so would conserve them' (author's translation). La Tour to Massachusetts General Court, 27 October 1644, MA, 2, ff. 484–5.

45 'The Sieur d'Aunay traded there in his time even to the extent of three thousand Moose [skins] a year, not counting Beaver and Otter, and this was the reason why he dispossessed the Sieur de la Tour of it.' Denys, *Description and Natural History*, 474; translation 121.

46 Ibid., 499; see also Le Blant, 'La Première Compagnie de Miscou,' 363–70.

47 Jenness, *The Isles of Shoals*, chaps. 1–9; on the incipient shift from migratory to residential fisheries, see Hornsby, *British Atlantic, American Frontier*, 73–7.

4. The 'Lost Colony' of New Scotland and Its Successors, to 1670

1 Charter, 10 September 1621, in Laing, ed., *Royal Letters, Charters, and Tracts*, 4.

2 Alexander's individual role is discussed more fully in Reid, 'Sir William Alexander and North American Colonization' (chap. 2 in this volume).

3 Burton et al., eds., *The Register of the Privy Council of Scotland*, 13: 616, 633–4, 649–51.

4 Propositions of Accommodation for the Settling of the Trade and Plantation in Canada or New France, 1628, HMC, *Twelfth Report, Appendix*, part 1, *The Manuscripts of the Earl Cowper*, 376–7; Grant to Sir William Alexander, 2 February 1628, in Thomson, ed., *The Register of the Great Seal of Scotland* [vol. 8], *A.D. 1620–1633*, no. 1202.

5 For fuller discussion, see Griffiths and Reid, eds., 'New Evidence on New Scotland,' 496–7.

6 Sir William Alexander's Information Touching his Plantation at Cape Breton and Port Royal, [c. 1630], BL, Egerton MSS, 2395, f. 23; Claude de Saint-Étienne de La Tour, quoted in Biggar, ed., *The Works of Samuel de Champlain*, 6: 176.

7 See Griffiths and Reid, eds., 'New Evidence on New Scotland,' 497.

8 Relation of Richard Guthry, [1629], ibid., 503.

9 Memorial of Lord Ochiltree, [1630], UKNA, CO1/5, no. 46.

10 For a thorough discussion of Ochiltree and his role, see Nicholls, '"The purpois is honorabill, and may conduce to the good of our service."'

11 Rev. Joseph Mead to Sir Martin Stuteville, 12 February 1630, in Slafter, ed., *Sir William Alexander and American Colonization*, 66; for the aboriginal visits

to Port Royal, see Relation of Richard Guthry, [1629], in Griffiths and Reid, eds., 'New Evidence on New Scotland,' 506–8. On identification of aboriginal groups in this era, see Bourque, 'Ethnicity on the Maritime Peninsula.'

12 Articles of Agreement, 6 October 1629, BL, Egerton MSS, 2395, f. 17. For further discussion, see Reid, *Acadia, Maine, and New Scotland*, 32–3 and 33n134.

13 Relation of Richard Guthry, [1629], in Griffiths and Reid, eds., 'New Evidence on New Scotland,' 507.

14 Biggar, *Works of Champlain*, 6: 172–5; see also George MacBeath, 'Claude de Saint-Étienne de La Tour,' DCB, 1: 596–8.

15 Reid, *Acadia, Maine, and New Scotland*, 82.

16 'all the places occupied in New France, Acadia, and Canada' (author's translation). Treaty of St-Germain-en-Laye, 29 March 1632, in *Mémoires des commissaires de sa majesté très-chretienne et de ceux de sa majesté brittanique*, 2: 9.

17 Charles I to Knights-Baronets, 15 August 1632, in Rogers, ed., *Stirling's Register*, 619; emphasis added. See also Reid, 'The Scots Crown and the Restitution of Port Royal.'

18 Sir Isaac Wake to Sir John Coke, 13 April 1632, UKNA, SP78/91, ff. 120–1.

19 See Reid, 'The Scots Crown and the Restitution of Port Royal,' 56–9.

20 See Alexander to Earl of Menteith, 21 January 1630, in Fraser, ed., *The Red Book of Menteith*, 2: 110.

21 See Lythe, *The Economy of Scotland in Its European Setting*, 57–61, 251; Devine and Lythe, 'The Economy of Scotland under James VI: A Revision Article,' 102–5.

22 Charles I to Knights-Baronets, 15 August 1632, in Rogers, ed., *Stirling's Register*, 619.

23 See D.C. Harvey, 'Sir William Alexander, Earl of Stirling,' DCB, 1: 50–4.

24 Charles I to the Exchequer, 27 June 1632, in in Rogers, ed., *Stirling's Register*, 602–3; see also the discussion in chap. 2 above.

25 See Morse, ed., *Pierre du Gua, Sieur de Monts*, 11.

26 For more detailed discussion, see Reid, *Acadia, Maine, and New Scotland*, 16–18.

27 Le Blant, 'L'avitaillement du Port-Royal d'Acadie par Charles de Biencourt et les marchands rochelais,' 138–64; MacDonald, *Fortune and La Tour*, 12–13.

28 See George MacBeath, 'Pierre Du Gua de Monts,' DCB, 1: 293–4.

29 Couillard-Després, *Charles de Saint-Étienne de La Tour*, 191–3; Concession to Razilly, 19 May 1632, AC, C11D, I, f. 52. For discussion of these and other

efforts to delegate royal authority in Acadia as a form of elite co-option, see Mancke and Reid, 'Elites, States, and the Imperial Contest for Acadia,' 36–8.

30 Deschamps, *Un colonisateur du temps de Richelieu*, 5; René Baudry, 'Charles de Menou d'Aulnay,' DCB, 1: 502–3; George MacBeath, 'Nicolas Denys,' DCB, 1: 256.

31 A.H. Clark, *Acadia*, 99–101.

32 Patent to Charles d'Aulnay, February 1647, AC, E, dossier 12.

33 Reid, *Acadia, Maine, and New Scotland*, 135–6.

34 The matter of claims and terminology is more fully discussed in Reid, 'The Conquest of "Nova Scotia"' (chap. 6 in this volume).

35 Warrant, 14 July 1656, UKNA, CO1/13, no. 4; Patent, 9 August 1656, ibid., no. 11. On the significance of the use of both of the terms, 'Acadia' and 'Nova Scotia,' see Reid, 'The Conquest of "Nova Scotia,"' 94–6.

36 Huia G. Ryder (in collaboration), 'William Crowne,' DCB, 1: 241–2, and 'Sir Thomas Temple,' ibid., 636–7; Faulkner and Faulkner, *The French at Pentagoet*, 21–3; Johnson, *John Nelson, Merchant Adventurer*, 10–13.

37 Notes Relating to America, c. 1667, UKNA, CO1/21, no. 174.

38 Sir Thomas Temple to Lord Fiennes, 6 September 1659, UKNA, CO1/13, no. 71; Buffinton, 'Sir Thomas Temple in Boston,' 311–14.

39 Thomas Lake to John Leverett, 2 September 1657, MA, 2, ff. 504–5.

40 Sir Thomas Temple to [Thomas Povey], [1660], UKNA, CO1/14, no. 64.

41 Warrant to Attorney-General, 7 July 1662, UKNA, SP44/7, 148; Bounds of Sir Thomas Temple's Patent, July 1662, UKNA, CO1/16, no. 86.

42 See Reid, *Acadia, Maine, and New Scotland*, 147, 156–7.

43 For assessment of eighteenth-century migrations, see Reid, '*Pax Britannica* or *Pax Indigena*?' (chap. 10 in this volume).

44 These factors and others are usefully summarized in Games, *Migration and the Origins of the English Atlantic World*, 13–17.

45 Armitage, 'Three Concepts of Atlantic History'; Bushnell and Greene, 'Peripheries, Centers, and the Construction of Early Modern American Empires,' esp. 2–3.

46 For fuller discussion, see Baker and Reid, 'Amerindian Power in the Early Modern Northeast' (chap. 8 in this volume).

47 Choquette, *Frenchmen into Peasants*, 247–77; Banks, *Chasing Empire across the Sea*, 30–1.

48 'have protested to us a hundred times that they have express orders to break off [negotiations] entirely' (author's translation). [French Plenipotentiaries] to Louis XIV, 3 April 1717, UKNA, SP103/99, 343–5.

5. 'The best Conditioned Gentleman in the World'?

1 Cotton Mather, 'Pietas in Patriam,' in Mather, *Magnalia Christi Americana*, 341–6.

2 This summary is condensed from Baker and Reid, *The New England Knight.*

3 Calef, *More Wonders of the Invisible World Displayed.*

4 Hutchinson, *The History of the Colony and Province of Massachusetts-Bay*, 2: 56–9.

5 Goold, 'Sir William Phips'; Bowen, 'Life of Sir William Phips,' 99–100.

6 Thayer, *Sir William Phips, Adventurer and Statesman*, 67–8.

7 Osgood, *The American Colonies in the Eighteenth Century*, 1: 169–70, 171, 300.

8 Barnes, 'Phippius Maximus.'

9 Miller, *The New England Mind: From Colony to Province*, 209.

10 Breen, *The Character of the Good Ruler*, 180, 187; Hall, *The Last American Puritan*, 265.

11 Sosin, *English America and the Revolution of 1688*, 204, 223–4.

12 Journal of John Knepp, 1–12 November 1683, BL, Egerton MSS, 2526, ff. 8–12.

13 See Montagu, *The Anatomy of Swearing*, 104–6.

14 Deposition of Timothy Clarke, 14 August 1694, UKNA, CO5/858, no. 42 (i), p. 36.

15 Petition of Jahleel Brenton to the Lords of the Treasury, [20 July 1693], UKNA, CO5/857, no. 87 (i); Deposition of David Edwards, 14 August 1694, UKNA, CO5/858, no. 42 (i), p. 31.

16 See Journal of Lords of Trade, 2 February 1694, UKNA, CO391/7, pp. 259–60; Minute of Lords of Trade, 2 February 1694, UKNA, CO5/858, no. 15; and William III to Phips, 15 February 1694, ibid., no. 16.

17 Deposition of Timothy Clarke, 14 August 1694, UKNA, CO5/858, no. 42 (i), p. 36; Deposition of Nathaniel Byfield, 31 August 1694, ibid., 41; Deposition of William Hill and Henry Francklyn, 17 July 1694, ibid., 34–5. The other depositions are also found ibid., 28–46. See also Articles of Jahleel Brenton, [November 1694], UKNA, CO5/858, no. 44.

18 Mather, 'Pietas in Patriam,' 281.

19 Hender Molesworth to William Blathwayt, 30 September 1684, CWBP, vol. 25, folder 1; Deposition of Henry Dickeson, 24 January 1691, MA, 36, f. 348a; Deposition of William Bryant, 29 January 1691, ibid., f. 349.

20 'Relation de la prise du Port-Royal par les habitans de Baston et de Selan commandez par Vuillam Phips le 21e May 1690,' in Doughty, *Report of the Work of the Archives Branch for the Year 1912*, appendix F, 69. On the pillag-

ing of Port Royal, see also *A Journal of the Proceedings in the Late Expedition to Port-Royal*, 6–7.

21 Deposition of John March and Nathaniel Hatch, 4 January 1693, UKNA, CO5/857, no. 18; Deposition of Joseph Short, [25 March 1693], ibid., no. 57 (i); Phips to the Earl of Nottingham, 15 February 1693, UKNA, CO5/751, no. 19.

22 Letter from Boston, [24 March 1693], UKNA, CO5/857, no. 41. On the contemporary sense of 'bigot' as one obstinately or unreasonably attached to another person, see OED, 2: 185.

23 See, for example, Deposition of Thomas Dobbins, 4 September 1694, UKNA, CO5/858, no. 42 (i), p. 82; and Deposition of Benjamin Eames, 17 August 1694, ibid., 85–6. These and other dealings between Phips and Short are discussed in greater detail in Baker and Reid, *The New England Knight.*

24 Phips to Nottingham, 15 February 1693, UKNA, CO5/751, no. 19; Nathaniel Byfield et al. to William Blathwayt, 20 February 1693, CWBP, vol. 4, folder 4; Deposition of John March, 17 September 1694, UKNA, CO5/858, no. 42 (i), p. 66; Deposition of Robert Smith, 4 September 1694, ibid., 67.

25 Mather, 'Pietas in Patriam,' 283. Mather used the term 'conversation' in the contemporary sense that referred to the keeping of company rather than purely to spoken interactions. See OED, 3: 868.

26 Crokat, *A Consolatory Letter*, preface. The details of Phips's successful search for patrons are discussed in Baker and Reid, *The New England Knight.*

27 AAS, Diary of Increase Mather, 6 August 1691.

28 See Davies, *Gentlemen and Tarpaulins*, 229–30.

29 See Pedigree of Francis Phipps, BODL, Rawlinson MSS, D865, 86; and Sir Henry Ashurst to William Stoughton, 14 November 1693, BODL, Ashurst Papers, Letterbook of Sir Henry Ashurst, 90.

30 'Monsieur demeneval estant arrivé a bord dud Commandant fut conduit en sa chambre dans le fond de laquelle il estoit assise. La Arrivant Mr demeneval luy fit une profonde reverence, Ce commandant y repondit en inclinant la teste a droite et a gauche a la maniere angloise ... La conversation estant ouverte se passa en compliment de part et d'autre Et durant autant de Temps quil en falloit pour faire debarquer 450. hommes a terre et se mettre en Bataille au port royal.' 'Relation de la prise du Port-Royal,' 68.

31 See *Journal of the Expedition to Port-Royal*, 6; 'Relation de la prise du Port-Royal,' 67–8.

32 Mémoire of Petit, Trouvé, Dubreuil, and Meneval, 27 May 1690, in *Collection de manuscrits*, 2: 8; *Expedition Journal*, 5.

33 See Foucault, *Language, Counter-Memory, Practice,* 124–36; also Weeks, 'Foucault for Historians,' 111.
34 Jones, *The Languages of Class,* 101–8.
35 Molesworth to Blathwayt, 30 September 1684, CWBP, vol. 25, folder 1.
36 Knepp journal, 6 October 1683, f. 5.
37 On antilanguages, see Halliday, *Language as Social Semiotic,* 164–82; Burke, 'Languages and Anti-Languages in Early Modern Italy'; and, on the relationship to piracy, Rediker, *Between the Devil and the Deep Blue Sea,* 278.
38 Rediker, *Between the Devil and the Deep Blue Sea,* 166.
39 Hender Molesworth to William Blathwayt, 18 November 1684, UKNA, CO1/56, no. 82.
40 Deposition of Daniel Turell, 29 January 1691, MA, 36, ff. 351–2.
41 Journal of Benjamin Bullivant, 18 March 1690 [*sic,* for a date between 22 and 27 March], UKNA, CO5/855, no. 94.
42 Meneval to Pontchartrain, 6 April 1691, in *Collection de Manuscrits,* 2: 42.
43 Ibid.
44 Joseph Robinau de Villebon to Pontchartrain, 1694, in Webster, ed., *Acadia at the End of the Seventeenth Century,* 74.
45 Sewall, *Diary of Samuel Sewall,* 1 November 1694, 322.
46 See Flynn, *Insult and Society,* 39–60; Moogk, '"Thieving Buggers" and "Stupid Sluts"'; and Garrioch, 'Verbal Insults in Eighteenth-Century Paris.'
47 Robert Fairfax to James Sotherne, 31 January 1693, UKNA, CO5/857, no. 22.
48 Deposition of Nathaniel Byfield, 31 August 1694, UKNA, CO5/858, no. 42 (i), p. 41. Other witnesses, however, did observe that Brenton had at least some supporters in the crowd. See Deposition of William Rous, 17 July 1694, ibid., 37.
49 Deposition of Hill and Francklyn, 10 September 1694, ibid., 12–13; see also Baker and Reid, 'Sir William Phips and the Decentring of Empire in Northeastern North America, 1690–1694.'
50 Richard Short to the Admiralty, [March 1693], UKNA, CO5/857, no. 44; Short to the Admiralty, 24 April 1693, ibid., no. 57.
51 Sir Nathaniel Rich to Increase Mather, 25 January 1694, in Hutchinson, *History of the Colony and Province of Massachusetts-Bay,* 2: 60.
52 Chidley Brooke to Benjamin Fletcher, 2 August 1693, UKNA, CO5/1038, no. 23.
53 See Dening, *Mr Bligh's Bad Language,* 55–62, 142–5.
54 St George, '"Heated" Speech and Literacy in Seventeenth-Century New England'; Kamensky, *Governing the Tongue,* 124–5; Stoughton, *New-Englands true interest,* 20.

55 Brooke to Fletcher, 2 August 1693, UKNA, CO5/1038, no. 23; [Nathaniel Byfield] to Joseph Dudley, 12 June 1694, UKNA, CO5/858, no. 31.

6. The Conquest of 'Nova Scotia'

1 'Journal of Colonel Nicholson at the Capture of Annapolis, 1710,' in *Collections of the Nova Scotia Historical Society*, 1: 85–6.
2 Articles of Capitulation, 2 October 1710, UKNA, CO5/9, no. 66; Joseph Dudley, Samuel Vetch, and John Moody to [the Earl of Sunderland?], 25 October 1709, ibid., no. 33.
3 Jérôme Phélypeau, comte de Pontchartrain, to François de Beauharnois de la Chaussaye, 24 December 1710, AC, B, f. 508.
4 On the Treaty of Ryswick, see Reid, 'Imperial Intrusions,' 84–5.
5 Commission to Nicholson, 18 March 1710; Instructions to Nicholson, 18 March 1710, in 'Journal of Colonel Nicholson,' 59–62.
6 Proclamation to the Inhabitants, 12 October 1710, UKNA, CO5/9, no. 73; Proclamation to British Subjects on the Continent of America, 12 October 1710, ibid., no. 74.
7 Vetch to Dartmouth, 22 January 1711, ibid., no. 84.
8 Council of War to Queen Anne, 14 October 1710, ibid., no. 72.
9 See McKay, 'Tartanism Triumphant'; also the frequently cited treatment of Scotland itself by Hugh Trevor-Roper, 'The Invention of Tradition.'
10 See Carter, *The Road to Botany Bay*, xiii–xxiii; Harley, *Maps and the Columbian Encounter*, 55–6, 97–9; and Harley, 'New England Cartography and the Native Americans.' On the significance of colonial toponymy, see also Krim, 'Acculturation of the New England Landscape: Native and English Toponymy of Eastern Massachusetts.'
11 Alexander, *An Encouragement to Colonies*, 32.
12 Charter in favour of Sir William Alexander, 10 September 1621, in Bourinot, 'Builders of Nova Scotia,' 104–21.
13 For details, see Reid, *Acadia, Maine, and New Scotland*, 23–5, 30–3, 37–41.
14 See Griffiths and Reid, eds., 'New Evidence on New Scotland.'
15 Ibid., 506–7; see also Bourque and Whitehead, 'Tarrentines and the Introduction of European Trade Goods in the Gulf of Maine,' 327–41.
16 Alexander, *An Encouragement to Colonies*, map facing p. 1.
17 Patent of Baronetcy in favour of Sir James Skene of Curriehill, 26 June 1630, in Skene, ed., *Memorials of the Family of Skene of Skene*, 197–8. See also Laing, ed., *Royal Letters, Charters, and Tracts*, 120–3.
18 See D'Entremont, 'Du nouveau sur les Melanson' and 'Les Melanson

d'Acadie sont français de père et anglais de mère'; and Melanson, *The Melanson Story*, 3–9.

19 Charles I to the Knights-baronets, 15 August 1632, in Rogers, ed., *Stirling's Register*, 619.

20 Charles I to Commissioners for the plantation of New Scotland, 24 April 1633, in Rogers, ed., *Stirling's Register*, 664; Charles I to the council and commissioners for passing the patents of knight baronets, 27 September 1633, ibid., 676; Ratification, 28 June 1633, in Innes, ed., *The Acts of the Parliament of Scotland*, 5: 43.

21 Alexander's role, and the problems encountered by New Scotland in its initial form, are discussed in greater detail in chaps. 2 and 4 above.

22 Charles I to Sir Ferdinando Gorges, 5 January 1635, in Rogers, ed., *Stirling's Register*, 818; Gorges to Sir Francis Windebank, 21 March 1635, UKNA, CO1/8, no. 52.

23 John Winthrop, Jr, to Lord Forbes, 23 December 1644, in *Winthrop Papers*, 6: 518–19.

24 On Lord Forbes, see Furgol, *A Regimental History of the Covenanting Armies*, 216–17. While the private interest of Winthrop was one definable influence on this approach to Forbes, there is also room for speculation – based in part on the use of the term 'brethren' in the letter, and in part on the pivotal role that Covenanting armies were widely expected to play in the English Civil War – as to whether it also represented a wider desire in New England for a religiously based alliance in North America at a time when the finely balanced state of the Civil War was being watched anxiously by Parliamentary sympathizers in Massachusetts and elsewhere.

25 On the relationship between La Tour, Gibbons, and Hawkins, see Deeds and Indentures, 1643, in *Suffolk Deeds*, 1: Nos. 6–9. For Winthrop's involvement, see Edward Winslow to William Bradford and others, 31 August 1644, Massachusetts Historical Society *Proceedings*, 1st ser. 16: 111.

26 See Reid, *Acadia, Maine, and New Scotland*, 97–9.

27 Deed, 13 May 1645, in *Suffolk Deeds*, 1: no. 10.

28 Robert Sedgwick to Oliver Cromwell, 1 July 1654, in Birch, ed., *A Collection of the State Papers of John Thurloe*, 2: 418–19.

29 See A.H. Clark, *Acadia*, 99–101, 107–8.

30 Bordeaux to Mazarin, 31 December 1654, CPA, 64, f. 298; Order of Council of State, 22 February 1655, MHS, Gay Transcripts, Sedgwick Papers, 5.

31 Order of the Council of State, 29 May 1656, in *Calendar of State Papers, Colonial Series, America and West Indies, 1574–1660*, 441; Huia G. Ryder (in col-

laboration), 'William Crowne,' DCB, 1: 241–2, and 'Sir Thomas Temple,' ibid., 1: 636–7; Johnson, *John Nelson, Merchant Adventurer,* 10–12.

32 'wished to justify the seizure of the forts through an English claim to all of that American coastline on the basis of first discovery' (author's translation). Bordeaux to Brienne, 18 February 1655, CPA, 65, ff. 44–9.

33 Treaty of Westminster, 3 November 1655, in Parry, ed., *The Consolidated Treaty Series,* 4: 12; Bordeaux to Brienne, 11 February 1655 (translation), in Birch, ed., *A Collection of the State Papers of John Thurloe,* 3: 135.

34 Warrant for Articles of Agreement, 14 July 1656, UKNA, CO1/13, No.4; Patent, 9 August 1656, ibid., no. 11.

35 Order in Council, 7 March 1662, BL, Egerton MSS, 2395, f. 341; Warrant, 5 April 1662, UKNA, CO1/16, no. 40; Warrant, 7 July 1662, UKNA, SP44/7, 148; Bounds of Sir Thomas Temple's Patent of Novia Scotia [*sic*], July 1662, UKNA, CO1/16, no. 86; Reid, *Acadia, Maine, and New Scotland,* 156–7.

36 'a man ... who has taken it into his head that he has just claims on Port Royal and on Acadia, because of an uncle to whom, he says, the colony belonged before the English restored it [to France] as a result of the Treaty of Breda' (author's translation). Louis de Buade de Frontenac et de Palluau to Minister of Marine, 15 September 1692, AC, C11A, 12, f. 27. On the tenuous basis of the passage of Temple's claim to his heirs – principally Nelson – see Johnson, *John Nelson, Merchant Adventurer,* 21–2.

37 Petition of William Vaughan et al., [5 December 1684], UKNA, CO1/56, no. 105.

38 For fuller discussion, see Reid, *Acadia, Maine, and New Scotland,* 137.

39 Answer to the French Ambassador's Claim, [1662], UKNA, CO1/16, no. 24.

40 *A Journal of the Proceedings in the Late Expedition to Port-Royal,* 7; emphasis in original. For more extended discussion, see Baker and Reid, *The New England Knight,* 81–94.

41 *A Journal of the Proceedings in the Late Expedition to Port-Royal,* 11; emphases in original.

42 Minute of Massachusetts Council, 4 June 1691, MA, 36, 108–9, 111; Samuel Ravenscroft to Francis Nicholson, 5 November 1691, UKNA, CO5/1037, no. 67; Johnson, *John Nelson, Merchant Adventurer,* 66–9.

43 Journal of the Lords of Trade, 7 September 1691, UKNA, CO391/7, 45; Massachusetts Charter, 7 October 1691, UKNA, CO5/940, 298–352.

44 Petition of John Nelson, [12 April 1697], UKNA, CO5/859, no. 87; Treaty of Ryswick, 20 September 1697, in Parry, ed., *Consolidated Treaty Series,* 21:

446–7. For Nelson's wider role as an adviser to the Board of Trade, see Johnson, *John Nelson, Merchant Adventurer*, 93–106.

45 Joseph Dudley, Samuel Vetch, and John Moody to [the Earl of Sunderland?], 25 October 1709, UKNA, CO5/9, no. 33. See also Reid, 'Unorthodox Warfare in the Northeast, 1703'; Donald F. Chard, 'The Impact of French Privateering on New England, 1689–1713'; Plank, *An Unsettled Conquest*, 40–54.

46 Waller, *Samuel Vetch*, passim. For a briefer biographical treatment, see also G.M. Waller, 'Samuel Vetch,' DCB, 2: 650–2.

47 Waller, *Samuel Vetch*, 80.

48 Ibid., 79–93; Johnson, *John Nelson, Merchant Adventurer*, 115–16. For Nelson's support of Vetch, see Deposition of John Nelson and John Alden, [1706], UKNA, CO5/864, no. 179.

49 John Chamberlain to [Charles Montague, Earl of Halifax], 27 February 1706, BL, Egerton MSS, 929, f. 90; Proposal for 'an Addition and Advantage to the Crown of England,' n.d., ibid., ff. 92–3. Also associated with this document were discussions of the value of northern New England as a source of naval stores, and of the possibility of establishing a Palatine colony between the Kennebec and St Croix Rivers. Ibid., ff. 94, 96–7. For a valuable commentary, see Alsop, 'Samuel Vetch's "Canada Survey'd,"' 46–7; also Alsop, 'The Age of the Projectors,' 43.

50 Dudley to Board of Trade, 2 October 1706, UKNA, CO5/864, no. 114.

51. Case of Samuel Vetch, [20 February 1707], UKNA, CO5/864, no. 89 (ii).

52 [Vetch], 'Canada Survey'd,' UKNA, CO323/6, no. 64; Alsop, 'Samuel Vetch's "Canada Survey'd,"' 47–58. See also the somewhat different political analysis in Waller, *Samuel Vetch*, 101–57, which should be read in the light of Alsop's critique.

53 Dudley to the Board of Trade, 1 March 1709, UKNA, CO5/865, no. 22; Dudley to the Board of Trade, 1 March 1709, ibid., no. 30.

54 Alsop, 'Samuel Vetch's "Canada Survey'd,"' 57–8; Rawlyk, *Nova Scotia's Massachusetts*, 109–23.

55 Vetch to Dartmouth, 22 January 1711, UKNA, CO5/9, no. 84; Vetch to Dartmouth, 8 August 1712, ibid., no. 109.

56 Board of Trade to Henry Boyle, 2 June 1709; Board of Trade to the Queen, [2 June 1709], UKNA, CO324/9, 294–307.

57 Board of Trade to James Vernon, 17 February 1699, UKNA, CO324/7, 12–30; John Nelson to Board of Trade, 12 April 1697, UKNA, CO5/859, no. 88; Nelson to Board of Trade, 2 November 1697, ibid., no. 129; Nelson to Board of Trade, 2 December 1697, UKNA, CO323/2, no. 79.

58 Johnson, *John Nelson, Merchant Adventurer*, 104–5, 114–18.

59 Board of Trade to Henry St John, 5 April 1712, UKNA, CO195/5, 267–9. On the role of treaty negotiations in the consolidation of territorial claims, and for a stimulating interpretation of the defensive character of British and other imperial aims in this period, see Alsop, 'The Age of the Projectors,' 48–52.

60 For the relevant article of the Treaty of Utrecht, see Treaty of Peace and Friendship, 11 April 1713, in Parry, ed., *Consolidated Treaty Series*, 27: 485.

61 Harley, 'New England Cartography and the Native Americans,' 312.

62 The connection between Mi'kmaq ship seizures and reports of the contemporary 'Tumults in Great Brittain' was reported on two separate occasions to an envoy from Annapolis Royal to the French and Mi'kmaq during the late summer of 1715. See Peter Capon, 'A Journall of a Voyage to Cape Britton on the Kings Account,' MA, 38A, 11–15.

7. Imperialism, Diplomacies, and the Conquest of Port Royal, 1710

1 Richard Philipps to James Craggs, July 1720, NSARM, RG1, vol. 14, 32; Philipps to Board of Trade, 27 September 1720, UKNA, CO217/3, no. 18.

2 'Those of your nation have never had leave from us to allow you the freedom of our country, as you would like to have' (author's translation). Memorial of John Henshaw et al., [29 August 1720], UKNA, CO217/3, no. 18 (i); Deposition of John Alden, 14 September 1720, ibid., no. 18 (xii); Antoine Couaret and Pierre Couaret to Philipps, 2 October 1720 [N.S.], ibid., no. 18 (xiv).

3 Matthew Prior to Oxford, 7 March 1713, UKNA, SP105/28, 97; Louis XIV to French Plenipotentiaries, 7 March 1713, UKNA, SP103/102, 314; Memoir of Duke of Shrewsbury, 7 March 1713, ibid., 320.

4 Philipps to St Ovide, 14 May 1720, NSARM, RG1, vol. 14, 16.

5 'we will quarrel with any and all of those who wish to inhabit our country without our consent' (author's translation). Antoine Couaret and Pierre Couaret to Philipps, 2 October 1720, UKNA, CO217/3, no. 18 (xiv).

6 French Proposal of Peace, 22 April 1711, UKNA, SP105/266, 4; British Demands, n.d., ibid., 8; Preliminary Articles, 27 September [8 Oct., N.S.] 1711, ibid., 27–33. For general discussion of the context of the negotiations, see the pro-Whig but informative account in Trevelyan, *England under Queen Anne.* More recent and specialized treatments of the negotiations regarding North America can be found in Hiller, 'Utrecht Revisited'; Laplante, 'Le traité d'Utrecht et la question des limites territoriales de l'Acadie'; and Miquelon, *New France*, 49–53.

7 Prior to Oxford, 29 December 1712, UKNA, SP105/266, 246.
8 'unending disputes between the parties' (author's translation). Plenipotentiaries to Louis XIV, 21 March 1712, UKNA, SP103/98, 380–3.
9 Prior's Negotiation in France, 23–5 July 1711, in HMC, *Report on the Manuscripts of His Grace the Duke of Portland Preserved at Welbeck Abbey*, vol. 5: 36.
10 Ibid., 37.
11 'they would also be the masters of the entry to the Gulf of St Lawrence'; 'an ancient domain which preserved communications among their main North American colonies' (author's translations). French Response to English Demands, 20 March 1712, UKNA, SP103/98, 343–5; [French Plenipotentiaries] to Louis XIV, 9 March 1712, ibid., 286.
12 'as also Acadia with the town of Port Royal, otherwise known as Annapolis Royal, and whatever depends on the said country' (author's translation). French Offers, [12 February 1712], UKNA, SP105/266, 60; Demands of Great Britain, n.d., Ibid., 62–4.
13 French Response, 20 March 1712, UKNA, SP103/98, 343–5.
14 'have protested to us a hundred times that they have express orders to break off [negotiations] entirely'; 'according to its ancient limits' (author's translations). [French Plenipotentiaries] to Louis XIV, 3 April 1712, UKNA, SP103/99, 26; [Henry St John], Mémoire touchant l'Amérique Septentrionale, 24 May 1712, UKNA, SP105/266, 71–2.
15 Mémoire of Torcy, 10 June 1712, UKNA, SP78/154, 300–3; French Responses, [13 June 1712], UKNA, SP103/99, 317–20.
16 Bolingbroke to Prior, 27 August 1713, UKNA, SP105/266, 87.
17 Bolingbroke to Prior, 29 September 1712, UKNA, SP105/266, 150–1.
18 Instructions to Shrewsbury, 11 December 1712, UKNA, SP105/266, 212–13.
19 Prior to Bolingbroke, 19 January 1713, UKNA, SP105/266, 304; Mémoire of Torcy, 14, 17 January 1713, UKNA, CO105/27, 21. See also Relation de la Conference de M. de Torcy avec M. Prior, 19 December 1712, CPA, vol. 240, 264–8.
20 'our disagreements over Newfoundland should not be the stumbling block' (author's translation). Bolingbroke to Prior, 19 January 1713, UKNA, SP105/266, 315–19; Bolingbroke to Prior, 19 January 1713, ibid., 321; Bolingbroke to Torcy, 20 January 1713, France, CPA, vol. 243, 131–5.
21 'with all the rights and prerogatives that the French have enjoyed' (author's translation). Prior to Bolingbroke, 28 December 1712, UKNA, SP105/266, 225–6; Proposition Concerted with Prior, 29 December 1712, UKNA, SP105/27, 13; see also the analysis in Hiller, 'Utrecht Revisited,' 30–1.

22 Louis XIV to Plenipotentiaries, 23 December 1712, UKNA, SP103/101, 278–9.

23 Louis XIV to Plenipotentiaries, 9 February 1713, UKNA, SP103/102, 140; Proposal Concerted with Prior, Note, 10 February 1713, UKNA, SP105/27, 13; Torcy to Plenipotentiaries, 9 February 1713, UKNA, SP103/102, 158.

24 Louis XIV to Plenipotentiaries, 7 March 1713, UKNA, SP103/102, 314; Dartmouth to Francis Nicholson, 20 May 1713, UKNA, CO324/32, 218; Warrant to Francis Nicholson, 23 June 1713, UKNA, CO217/1, no. 19; Treaty of Peace and Friendship, 11 April 1713, in Parry, ed., *The Consolidated Treaty Series,* 27: 485. An original Latin text of the treaty is in UKNA, SP108/72.

25 Mémoire of Torcy, 14, 17 January 1713, UKNA, SP105/27, 21.

26 Bellomont to Board of Trade, 20 April 1700, UKNA, CO5/861, no. 31; Mémoire of Bégon, [8 November 1718], MHS, Parkman Papers, vol. 9, 18.

27 'subjects or friends'; 'which are those who shall or ought to be counted as subjects and friends of France, or of Great Britain' (author's translations). Treaty of Peace and Friendship, 11 April 1713, in Parry, ed., *The Consolidated Treaty Series,* 27: 486–7.

28 Eccles, 'Sovereignty-Association, 1500–1783,' 485; White, *The Middle Ground,* 142.

29 'Protestant foreigners' (author's translation). D'Aulnay to Pierre Séguier, 10 September 1647, BN, Fonds français, 17387, no. 21, 218; see also Reid, *Acadia, Maine, and New Scotland,* 97–8.

30 Proceedings of Portsmouth Conference, 13 July 1713, MA, vol. 29, 11.

31 Proceedings of Casco Conference, 15–18 July 1713, ibid., 19.

32 Ibid.

33 'I have my territory, which I have not given, and shall not give, to anyone. I wish always to be its master; I move throughout it, and when anyone wishes to live there he will pay' (author's translation). Letter of [Sébastien] Rale, 9 September 1713, MHS, Parkman Papers, vol. 31, 129–31; see also Submission and Agreement of the Eastern Indians, 13 July 1713, UKNA, CO5/931, no. 10.

34 No original text of the 1678 treaty has survived, but its terms were summarized in Williamson, *The History of the State of Maine,* 2: 552–3.

35 See Baker and Reid, *The New England Knight,* 167–9.

36 See, for example, Heads and Propositions, 3 June 1701, UKNA, CO5/862, no. 101 (i); Memorial of Sagadahoc Conference, 27 July 1702, ibid., no. 125 (ii).

37 Council and Assembly of Massachusetts Bay, 12 July 1704, UKNA, CO5/863, no. 105.

38 'Monsieur Dudley ... has spared no effort this year'; 'expressing to them the regret they feel at being in a state of war with them' (author's translations). Vaudreuil to the Minister, 3 November 1710, AC, C11A, vol. 31, 52.
39 Letter of [Sébastien] Rale, 9 September 1713, MHS, Parkman Papers, vol. 31, 129–31.
40 Thomas Bannister to Board of Trade, 15 July 1715, UKNA, CO5/866, no. 53.
41 Proceedings of the Arrowsic Conference, 9–12 August 1717, UKNA, CO5/868, 197–8.
42 Vetch to Dartmouth, 24 June 1712, UKNA, CO5/9, no. 108.
43 Gaulin to Dudley, 8 July 1713, MA, vol. 51, 265–7.
44 Proceedings of Portsmouth conference, 11 July 1713, MA, vol. 29, 7.
45 Minutes of Massachusetts General Court, 10 February 1714, MA, General Court Records, vol. 9, 345–7.
46 Caulfeild to Nicholson, [1713?], NSARM, RG1, vol. 15, 1.
47 Nicholson to Caulfeild, 3 July 1714, NSARM, RG1, vol. 15, 9–12.
48 'I proclaim no foreign king in my country' (author's translation). Answer of the Penobscot, [April 1713], UKNA, CO217/1, no. 125 (iii).
49 Dudley to Board of Trade, 31 July 1715, UKNA, CO5/866, no. 69; Journal of Peter Capon, 31 August 1715, MA, vol. 38A, 11.
50 David Jeffries and Charles Shepreve to Robert Mears, 6 July 1715, UKNA, CO217/2, no. 2 (i).
51 Journal of Peter Capon, 29 October 1715, MA, vol. 38A, 15.
52 Letter of Christopher Aldridge, 24 May 1715, quoted in Francis Nicholson to William Popple, 16 August 1715, UKNA, CO217/2, no. 3.
53 Shirreff to Board of Trade, 24 May 1715, UKNA, CO217/1, no. 120.
54 Caulfeild to Board of Trade, 1 November 1715, UKNA, CO217/2, no. 8.
55 [Shirreff] to Board of Trade, 18 March 1715, UKNA, CO217/1, no. 96.
56 Instructions to Philipps, 14 July 1719, UKNA, CO5/189, 427–8.
57 Board of Trade to George I, 8 September 1721, UKNA, CO324/10, 412–18.
58 Doucett to Board of Trade, 10 February, 20 June 1718, UKNA, CO217/2, nos. 51, 54.
59 Philipps to Board of Trade, 3 January 1720, UKNA, CO217/3, no. 5.
60 'our father' (author's translation). Philipps to the Lords Justices, 26 May 1720, UKNA, CO217/3, no. 6; Speech of the St. John's Indians, 26 July 1720, ibid., no. 18 (x); Speech of Philipps, 27 July 1720, ibid., no. 18 (xi); Minutes of Nova Scotia Council, 26 July 1720, in MacMechan, ed., *Nova Scotia Archives III*, 11.
61 See Wicken, '26 August 1726,' 16–18.

62 'We are your friends, and ... we hope for the same of you' (author's translation). Speech of François de Salle, 10 November 1720, UKNA, CO217/3, no. 19 (ii); Speech of Passamaquoddy, 10 November 1720, ibid., no. 19 (i); Philipps to Board of Ordnance, 28 December 1720, NSARM, RG1, vol. 14, 65.

63 Wicken, '26 August 1726,' 13–17.

64 *Boston Courant*, 31 December 1722–7 January 1723.

65 Vetch to Dartmouth, 22 January 1711, UKNA, CO5/9, no. 85; Vetch to Board of Trade, 26 November 1711, UKNA, CO217/1, no. 1.

66 Letter of George Vane, 5 May 1712, UKNA, CO217/31, No.6. See also Principal Inhabitants of Port Royal to Vaudreuil, 13 November 1710, AC, C11D, vol. 7, 98–9; Journal of Richard King, 25 June 1711, UKNA, CO5/898, no. 11 (i); Dunn, *A History of Port Royal/Annapolis Royal*, 95–102; and Plank, *An Unsettled Conquest*, 59–60.

67 Undertaking of Annapolis Royal Inhabitants, August 1714, UKNA, CO217/1, no. 56; Proceedings at Annapolis Royal, 19–20 August 1714, ibid., no. 67; Nova Scotia Council Record, 20 August 1714, ibid., no. 68; Proceedings at Minas, 27 August 1714, ibid., no. 72; Pontchartrain to d'Iberville, 24 April 1715, UKNA, CO194/5, no. 93 (iii).

68 Francis Spelman and Andrew Simpson to Board of Trade, 2 September 1715, UKNA, CO217/2, no. 6; Nicholson to Popple, 16 August 1715, ibid., no. 3; see also Samuel Vetch to Board of Trade, 2 September 1715, ibid., no. 5.

69 [William Shirreff] to Board of Trade, 18 March 1715, UKNA, CO217/1, no. 96; Caulfeild to Board of Trade, 23 November 1715, UKNA, CO217/2, no. 14; John Doucett to Board of Trade, 20 June 1718, ibid., no. 54. See also Griffiths, *From Migrant to Acadian*, 262–7; and Pothier, 'Acadian Emigration to Ile Royale after the Conquest of Acadia.'

70 A.H. Clark, *Three Centuries and the Island*, 25–6; Harvey, *The French Régime in Prince Edward Island*, 30–9. On the proprietor, see Yves Zoltvany, 'Louis de La Porte de Louvigny,' DCB, 2: 345–7.

71 Representation of Governor and Officers, [1720], UKNA, CO217/3, no. 18 (xviii).

72 Doucett to Philipps, 13 December 1718, UKNA, CO217/2, no. 64.

73 Declaration of French Inhabitants of Nova Scotia, 13 January 1715, UKNA, CO217/1, no. 124 (xiii); Declaration of French Inhabitants of Nova Scotia, 22 January 1715, ibid., no. 124 (xii). See also Basque, *Des hommes de pouvoir*, 60–1.

74 French Inhabitants to Doucett, [1717], UKNA, CO217/2, no. 47 (ii);

French Inhabitants of Les Mines to Doucett, 10 February 1718, ibid., no. 51 (iv). See also Griffiths, *From Migrant to Acadian*, 270–4.

75 French Inhabitants of the River to Philipps, [1720], UKNA, CO217/3, no. 6 (v); French Inhabitants of Minas to Philipps, [1720], ibid., no. 6 (xv); see also John Adams to Philipps, 14 May 1720, ibid., no. 6 (xvi).

76 Vetch to Board of Trade, 9 March 1715, UKNA, CO217/1, no. 93; see also Sir Charles Hobby to Board of Trade, Ibid., no. 94.

77 Caulfeild to Board of Trade, 1 November 1715, UKNA, CO217/2, no. 8; Address of Inhabitants and Merchants of Annapolis Royal, 5 February 1718, ibid., no. 49 (ii).

78 T.G. Barnes, '"The Dayly Cry for Justice,"' 16.

79 See Paul Mascarene, Description of Nova Scotia, 1720, UKNA, CO217/3, no. 18 (xx); and Philipps to Board of Trade, 27 September 1720, ibid., no. 18.

80 Board of Trade to George I, 30 May 1718, UKNA, CO218/1, 369–70.

81 'to treat between me, or those whom I may depute, and the ... inhabitants' (author's translation). Philipps to French Inhabitants of Annapolis River, 30 April 1720, UKNA, CO217/3, no. 6 (vii); Philipps to Lords Justices, 26 May 1720, ibid., no. 6 (i).

82 Board of Trade to Philipps, 28 December 1720, UKNA, CO218/1, 496–7.

83 Board of Trade to James Craggs, 18 March 1719, UKNA, CO5/915, 263–4; Board of Trade to Lords Justices, 5 June 1719, UKNA, CO218/1, 411–15.

84 Greene, 'Negotiated Authorities'; Marshall, *The Making and Unmaking of Empires*, 72–6.

85 Mancke, 'Chartered Enterprises and the Evolution of the British Atlantic World'; Walters, '*Mohegan Indians v. Connecticut* (1705–1773) and the Legal Status of Aboriginal Customary Laws and Government in British North America,' esp. 789–803. See also Baker and Reid, *The New England Knight*, 253–4.

86 See Plank, 'The Culture of Conquest,' 84–5.

87 See J.A. Murray and Joseph Martin to Bolingbroke, 27 July 1714, UKNA, SP103/16; Letter of Martin Bladen, 29 December 1732, ibid.

88 Philipps to Board of Trade, 27 September 1720, UKNA, CO217/3, no. 18.

8. Amerindian Power in the Early Modern Northeast

1 Bellomont to Board of Trade, 20 April 1700, UKNA, CO5/861, no. 31.

2 'to pillage and destroy the habitations on the south shore of the St Lawrence, and even of all Canada'; 'would be easy for them, those natives

knowing perfectly all the settlements of New France' (authors' translations). Mémoire of Bégon, [8 November 1713], MHS, Parkman Papers, vol. 9, 18.

3 See Robert C. Ritchie, 'Richard Coote,' ODNB, entry 6247; and Yves F. Zoltvany, 'Michel Bégon de La Picardière,' DCB, 3: 57–63.

4 Bellomont to Board of Trade, 20 April 1700, UKNA, CO5/851, no. 31; Malone, *The Skulking Way of War.*

5 Bellomont to Board of Trade, 20 April 1700, UKNA, CO5/851, no. 31.

6 Exceptions to this pattern, relating directly to the period covered by this essay, will be identified below. For an important recent analysis of the imperatives governing native-English conflict in an earlier period, see Kupperman, *Indians and English,* 212–40.

7 Bellomont to Board of Trade, 20 April 1700, UKNA, CO5/861, no. 31.

8 See Morrison, 'The Bias of Colonial Law,' esp. 374–5, 386–7.

9 Native American nomenclature and territorial range in northern New England is currently a much debated topic. While the *Handbook of North American Indians* uses the terms 'Eastern Abenaki' and 'Western Abenaki' to divide the peoples of northern New England, current research has largely dismissed these terms. Thus, this essay uses the term 'Wabanaki' to refer to the peoples of northern New England. See Dean Snow, 'Eastern Abenaki,' in Trigger, ed., *Handbook of North American Indians,* 15: 134–47; Bourque, 'Ethnicity on the Maritime Peninsula, 1600–1759'; and Prins, 'Children of Gluskap.'

10 Leach, *Flintlock and Tomahawk,* 242–4; Peckham, *The Colonial Wars,* 16. See also Leach, *Arms for Empire,* 2–3.

11 Paret, 'Colonial Experience and European Military Reform at the End of the Eighteenth Century,' 52–3.

12 Hirsch, 'The Collision of Military Cultures in Seventeenth-Century New England.'

13 Calloway, *New Worlds for All,* 93.

14 Malone, *The Skulking Way of War,* 126–8. For Malone and other historians, moreover, King Philip's War was decisive. Philip Ranlet, for example, wrote in 1988 that it 'largely eliminated the Indian threat to English expansion in New England.' Ranlet, 'Another Look at the Causes of King Philip's War,' 79.

15 Roberts, *The Military Revolution.* See also Black, *European Warfare,* 1–33, 234–6; Bowen, *War and British Society,* 7–11; G. Clark, *War and Society in the Seventeenth Century,* 73; Duffy, ed., *The Military Revolution and the State*; Lenman, *Britain's Colonial Wars,* 1–10; and Parker, *The Military Revolution,* 4–5, 118–19 and passim.

16 Parker, *The Military Revolution*, 118–19.
17 Black, *European Warfare*, 16–19.
18 See Lepore, *The Name of War*, 115–19.
19 Richter, 'War and Culture: The Iroquois Experience,' 528–9.
20 Ibid., 559 and passim. For detailed analysis of the Great Peace, see Havard, *The Great Peace of Montreal of 1701*.
21 Richter, *The Ordeal of the Longhouse*, 245–6.
22 Haefeli and Sweeney, 'Revisiting *The Redeemed Captive*,' 16–18.
23 Melvoin, *New England Outpost*, 290–1.
24 Steele, *Warpaths*, 247; see also 131–74 on the 1687–1748 period. In only 44 pages of a substantial book, those years were characterized as seeing the establishment of recurring patterns of conflict that were based in northeastern North America on 'a local balance of violence' and thus rendered essentially sterile.
25 Starkey, *European and Native American Warfare*, viii.
26 Ibid., 41–2, 60, 80–2, 131–5, 167–9. For a more extended historiographical discussion, see also Lee, 'Early American Ways of War,' esp. 271–6.
27 Baker, 'Trouble to the Eastward,' 2–8, 178–220; Calloway, *The Western Abenakis of Vermont*, 88–89; Pulsipher, *Subjects unto the Same King*, 222, 261–2. For a brief survey of the earlier historiography of King Philip's War in Maine see Morrison, *The Embattled Northeast*, 224–5. James Drake goes so far as to classify the struggle on the northern frontier as one completely separate from King Philip's War. He bases this distinction on the marginality of the English settlements as well as on the family-band nature of Native society in the region, which contrasted with chiefdoms in southern New England. While Drake sees King Philip's War as a civil war, he believes events to the north constituted a separate 'frontier war' between competing societies. Drake, *King Philip's War*, 24–7. For a more general interpretation of the polarization following King Philip's War of those aboriginal groups who chose accommodation with the English and those who did not, see also Pulsipher, '"The Overture of this New-Albion World,"' 360–1, 375–8, and passim.
28 See Baker, 'Trouble to the Eastward'; Baker and Reid, *The New England Knight*, esp. 156–77; Bourque, *Twelve Thousand Years*, 129–208; Miquelon, *New France, 1701–1744*, 32–123 passim; Morrison, *The Embattled Northeast*; and Sévigny, *Les Abénaquis*.
29 Petition of Edward Rishworth et al., 27 May 1677, DHSM, 6: 169–70.
30 No original text of the treaty survives. A summary is found in Williamson, *The History of the State of Maine*, 1: 552–3. See also Pulsipher, *Subjects unto the Same King*, 235–7.

31 Submission and Agreements of the Eastern Indians, 11 August 1693, UKNA, CO5/857, no. 37 (i); Articles Signed by Sir William Phips to the Eastern Indians, 11 August 1693, ibid., no. 37 (iv).

32 For fuller discussion of this point, see Baker and Reid, *The New England Knight*, 167–9; more generally, see also Ghere, 'Mistranslations and Misinformation.'

33 Renewed Submission of the Eastern Indians, 27 January 1699, MA, 30, ff. 439–42.

34 Journal of Commissioners, 15–22 July 1713, DHSM, 23: 45–50.

35 Proceedings of Arrowsic Conference, 9–12 August 1717, UKNA, CO5/868, ff. 195–201.

36 Proceedings of Boston Conference, 16 November–7 December 1725, UKNA, CO5/898, ff. 178–88; Submission and Agreement of the Eastern Indians, 15 December 1725, ibid., ff. 173–4; Promises of William Dummer, 15 December 1725, ibid., 175–6.

37 'Indian Explanation of the Treaty of Casco Bay, 1727,' in Calloway, ed., *Dawnland Encounters*, 118.

38 Morrison, *The Embattled Northeast*, passim; Morrison, 'The Bias of Colonial Law.'

39 Proceedings of Arrowsic Conference, 9–12 August 1717, UKNA, CO5/868, f. 198.

40 Declaration of Francis Card, 22 January 1677, DHSM, 6: 150–1.

41 Kennebec *Sakamows* to Massachusetts Governor, 1 July 1677, MA, 30, ff. 241–2.

42 Records of New Hampshire Council, 5 August 1699, UKNA, CO5/787, pp. 503–4.

43 'I have my land that I have not given, and will not be giving, to anyone. I wish always to be the master of it. I know its extent, and when anyone wishes to come and live there, he will pay' (authors' translation). Sébastien Rale to Governor Vaudreuil, 9 September 1713, in *Recherches historiques*, 37: 290.

44 'the entire Wabanaki nation spread out throughout the continent and in Canada, and all the Catholic natives, Hurons, Iroquois, Mi'kmaqs, and other allies of the Wabanaki' (authors' translation). Letter of Eastern Indians, 28 July 1721, UKNA, CO5/869, ff. 106–7.

45 Report of Commander of St George's Fort, 21 July 1724, DHSM, 6: 165.

46 See Harris, ed., and Matthews, cart., *Historical Atlas of Canada*, volume 1, passim. For purposes of this description, we have included only the mainland portions of northeastern North America, as opposed to also including Newfoundland.

47 See White, *The Middle Ground.*
48 Samuel Shute to Board of Trade, [8 September 1721], UKNA, CO5/868, ff. 128–9.
49 Shute to Vaudreuil, 14 March 1722, UKNA, CO5/10, f. 284.
50 Bellomont to Board of Trade, 17 October 1700, UKNA, CO5/1045, no. 1.
51 Edward Randolph to Lords of Trade, 5 September 1689, UKNA, CO5/855, no. 34.
52 William Redford to Sir William Phips, [July 1694], UKNA, CO5/940, no. 40 (i).
53 Joseph Dudley to Board of Trade, 11 February 1703, UKNA, CO5/863, no. 10; Proceedings of Portsmouth Conference, 23 July 1714, DHSM, 23: 65.
54 Dudley to Board of Trade, 31 July 1715, UKNA, CO5/866, no. 69. The gloss of 'apprehensive' for 'doubtfull' is based on the fuller context of Dudley's remarks. The paragraph reads in full: 'Upon the whole, I am very doubtfull these Beginnings will poyson the Indians all along the Coast, as They have done Thrice within these Thirty years past, to the great Disadvantage of his Majesty's Governments in North America, and in the present mischief, the new Settlement at Cape Breton will be much more hurtfull to us, than all Their old Plantations at Port Royal and the Bay of Fundee; of which I humbly hope there will be some Consideration and resolves taken by his Majesty, to Secure the Settlement on the Shoar Eastward, and the fishery the whole Length of the Coast from Newfoundland to Cape Cod, which is humbly offer'd to your Lordships Consideration.' See also OED, 4: 983–4.
55 Letter from Boston, 24 October 1689, UKNA, CO5/855, no. 41.
56 Thomas Bannister to Board of Trade, UKNA, CO5/866, no. 53; Letter of [Thomas Moore?], 16 May 1723, UKNA, CO5/898, no. 31. The latter informant believed that a slave revolt in Boston might add force to a Wabanaki attack.
57 Shute's Answers to Queries [of Board of Trade], [17 February 1720], UKNA, CO5/867, no. 66 (i).
58 Address of the Council and Assembly of Massachusetts to Queen Anne, 20 October 1708, UKNA, CO5/865, no. 16 (i).
59 Address of the Council and Assembly of Massachusetts to Queen Anne, 12 July 1704, UKNA, CO5/863, no. 105.
60 Dudley to Board of Trade, 10 March 1705, UKNA, CO5/863, no. 132.
61 'Nova Scotia otherwise known as Acadia, in its entirety, according to its ancient boundaries, as also ... the town of Port-Royal, now called Annapolis Royal, and in general ... all that depends on the said lands and islands of that country'; 'subject to Great Britain'; '[aboriginal] Nations of

America'; 'the [native] Americans who are subjects or friends of France' (authors' translations). Treaty of Utrecht, 11 April 1713, in Parry, ed., *The Consolidated Treaty Series*, 27: 485–7.

62 'the lands inhabited by the natives from the first English fort at Casco Bay as far as the Bay of Fundy, where Beaubassin is located' (authors' translation). Mémoire of Bégon, [8 November 1713], MHS, Parkman Papers, vol. 9: 9, 14–15.

63 See Black, *British Foreign Policy in the Age of Walpole*, 2–11.

64 Vaudreuil to Shute [contemporary translation], 28 October 1723, UKNA, CO5/10, f. 293.

65 Vaudreuil to Dummer [contemporary translation], 29 October 1724, UKNA, CO5/869, f. 127.

66 Report of Commissioners, 1725, UKNA, CO5/869, f. 196.

67 Baker, 'Finding the Almouchiquois'; Stewart-Smith, 'The Pennacook Indians and the New England Frontier,' 87, 228–32; Hope Hood et al. to Peter Coffin, 3 January 1686, NHARM, Rockingham County Deeds, vol. 2, 366.

68 Baker, 'Finding the Almouchiquois'; Baker, 'Trouble to the Eastward,' 196–7; Baker, 'A Scratch with a Bear's Paw,' 240–2; Bourque, 'Ethnicity on the Maritime Peninsula,' 266–76; William Hubbard, 'A Narrative of the Troubles with the Indians in New England from Piscataqua to Pemaquid,' 154–6.

69 See also Baker and Reid, *The New England Knight*, 169–73.

70 *Province Laws (Massachusetts)*, 1694–5, chap. 6, 172–3; ibid., 1699–1700, chap. 13, 384–5.

71 Proceedings of Portsmouth Conference, 27 July 1714, DHSM, 23: 72.

72 Minutes of General Court, 10 February 1714, MA, Massachusetts General Court Records, 9: 346.

73 Minutes of General Court, 27 May 1714, ibid., 374.

74 Morrison, *The Embattled Northeast*, 173–85.

75 See McManis, *Colonial New England*, 68–9.

76 'These are not the words of four or five natives whom you can bring around to your point of view by your gifts, your lies, and your trickery. This is the expression of the entire Wabanaki nation, spread throughout this continent and in Canada, and all the other Christian natives their allies' (authors' translation). Letter of Eastern Indians, 28 July 1721, UKNA, CO5/869, ff. 106–7. For further discussion of Wabanaki-Mi'kmaq and related alliances, see Wicken, *Mi'kmaq Treaties on Trial*, 55–7. A published English translation of the Wabanaki letter of 1721, can be found in Crochet, trans., 'Eastern Indians' Letter to the Governour.'

77 Morrison, *The Embattled Northeast,* 165–93; Submission and Agreements of the Eastern Indians, 11 August 1693, UKNA, CO5/751, no. 37 (i); Eastern Indians to Bellomont, 8 September 1699, MA, 30, ff. 447–8.

78 Proceedings of Arrowsic Conference, 9–12 August 1717, UKNA, CO5/868, f. 198.

79 Baker, 'New Evidence on the French Involvement in King Philip's War'; Morrison, *The Embattled Northeast,* 136–43, 159–64.

80 See Douglas Hay, 'Wowurna,' DCB, 2: 668–70.

81 Vaudreuil to Dummer [contemporary translation], 29 October 1724, UKNA, CO5/869, f. 127.

82 Richter, *The Ordeal of the Longhouse,* 244.

83 Calloway, *The Western Abenaki,* 113–31; Plank, *An Unsettled Conquest,* 78–9.

84 Letter from Boston, 16 May 1723, UKNA, CO5/898, no. 31.

85 Baker and Reid, *The New England Knight,* 134–55; Baker and Kences, 'Maine, Indian Land Speculation, and the Essex County Witchcraft Outbreak of 1692'; Norton, *In the Devil's Snare.*

86 Slotkin, *Regeneration through Violence,* 78–93; Slotkin and James K. Folsom, 'Introduction,' in Slotkin and Folsom, eds., *So Dreadfull a Judgment,* 3–4, 30–9; Lepore, *The Name of War,* ix–xxiii. The modern historiography of King Philip's War starts with Leach, *Flintlock and Tomahawk* and prominently includes the debate between Francis Jennings and Alden Vaughan over the nature of the war and Anglo–Indian relations in early New England. See Vaughan, *New England Frontier*; and Jennings, *The Invasion of America.* For the English desperation, and the idea of an English pale, see the most recent history of the war: Drake, *King Philip's War,* 121–6.

87 Heads and Propositions, 3 June 1701, UKNA, CO5/862, no. 101 (i).

88 Memorial of Sagadahoc Conference, 27 July 1702, UKNA, CO5/862, no. 125 (ii).

89 Submission and Agreement of the Eastern Indians, 13 July 1713, UKNA, CO5/931, no. 10.

90 Vaudreuil to Minister of Marine, AC, C11A, vol. 31, f. 52.

91 'if you wish'; 'I ask you' (authors' translations). Sébastien Rale to Vaudreuil, 9 September 1713, *Recherches historiques,* 37: 289.

92 Ghere, 'Eastern Abenaki Autonomy and French Frustrations.'

93 Lord William Campbell to Lord Hillsborough, 25 October 1768, UKNA, CO217/45, no. 27. On the military pressures operating in the second half of the eighteenth century in other parts of the empire, see Bayly, 'The British and Indigenous Peoples,' 24–9; and Way, 'The Cutting Edge of Culture.'

94 Anderson, *The Crucible of War,* 734.

95 White, 'The Winning of the West.'
96 Board of Trade to Crown, 8 September 1721, UKNA, CO324/10, pp. 296–431.
97 Desbarats, 'The Cost of Early Canada's Native Alliances,' 610. Though see also Havard, *The Great Peace*, 180–1, for an interpretation of the Great Peace as a genuine triumph for a form of colonialism based on adaptation to and cultural exchange with aboriginal nations.
98 Shute to Vaudreuil, 14 March 1722, UKNA, CO5/10, f. 284.

9. The Sakamow's Discourtesy and the Governor's Anger

1 Thomas Smart to Admiralty, 4 November 1717, UKNA, ADM1/2451, Captains' Letters, 'S,' 1715–1717. On the arrival of the sloop, see 'Journal of the Rev. Joseph Baxter,' 46–7.
2 Logbook of *Squirrel*, 9 August 1717, UKNA, ADM51/926.
3 Smart to Admiralty, 4 November 1717, UKNA, ADM1/2451, Captains' Letters, 'S,' 1715–1717; Logbook of *Squirrel*, 10–18 August 1717, UKNA, ADM51/926; Account of Work Done On Board His Majesty's Ship Squirrell, 4 September 1717, UKNA, ADM1/2452, Captains' Letters, 'S,' 1718–1723. For Smart's arrival in Boston, see Smart to Admiralty, 28 July 1717, UKNA, ADM1/2451, Captains' Letters, 'S,' 1715–1717.
4 Logbook of *Squirrel*, 5 August 1717, UKNA, ADM51/926. Casco Bay had been the location of numerous British-Wabanaki conferences in the past, and therefore was an area of symbolic diplomatic significance.
5 Ibid., 10–13 August 1717. The designation 'Indian king' presumably referred to Moxus, the most experienced and prestigious *sakamow* present, although no such title existed either in the letter or the spirit.
6 William Pencak, 'Samuel Shute,' ODNB, entry 25488.
7 The treaty, for which no full text is known to survive, is summarized in Williamson, *The History of the State of Maine*, 1: 552–3.
8 An outline of these developments can be found in Baker and Reid, *The New England Knight*, 135–9, 156–77.
9 See Bellomont to Board of Trade, 20 April 1700, UKNA, CO5/861, no. 31.
10 Heads and Propositions, 3 June 1701, UKNA, CO5/862, no. 101 (i).
11 Submission and Agreement, 13 July 1713, UKNA, CO5/931, no. 10.
12 Rale to Philippe de Rigaud de Vaudreuil, 9 September 1713, in *Recherches historiques*, 37: 290.
13 MA, Massachusetts General Court Records, vol. 9, 374–5.
14 Moody, 'The Maine Frontier,' 357, 368–9; Kershaw, *'Gentlemen of Large Prop-*

erty and Judicious Men,' 18–19. For the native context of the era, see also Bourque, *Twelve Thousand Years*, 182–6.

15 Moody, 'The Maine Frontier,' 357–62; Kershaw, *'Gentlemen of Large Property and Judicious Men,'* 18–19; C.E. Clark, *The Eastern Frontier*, 121–3.

16 A Conference of His Excellency the GOVERNOUR, with the *Sachems* and Chief Men of the Eastern *Indians*, 9–12 August 1717, UKNA, CO5/868 (hereafter Arrowsic Conference), f. 195. This is a printed record of the conference, with the following publication details: 'BOSTON: Printed by *B. Green*, Printer to His Excellency the GOVERNOUR & COUNCIL: And Sold by *Benj. Eliot*, at his Shop below the Town-house. 1717.'

17 Arrowsic Conference, f. 195. See also Gordon M. Day, 'Atecouando,' DCB, 2: 25–6; Douglas Hay, 'Wowurna,' DCB, 2: 668–70. Other identifications are from the records of previous treaties and meetings.

18 See W.S. MacNutt, 'John Gyles,' DCB, 3: 272–3.

19 Noyes, Libby, and Davis, *Genealogical Dictionary of Maine and New Hampshire*, 389–90.

20 Referring to Wiwurna by an English name, 'Captain Jo,' the Massachusetts missionary Joseph Baxter commented that he 'understood English pretty well.' 'Journal of the Rev. Joseph Baxter,' 49.

21 Arrowsic Conference, f. 200.

22 Thomas Bannister to Board of Trade, 15 July 1715, UKNA, CO5/866, no. 53.

23 Arrowsic Conference, ff. 195–201.

24 Ibid., ff. 195–7.

25 Ibid., f. 197.

26 Ibid.

27 Ibid., ff. 197–8.

28 'Journal of the Rev. Joseph Baxter,' 49–51; see also Hay, 'Wowurna,' DCB, 2: 668.

29 Arrowsic Conference, f. 198.

30 See DePaoli, 'Beaver, Blankets, Liquor, and Politics'; Carroll, *The Timber Economy of Puritan New England*, 110.

31 Arrowsic Conference, f. 198.

32 See Deed, 7 July 1684, in *York Deeds*, 4: 14–16.

33 Arrowsic Conference, ff. 198–9.

34 'Journal of the Rev. Joseph Baxter,' 48.

35 For fuller statements of the French position, see Mémoire of Michel Bégon, [8 November 1713], MHS, Parkman Papers, vol. 9, 14–15; Vaudreuil to Shute, 28 October 1723, UKNA, CO5/10, f. 293.

36 Logbook of *Squirrel*, 11 August 1717, UKNA, ADM51/926.
37 'Journal of the Rev. Joseph Baxter,' 48.
38 Arrowsic Conference, f. 199.
39 Ibid., ff. 199–201; Logbook of *Squirrel*, 13–18 August 1717, UKNA, ADM51/926.
40 Shute to Board of Trade, 9 November 1717, UKNA, CO5/866, no. 137.
41 Shute to Rale, 21 February 1718, in *Collections of the Massachusetts Historical Society*, 5 (Boston, 1798), 117.
42 Arrowsic Conference, f. 200; 'Journal of the Rev. Joseph Baxter,' 48.
43 Shute to Rale, 21 February 1718, in *Collections of the Massachusetts Historical Society*, 5: 117; Arrowsic Conference, ff. 199–200.
44 Shute to Rale, 21 February 1718, in *Collections of the Massachusetts Historical Society*, 5: 118.
45 Kershaw, *'Gentlemen of Large Property and Judicious Men,'* 19; Moody, 'Maine Frontier,' 366–7.
46 Report of Commissioners, [15 July 1720], DHSM, 23: 83–4.
47 Richard Waldron to Lieutenant-Governor William Dummer and Council, 25 August 1720, DHSM, 9: 458.
48 Conference at Georgetown [Arrowsic], 25 November 1720, DHSM, 23: 97–108.
49 Letter of the Eastern Indians, 28 July 1721, UKNA, CO5/869, ff. 106–7.
50 Shute to Board of Trade, [8 September 1721], UKNA, CO5/868, f. 128; Vaudreuil to Rale, 25 September 1721, ibid., f. 190.
51 See Gyles to Shute, 10 August 1720, DHSM, 9: 456; John Wentworth to Shute, 17 August 1720, ibid., 459.

10. *Pax Britannica* or *Pax Indigena*?

1 See Barnes, 'Francis Legge, Governor of Loyalist Nova Scotia'; Brebner, *The Neutral Yankees of Nova Scotia* and *North Atlantic Triangle*; Kerr, *The Maritime Provinces of British North America and the American Revolution*, 'The Merchants of Nova Scotia and the American Revolution,' and 'Nova Scotia in 1775–6'; R.S. Longley, 'The Coming of the New England Planters to the Annapolis Valley'; Rawlyk, *Revolution Rejected*; Stewart and Rawlyk, *A People Highly Favoured of God*; and Wright, *Planters and Pioneers*.
2 Conrad, ed., *They Planted Well*, esp. 'Introduction,' 9–11; Conrad, ed., *Making Adjustments* and *Intimate Relations*; and Conrad and Moody, eds., *Planter Links*.
3 Wicken, 'Mi'kmaq Land in Southwestern Nova Scotia, 1771–1823.'
4 See Griffiths, *From Migrant to Acadian*; Mancke, 'Another British America';

Plank, *An Unsettled Conquest*; Reid, *Acadia, Maine, and New Scotland*; Reid et al., *The 'Conquest' of Acadia*; and Wicken, *Mi'kmaq Treaties on Trial.*

5 Upton, *Micmacs and Colonists*, xiii–xiv, 61–78 (quotations from xiv).

6 Brebner, *The Neutral Yankees*, 71.

7 Patterson, '1744–1763,' 149–50. See also Patterson, 'Indian-White Relations in Nova Scotia,' esp. 54–9.

8 Paul, *We Were Not the Savages*, 166.

9 The significance of historical interpretation in legal cases involving aboriginal treaty rights suggests a rider to Allan Greer's persuasive recent argument for greater attention to pre-Confederation Canadian history, by illustrating that some elements of pre-Confederation history can be 'useful' even in an applied sense. See Greer, 'Canadian History: Ancient and Modern.'

10 Brebner, *The Neutral Yankees of Nova Scotia*, 299, 313–14, 446–7, and passim; see also Brebner, *North Atlantic Triangle*, 55–6. Brebner's interpretations did not go unopposed, and Viola Florence Barnes in particular offered an interpretation based on transatlantic rather than continental linkages. See Reid, 'Viola Barnes, the Gender of History, and the North Atlantic Mind.'

11 For a recent exploration of these issues in a different geographical and chronological context, see Baker and Reid, 'Amerindian Power in the Early Modern Northeast: A Reappraisal' (chap. 8 in this volume).

12 For population estimates, see Reid et al., *The 'Conquest' of Acadia*, ix. I have excluded the Passamaquoddy and Penobscot populations of the southwestern portion of the territory claimed for Nova Scotia as being outside the areas primarily occupied by Planter-era settlers. The figure given for Annapolis Royal excludes intermittent wartime reinforcements.

13 Richter, 'Native Peoples of North America and the Eighteenth-Century British Empire,' 348.

14 For more general discussion of the environmental role of agriculture, see Cronon, *Changes in the Land*, esp. 127–56; Delâge, *Bitter Feast*, 250–8; Anderson, 'King Philip's Herds' and *Creatures of Empire*, esp. 209–42.

15 Wicken, 'Encounters with Tall Sails and Tall Tales,' 227–43.

16 Reid et al., *The 'Conquest' of Acadia*, 205.

17 Mancke, 'Another British America,' 16–17.

18 Labaree, ed., *Royal Instructions to British Colonial Governors*, 2: 537–42, 583–5. For more general discussion of the foundation of Halifax and its strategic antecedents, see Fingard, Guildford, and Sutherland, *Halifax: The First 250 Years*, 8–16; MacNutt, *The Atlantic Provinces*, 53–6; and Patterson, '1744–1763,' 127–8.

19 Gwyn, *Excessive Expectations*, 7, 27.

20 See Hornsby, *British Atlantic, American Frontier*, 206–8; Plank, *An Unsettled Conquest*, 126–9; Paul, *We Were Not the Savages*, 111–12; David A. Charters and Stuart R.J. Sutherland, 'Joseph Goreham (Gorham),' DCB, 4: 308–10; and John David Krugler, 'John Gorham,' DCB, 3: 260–1.

21 Minutes of Nova Scotia Council, 13, 14, 16 February 1760, NSARM, RG1, vol. 188, 124–32.

22 Treaty, 23 February 1760, UKNA, CO217/18, ff. 18–31; Wicken, *Mi'kmaq Treaties on Trial*, 196–202.

23 Lawrence to Board of Trade, 11 May 1760, UKNA, CO217/17, ff. 59–60.

24 Treaty with LaHave Mi'kmaq, 10 March 1760, BL, Andrew Brown Papers, Additional Manuscripts, vol. 19071, no. 37.

25 Wicken, *Mi'kmaq Treaties on Trial*, 203–9.

26 Proclamation, 12 October 1758, UKNA, CO217/16, f. 311; Proclamation, 11 January 1759, UKNA, CO217/16, f. 315.

27 See Jean Daigle and Robert LeBlanc, 'Acadian Deportation and Return,' and Graeme Wynn and Debra McNabb, 'Pre-Loyalist Nova Scotia,' in Harris, ed., and Matthews, cart., *Historical Atlas of Canada*, vol. 1, plates 30, 31. The townships not in areas of substantial earlier Acadian settlement were those of Barrington, Chester, Liverpool, Maugerville, and Yarmouth, while the other townships included upland as well as marshland allocations.

28 Record of Governor's Farm Ceremony, 25 June 1761, UKNA, CO217/18, ff. 277–83.

29 Lawrence to Board of Trade, 20 April, 20 September 1759, UKNA, CO217/16, ff. 317–18, 322.

30 Minutes of Nova Scotia Council, 16 July 1759, NSARM, RG1, vol. 188, 88–90.

31 Belcher to Board of Trade, 12 December 1760, UKNA, CO217/18, f. 81.

32 Minutes of Nova Scotia Council, 5 June 1760, NSARM, RG1, vol. 188, 149. Morris's letter, recorded in the minutes, was written on 1 June 1760.

33 Beverley and Moody, eds., *The Life and Journal of the Rev. Mr. Henry Alline*, 33; see also Bumsted, *Henry Alline*, 9–10.

34 Minutes of Nova Scotia Council, 8 August 1763, NSARM, RG1, vol. 188, 395–8.

35 Wicken, *Mi'kmaq Treaties on Trial*, 221–2.

36 Belcher to Council and Assembly, 23 March 1762, UKNA, CO217/19, f. 31.

37 Proclamation, 4 May 1762, UKNA, CO217/19, ff. 27–8; Belcher to Board of Trade, 2 July 1762, UKNA, CO217/19, ff. 22–3.

38 Board of Trade to Montague Wilmot, UKNA, CO218/6, ff. 194–5.

39 Wilmot to Board of Trade, 28 January 1764, UKNA, CO217/21, f. 7; Michael Francklin to Lord Shelburne, 10 November 1766, UKNA, CO217/22, f. 4. For the text of the Royal Proclamation of 1763, see *Report of the Public Archives for the Year 1918*, 323–9.
40 Belcher to Board of Trade, 7 September 1762, UKNA, CO217/19, ff. 70–9.
41 Sebastian Zouberbuhler, John Creighton, and Leonard Christopher Rudolf to Belcher, 15 July 1762, UKNA, CO217/19, f. 118; Memorial of Principal Inhabitants of Lunenburg, 15 July 1782, UKNA, CO217/19, f. 120.
42 Letter of Belcher, 17 July 1762, UKNA, CO217/19, f. 116.
43 Petition of King's County Inhabitants, [July 1762], NSARM, RG1, vol. 284, Brown Transcripts, no. 10; Minutes of Council of War, 21 July 1762, NSARM, RG1, vol. 188A, 11–12.
44 Minutes of Council of War, 11 August 1762, NSARM, RG1, vol. 188A, 18–19; Belcher to Amherst, 12 August 1762, UKNA, CO217/43, ff. 103–4.
45 Belcher to Board of Trade, 7 September 1762, UKNA, CO217/19, ff. 70–9.
46 Richard Bulkeley to William Forster, 28 July 1763, NSARM, RG1, vol. 136, 51.
47 Michael Francklin to [Sir Hugh Palliser], 11 September 1766, UKNA, CO217/44, f. 80; Palliser to Francklin, 16 October 1766, UKNA, CO217/44, ff. 81–3.
48 Richard Bulkeley to John Anderson, Jeremiah Mears, Francis Peabody, and James Simonds, 20 December 1766, NSARM, RG1, vol. 136, 101–2.
49 See, for example, Wilmot to Board of Trade, 10 December 1763, UKNA, CO217/20, ff. 356–7.
50 Wilmot to Board of Trade, 24 June 1764, UKNA, CO217/21, f. 193.
51 Green to Board of Trade, 24 August 1766, UKNA, CO217/21, ff. 262–3.
52 Francklin to Board of Trade, 3 September 1766, UKNA, CO217/21, f. 345.
53 Minutes of Nova Scotia Council, 11 July 1768, NSARM, RG1, vol. 189, 104–5.
54 Campbell to Lord Hillsborough, 12 September 1768, UKNA, CO217/45, ff. 245–6; Campbell to Lord Barrington, 12 September 1768, UKNA, CO217/45, f. 251. See also Francis A. Coghlan, 'Lord William Campbell,' DCB, 4: 131–2.
55 Campbell to Lord Hillsborough, 25 October 1768, UKNA, CO217/45, ff. 272–3.
56 Campbell to Lord Hillsborough, 13 January 1769, UKNA, CO217/25, f. 112.
57 Minutes of Nova Scotia Council, 8, 11, 22 August 1763, NSARM, RG1, vol. 188, 395–407.

58 Beamsley Glasier to [Saint John River Society], 14 December 1764, *New Brunswick Historical Society Collections*, 6: 310. See also D. Murray Young, 'Beamsley Perkins Glasier,' DCB, 4: 299–301.
59 Minutes of Nova Scotia Council, 18 July 1768, NSARM, RG1, vol. 189, 119–23.
60 See also Claude Galarneau, 'Charles-François Bailly de Messein,' DCB, 4: 41–4.
61 Bulkeley to John Anderson, NSARM, RG1, vol. 136, 139.
62 Campbell to Lord Hillsborough, 22 December 1770, UKNA, CO217/48, ff. 11–12.
63 Report of the Present State and Condition of His Majesty's Province of Nova Scotia, 1773, UKNA, CO217/50, ff. 19–20.
64 Robinson and Rispin, *Journey Through Nova-Scotia*, 27.
65 Gwyn, *Excessive Expectations*, 25.
66 Armstrong, 'Neutrality and Religion in Revolutionary Nova Scotia,' 50; Wynn, 'Late Eighteenth-Century Agriculture on the Bay of Fundy Marshlands,' 88. See also Campbell to Lord Shelburne, 27 February, 21 May 1767, UKNA, CO217/44, ff. 167, 293–5.
67 Alan R. MacNeil, 'The Acadian Legacy and Agricultural Development in Nova Scotia, 1760–1861,' 7–9; Wynn, 'Late Eighteenth-Century Agriculture on the Bay of Fundy Marshlands,' 80–9.
68 See Upton, *Micmacs and Colonists*, 68–71.
69 Ibid., 72–8; Augustine, '*Lsipogtog*, "River of Fire,"' 5–6; Clarke, *The Siege of Fort Cumberland*, 73–5, 82–3. My thanks to Stephen Augustine for permission to cite his unpublished report.
70 Upton, *Micmacs and Colonists*, 82–3; MacNutt, *New Brunswick*, 78.
71 See Allen, ed., *The Loyal Americans*, passim.
72 Gwyn, 'The Mi'kmaq, Poor Settlers, and the Nova Scotia Fur Trade.'
73 Mancke, 'Another British America,' 1–2 and passim.
74 P.J. Marshall, 'The British in Asia,' 505.
75 See Mancke, 'Imperial Transitions'; and Armitage, *The Ideological Origins of the British Empire*, 170–98.
76 Reid et al., *The 'Conquest' of Acadia*, 208.
77 See Reid, 'Change and Continuity in Nova Scotia'; and Hoffman, *Florida's Frontiers*.
78 See White, *The Middle Ground*, 59–60.
79 Clarke, *The Siege of Fort Cumberland*, 4–44.
80 See, among other works, Bell, *Early Loyalist Saint John*; Condon, *The Envy of the American States*; W.G. Godfrey, 'Thomas Carleton,' DCB, 4: 155–63; W.G.

Godfrey, 'James Glenie,' DCB, 5: 347–58; and MacKinnon, *This Unfriendly Soil.*

11. Chronologies, Counterfactuals, Trajectories, and Encounter 1604

1 See Reid, *Acadia, Maine, and New Scotland,* 18; also Gustave Lanctôt, 'Troilus de La Roche de Masguez,' DCB, 1: 421–2.

2 Huia Ryder (in collaboration), 'Jean de Biencourt de Poutrincourt et de Saint-Just,' DCB, 1: 96.

3 Marcel Trudel, 'Samuel de Champlain,' DCB, 1: 187.

4 Codignola, 'Competing Networks,' 541–3.

5 Carr, *What Is History?* 128–34.

6 Bury, 'Cleopatra's Nose'; see also Marwick, *The Nature of History,* 77–8.

7 Bury, 'Cleopatra's Nose,' 61.

8 For examples of critical discussions of Bury and of counterfactualism itself, see Carr, *What Is History?* 141; Marwick, *The Nature of History,* 118; Thompson, 'The Poverty of Theory or An Orrery of Errors,' 107–8; and Tosh, *The Pursuit of History,* 199.

9 Martin, *Past Futures,* 192.

10 Ibid., 212.

11 Lorenz, *The Essence of Chaos*; Lorenz, *The Nature and Theory of the General Circulation of the Atmosphere.* See also Smith, *Explaining Chaos,* 1–13.

12 Lorenz, *The Essence of Chaos,* 181–4.

13 Smith, *Explaining Chaos,* 1–13; quotations from 1, 13. Among other useful discussions of chaos theory, and of the more general question of nonlinear approaches to science, are those in Kellett, *In the Wake of Chaos* and Nicolis, *Introduction to Nonlinear Science.*

14 Examples are provided in Niall Ferguson, 'Introduction. Virtual History: Towards a "Chaotic" Theory of the Past,' in Ferguson, ed., *Virtual History,* 8–19; though see also Cowley, ed., *What If?*

15 Ferguson, ed., *Virtual History,* 86.

16 Ibid., 83–9.

17 Niall Ferguson, 'Afterword. A Virtual History, 1646–1996,' in Ferguson, ed., *Virtual History,* 416–40.

18 This paragraph is based primarily on Barkham, 'The Documentary Evidence for Basque Whaling Ships in the Strait of Belle Isle'; Bourque and Whitehead, 'Trade and Alliances in the Contact Period'; Cell, *English Enterprise in Newfoundland*; Harrington, '"Wee Tooke Great Store of Cod-fish"';

Quinn, *England and the Discovery of America*; and Turgeon, 'French Fishers, Fur Traders, and Amerindians during the Sixteenth Century.'

19 These episodes are conveniently summarized in the relevant passages of Quinn, *North America from Earliest Discovery to First Settlements.*

20 Mancke, 'Negotiating an Empire,' 235–6.

21 I owe the term 'unstable space' to Graeme Wynn, 'Peeping through the Cracks.'

22 This discussion is primarily based on Davis, 'Early Societies'; Jones, 'Virgin Soils Revisited'; Pastore, 'The Collapse of the Beothuk World' and 'The Sixteenth Century: Aboriginal Peoples and European Contact'; Reid et al., *The 'Conquest' of Acadia*; Wicken, 'Encounters with Tall Sails and Tall Tales,' esp. 160–205; and Wicken, *Mi'kmaq Treaties on Trial.*

23 See Reid, 'Réflexions actuelles sur l'Acadie du XVIIe siècle' (translated in this volume as chap. 13).

12. Champlain: Longevity and Commemoration

1 Dionne, *Samuel Champlain, fondateur de Québec et père de la Nouvelle-France*; Samuel Eliot Morison, *Samuel de Champlain, Father of New France.*

2 Charles W. Colby, *The Founder of New France*; Ralph Flenley, *Samuel de Champlain, Founder of New France.*

3 Bishop, *Champlain: The Life of Fortitude.*

4 Armstrong, *Champlain.*

5 Marcel Trudel, 'Samuel de Champlain,' DCB, 1: 186–99; Trudel, *Histoire de la Nouvelle-France,* vols. 1, 2, 3-I, and 3-II. The series dealing with the history of New France is also available in an abridged, English-language edition. Trudel, *The Beginnings of New France.*

6 Trigger, *Natives and Newcomers*; Delâge, *Bitter Feast.*

7 Warkentin and Podruchny, eds., *Decentring the Renaissance.* See, especially, the essays by Deborah Doxtator, Gilles Thérien, Réal Ouellet with Mylene Tremblay, Lynn Berry, and Conrad Heidenreich.

8 The following outline of Champlain's colonial experiences is a composite account based on the secondary works cited above.

9 Quinn, 'Henri Quatre and New France,' 19.

10 Biggar, ed., *The Works of Samuel de Champlain,* 1: 136–7.

11 The traditional estimation of Champlain's age at his death has been that he was 65 years of age or perhaps a little older. See Trudel, 'Samuel de Champlain,' DCB, 1: 186. However, in 1978 an intriguing and plausible argument was put forward by Jean Liebel that he was a decade younger.

See Liebel, 'On a vieilli Champlain.' Even so, he would have been at an advanced age for his time.

12 Quoted in Armstrong, *Champlain*, 263.
13 Extract from the Letters of the Chamber of Commerce, 9 February 1618, in Biggar, *Works of Champlain*, 2: 348.
14 Champlain to Chamber of Commerce, [1618], ibid., 2: 339–45.
15 Champlain to the King and Lords of his Council, [1618], ibid., 2: 326.
16 Ibid., 326–39.
17 Biggar, *Works of Champlain*, 5: 313.
18 Ibid., 4: 319–21. Much of this paragraph is based on Trigger, *Natives and Newcomers*, 180–1, 198–200, 315–19; also Trigger, 'Champlain Judged by His Indian Policy.'
19 See Doxtator, 'Inclusive and Exclusive Perceptions of Difference,' 35–6; Conrad E. Heidenreich, 'The Beginning of French Exploration out of the St. Lawrence Valley,' 238–45.
20 See Delâge, *Bitter Feast*, 96–7.
21 Biggar, *Works of Champlain*, 3: 31–2.

13. Reflections on Seventeenth-Century Acadia

1 MacLennan, *On Being a Maritime Writer*, 19.
2 Rudin, 'The Champlain–De Monts Tercentenary,' 9–10, 15; on the anniversary observances of a century ago, see also Marquis, 'Celebrating Champlain in the Loyalist City.'
3 J.W. Longley, 'De Monts' Tercentenary at Annapolis Royal, N.S.,' *Acadiensis* 5 (1905), 5; W.F. Ganong, 'A Visitor's Impressions of the Champlain Tercentenary, St. John, June 21–24, 1904,' ibid., 21.
4 On the Sylliboy case, see Whitehead, *The Old Man Told Us*, 327–30.
5 See Bailey, 'Retrospective Thoughts of an Ethnohistorian.'
6 Reid, *Six Crucial Decades*, 1–26.
7 See Griffiths, 'Mating and Marriage in Early Acadia,' 122; and Griffiths, *From Migrant to Acadian*, 34–7.
8 See A.H. Clark, *Acadia*, 100–1.

14. Epilogue

1 Joe, *The Poems of Rita Joe*, 10. This passage and the succeeding quotation from Guy Arsenault were also cited in a related context in Reid, 'The Nova Scotia Historian,' 107.

2 'Your house is your home. Shediac by the sea, Bouctouche *sur mer*, I hunger for Acadie and I thirst to be able to speak' (author's translation). Arsenault, *Acadie Rock*, 21. An important anthology of Acadian writing, including work from the poets of the 1970s, is Maillet, LeBlanc, and Émont, eds., *Anthologie de textes littéraires acadiens.* For more general reflections on developments during the 1970s, see Reid, 'The 1970s,' esp. 476–83.

3 See Whitehead, *The Old Man Told Us*, 208, 239, 271–2, 302, 327, 328, 339, 342.

4 Miller, 'The Invisible Historian,' 18.

5 See Pichette, *Le pays appelé l'Acadie*, esp. 31–64; also the preface by Herménégilde Chiasson, 9–18.

Bibliography

Manuscript Sources

American Antiquarian Society
- Diary of Increase Mather.
Archives du ministère des Affaires étrangères, France
- Correspondance politique, Angleterre, vols. 64, 65, 240, 243 (LAC, R11663-7-X-F).
Archives Nationales, France
- Archives des Colonies, Séries B, C11A, C11D, E.
Bibliothèque Nationale, France
- Fonds français, 17397, 18593 (LAC, R11313-1-O-F).
Bodleian Library
- Ashurst Papers.
- Rawlinson Manuscripts, D865.
British Library
- Additional Manuscripts, vol. 19071.
- Egerton Manuscripts, vols. 929, 2395, 2526.
Colonial Williamsburg Foundation
- William Blathwayt Papers, vols. 4, 25.
Maine Historical Society, Archives
- Champernowne/Gerrish/Pepperrell Papers.
Massachusetts Historical Society
- Gay Transcripts, Sedgwick Papers.
- Parkman Papers, vols. 9, 31.
Massachusetts State Archives
- General Court Records, vol. 9.
- Massachusetts Archives, 2; 29; 30; 36; 38A; 51.

National Archives, United Kingdom
- Admiralty Papers, ADM1; ADM51.
- Colonial Papers, CO1, CO5, CO194, CO195, CO217, CO218, CO323, CO324, CO391.
- State Papers, SP16; SP44; SP78; SP103; SP105; SP108.

National Archives of Scotland
- Privy Seal Register, PS5/1.
- Yule Collection, GD90/SEC3/23, 3.

New Hampshire Archives and Records Management
- Rockingham County Deeds, vol. 2.

Nova Scotia Archives and Records Management
- Nova Scotia Records, RG1.

Printed Primary Sources

Acadiensis. Vol. 5. Saint John, NB: 1905.

Alexander, Sir William Alexander. *An Encouragement to Colonies.* London: William Stansby, 1624.

Beverley, James, and Barry Moody, eds. *The Life and Journal of the Rev. Mr. Henry Alline.* Hantsport, NS: Lancelot Press, 1982.

Biggar, Henry Percival Biggar, ed. *The Works of Samuel de Champlain.* 6 vols. Toronto: Champlain Society, 1922–36.

Birch, Thomas, ed. *A Collection of the State Papers of John Thurloe Esq.* 7 vols. London: Printed for the Executor of F. Gyles, 1742.

Boston Courant (newspaper). 1722–3.

Burton, John Hill, et al., eds. *The Register of the Privy Council of Scotland.* 38 vols. Edinburgh: H.M. General Register House, 1877–1970.

Calef, Robert. *More Wonders of the Invisible World Displayed.* London: N. Hillar and J. Collyer, 1700.

Calendar of State Papers, Colonial Series, America and West Indies, 1574–1660. Edited by W. Noel Sainsbury. London: Public Record Office, 1860.

Calloway, Colin G., ed. *Dawnland Encounters: Indians and Europeans in Northern New England.* Hanover: University Press of New England, 1991.

Collection de manuscrits contenant lettres, mémoires, et autres documents historiques relatifs à la Nouvelle-France recueillis aux Archives de la Province de Québec ou copiés à l'étranger. 4 vols. Quebec: A. Côté, 1883–5.

Collections of the Massachusetts Historical Society. Vol. 5. Boston: Massachusetts Historical Society, 1798.

Collections of the Nova Scotia Historical Society. Vol. 1. Halifax: Nova Scotia Historical Society, 1879.

Crochet, Monique, trans. 'Eastern Indians' Letter to the Governour.' *Maine Historical Society Quarterly* 13:3 (Winter 1974), 178–84.

Crokat, Gilbert. *A Consolatory Letter, Written to Lady Shovell on the Surprising and Calamitous Loss of her Husband and Two Only-Sons.* London: George Strahan, 1708.

Denys, Nicolas. *The Description and Natural History of the Coasts of North America (Acadia).* Edited by William F. Ganong. Toronto: Champlain Society, 1908.

Documentary History of the State of Maine. Edited by William Willis et al. Maine Historical Society *Collections,* Series 2. 24 vols. Portland, ME, and Cambridge, MA, 1869–1916: 3, *The Trelawny Papers,* edited by James Phinney Baxter; 6, 9, 23, *The Baxter Manuscripts,* edited by James Phinney Baxter; 7, *The Farnham Papers,* edited by Mary Frances Farnham.

Doughty, Arthur G. *Report of the Work of the Archives Branch for the Year 1912.* Ottawa: King's Printer, 1913.

Fraser, William, ed. *Memoirs of the Maxwells of Pollok.* 2 vols. Edinburgh: Privately published, 1863.

– ed. *The Red Book of Menteith.* 2 vols. Edinburgh: Privately published, 1880.

Gorges, Sir Ferdinando. 'A Brief Narration of the Original Undertakings for the Advancement of Plantations in America.' Maine Historical Society *Collections,* series 1, 2. Portland, 1847.

Great Britain, Historical Manuscripts Commission. *Report on the Manuscripts of His Grace the Duke of Portland Preserved at Welbeck Abbey.* Vol. 5. Norwich: HMSO, 1899.

– *Twelfth Report, Appendix.* Part 1, *The Manuscripts of the Earl Cowper, K.G., Preserved at Melbourne Hall, Derbyshire.* London: HMSO, 1888.

Griffiths, N.E.S., and John G. Reid, eds. 'New Evidence on New Scotland, 1629.' *William and Mary Quarterly,* 3rd ser., 49 (1992), 492–508.

Hubbard, William. 'A Narrative of the Troubles with the Indians in New England from Piscataqua to Pemaquid.' In *The History of the Indian Wars in New England,* edited by Samuel G. Drake, 1–277. New York: Burt Franklin, 1971; first published 1677.

Innes, Cosmo, et al., eds. *The Acts of the Parliament of Scotland.* 12 vols. Edinburgh: Great Britain, Record Commission, 1844–75.

Josselyn, John. *An Account of Two Voyages to New-England.* Massachusetts Historical Society *Collections,* Series 3, 3. Boston, 1833.

A Journal of the Proceedings in the Late Expedition to Port-Royal. Boston: Benjamin Harris, 1690.

'Journal of the Rev. Joseph Baxter, of Medfield, Missionary to the Eastern Indians in 1717.' Edited by Elias Nason. *New England Historical and Genealogical Register* 21 (1867), 45–60.

Labaree, Leonard Woods, ed. *Royal Instructions to British Colonial Governors, 1670-1776.* 2 vols. New York: Octagon Books, 1967; first published 1935.

Laing, David, ed. *Royal Letters, Charters, and Tracts, Relating to the Colonization of New Scotland and the Institution of the Order of Knights Baronets of Nova Scotia, 1621 to 1638.* Edinburgh: Bannatyne Club, 1867.

MacMechan, Archibald, ed. *Nova Scotia Archives III: Original Minutes of His Majesty's Council at Annapolis Royal, 1720-1739.* Halifax: McAlpine, 1908.

MacQueen, John, and Tom Scott, eds. *The Oxford Book of Scottish Verse.* Oxford: Clarendon Press, 1966.

Massachusetts Historical Society. *Proceedings.* 1st ser., 16. Boston, 1878.

Mather, Cotton. *Magnalia Christi Americana: Books I and II.* Edited by Kenneth B. Murdock with Elizabeth W. Miller. Cambridge, MA: Harvard University Press, 1977.

Mémoires des commissaires de sa majesté très-chretienne et de ceux de sa majesté brittanique. 3 vols. Amsterdam and Leipzig: J. Schreuder and Pierre Mortier le jeune, 1755.

Moody, Robert E., ed. *The Letters of Thomas Gorges, Deputy Governor of the Province of Maine, 1640-1643.* Portland: Maine Historical Society, 1978.

Morse, William Inglis, ed. *Pierre du Gua, Sieur de Monts: Records, Colonial and 'Saintongeois.'* London: B. Quaritch, 1939.

New Brunswick Historical Society Collections. Vol. 6. Saint John: New Brunswick Historical Society, 1905.

Parry, Clive, ed. *The Consolidated Treaty Series.* 231 vols. Dobbs Ferry, NY: Oceana Publications, 1969–81.

Province and Court Records of Maine. Edited by Charles Thornton Libby et al. 5 vols. Portland: Maine Historical Society, 1928–75.

Province Laws, Massachusetts. 1694–5; 1699–1700.

Recherches historiques: Bulletin d'archéologie, d'histoire, de biographie, de bibliographie, de numisnatique, etc., etc. Vol. 37. Lévis: Pierre-Georges Roy, 1931.

Report of the Public Archives for the Year 1918. Ottawa: King's Printer, 1920.

Robinson, John, and Thomas Rispin. *Journey Through Nova-Scotia Containing a Particular Account of the Country and its Inhabitants.* Sackville, NB: Ralph Pickard Bell Library, Mount Allison University, 1981; first published 1774.

Rogers, Charles, ed. *The Earl of Stirling's Register of Royal Letters Relative to the Affairs of Scotland and Nova Scotia from 1615 to 1635.* Edinburgh: Privately published, 1885.

Sewall, Samuel. *Diary of Samuel Sewall.* Edited by M. Halsey Thomas. 2 vols. New York: Farrar, Straus and Giroux, 1973.

Skene, William Forbes, ed. *Memorials of the Family of Skene of Skene.* Aberdeen: New Spalding Club, 1887.

Slafter, Edmund F., ed. *Sir William Alexander and American Colonization.* Boston: Prince Society, 1873.

Stoughton, William. *New-Englands true interest; not to lie: or, A treatise declaring from the word of truth the terms on which we stand, and the tenure by which we hold our hitherto-continued precious and pleasant things: Shewing what the blessed God expecteth from his people, and what they may rationally look for from him: Delivered in a sermon preached in Boston in New-England, April 29, 1668.* Cambridge, MA: Printed by S.G. and M.J., 1670.

Suffolk Deeds. Vol. 1. Boston: Rockwell and Churchill, 1881.

Thomson, John Maitland, ed. *The Register of the Great Seal of Scotland* [Vol. 8], *A.D. 1620-1633.* Edinburgh: H.M. General Register House, 1894.

Urquhart, Thomas, ed. *Tracts of the Learned and Celebrated Antiquarian Sir Thomas Urquhart of Cromarty.* Edinburgh: Charles Herriott, 1774.

Webster, John Clarence, ed. *Acadia at the End of the Seventeenth Century: Letters, Journals and Memoirs of Joseph Robineau de Villebon, Commandant in Acadia, 1690-1700, and Other Contemporary Documents.* Saint John, N.B.: New Brunswick Museum, 1934.

Whitehead, Ruth Holmes. *The Old Man Told Us: Excerpts from Micmac History.* Halifax: Nimbus, 1991.

Winthrop, John. *Winthrop's Journal.* Edited by James Kendall Hosmer. 2 vols. New York: C. Scribner's Sons, 1908.

Winthrop Papers. Massachusetts Historical Society *Collections,* Series 4, 6–7. Boston, 1863–71.

York Deeds. 18 vols. Portland: Maine Historical Society, 1887–1911.

Secondary Sources

Allen, Robert S., ed. *The Loyal Americans: The Military Rôle of the Loyalist Provincial Corps and Their Settlement in British North America, 1775–1784* Ottawa: National Museum of Man / National Museums of Canada, 1983.

Alsop, James D. 'The Age of the Projectors: British Imperial Strategy in the North Atlantic in the War of the Spanish Succession.' *Acadiensis* 21:1 (Autumn 1991), 30-53.

– 'Samuel Vetch's "Canada Survey'd": The Formation of a Colonial Strategy, 1706–1710.' *Acadiensis* 12:1 (Autumn 1982), 39–58.

Anderson, Fred. *The Crucible of War: The Seven Years' War and the Fate of Empire in British North America, 1754–1766.* New York: Knopf, 2000.

Anderson, Virginia DeJohn. *Creatures of Empire: How Domestic Animals Transformed Early America.* New York: Oxford University Press, 2004.

– 'King Philip's Herds: Indians, Colonists, and the Problem of Livestock in

Early New England.' *William and Mary Quarterly*, 3rd ser., 51 (1994), 601–24.

Andrews, Charles McLean. *The Colonial Period of American History*. 4 vols. New Haven: Yale University Press, 1934–8.

Armitage, David. *The Ideological Origins of the British Empire*. Cambridge: Cambridge University Press, 2000.

– 'Three Concepts of Atlantic History.' In David Armitage and Michael J. Braddick, eds., *The British Atlantic World, 1500-1800*, 11–27. New York: Palgrave Macmillan, 2002.

Armitage, David, and Michael J. Braddick, eds. *The British Atlantic World, 1500-1800*. New York: Palgrave Macmillan, 2002.

Armstrong, Joe C.W. *Champlain*. Toronto: Macmillan, 1987.

Armstrong, M.W. 'Neutrality and Religion in Revolutionary Nova Scotia.' *New England Quarterly* 19 (1946), 50-62.

Arsenault, Guy. *Acadie Rock*. Moncton: Éditions d'Acadie, 1973.

Augustine, Stephen. '*Lsipogtog*, "River of Fire": A Historical Analysis.' Report to the Big Cove Band, 2003.

Axtell, James. *Beyond 1492: Encounters in Colonial North America*. New York: Oxford University Press, 1992.

– 'Beyond 1992.' In James Axtell, *Beyond 1492: Encounters in Colonial North America*, 267–316. New York: Oxford University Press, 1992.

– 'Columbian Encounters: 1992–1995.' *William and Mary Quarterly*, 3rd ser., 52 (1995), 649–96.

– 'The Ethnohistory of Early America.' *William and Mary Quarterly*, 3rd ser., 35 (1978), 110-44.

– 'The White Indians of Colonial America.' *William and Mary Quarterly*, 3rd ser., 32 (1975), 55–88.

Bailey, Alfred G. 'Retrospective Thoughts of an Ethnohistorian.' Canadian Historical Association, *Historical Papers/Communications historiques, 1977: A Selection from the Papers Presented at the 1977 Annual Meeting Held at Fredericton*, 15–29.

Bailyn, Bernard. *The New England Merchants in the Seventeenth Century*. Cambridge, MA: Harvard University Press, 1955.

Baker, Emerson W. 'Finding the Almouchiquois: Native American Families, Territories and Land Sales in Southern Maine.' *Ethnohistory* 51 (2004), 73–100.

– 'New Evidence on the French Involvement in King Philip's War.' *Maine Historical Society Quarterly* 28:2 (1988), 85–91.

– '"A Scratch with a Bear's Paw": Anglo-Indian Land Deals in Early Maine.' *Ethnohistory* 36 (1989), 235–56.

– 'Trouble to the Eastward: The Failure of Anglo–Indian Relations in Early Maine.' PhD thesis, College of William and Mary, 1985.

Baker, Emerson W., Edwin A. Churchill, Richard S. D'Abate, Kristine L. Jones, Victor A. Konrad, and Harald E.L. Prins, eds. *American Beginnings: Exploration, Culture, and Cartography in the Land of Norumbega.* Lincoln: University of Nebraska Press, 1994.

Baker, Emerson W., and James Kences. 'Maine, Indian Land Speculation, and the Essex County Witchcraft Outbreak of 1692.' *Maine History* 40:3 (2001), 159–89.

Baker, Emerson W., and John G. Reid. 'Amerindian Power in the Early Modern Northeast: A Reappraisal.' *William and Mary Quarterly,* 3rd ser., 61 (2004), 77–106.

– *The New England Knight: Sir William Phips, 1651–1695.* Toronto: University of Toronto Press, 1998.

– 'Sir William Phips and the Decentring of Empire in Northeastern North America, 1690-1694.' In Germaine Warkentin and Carolyn Podruchny, eds., *Decentring the Renaissance: Canada and Europe in Multidisciplinary Perspective, 1500-1700,* 287–302. Toronto: University of Toronto Press, 2001.

Banks, Charles Edward. *History of York, Maine.* 2 vols. Boston: Calkins Press, 1931–5.

Banks, Kenneth J. *Chasing Empire across the Sea: Communications and the State in the French Atlantic, 1713–1763.* Montreal and Kingston: McGill-Queen's University Press, 2002.

Barkham, Selma. 'The Documentary Evidence for Basque Whaling Ships in the Strait of Belle Isle.' In G.M. Story, ed., *Early European Settlement and Exploitation in Atlantic Canada: Selected Papers,* 53–95. St John's: Memorial University of Newfoundland, 1982.

Barnes, Thomas Garden. '"The Dayly Cry for Justice": The Juridical Failure of the Annapolis Royal Regime, 1713–1749.' In Philip Girard and Jim Phillips, eds., *Essays in the History of Canadian Law,* vol. 3, *Nova Scotia,* 10-41. Toronto: University of Toronto Press, for The Osgoode Society, 1990.

Barnes, Viola F. 'Francis Legge, Governor of Loyalist Nova Scotia, 1773–1776.' *New England Quarterly* 4 (1931), 420-47.

– 'Phippius Maximus.' *New England Quarterly* 1 (1928), 532–53.

Basque, Maurice. 'Family and Political Culture in Pre-Conquest Acadia.' In John G. Reid et al., *The 'Conquest' of Acadia, 1710: Imperial, Colonial, and Abo riginal Constructions,* 48–63. Toronto: University of Toronto Press, 2004.

– *Des hommes de pouvoir: Histoire d'Otho Robichaud et de sa famille, notables acadiens de Port-Royal et de Néguac.* Néguac: Société historique de Néguac, 1996.

– 'The Third Acadia: Political Adaptation and Societal Change.' In John G.

Reid et al., *The 'Conquest' of Acadia, 1710: Imperial, Colonial, and Aboriginal Constructions*, 155–77. Toronto: University of Toronto Press, 2004.

Basque, Maurice, with the collaboration of Eric Snow. *La Société Nationale de l'Acadie: Au coeur de la réussite d'un peuple.* Moncton: Les Éditions de la Francophonie, 2006.

Baudry, René. 'Charles d'Aulnay et la Compagnie de la Nouvelle France.' *Revue d'histoire de l'Amérique française* 11 (1957–8), 218–41.

Baxter, James Phinney. *George Cleeve of Casco Bay, 1630-1667.* Portland: Gorges Society, 1885.

Bayly, C.A. 'The British and Indigenous Peoples, 1760-1860: Power, Perception and Identity.' In Martin Daunton and Rick Halpern, eds., *Empire and Others: British Encounters with Indigenous Peoples, 1600-1850*, 19–41. Philadelphia: University of Pennsylvania Press, 1999.

– *Imperial Meridian: The British Empire and the World, 1780-1830.* London: Longman, 1989.

Bell, D.G. *Early Loyalist Saint John: The Origin of New Brunswick Politics, 1783–1786.* Fredericton: New Ireland Press, 1983.

Benes, Peter, ed. *New England Prospect: Maps, Place Names, and the Historical Landscape, Proceedings of the Fifth Dublin Seminar for New England Folklife.* Boston: Boston University, [1980].

Berger, Carl. *The Writing of Canadian History: Aspects of English Canadian Historical Writing,1900-1970.* Toronto: Oxford University Press, 1976.

Bernard, Antoine. *Le drame acadien depuis 1604.* Montreal: Les clercs de Saint-Viateur, 1936.

Bishop, Morris. *Champlain: The Life of Fortitude.* New York: Knopf, 1948.

Black, Jeremy. *British Foreign Policy in the Age of Walpole.* Edinburgh: John Donald, 1985.

– *European Warfare, 1660-1815.* New Haven: Yale University Press, 1994.

Bond, Beverley W., Jr. *The Quit-Rent System in the American Colonies.* New Haven: Yale University Press, 1919.

Bourinot, John G. 'Builders of Nova Scotia.' Royal Society of Canada, *Proceedings and Transactions*, 2nd ser., 5 (1899), section 2, 1–198.

Bourque, Bruce J. 'Ethnicity on the Maritime Peninsula, 1600-1759.' *Ethnohistory* 36 (1989), 257–84.

Bourque, Bruce J., with contributions by Steven L. Cox and Ruth H. Whitehead. *Twelve Thousand Years: American Indians in Maine.* Lincoln: University of Nebraska Press, 2001.

Bourque, Bruce J., and Ruth Holmes Whitehead. 'Tarrentines and the Introduction of European Trade Goods in the Gulf of Maine.' *Ethnohistory* 32 (1985), 327–41.

– 'Trade and Alliances in the Contact Period.' In Emerson W. Baker et al., eds., *American Beginnings: Exploration, Culture, and Cartography in the Land of Norumbega*, 131–47. Lincoln: University of Nebraska Press, 1994.

Bowen, Francis. 'Life of Sir William Phips.' In Jared Sparks, ed., *American Biography*, vol. 10, 3–100. New York: Harper and Brothers, 1902 (first published 1854).

Bowen, H.V. *War and British Society, 1688–1815*. Cambridge: Cambridge University Press, 1998.

Brebner, John Bartlet. *The Neutral Yankees of Nova Scotia: A Marginal Colony during the Revolutionary Years*. New York: Columbia University Press, 1937.

– *North Atlantic Triangle: The Interplay of Canada, the United States, and Great Britain*. 2nd ed. Toronto: McClelland & Stewart, 1966.

Breen, T.H. *The Character of the Good Ruler: A Study of Puritan Political Ideas in New England, 1630-1730*. New Haven: Yale University Press, 1970.

Brewer, John. *The Sinews of Power: War, Money, and the English State, 1688–1783*. New York: Alfred A. Knopf, 1989.

Brown, George W., et al., eds. *Dictionary of Canadian Biography*. 15 vols. to date. Toronto: University of Toronto Press, 1966–.

Buckner, Phillip A., and John G. Reid, eds. *The Atlantic Region to Confederation: A History*. Toronto and Fredericton: University of Toronto Press and Acadiensis Press, 1994.

Buffinton, Arthur Howland. 'Sir Thomas Temple in Boston: A Case of Benevolent Assimilation.' *Publications of the Colonial Society of Massachusetts* 27 (1932), 308–19.

Bumsted, J.M. *Henry Alline, 1748–1784*. Toronto: University of Toronto Press, 1971.

Burke, Peter. 'Languages and Anti-Languages in Early Modern Italy.' *History Workshop Journal* 11 (Spring 1981), 24–32.

Burke, Peter, and Roy Porter, eds. *The Social History of Language*. Cambridge: Cambridge University Press, 1987.

Burrage, Henry Sweetser. *The Beginnings of Colonial Maine, 1602–1658*. Portland: Printed for the State, 1914.

Bury, J.B. 'Cleopatra's Nose.' In J.B. Bury, *Selected Essays of J.B. Bury*, 60-9. Edited by Harold Temperley. Cambridge: Cambridge University Press, 1930.

– *Selected Essays of J.B. Bury*. Edited by Harold Temperley. Cambridge: Cambridge University Press, 1930.

Bushnell, Amy Turner, and Jack P. Greene. 'Peripheries, Centers, and the Construction of Early Modern American Empires: An Introduction.' In Christine Daniels and Michael V. Kennedy, eds., *Negotiated Empires: Centers and Peripheries in the Americas, 1500-1820*, 1–14. New York: Routledge, 2002.

Cain, P.J., and A.G. Hopkins. *British Imperialism: Innovation and Expansion, 1688–1914.* London: Longman, 1993.

Calloway, Colin G. *New Worlds for All: Indians, Europeans, and the Remaking of Early America.* Baltimore: Johns Hopkins University Press, 1997.

– *The Western Abenakis of Vermont, 1600-1800: War, Migration and the Survival of an Indian People.* Norman: University of Oklahoma Press, 1990.

Carr, E.H. *What Is History?* New York: Vintage Books, 1961.

Carroll, Charles F. *The Timber Economy of Puritan New England.* Providence: Brown University Press, 1973.

Carter, Paul. *The Road to Botany Bay: An Essay in Spatial History.* London: Faber, 1987.

Cell, Gillian T. *English Enterprise in Newfoundland, 1577–1660.* Toronto: University of Toronto Press, 1969.

Chard, Donald F. 'The Impact of French Privateering on New England, 1689–1713.' *American Neptune* 35 (1975), 153–65.

Chet, Guy. *Conquering the American Wilderness: The Triumph of European Warfare in the Colonial Northeast.* Amherst: University of Massachusetts Press, 2003.

Choquette, Leslie. *Frenchmen into Peasants: Modernity and Tradition in the Peopling of French Canada.* Cambridge, MA: Harvard University Press, 1997.

Christmas, Peter. 'Foreword.' In Dianne O'Neill, curator, *At the Great Harbour: 250 Years on the Halifax Waterfront,* iv. Halifax: Art Gallery of Nova Scotia, 1999.

Clark, Andrew Hill. *Acadia: The Geography of Early Nova Scotia to 1760.* Madison: University of Wisconsin Press, 1968.

– *Three Centuries and the Island: A Historical Geography of Settlement and Agriculture in Prince Edward Island, Canada.* Toronto: University of Toronto Press, 1959.

Clark, Charles E. *The Eastern Frontier: The Settlement of Northern New England, 1610-1763.* New York: Knopf, 1970.

Clark, Sir George. *War and Society in the Seventeenth Century.* Cambridge: Cambridge University Press, 1958.

Clarke, Ernest. *The Siege of Fort Cumberland, 1776: An Episode in the American Revolution.* Montreal and Kingston: McGill-Queen's University Press, 1995.

Coates, Ken. *The Marshall Decision and Native Rights.* Montreal and Kingston: McGill-Queen's University Press, 2000.

Codignola, Luca. *The Coldest Harbour of the Land: Simon Stock and Lord Baltimore's Colony in Newfoundland, 1621–1649.* Kingston and Montreal: McGill-Queen's University Press, 1988.

– 'Competing Networks: Roman Catholic Ecclesiastics in French North America, 1610-58.' *Canadian Historical Review* 80 (1999), 539–84.

Colby, Charles W. *The Founder of New France: A Chronicle of Champlain.* Glasgow: Brook & Co., 1915.

Condon, Ann Gorman. *The Envy of the American States: The Loyalist Dream for New Brunswick.* Fredericton: New Ireland Press, 1984.

Conrad, Margaret, ed. *Intimate Relations: Family and Community in Planter Nova Scotia, 1759–1800.* Fredericton: Acadiensis Press, 1995.

– *Looking Into Acadie: Three Illustrated Studies.* Halifax: Nova Scotia Museum, [1999].

– *Making Adjustments: Change and Continuity in Planter Nova Scotia, 1759–1800.* Fredericton: Acadiensis Press, 1991.

– *They Planted Well: New England Planters in Maritime Canada.* Fredericton: Acadiensis Press, 1988.

Conrad, Margaret, and Barry Moody, eds. *Planter Links: Community and Culture in Colonial Nova Scotia.* Fredericton: Acadiensis Press, 2001.

Couillard-Després, Azarie. *Charles de Saint-Étienne de La Tour, gouverneur, lieutenant-général en Acadie, et son temps, 1593–1666.* Arthabaska, QC: Imprimerie d'Arthabaska, 1930.

Cowley, Robert, ed. *What If? The World's Foremost Military Historians Imagine What Might Have Been.* New York: Putnam, 1999.

Cronon, William. *Changes in the Land: Indians, Colonists, and the Ecology of New England.* New York: Hill and Wang, 1983.

Daniels, Christine, and Michael V. Kennedy, eds. *Negotiated Empires: Centers and Peripheries in the Americas, 1500-1820.* New York: Routledge, 2002.

Daunton, Martin, and Rick Halpern, eds. *Empire and Others: British Encounters with Indigenous Peoples, 1600-1850.* Philadelphia: University of Pennsylvania Press, 1999.

Davies, J.D. *Gentlemen and Tarpaulins: The Officers and Men of the Restoration Navy.* Oxford: Clarendon Press, 1991.

Davis, Stephen A. 'Early Societies: Sequences of Change.' In Phillip A. Buckner and John G. Reid, eds., *The Atlantic Region to Confederation: A History,* 3–21. Toronto and Fredericton: University of Toronto Press and Acadiensis Press, 1994.

Dawson, Joan. 'Colonists or Birds of Passage? A Glimpse of the Inhabitants of LaHave, 1632–1636.' *Nova Scotia Historical Review* 9:1 (1989), 42–61.

Dechêne, Louise. *Habitants and Merchants in Seventeenth-Century Montreal.* Translated by Liana Vardi. Montreal and Kingston: McGill-Queen's University Press, 1992; first published 1974.

Delâge, Denys. *Le pays renversé: Amérindiens et Européens en Amérique du Nord-Est, 1600-1664.* Montreal: Boréal, 1985. Published in English translation as *Bitter Feast: Amerindians and Europeans in Northeastern North America, 1600-64*, translated by Jane Brierley. Vancouver: UBC Press, 1993.

Demos, John. *The Unredeemed Captive: A Family Story from Early America.* New York: Knopf, 1994.

Dening, Greg. *Mr Bligh's Bad Language: Passion, Power and Theatre on the Bounty.* Cambridge: Cambridge University Press, 1992.

D'Entremont, Clarence-J. 'Du nouveau sur les Melanson.' *La société historique acadienne: Les cahiers* 3:8 (July–September 1970), 339–52.

– 'Les Melanson d'Acadie sont français de père et anglais de mère.' *La société historique acadienne: Les cahiers* 4: 10 (July–September 1973), 416–19.

DePaoli, Neill. 'Beaver, Blankets, Liquor, and Politics: Pemaquid's Fur Trade, 1614–1760.' *Maine Historical Society Quarterly* 33 (1993–4), 166–201.

Desbarats, Catherine. 'The Cost of Early Canada's Native Alliances: Reality and Scarcity's Rhetoric.' *William and Mary Quarterly*, 3rd ser., 52 (1995), 609–30.

Deschamps, Léon. *Un colonisateur du temps de Richelieu, Isaac de Razilly, biographie, mémoire inédit.* Paris: Institut géographique de Paris, 1887.

Devine, T.M., and S.G.E. Lythe. 'The Economy of Scotland under James VI: A Revision Article.' *Scottish Historical Review* 50 (1971), 91–106.

Dionne, N.E. *Samuel Champlain, fondateur de Québec et père de la Nouvelle-France: histoire de sa vie et de ses voyages.* 2 vols. Quebec: A. Coté, 1891–1906.

Donovan, Kenneth. 'Slaves and Their Owners in Ile Royale, 1713–1760.' *Acadiensis* 25:1 (Autumn 1995), 3–32.

Doxtator, Deborah. 'Inclusive and Exclusive Perceptions of Difference: Native and Euro-Based Concepts of Time, History, and Change.' In Germaine Warkentin and Carolyn Podruchny, eds., *Decentring the Renaissance: Canada and Europe in Multidisciplinary Perspective, 1500-1700*, 33–47. Toronto: University of Toronto Press, 2001.

Doyle-Bedwell, Patricia. 'How French Settlement Affected Mi'kmaq People.' At http://www.cbc.ca/news/background/champlainanniversary/micmac.html.

Drake, James D. *King Philip's War: Civil War in New England, 1675–1676.* Amherst: University of Massachusetts Press, 1999.

Duffy, Michael, ed. *The Military Revolution and the State, 1500-1800.* Exeter: University of Exeter, 1980.

Dunn, Brenda. *A History of Port Royal/Annapolis Royal, 1605–1800.* Halifax: Nimbus, 2004.

Dwyer, John, Roger A. Mason, and Alexander Murdoch, eds., *New Perspectives on the Politics and Culture of Early Modern Scotland.* Edinburgh: John Donald, 1982.

Eccles, W.J. *Essays on New France.* Toronto: Oxford University Press, 1987.
– *Frontenac: The Courtier Governor.* Toronto: McClelland & Stewart, 1959.
– 'Sovereignty-Association, 1500-1783.' *Canadian Historical Review* 65 (1984), 475–510.
Faragher, John Mack. *A Great and Noble Scheme: The Tragic Story of the Expulsion of the French Acadians from Their American Homeland.* New York: Norton, 2005.
Faulkner, Alaric, and Gretchen Fearon Faulkner. *The French at Pentagoet, 1635–1674: An Archaeological Portrait of the Acadian Frontier.* Augusta, ME, and Saint John, NB: Maine Historic Preservation Commission and New Brunswick Museum, 1987.
Ferguson, Niall, ed. *Virtual History: Alternatives and Counterfactuals.* London: Picador, 1997.
Fingard, Judith, Janet Guildford, and David Sutherland. *Halifax: The First 250 Years.* Halifax: Formac, 1999.
Flenley, Ralph. *Samuel de Champlain, Founder of New France.* Toronto: Macmillan, 1924.
Flynn, Charles P. *Insult and Society: Patterns of Comparative Interaction.* Port Washington, NY: Kennikat Press, 1977.
Forbes, E.R., and D.A. Muise, eds. *The Atlantic Provinces in Confederation.* Toronto and Fredericton: University of Toronto Press and Acadiensis Press, 1993.
Foucault, Michel. *Language, Counter-Memory, Practice: Selected Essays and Interviews.* Edited by Donald F. Bouchard. Ithaca, NY: Cornell University Press, 1977.
Furgol, Edward M. *A Regimental History of the Covenanting Armies, 1639–1651.* Edinburgh: John Donald, 1990.
Games, Alison. *Migration and the Origins of the English Atlantic World.* Cambridge, MA: Harvard University Press, 1999.
Garrioch, David. 'Verbal Insults in Eighteenth-Century Paris.' In Peter Burke and Roy Porter, eds., *The Social History of Language,* 104–19. Cambridge: Cambridge University Press, 1987.
Ghere, David L. 'Eastern Abenaki Autonomy and French Frustrations, 1745–1760.' *Maine History* 34:1 (1994), 2–21.
– 'Mistranslations and Misinformation: Diplomacy on the Maine Frontier, 1725 to 1755.' *American Indian Culture and Research Journal* 8:4 (1984), 3–26.
Girard, Philip, and Jim Phillips, eds. *Essays in the History of Canadian Law,* vol. 3, *Nova Scotia.* Toronto: University of Toronto Press, for The Osgoode Society, 1990.
Goold, William. 'Sir William Phips.' *Maine Historical Society Collections* 9 (1887), 1–72.

Greene, Jack P. *Negotiated Authorities: Essays in Colonial Political and Constitutional History.* Charlottesville: University Press of Virginia, 1994.

– 'Negotiated Authorities: The Problem of Governance in the Extended Polities of the Early Modern Atlantic World,' in Greene *Negotiated Authorities,* 1–24.

Greer, Allan. 'Canadian History: Ancient and Modern.' *Canadian Historical Review* 77 (1996), 575–90.

Griffiths, N.E.S. *From Migrant to Acadian: A North American Border People, 1604–1755.* Montreal and Kingston: McGill-Queen's University Press, 2005.

– 'Mating and Marriage in Early Acadia.' *Renaissance and Modern Studies* 35 (1992), 109–27.

Gwyn, Julian. *Excessive Expectations: Maritime Commerce and the Economic Development of Nova Scotia, 1740-1870.* Montreal and Kingston: McGill-Queen's University Press, 1998.

– 'The Mi'kmaq, Poor Settlers, and the Nova Scotia Fur Trade, 1783–1853.' *Journal of the Canadian Historical Association,* new ser., 14 (2003), 65–91.

Haefeli, Evan, and Kevin Sweeney. *Captors and Captives: The 1704 French and Indian Raid on Deerfield.* Amherst: University of Massachusetts Press, 2003.

– 'Revisiting *The Redeemed Captive*: New Perspectives on the 1704 Attack on Deerfield.' *William and Mary Quarterly,* 3rd ser., 52 (1995), 3–46.

Hall, David D., and David Grayson Allen, eds. *Seventeenth-Century New England.* Boston: Colonial Society of Massachusetts, 1984.

Hall, Michael G. *The Last American Puritan: The Life of Increase Mather, 1639–1723.* Middletown, CT: Wesleyan University Press, 1988.

Halliday, M.A.K. *Language as Social Semiotic: The Social Interpretation of Language and Meaning.* London: Edward Arnold, 1978.

Harley, J.B. *Maps and the Columbian Encounter: An Interpretive Guide to the Travelling Expedition, American Geographical Society Collection.* Milwaukee: Golda Meir Library, University of Wisconsin, 1990.

– 'New England Cartography and the Native Americans.' In Emerson W. Baker et al., eds., *American Beginnings: Exploration, Culture, and Cartography in the Land of Norumbega,* 287–313. Lincoln: University of Nebraska Press, 1994.

Harrington, Faith. '"Wee Tooke Great Store of Cod-fish": Fishing Ships and First Settlements on the Coast of New England, 1600-1630.' In Emerson W. Baker et al., eds., *American Beginnings: Exploration, Culture, and Cartography in the Land of Norumbega,* 191–216. Lincoln: University of Nebraska Press, 1994.

Harris, R. Cole, ed., and Geoffrey Matthews, cart. *Historical Atlas of Canada,* vol. 1, *From the Beginning to 1800.* Toronto: University of Toronto Press, [1987].

Harvey, D.C. *The French Régime in Prince Edward Island.* New Haven: Yale University Press, 1926.

Hautecoeur, Jean-Paul. *L'Acadie du discours: Pour une sociologie de la culture acadienne.* Quebec: Les presses de l'Université Laval, 1975.

Havard, Gilles. *Empire et métissages: Indiens et Français dans le Pays d'en Haut, 1660-1715.* Quebec and Paris: Septentrion and Presses de l'Université Paris-Sorbonne, 2003.

– *The Great Peace of Montreal of 1701: French-Native Diplomacy in the Seventeenth Century.* Montreal and Kingston: McGill-Queen's University Press, 2001.

Havard, Gilles, and Cécile Vidal. *Histoire de l'Amérique française.* Paris: Flammarion, 2003.

Heidenreich, Conrad E. 'The Beginning of French Exploration out of the St Lawrence Valley: Motives, Methods, and Changing Attitudes towards Native People.' In Germaine Warkentin and Carolyn Podruchny, eds., *Decentring the Renaissance: Canada and Europe in Multidisciplinary Perspective, 1500-1700,* 236–51. Toronto: University of Toronto Press, 2001.

Hill, George. *An Historical Account of the Plantation of Ulster at the Commencement of the Seventeenth Century, 1608–1630.* Belfast: M'Caw & Co., 1877.

Hiller, J.K. 'Utrecht Revisited: The Origins of French Fishing Rights in Newfoundland Waters.' *Newfoundland Studies* 7:1 (1991), 23–39.

Hirsch, Adam J. 'The Collision of Military Cultures in Seventeenth-Century New England.' *Journal of American History* 74 (1997–8), 1187–1212.

Hobsbawm, Eric, and Terence Ranger, eds. *The Invention of Tradition.* Cambridge: Cambridge University Press, 1983.

Hoffman, Paul E. *Florida's Frontiers.* Bloomington: Indiana University Press, 2002.

Hornsby, Stephen J. *British Atlantic, American Frontier: Spaces of Power in Early Modern British America.* Hanover, NH: University Press of New England, 2005.

Hornsby, Stephen J., and John G. Reid, eds. *New England and the Maritime Provinces: Connections and Comparisons.* Montreal and Kingston: McGill-Queen's University Press, 2005.

Huskins, Bonnie, and Michael Boudreau. 'Life after Île Ste-Croix.' *Acadiensis* 35:2 (Spring 2006), 180-7.

Hutchinson, Thomas. *The History of the Colony and Province of Massachusetts-Bay.* Edited by Lawrence Shaw Mayo. 3 vols. Cambridge, MA: Harvard University Press, 1936.

Insh, George Pratt. *Scottish Colonial Schemes, 1620-1686.* Glasgow: Maclehose, Jackson & Co., 1922.

Inwood, Kris, ed. *Farm, Factory and Fortune: New Studies in the Economic History of the Maritime Provinces.* Fredericton: Acadiensis Press, 1993.

Isaac, Thomas. *Aboriginal and Treaty Rights in the Maritimes: The* Marshall *Decision and Beyond.* Saskatoon: Purich Publishing, 2001.

Jenness, John Scribner. *The Isles of Shoals: An Historical Sketch.* New York: Hurd and Houghton, 1873.

Jennings, Francis. *The Invasion of America: Indians, Colonialism, and the Cant of Conquest.* Chapel Hill: University of North Carolina Press, 1975.

Joe, Rita. *The Poems of Rita Joe.* Halifax: Abanaki Press, 1978.

Johnson, Richard R. 'Charles McLean Andrews and the Invention of American Colonial History.' *William and Mary Quarterly,* 3rd ser., 43 (1986), 528–41.

– *John Nelson, Merchant Adventurer: A Life between Empires.* New York: Oxford University Press, 1991.

Jones, David S. 'Virgin Soils Revisited.' *William and Mary Quarterly,* 3rd ser., 60 (2003), 703–42.

Jones, Gareth Stedman. *The Languages of Class: Studies in English Working Class History, 1832–1982.* Cambridge: Cambridge University Press, 1983.

Kamensky, Jane. *Governing the Tongue: The Politics of Speech in Early New England.* New York: Oxford University Press, 1997.

Kellett, Stephen H. *In the Wake of Chaos: Unpredictable Order in Dynamical Systems.* Chicago: University of Chicago Press, 1993.

Kerr, Wilfred Brenton. *The Maritime Provinces of British North America and the American Revolution.* New York: Russell and Russell, 1970; first published 1941.

– 'The Merchants of Nova Scotia and the American Revolution.' *Canadian Historical Review* 13 (1932), 20-36.

– 'Nova Scotia in 1775–6.' *Dalhousie Review* 12 (1932–3), 97–107.

Kershaw, Gordon E. *'Gentlemen of Large Property and Judicious Men': The Kennebec Proprietors, 1749–1775.* Portland: Maine Historical Society, 1975.

Krim, Arthur J. 'Acculturation of the New England Landscape: Native and English Toponymy of Eastern Massachusetts.' In Peter Benes, ed., *New England Prospect: Maps, Place Names, and the Historical Landscape, Proceedings of the Fifth Dublin Seminar for New England Folklife,* 69–88. Boston: Boston University, [1980].

Kupperman, Karen Ordahl. *Indians and English: Facing off in Early America.* Ithaca, NY: Cornell University Press, 2000.

Lahey, Raymond J. 'Avalon: Lord Baltimore's Colony in Newfoundland.' In G.M. Story, ed., *Early European Settlement and Exploitation in Atlantic Canada,* 115–37. St John's: Memorial University of Newfoundland, 1982.

Laplante, Corinne. 'Le traité d'Utrecht et la question des limites territoriales de l'Acadie.' *La société historique acadienne: Les cahiers* 6:1 (1975), 25–42.

Leach, Douglas Edward. *Arms for Empire: A Military History of the British Colonies in North America, 1607–1763.* New York: Macmillan, 1973.

– *Flintlock and Tomahawk: New England in King Philip's War.* New York: Macmillan, 1958.

– *The Northern Colonial Frontier, 1607–1763.* New York: Holt, Rinehart, and Winston, 1966.

LeBlanc, Ronnie-Gilles. 'Critique du film documentaire *Life after Île Sainte-Croix.*' *CHA Bulletin* 32:1 (2006), 1–3.

LeBlanc, Ronnie-Gilles, ed. *Du Grand Dérangement à la Déportation: Nouvelles perspectives historiques.* Moncton: Chaire d'études acadiennes, Université de Moncton, 2005.

Le Blant, Robert. 'L'avitaillement du Port-Royal d'Acadie par Charles de Biencourt et les marchands rochelais, 1615–1618.' *Revue d'histoire des colonies* 44 (1958), 138–64.

– *Un colonial sous Louis XIV: Philippe de Pastour de Costebelle, gouverneur de Terre-Neuve, puis de l'Île Royale, 1661–1717.* Dax: Pradeu, 1937.

– 'Les compagnies du Cap-Breton, 1629–1647.' *Revue d'histoire de l'Amérique française* 16 (1962–3), 81–94.

– *Une figure légendaire de l'histoire acadienne: Le Baron de Saint-Castin.* Dax: Pradeu, 1934.

– 'La première compagnie de Miscou, 1635–1645.' *Revue d'histoire de l'Amérique française* 17 (1963–4), 363–70.

Lee, Wayne E. 'Early American Ways of War: A New Reconnaissance, 1600-1815.' *Historical Journal* 44 (2001), 269–89.

Lenman, Bruce. *Britain's Colonial Wars, 1688–1783.* London: Longman, 2001.

Lepore, Jill. *The Name of War: King Philip's War and the Origins of American Identity.* New York: Knopf, 1998.

Liebel, Jean. 'On a vieilli Champlain.' *Revue d'histoire de l'Amérique française* 32 (1978–9), 228–37.

Longley, R.S. 'The Coming of the New England Planters to the Annapolis Valley.' *Collections of the Nova Scotia Historical Society* (Halifax, 1961), 81–101.

Lorenz, Edward N. *The Essence of Chaos.* Seattle: University of Washington Press, 1993.

– *The Nature and Theory of the General Circulation of the Atmosphere.* [Washington, DC]: World Meteorological Organization, 1967.

Louis, W. Roger, editor-in-chief. *The Oxford History of the British Empire.* 5 vols. Oxford: Oxford University Press, 1998–9.

Lythe, S.G.E. *The Economy of Scotland in Its European Setting,* 1550-1625. Edinburgh: Oliver and Boyd, 1960.

MacDonald, M.A. *Fortune and La Tour: The Civil War in Acadia.* Toronto: Methuen, 1983.

– *Robert Le Blant, historien et chef de file de la recherche sur les débuts de la Nouvelle-France: Bibliographie commentée.* Saint John: New Brunswick Museum, 1986.

McGrail, Thomas H. *Sir William Alexander, First Earl of Stirling: A Biographical Study.* Edinburgh: Oliver and Boyd, 1940.

Macinnes, A.I. 'Scottish Gaeldom, 1638–1651: The Vernacular Response to the Covenanting Dynamic.' In John Dwyer, Roger A. Mason, and Alexander Murdoch, eds., *New Perspectives on the Politics and Culture of Early Modern Scotland,* 59–94. Edinburgh: John Donald, 1982.

McKay, Ian. 'Tartanism Triumphant: The Construction of Scottishness in Nova Scotia, 1933–1954.'' *Acadiensis* 21:2 (Spring 1992), 5–47.

Mackenzie, William Cook. *History of the Outer Hebrides.* Paisley: Alexander Gardner, 1903.

MacKinnon, Neil. *This Unfriendly Soil: The Loyalist Experience in Nova Scotia, 1783–1791.* Kingston and Montreal: McGill-Queen's University Press, 1986.

MacLennan, Hugh. *On Being a Maritime Writer.* Sackville, NB: Mount Allison University, [1984].

McManis, Douglas R. *Colonial New England: A Historical Geography.* New York: Oxford University Press, 1975.

MacNeil, Alan R. 'The Acadian Legacy and Agricultural Development in Nova Scotia, 1760-1861.' In Kris Inwood, ed., *Farm, Factory and Fortune: New Studies in the Economic History of the Maritime Provinces,* 1–16. Fredericton: Acadiensis Press, 1993.

MacNutt, W.S. *The Atlantic Provinces: The Emergence of Colonial Society.* Toronto: McClelland & Stewart, 1965.

– *New Brunswick, A History: 1784–1867.* Toronto: Macmillan, 1963.

Maillet, Marguerite, Gérard LeBlanc, and Bernard Émont, eds. *Anthologie de textes littéraires acadiens, 1606–1975.* Moncton: Éditions d'Acadie, 1979.

Malone, Patrick M. *The Skulking Way of War: Technology and Tactics among the New England Indians.* 2nd ed. Baltimore: Johns Hopkins University Press, 1993.

Mancke, Elizabeth. 'Another British America: A Canadian Model for the Early Modern British Empire.' *Journal of Imperial and Commonwealth History,* 25 (1997), 1–36.

– 'Chartered Enterprises and the Evolution of the British Atlantic World.' In Elizabeth Mancke and Carole Shammas, eds., *The Creation of the British Atlantic World,* 237–62. Baltimore: Johns Hopkins University Press, 2005.

– 'Early Modern Expansion and the Politicization of Oceanic Space.' *Geographical Review* 89 (April 1999), 225–36.

– 'Imperial Transitions.' In John G. Reid et al., *The 'Conquest' of Acadia, 1710: Imperial, Colonial, and Aboriginal Constructions*, 178–202. Toronto: University of Toronto Press, 2004.

– 'Negotiating an Empire: Britain and Its Overseas Peripheries, c. 1550-1780.' In Christine Daniels and Michael V. Kennedy, eds., *Negotiated Empires: Centers and Peripheries in the Americas, 1500-1820*, 235–65. New York: Routledge, 2002.

Mancke, Elizabeth, and John G. Reid. 'Elites, States, and the Imperial Contest for Acadia.' In John G. Reid et al., *The 'Conquest' of Acadia, 1710: Imperial, Colonial, and Aboriginal Constructions*, 25–47. Toronto: University of Toronto Press, 2004.

Mancke, Elizabeth, and Carole Shammas, eds. *The Creation of the British Atlantic World*. Baltimore: Johns Hopkins University Press, 2005.

Marquis, Greg. 'Celebrating Champlain in the Loyalist City: Saint John, 1904–10.' *Acadiensis* 33:2 (Spring 2004), 27–43.

Marshall, P.J. 'The British in Asia: Trade to Dominion, 1700-1765.' In W. Roger Louis, editor-in-chief, *The Oxford History of the British Empire*, 2: 487–507. 5 vols. Oxford: Oxford University Press, 1998–9.

– 'Empire and Authority in the Later Eighteenth Century.' *Journal of Imperial and Commonwealth History* 15 (1987), 105–22.

– *The Making and Unmaking of Empires: Britain, India, and America, c. 1750-1783*. Oxford: Oxford University Press, 2005.

Martin, Ged. *Past Futures: The Impossible Necessity of History*. Toronto: University of Toronto Press, 2004.

Marwick, Arthur. *The Nature of History*. London: Macmillan, 1970.

Massignon, Geneviève. *Les parlers français d'Acadie: Enquête linguistique*. Paris: C. Klincksieck, 1962.

– 'La seigneurie de Charles de Menou d'Aulnay, gouverneur de l'Acadie, 1635–1650.' *Revue d'histoire de l'Amérique française* 16 (1962–3), 469–501.

Matthews, Colin, et al., eds. *Oxford Dictionary of National Biography*. Online edition: updated January 2007.

Melanson, Margaret C. *The Melanson Story: Acadian Family, Acadian Times*. Toronto: Margaret C. Melanson, 2003.

Melvoin, Richard I. *New England Outpost: War and Society in Colonial Deerfield*. New York: Norton, 1989.

Miller, J.R. 'The Invisible Historian.' *Journal of the Canadian Historical Association*, new ser., 8 (1997), 3–18.

Miller, Perry. *The New England Mind: From Colony to Province*. Cambridge, MA: Harvard University Press, 1953.

Miquelon, Dale. *Dugard of Rouen: French Trade to Canada and the West Indies,*

1729–1770. Montreal and London: McGill-Queen's University Press, 1978.

– *New France, 1701–1744: 'A Supplement to Europe.'* Toronto: McClelland & Stewart, 1987.

Montagu, Ashley. *The Anatomy of Swearing.* New York: Macmillan, 1968.

Moody, Robert Earle. 'The Maine Frontier, 1607 to 1763.' PhD thesis, Yale University, 1933.

Moogk, Peter. '"Thieving Buggers" and "Stupid Sluts": Insults and Popular Culture in New France.' *William and Mary Quarterly,* 3rd ser., 36 (1979), 524–47.

Morison, Samuel Eliot. *Samuel de Champlain, Father of New France.* Boston: Little Brown, 1972.

Morrison, Kenneth M. 'The Bias of Colonial Law: English Paranoia and the Abenaki Arena of King Philip's War, 1675–1678.' *New England Quarterly* 53 (1980), 363–78.

– *The Embattled Northeast: The Elusive Ideal of Alliance in Abenaki–Euramerican Relations.* Berkeley: University of California Press, 1984.

Nelles, H.V. *The Art of Nation-Building: Pageantry and Spectacle at Quebec's Tercentenary.* Toronto: University of Toronto Press, 1999.

Nicholls, Andrew D. '"The purpois is honorabill, and may conduce to the good of our service": Lord Ochiltree and the Cape Breton Colony, 1629–1631.' *Acadiensis* 34:2 (Spring 2005), 109–23.

Nicolis, G. *Introduction to Nonlinear Science.* Cambridge: Cambridge University Press, 1995.

Norton, Mary Beth. *In the Devil's Snare: The Salem Witchcraft Crisis of 1692.* New York: Alfred A. Knopf, 2002.

Noyes, Sybil, Charles T. Libby, and Walter G. Davis. *Genealogical Dictionary of Maine and New Hampshire.* Baltimore: Genealogical Publishing Co., 1979; first published 1928–39.

O'Neill, Dianne, curator. *At the Great Harbour: 250 Years on the Halifax Waterfront.* Halifax: Art Gallery of Nova Scotia, 1999.

Osgood, Herbert L. *The American Colonies in the Eighteenth Century.* 4 vols. New York: Columbia University Press, 1924–5.

Oxford English Dictionary. 2nd ed. 20 vols. Oxford: Clarendon Press, 1989.

Paret, Peter. 'Colonial Experience and European Military Reform at the End of the Eighteenth Century.' *Bulletin of the Institute of Historical Research* 37 (1964), 47–59.

Parker, Geoffrey. *The Military Revolution: Military Innovation and the Rise of the West, 1500-1800.* Cambridge: Cambridge University Press, 1988.

Pastore, Ralph. 'The Collapse of the Beothuk World.' *Acadiensis* 19:1 (Fall 1989), 52–71.

– 'The Sixteenth Century: Aboriginal Peoples and European Contact.' In Phillip A. Buckner and John G. Reid, eds., *The Atlantic Region to Confederation: A History*, 22–39. Toronto and Fredericton: University of Toronto Press and Acadiensis Press. 1994.

Patterson, Stephen E. 'Indian–White Relations in Nova Scotia, 1749–61: A Study in Political Interaction.' *Acadiensis* 23:1 (Autumn 1993), 23–59.

– '1744–1763: Colonial Wars and Aboriginal Peoples.' In Phillip A. Buckner and John G. Reid, eds., *The Atlantic Region to Confederation: A History*, 125–55. Toronto and Fredericton: University of Toronto Press and Acadiensis Press. 1994.

Paul, Daniel N. *We Were Not the Savages: A Micmac Perspective on the Collision of European and Aboriginal Civilization.* Halifax: Nimbus, 1993.

Peckham, Howard H. *The Colonial Wars, 1689–1762.* Chicago: University of Chicago Press, 1964.

Pichette, Robert. *Le pays appelé l'Acadie: Réflexions sur les commémorations.* Moncton: Centre d'études acadiennes, Université de Moncton, 2006.

Plank, Geoffrey Gilbert. 'The Culture of Conquest: The British Colonists and Nova Scotia, 1690–1759.' PhD thesis, Princeton University, 1994.

– *An Unsettled Conquest: The British Campaign against the Peoples of Acadia.* Philadelphia: University of Pennsylvania Press, 2001.

Pope, Peter E. *Fish into Wine: The Newfoundland Plantation in the Seventeenth Century.* Chapel Hill, NC: University of North Carolina Press, 2004.

Pothier, Bernard. 'Acadian Emigration to Ile Royale after the Conquest of Acadia.' *Histoire sociale/Social History* 3 (1970), 116–31.

Preston, Richard A. *Gorges of Plymouth Fort.* Toronto: University of Toronto Press, 1953.

– 'The Laconia Company of 1629: An English Attempt to Intercept the Fur Trade.' *Canadian Historical Review* 31 (1950), 125–44.

Prins, Harald. 'Children of Gluskap: Wabanaki Indians on the Eve of the European Invasion.' In Emerson Baker et al., eds., *American Beginnings: Exploration, Culture and Cartography in the Land of Norumbega*, 95–117. Lincoln: University of Nebraska Press, 1994.

Pritchard, James. *In Search of Empire: The French in the Americas, 1670-1730.* Cambridge: Cambridge University Press, 2004.

Pulsipher, Jenny Hale. '"The Overture of this New-Albion World": King Philip's War and the Transformation of New England.' PhD thesis, Brandeis University, 1999.

– *Subjects unto the Same King: Indians, English, and the Contest for Authority in Colonial New England.* Philadelphia: University of Pennsylvania Press, 2005.

Quennell, Peter. *Shakespeare: A Biography.* Cleveland and New York: World Publishing Co., 1963.

Quinn, David B. *England and the Discovery of America, 1481–1620.* New York: Knopf, 1974.

– 'Henri Quatre and New France.' *Terra Incognitae: The Journal for the History of Discoveries* 22 (1990), 13–28.

– *North America from Earliest Discovery to First Settlements: The Norse Voyages to 1612.* New York: Harper and Row, 1977.

Rameau de Saint-Père, Edmé. *Une colonie féodale en Amérique: L'Acadie, 1604–1710.* Paris: Didier, 1877.

Ranlet, Philip. 'Another Look at the Causes of King Philip's War.' *New England Quarterly* 61 (1988), 79–100.

Rawlyk, George A. *Nova Scotia's Massachusetts: A Study of Massachusetts–Nova Scotia Relations, 1630 to 1784.* Montreal: McGill-Queen's University Press, 1973.

– *Revolution Rejected, 1775–1776.* Scarborough, ON: Prentice-Hall, 1968.

Rediker, Marcus. *Between the Devil and the Deep Blue Sea: Merchant Seamen, Pirates, and the Anglo-American Maritime World, 1700-1750.* Cambridge: Cambridge University Press, 1987.

Reid, John G. *Acadia, Maine, and New Scotland: Marginal Colonies in the Seventeenth Century.* Toronto: University of Toronto Press, 1981.

– 'Change and Continuity in Nova Scotia, 1758–1775.' In Margaret Conrad, ed., *Making Adjustments: Change and Continuity in Planter Nova Scotia, 1759–1800,* 45–59. Fredericton: Acadiensis Press, 1991.

– 'European Expectations of Acadia and the Bermudas, 1603–1624.' *Histoire sociale/Social History* 20 (1987), 319–35.

– 'How Wide Is the Atlantic Ocean? Not Wide Enough!' *Acadiensis* 34:2 (Spring 2005), 81–7.

– 'Imperial Intrusions, 1687–1720.' In Phillip A. Buckner and John G. Reid, eds., *The Atlantic Region to Confederation: A History,* 78–103. Toronto and Fredericton: University of Toronto Press and Acadiensis Press, 1994.

– *Maine, Charles II, and Massachusetts: Governmental Relationships in Early Northern New England.* Portland: Maine Historical Society, 1977.

– 'Maine and the Royal Commission of 1664–1666.' MA thesis, Memorial University of Newfoundland, 1972.

– 'The 1970s: Sharpening the Sceptical Edge.' In E.R. Forbes and D.A. Muise, eds., *The Atlantic Provinces in Confederation,* 460-504. Toronto and Fredericton: University of Toronto Press and Acadiensis Press, 1993.

– 'The Nova Scotia Historian: A Creature of Paradox?' *Journal of the Royal Nova Scotia Historical Society* 5 (2002), 106–21.
– '*Pax Britannica* or *Pax Indigena*? Planter Nova Scotia (1760-1782) and Competing Strategies of Pacification.' *Canadian Historical Review* 85 (2004), 669–92.
– 'Réflexions actuelles sur l'Acadie du XVIIe siècle.' *Port Acadie: Revue interdisciplinaire en études acadiennes* 5 (Spring 2004), 11–24.
– 'The Scots Crown and the Restitution of Port Royal, 1629–1632.' *Acadiensis* 6:2 (Spring 1977), 39–63.
– *Sir William Alexander and North American Colonization: A Reappraisal.* Edinburgh: Centre of Canadian Studies, University of Edinburgh, 1990.
– *Six Crucial Decades: Times of Change in the History of the Maritimes.* Halifax: Nimbus, 1987.
– 'Unorthodox Warfare in the Northeast, 1703.' *Canadian Historical Review* 73 (1992), 211–20.
– 'Viola Barnes, the Gender of History, and the North Atlantic Mind.' *Acadiensis* 33:1 (Autumn 2003), 3–20.
Reid, John G., Maurice Basque, Elizabeth Mancke, Barry Moody, Geoffrey Plank, and William Wicken. *The 'Conquest' of Acadia, 1710: Imperial, Colonial, and Aboriginal Constructions.* Toronto: University of Toronto Press, 2004.
Richter, Daniel K. *Facing East from Indian Country: A Native History of Early America.* Cambridge, MA: Harvard University Press, 2001.
– 'Native Peoples of North America and the Eighteenth-Century British Empire.' In W. Roger Louis, editor-in-chief, *The Oxford History of the British Empire,* 2: 347–71. 5 vols. Oxford: Oxford University Press, 1998–9.
– *The Ordeal of the Longhouse: The Peoples of the Iroquois League in the Era of European Colonization.* Chapel Hill: University of North Carolina Press, 1992.
– 'War and Culture: The Iroquois Experience.' *William and Mary Quarterly,* 3rd ser., 40 (1983), 528–59.
Roberts, Michael. *The Military Revolution, 1560-1660.* Belfast: M. Boyd, 1956.
Rudin, Ronald. 'The Champlain–De Monts Tercentenary: Voices from Nova Scotia, New Brunswick and Maine, June 1904.' *Acadiensis* 33:2 (Spring 2004), 3–26.
– *Founding Fathers: The Celebration of Champlain and Laval in the Streets of Quebec, 1878–1908.* Toronto: University of Toronto Press, 2003.
– *Making History in Twentieth-Century Quebec.* Toronto: University of Toronto Press, 1997.
Rudin, Ronald, in collaboration with Leo Aristimuño. *Life after Ile Ste.-Croix.* Distributed by National Film Board, 2006.

Rutman, Darrett B. *Winthrop's Boston: Portrait of a Puritan Town, 1630-1649.* Chapel Hill: University of North Carolina Press, 1965.

St George, Robert. '"Heated" Speech and Literacy in Seventeenth-Century New England.' In David D. Hall and David Grayson Allen, eds., *Seventeenth-Century New England,* 275–322. Boston: Colonial Society of Massachusetts, 1984.

Salisbury, Neal. 'The Indians' Old World: Native Americans and the Coming of Europeans.' *William and Mary Quarterly,* 3rd ser., 53 (1996), 435–58.

– *Manitou and Providence: Indians, Europeans, and the Making of New England, 1500-1643.* New York : Oxford University Press, 1982.

Séguin, Robert-Lionel. *La civilisation traditionnelle de l'"habitant' aux 17e et 18e siècles: Fonds matériel.* Montreal: Fides, 1967.

Sévigny, P.-André. *Les Abénaquis: Habitat et migrations, 17e et 18e siècles.* Montreal: Bellarmin, 1976.

Shammas, Carole. 'Introduction.' In Elizabeth Mancke and Carole Shammas, eds., *The Creation of the British Atlantic World,* 1–16. Baltimore: Johns Hopkins University Press, 2005.

Slotkin, Richard. *Regeneration through Violence: The Mythology of the American Frontier, 1600-1860.* Middletown, CT: Wesleyan University Press, 1973.

Slotkin, Richard, and James K. Folsom, eds. *So Dreadfull a Judgment: Puritan Responses to King Philip's War, 1676–1677.* Middletown, CT: Wesleyan University Press, 1978.

Smith, Peter. *Explaining Chaos.* Cambridge: Cambridge University Press, 1998.

Sosin, J.M. *English America and the Revolution of 1688: Royal Administration and the Structure of Provincial Government.* Lincoln: University of Nebraska Press, 1982.

Starkey, Armstrong. *European and Native American Warfare, 1675–1815.* Norman: University of Oklahoma Press, 1998.

Steele, Ian K. *Warpaths: Invasions of North America.* New York: Oxford University Press, 1994.

Stevenson, Robert B.K. 'The "Stirling" Turners of Charles I, 1632–9.' *British Numismatic Journal* 29 (1958–9), 128–37.

Stewart, Gordon, and George Rawlyk. *A People Highly Favoured of God: The Nova Scotia Yankees and the American Revolution.* Toronto: Macmillan, 1972.

Stewart-Smith, David. 'The Pennacook Indians and the New England Frontier, 1604–1733.' PhD thesis, The Union Institute, 1998.

Story, G.M., ed. *Early European Settlement and Exploitation in Atlantic Canada.* St John's: Memorial University of Newfoundland, 1982.

Taylor, Alan. *American Colonies.* New York: Viking Penguin, 2001.

– *The Divided Ground: Indians, Settlers, and the Northern Borderland of the American Revolution.* New York: Knopf, 2006.

Taylor, M. Brook. *Promoters, Patriots, and Partisans: Historiography in Nineteenth-Century English Canada.* Toronto: University of Toronto Press, 1989.

Thayer, Henry O. *Sir William Phips, Adventurer and Statesman: A Study in Colonial Biography.* Portland: Maine Historical Society, 1927.

Thompson, E.P. 'The Poverty of Theory or An Orrery of Errors.' In E.P. Thompson, *The Poverty of Theory and Other Essays,* 1–210. New York: Monthly Review Press, 1978.

– *The Poverty of Theory and Other Essays.* New York: Monthly Review Press, 1978.

Tosh, John. *The Pursuit of History: Aims, Methods, and New Directions in the Study of Modern History.* 2nd ed. London: Longman, 1991.

Trevelyan, George Macaulay. *England under Queen Anne: The Peace and the Protestant Succession.* London: Longman, 1934.

Trevor-Roper, Hugh. 'The Invention of Tradition: The Highland Tradition of Scotland.' In Eric Hobsbawm and Terence Ranger, eds., *The Invention of Tradition,* 15–41. Cambridge: Cambridge University Press, 1983.

Trigger, Bruce G. 'Champlain Judged by his Indian Policy: A Different View of Early Canadian History.' *Anthropologica* 13 (1971), 85–114.

– *The Children of Aataentsic: A History of the Huron People to 1660.* 2 vols. Kingston and Montreal: McGill-Queen's University Press, 1976.

– *Natives and Newcomers: Canada's 'Heroic Age' Reconsidered.* Kingston and Montreal: McGill-Queen's University Press, 1985.

Trigger, Bruce G., ed. *Handbook of North American Indians.* Vol. 15, *Northeast.* Washington: Smithsonian Institution, 1978.

Trudel, Marcel. *The Beginnings of New France, 1524–1663.* Toronto: McClelland & Stewart, 1973.

– *Histoire de la Nouvelle-France.* Vol. 1, *Les vaines tentatives, 1524–1603.* Montreal: Fides, 1963.

– *Histoire de la Nouvelle-France.* Vol. 2, *Le comptoir, 1603–1627.* Montreal: Fides, 1966.

– *Histoire de la Nouvelle-France.* Vol. 3, *La seigneurie des cent-associés, 1627–1663,* I, *les événements.* Montreal: Fides, 1979.

– *Histoire de la Nouvelle-France.* Vol. 3, *La seigneuire des cent-associés, 1627–1663,* II, *la société.* Montreal: Fides, 1983.

Turgeon, Laurier. 'French Fishers, Fur Traders, and Amerindians during the Sixteenth Century: History and Archaeology.' *William and Mary Quarterly,* 3rd ser., 55 (1998), 585–610.

– *Patrimoines métissés: Contextes coloniaux et postcoloniaux.* Quebec and Paris: Presses de l'Université Laval and Éditions de la Maison des sciences de l'homme, 2003.

Upton, L.F.S. *Micmacs and Colonists: Indian–White Relations in the Maritimes, 1713–1867.* Vancouver: University of British Columbia Press, 1979.

Van Deventer, David Earl. 'The Emergence of Provincial New Hampshire.' PhD thesis, Case Western Reserve University, 1969.

Vaughan, Alden T. *New England Frontier: Puritans and Indians, 1620-1675.* Boston: Little, Brown, 1965.

Wallace, Birgitta. 'An Archaeologist Discovers Early Acadia.' In Margaret Conrad, ed., *Looking into Acadie: Three Illustrated Studies.* Halifax: Nova Scotia Museum, [1999].

Waller, G.M. *Samuel Vetch: Colonial Enterpriser.* Chapel Hill: University of North Carolina Press, 1960.

Walters, Mark D. '*Mohegan Indians v. Connecticut* (1705–1773) and the Legal Status of Aboriginal Customary Laws and Government in British North America.' *Osgoode Hall Law Journal* 33 (1995), 785–829.

Warkentin, Germaine, and Carolyn Podruchny, eds. *Decentring the Renaissance: Canada and Europe in Multidisciplinary Perspective, 1500-1700.* Toronto: University of Toronto Press, 2001.

Washburn, Wilcomb E. *The Indian in America.* New York: Harper Colophon, 1975.

Way, Peter. 'The Cutting Edge of Culture: British Soldiers Encounter Native Americans in the French and Indian War.' In Martin Daunton and Rick Halpern, eds., *Empire and Others: British Encounters with Indigenous Peoples, 1600-1850,* 123–48. Philadelphia: University of Pennsylvania Press, 1999.

Weeks, Jeffrey. 'Foucault for Historians.' *History Workshop Journal* 14 (Autumn 1982), 106–19.

White, Richard. *The Middle Ground: Indians, Empires, and Republics in the Great Lakes Region, 1650-1815.* New York: Cambridge University Press, 1991.

– 'The Winning of the West: The Expansion of the Western Sioux in the Eighteenth and Nineteenth Centuries.' *Journal of American History* 65 (1978–9), 319–43.

Wicken, William C. 'Encounters with Tall Sails and Tall Tales: Mi'kmaq Society, 1500–1760.' PhD thesis, McGill University, 1994.

– 'Mi'kmaq Land in Southwestern Nova Scotia, 1771–1823.' In Margaret Conrad, ed., *Making Adjustments: Change and Continuity in Planter Nova Scotia, 1759–1800,* 113–22. Fredericton: Acadiensis Press, 1991.

– *Mi'kmaq Treaties on Trial: History, Land, and Donald Marshall Junior.* Toronto: University of Toronto Press, 2002.

– 'Passamaquoddy Identity and the Marshall Decision.' In Stephen J. Hornsby and John G. Reid, eds., *New England and the Maritime Provinces: Connections and Comparisons,* 50–8. Montreal and Kingston: McGill-Queen's University Press, 2005.

– '26 August 1726: A Case Study in Mi'kmaq–New England Relations in the Early 18th Century.' *Acadiensis* 23:1 (Autumn 1993), 5–22.

Williamson, William D. *The History of the State of Maine: From Its First Discovery, A.D. 1602, to the Separation, A.D. 1820.* 2 vols. Hallowell, ME: Glazier and Masters, 1832.

Wilson, Kathleen. 'Introduction: Histories, Empires, Modernities.' In Kathleen Wilson, ed., *A New Imperial History: Culture, Identity and Modernity in Britain and the Empire, 1660–1840,* 1–26. Cambridge: Cambridge University Press, 2004.

Wilson, Kathleen, ed. *A New Imperial History: Culture, Identity and Modernity in Britain and the Empire, 1660-1840.* Cambridge: Cambridge University Press, 2004.

Winius, George. 'The "Shadow Empire" of Goa in the Bay of Bengal.' *Itinerario* 7:2 (1983), 83–101.

Wormald, Jenny. *Court, Kirk, and Community: Scotland 1470-1625.* Toronto: University of Toronto Press, 1981.

Wright, Esther Clark. *Planters and Pioneers.* 2nd ed. Hantsport, NS: Lancelot Press, 1982; first published 1978.

Wynn, Graeme. 'Late Eighteenth-Century Agriculture on the Bay of Fundy Marshlands.' *Acadiensis* 8:2 (Spring 1979), 80–9.

– 'Peeping through the Cracks: Seeking Connections, Comparisons, and Understanding in Unstable Space.' In Stephen J. Hornsby and John G. Reid, eds., *New England and the Maritime Provinces: Connections and Comparisons,* 295–313. Montreal and Kingston: McGill-Queen's University Press, 2005.

Web Sites

Deportation of the Acadians, commemoration at Grand Pré (28 July 2005): http://www.commemoration250.ca/

Harvard University, International Seminar on the History of the Atlantic World, list of working papers: http://www.fas.harvard.edu/~atlantic/compwp.html

Donald Marshall case, ruling: http://scc.lexum.umontreal.ca/en/1999/1999rcs3-456/1999rcs3-456.html

Stephen Marshall and Joshua Bernard cases, ruling: http://scc.lexum.umontreal.ca/en/2005/2005scc43/2005scc43.html

Port Royal anniversary, commemoration of landing of de Monts and Champlain: http://www.portroyal400.com/

Royal proclamation in commemoration of the *Grand dérangement*: http://laws.justice.gc.ca/en/otherreg/SI-2003-188/188971.html

St Croix River commemoration (June–July 2004), plan of events: http://www.pc.gc.ca/lhn-nhs/nb/stcroix/ne/ne2_e.asp; background and commentaries, http://www.cbc.ca/news/background/champlainanniversary/

Index

www.ingramcontent.com/pod-product-compliance
Lightning Source LLC
LaVergne TN
LVHW040757070826
844660LV00025B/1173

* 9 7 8 0 8 0 2 0 9 4 1 6 2 *